110 Miles Behind the Lines

Book One

Robert Marabito

110 Miles Behind the Lines: Book One
©2013 Robert Marabito

Edited by Janet Elaine Smith
Designed by Star Publish LLC

Trade Paperback
ISBN: 978-1-935188-54-4

A Star Publish LLC Publication
www.starpublishllc.com
Published in 2013
Printed in the United States of America and United Kingdom

Acknowledgments

The Ford Motor M161 Army jeep for its hustle and bustle and wheelies.

The soldiers, sergeants and officers of the Berlin Brigade for their support, especially the soldiers of the 592nd Signal Company, about whom this novel was written.

Soldiers, sergeants and officers of the 1st Armored Division, Wiesbaden, Germany, for their re-education 35 years later of all things Army. "Attention! Right Face!"

Willi Brand, "Bürgermeister"and Mayor of West Berlin, for that moment of history at the time, November 22, 1963.

Janet Elaine Smith, author of more than 20 novels, for her professional coaching and support that got this novel published, and to her grandmother, Annie Hallett, who taught her enough German when Janet was a little girl to make some sense out of the German/English words in the book.

110 Miles Behind the Lines

Book One

SP
A Star Publish Book

Table of Contents

Preface 9
Prologue 11
1. 592nd Signal Company 15
2. Mess Hall 38
3. Keystone Grunts..67
4. The Checkpoint 106
5. The Golden Sun 124
6. Gestapo 153
7. Radio Room 165
8. Kennedy 189
9. A Carton of Cigarettes..209
10. The Brits...216
11. Convoy 238
12. Pay Call 301
13. The Old Man 322
14. The Old Eden Saloon 355
15. The Soldier...394
16. Cookie Nast..406
17. Vietnam I..427

noncommissioned officer (NCO)
= Unteroffizier

Preface

I have written a novel that needed to be written. Actually, it is two novels. The titles: *110 Miles Behind the Lines*, Volumes 1& 2. Call it a cross between Joseph Heller's *Catch 22* and the book, *MASH*. It is a story about army training and discipline that we American soldiers went through—all servicemen went through—Army, Navy, Marines and Air Force. From World War II to Korea, from the Cold War and Vietnam to the present (Afganistan). We who served experienced the same rough and tumble training whether in the field or in the barracks. It is called "discipline" with that senior NCO slap on the back. "Right shoulder. Arms!" "Left shoulder. Arms!" "Forward... Trip!"

110 Miles Behind the Lines is a story about one company, the 592nd Signal Company of the U.S. Army's Berlin Brigade as seen from the eyes of the enlisted and draftee soldiers. It was the turbulent Cold War years in West Berlin. However, the novel is not about turbulence, but about how these young men—really several young man of low rank— saw the army. The years are 1963 to 1965.

The two novels also show how American soldiers related to the German population of West Berlin at the time. The adventures they shared. Also, the stories reveal the mentality of post war Germany. It was a mentality that, though 13 years after World War II, still burdened German thinking: correctness, discipline, arrogance and that weight of the past, that National Socialist past. It still lingered.

One chapter tells of the German jubilation at the visit of President Kennedy to the city. Another of his death and how the Germans reacted to it. They marched...and they wept. There are personal tragedies as well as one love story, and stories about how American soldiers related to the Berlin women. They jitterbugged. Call it "Dirty Dancing." The British,

9

known for their love of darts, play in another chapter. The Keystone Grunts, too, in their vehicles, the Ford Motor M151 Jeeps. Zip! Zoom! Wheelies! That alternate life style surfaces in one chapter. A field exercise dominates another. Racism as well. It plays a background role. And there are ghosts. In West Berlin there are always ghosts. There is Cold War tension. One sees it in the chapter about Check Point Charlie where two female UCLA students confront the Berlin Wall. The Wall almost came down. And there is more: two books, 38 chapters total. Have a good read.

Prologue

The two Russian soldiers laid the charge at the base of the cellar wall. They were combat engineers. Their squad had already blown through two building cellars and fought their way from floor to floor until the buildings were cleared of the *Wehrmacht* defenders. It had to be that way. The *Wehrmacht* controlled the streets and buildings of central Berlin, the Russian army, the sewers and the cellars. Only in this way could the Russians outflank the die-hard Germans.

In the cellar of the third building, a Russian sergeant looked around. He waved his soldiers and engineers back. Satisfied, he set the fuse to the charge. Crouched in filthy battle fatigues and lying on the crummy floor, the squad of soldiers cradled their burp guns and held their ears. The chamber fell silent. On the street above, the muffled rat-tat and thuds of the unending battle could be heard. It was a strange way to spend a spring day. BOOM!

The explosion stunned them. No matter how often they had laid charges and blown cellar walls, the concussion from the blast shocked the men in the compressed chambers. No one of the engineer squad ever got used to it. Dirt, stone and dust pounded through the doorway and into the chamber, momentarily blinding them. As the dust settled, the engineers rushed the just-blown hole and raced into the next cellar room, burp guns pointing, ready to fire. The explosive charge had done its job. They expected resistance, but got none. Then they stopped. They looked around, then at each other and began to grin. The Russian engineer squad found themselves standing in a large wine cellar.

There, in the gloom of the room, were rows of carefully laid bottles of vintage wine— German Mosel and Rheinhessen—all set neatly on dark wood racks. There were bottles of French Bordeaux and Chablis and a rack of champagne, all corked, the neck of the bottles wrapped in gold. Such abundance! The engineer squad, dirty, feeling crummy, could only blink, not believing their good fortune. They had stumbled into a hedonist's gold mine.

One of the racks had been knocked over by the blast. Some of its precious cargo lay shattered on the floor, many of the bottles still unbroken, waiting to be vandalized. Crouching, the soldiers checked between the wine racks and around corners of the cellar. No enemy.

"Okay, men, don't get any ideas. This is now property of the Red Army," said the squad's captain sternly. "Let's go! Follow me!" he ordered as he hustled toward the base of the staircase leading to the floor above. At the staircase and crouching, he looked back…and found himself alone. There was no back up man. His squad was busy popping champagne corks and laughing as they popped. They began to drink up the booty, for they knew that if they didn't stop to drink the cache on the spot they would never see it again. To them, property of the Red Army meant property of the senior officers who, no doubt, would consume it at their leisure.

The squad of Russian engineers sprayed each other, gorged themselves, drank and laughed, while sitting on the floor, never mind the rat-tat-tat and thunder from the street battle above. They had not seen drink in such abundance except at weddings and baptisms back home, and that was years ago in 1940, before the war. This was April 1945, five years later. Except for an occasional bottle of vodka tossed to them between missions or what they managed to grab for themselves out of captured German towns, they never had drink like this. Discipline broke down. Shattering wine bottles at the neck, they drank.

A foaming bottle of champagne was thrust into the captain's hand by his engineer sergeant, the one who had laid the charge. The captain stared at it, trembling. It was as if a woman had just bared her breasts in front of him. To go to war, or to go to party in the middle of war, that was the conflict of judgment he struggled with. Above, on the street, the gun fire and thuds of the unending battle continued. He holstered his side arm. "Okay, sergeant, but just this once. The men have permission to break." Now, the captain himself drank, and drank deeply.

The Battle of Berlin had been going on since March. The fighting had been continuous. The die-hard, fanatical SS defenders were putting up unexpected resistance. Between the months of March and May, before the city finally fell to the Russian Army, it would cost the lives of 20,000 Soviet soldiers.

The wine cellar party didn't last. In the jubilation there was a sudden flash. An explosion! An SS defender had come down the cellar steps and tossed a stick grenade into the chamber. As luck would have it, only two of the engineers were wounded. The stick grenade fell between two of the wine racks. The heavy oak frames and bottles took the explosion's shock.

Returning fire, the engineers drove the SS defender back up the staircase. A short fire- fight raged. The SS defender was hit and dropped his machine pistol. Another SS defender retreated to the upper floors. From above there was an explosion, then the unmistakable sound of burp guns and shouts in Russian. Caught on the staircase, the SS man was hit. A third tried to surrender but was shot point blank. No prisoners today. The building was taken.

The job done, the engineer squad from the cellar embraced the infantry team that had advanced from the floor above. When told what was in the cellar, the infantry team posted a guard and went into the cellar themselves to share the cache. They did it quickly. Understanding, their officer-in-command looked away.

Now, satiated and half-drunk, the Russian engineer squad stumbled up the stairs, some with wine bottles shoved in their ammo belts. They entered what was a large kitchen. Among the broken cookery they passed two German defenders dead on the floor. Along one wall, pots and pans and cooking utensils still hung, amazingly, from hooks as if waiting to be used for an order of chicken souffle. The table was pushed to one side. On a massive cast iron stove laid another dead German, a metal ladle shoved in his hand in memorial. Laughing, and just a little tipsy, the Russian engineers passed him and pushed through the swinging doors and entered the grand hall.

Looking around, they saw it was an enormous ballroom with a baroque ceiling and wall frescos of German knights and kings. One fresco was of Bismarck and an entourage hailing the German Kaiser, Wilhelm I. Several large, crystal glass chandeliers hung from the ceiling. There were enormous arched windows, of which one had been blown out. Elegant furniture that had once seated princes and barons lay broken and scattered on the floor. All the majestic wall mirrors had been smashed except one; a Russian soldier stood in front of it his helmet under his arm, combing his hair. Here and there lay a dead *Wehrmacht* defender. Near the blown arch window, an operation command post had been set up. Outside, a T34 tank could be seen firing into the adjacent building. There were the occasional zips of enemy rounds overhead.

The engineer captain called his squad together for a quick briefing. The order: another building to blow. After checking their supply of charges, the men ran out into the street, gaily this time, into the heat of the Battle of Berlin.

The Russian engineer captain was about to follow, but paused. He blinked and tilted his head. "Wha´?" Around him, the cacophony of combat, a moment before so vibrant and loud, had stopped. The churning, rapping, crunching of war had ceased. It was as if every soldier, every tank, every artillery piece had run out of ordinance. Amazingly, the world had fallen silent. But why? Had someone thrown a switch? In the dearth of the silence, the Russian captain heard a tinkling. It had the delight of a robin's chirp in spring, the chime of a baby's cry. It made him think of his daughter back home, whom he had not seen for three years. Emotional, he looked up and saw two enormous chandeliers hanging from the grand hall's baroque ceiling. It was the chandelier's fist size crystals. They tinkled as if in a vacuum.

"Whatever was this place? Whatever was this place?" he called out loud, his voice echoing in the chamber. "Versailles!"

Suddenly, there was the sound of gunfire. The Battle of Berlin had resumed. The pause, whatever it was, was over. Moving quickly, the Russian captain followed his engineer squad and ran out of the grand hall into the afternoon's heated conflict and smoke. Eighteen years later, the whistle blew.

The 592nd Signal Company

The whistle blew. It echoed up and down the neon-lit hallways of the barracks as the PltSgts went from room to room, floor to floor, up and down the corridors hollering, yelling, "Wake up! Wake up! It's reveille! Hit the deck, y'all!" It was 0520 in the morning and another day of soldiering for the men of the 592nd Signal Company, Berlin Brigade. "Wake up! Wake up! Oudda-da-fart-sack! Wake up, ya hear!" Another whistle blew, and another.

From the bunks, snores sputtered like cropdusters over cotton fields as half-asleep young men struggled to lift the dead weight of their bodies. Without the shrill cries of the company platoon sergeants and their staccato pestering, soldiers would never leave their beloved bunks. It took NCOs, the US Army's equivalent of surrogate mothers, to raise them from the dead and drive them into pasture (formation) like the temple slaves masters of old. Master Sergeant, M.Sgt Humphry Sweechek, of the third platoon ("Sergeant Sweetcheeks" behind his back) was one of those slave masters. He was clamorous, blustery, a typical hard-nose army nanny. "Snap to! Snap to!" he barked.

At 6'2", 210 Lbs, and a Korean War veteran, the MSgt had a vocal slap that made soldiers tremble, though his bite had all the sting of a campfire marshmallow. His men liked and respected him, but detested his morning reveille. "Wake up, you girls!" he would bellow in a voice devoid of compassion as he pushed open the doors to the soldiers' quarters. He did it with a BANG!, flipping of the light switch, then storming the room. He walked around the foot lockers clapping his hands, barking and bellowing, pulling off a blanket here, kicking a bunk there. He would do the same in the next room, and the next, with all the sensitivity of an East Asian monsoon until he had his brood of whiny draftees and enlistees on their feet and hustling.

15

At one room he pushed open the door and stormed in, a bark hanging on the edge of his tongue, locked and loaded and ready to fire. But the bark jammed. He gagged and jumped back into the hallway to catch his breath. The soldiers' quarter was a vacuum devoid of air. It was as if all of the oxygen had been sucked out of it. To breathe was to inhale a moist cocktail of methane and chloride gas. "Beer breath!" muttered the MSgt. He knew it well. He was not sure if the men inside were still alive, for the room's two windows were shut. In such an emergency, long experience had taught him to carry a drill instructor's first weapon of defense. A whistle! He took it out. Inhaling, he stepped back into the room and blew, leaving his comatose soldiers flailing and levitating above their bunks.

MSgt Sweechek kicked open the doors of every room on the second floor until his brood of 32, half-asleep fighting men were on their feet and in their fatigues. Half-shaved and with flies unbuttoned from a quick pee, they doubletimed down the hallway toward the stairwell, bouncing off one other as they hustled. They bounced off the men rushing down from the third floor, and bounced off those rushing in from the first. Bumbling and stumbling and bouncing off the walls, the soldiers of the 592nd Signal Company spilled out the double doors of the barracks entrance and into the chill of the north German morning. Outside they stiffened as if slapped in the face, shocked by the bitter air. "Ch-a-rist, its cold!"

Up and down the *Altdorfer Strasse*, the street, it was the same. The other companies of Berlin Brigade Special Troops were also falling out: Service Company, Headquarters Company, the 287 MP Company, all shouting and clamoring, the noise reverberating the length and breadth of the Andrews Barracks Army Post.

Out of the tangle of torsos and limbs, pushing and shoving, the Signal Company's three platoons formed up and stood in rank four squads deep, a compliment of 93 men. It was now 0530. Somewhere on the post compound the trumpets for reveille could be heard.

Following the soldiers, and sauntering confidently, came the company's three platoon Sgts. They took their places in front of the platoons. "Dress right-dress! Ready! Front! Coveeer!" they ordered, their shouts rich, carrying on the morning air. It was the month of November 1963, and the 592nd Signal Company, Berlin Brigade was about to begin another day of soldiering.

In the third platoon, Specialist E-4 Roger Robuck had his fatigue cap pulled low on his eyebrows. His eyes were open slits as if he had just seen light for the first time in his life. The fresh air made them smart. He had been on overnight pass, barhopping, and did not get much sleep. He had finished up the evening at the Golden Sun *Kneipe*, the local GI bar across the street from the army post. He had just gotten back to the company and into his bunk when the reveille whistles blew. Now, standing in the ranks, he paid the consequences--a raging hangover, and a headache that could be heard, or so he thought, if he thought at all--the length of the *Altdorfer Strasse*.

Also with the rank of Specialist E-4, Frank Bravo leaned on the barracks door; he could go no further. He trembled, hacking and coughing. He fought for breath, discharging the secondary smoke he had absorbed from the evening's beer party.

He and some of the men of the third platoon had thrown a "Hail and Farewell" goodbye fest at the Golden Sun Bar for their long time buddy, Saul Rosenblum. He had re-enlisted. Having done that, he was promoted to the rank of Sgt E-5 with an extended tour of duty. His promotion was part of the festivity and a reason to celebrate. He, Rosenblum, was force-fed boilermakers, the soldier's "bon voyage" beverage of choice. Following his honorary collapse, he was shoulder-carried to the RTO station and the army duty train waiting there. The duty train would take him and other rotating Brigade soldiers to the German port of Bremenhaven, there to board the army troop ship for the States and home.

For Bravo, at the barracks doorway and trembling from the evening's hangover, that was all history. He hung there, supported by the door grip. He dared not let go for fear of collapsing. He looked around, trying to orient himself, his thoughts unfocused. When the floor whistle blew at reveille he had awoken with a woman's brazier, size 42 triple D, wrapped around his head, his face buried deep inside one scented cup. "Wa, how?" He begged to remember, but could not. Bravo wanted to cry. Someone grabbed him by the shoulder. It was Paul Pereski, another signalman with that E-4 rank. He, too, appeared distressed.

"Frank, where's the formation?" Pereski blubbered. "I know it's here, but I can't see it." Pereski had also been to Saul Rosenblum's 'Hail and Farewell' festivity and drank too much. He was one of the soldiers Platoon Sergeant Sweechek's whistle left levitating above his bunk. Now, holding on for dear life, Bravo had become his life buoy in a raising tide of ataxia. "Frank, ya gotta help me," he slurred through his hangover.

Struggling with his own disorientation, Bravo slurred back, "The formation's that-a-way. Problem is, which one of those revolving platoons is the third?"

"Pick one," Pereski begged.

Leaning shoulder-to-shoulder against each other at a perfect 45-degree angle, the two signalmen managed the great divide of 20 yards, the distance from the barracks entrance to the formation standing at parade rest at the street.

"Just what the hell you men doing over here?" demanded the Service Company Platoon Sgt. Service Company was holding its own reveille formation next door. "Signal Company's that-a-way, you bum heads!" he shouted, pushing Bravo and Pereski in the direction. Stumbling, and still at a perfect 45 degree angle and shoulder-to-shoulder, Bravo and Pereski finally reached the ranks of the third platoon. Immediately, rough hands grabbed them and passed them along the ranks, helter-skelter, until they reached their slots in the platoon formation.

Again, Platoon Sgt Sweechek shouted the order of, "Dress-right-dress! Ready! Front! COVEEER!"

Spc-4 Albert Lavoss was already in rank. He stood at rest, but hunchbacked. Lavoss was a large man with a Lou Costello baby face. Gingerly, he reached up and touched the wounds on his cheeks. He had slashed himself shaving and covered the cuts with bits of toilet paper.

At age 26 and six years in service, Lavoss already showed signs of a soldier's drinker disease—the swollen nose, the tremulous hand, the butchered chin from too many unsteady shaves. Lavoss, too, was at the Golden Sun *Kneipe* and Rosenblum's "Hail and Farewell" festivity. For him, it was that final *Weinbrand* (whiskey) duel with Rosenblum that had leveled him. He did win the contest and collected the $5 bet. It took eleven shots and a series of inspiring cheers before Rosenblum threw in the towel—and threw up. Now, swaying in the cold November air, Spc-4 Lavoss, as rank E4s are called, touched his wounded cheeks, hating himself for the evening's indulgence.

Another third platoon man was Spc-4 Robert Yorit. He stepped out of the company barracks, refreshed. He looked sharp in his starched olive drab work fatigues. Stretching, he slapped himself on the chest with a "Me Tarzan! You Jane!" vigor. The evening before he had Radio Room duty until 2400 hours and missed Rosenblum's celebration at the

Golden Sun Bar, where most of the squad had been. Pink cheeked and clear eyed, he felt exhilarated by the pine scent of the Berlin morning air. He glanced around, mischief in his eyes. Then, with an arm's wide swing of ebullient panache, he moved as if to sweep up an invisible bouquet of flowers from the ground. The act raised eyebrows, if not the interest from the inert ranks. Yorit looked, transfixed, into his hands. Opening his arms wide, he pointed his toes as far as his combat boots would allow and stepped into the classical dance position number three. Suddenly, he sprang into the air and did a graceful pirouette, followed by a grand elevation, a move perfected in Miss Simmon's modern dance class at Kent State University back in Ohio. He landed two steps from his place in the first squad of the third platoon. In two bounds Yorit had traversed the 20 meters of space from the barracks entrance to the sidewalk formation. Light applause came from the ranks. The company was coming together.

The full compliment of three platoons was now in formation and waiting when, from somewhere above, there came a sudden scream. It erupted from inside the now supposed-to- be empty barracks. It was not a life threatening scream but a controlled melodious one, a kind of animal message. The whole of the formation looked up.

From a second story window stood Spc E4 Jimmy Lightpony, a Shoshone. He was conversing with nature as was his nature, since he was the only Plains Indian soldier in the company. He was in an attitude of prayer, with arms outstretched, face uplifted to the slate autumn sky; his palms up as if feeling for rain. He jumped on the window's ledge. There he hesitated. Then, crying "Geronimo!" or some such thing, he leaped.

There were several gasps from the formation below. He dropped 30 feet to the ground, landing in the space between the barracks and the hedge row. Two men sprang from their places in the formation to help him should he be injured; it would give them a chance to get some hands on first aid training. It wasn't. Lightpony had landed and bounced the way Plains Indians do when thrown from a horse—on his feet. He popped up from behind the hedge row bush and loped to his place in the third platoon.

"Now there's a man who is definitely Jump School material," said Yorit, observing.

"I'd like to see him do that with a hundred pound pack on his back," slurred Robuck from under his cap.

"Or Flight School, if he can flap his ears," said Lavoss with heavy eyelids.

In front of the platoon, MSgt Sweechek was not amused. In spite of repeated warnings, it was the third time in a month that Lightpony had jumped out of the barracks window. Frowning disapproval, he looked over at the 2nd Platoon NCO, SFC Cabul. He was from Hawaii.

Sgt Cabul appeared comatose, and was. He stood at parade rest in front of his men, only he swayed. He seemed oblivious to Lightpony's antics. He, too, had been to the Golden Sun Bar the night before. He had not intended to get involved in the "Hail and Farewell" festivity, but bought a couple of rounds anyway. Everybody was buying drinks at the bar. Now, like the professional soldier he was, he stood in front of his platoon, half-plastered, but in control.

Then MSgt Sweechek looked over at the first platoon's SFC, Oats. He was the strong man who never smiled. SFC Oats looked back at Sweechek and gave him what the Army calls the "Air Force response"—a shrug.

Suddenly, the double doors of the barracks flew open. The formation murmurs died down. All eyes focused on the double doors. Framed in the doorway against the dark background of the stairwell stood the company's 1stSgt, Luis (No, I'm not a Dago, I'm a Spic) Persilla. Firm jawed and narrow eyed, he looked around. Satisfied, and taking a deep breath, he stepped into the morning's chilly air.

And who was 1stSgt Luis Persilla? He was a hard-nosed, no-nonsense soldier with 25 years of time and grade. He had fought both in World War II and Korea. His only problem was his image; he was five foot one. Height was his bitter pill. Like most men born short, he suffered a lifetime of ridicule, especially in the macho environment of the US Army. In defense of his size he once said, "The officers love it when an NCO must look up to them to salute, so there!"

To maintain his self-esteem, he wore elevated boots with two-inch soles and three-inch heels. When he marched, it gave him a roly-poly gait of a stunt man on a high wire. Back home in the Bronx, the Puerto Rican neighborhood where he grew up, he had to fist fight his way up the gang ladder to be recognized. In the Army it was the same. No one dared smile at him, let alone wisecrack about his size, not even the officers. It was why he made the Army a career. His rank of E-8-MSgt—not to forget the army high-heel boots—bestowed on him the psychological stature necessary to run sections and command companies. That, plus his well practiced growl which some said was a cross between a hyena and Vince Lombardi, made draftees fear to giggle.

Like many a career man, 1stSgt Persilla led by example. He followed Ft. Bragg standards and expected as much from his sergeants. His fatigues were double starched. His spit-shined boots put mirrors to shame. In the sunshine, his belt buckle was a shooting star. He shaved so close it was suspected he plucked his beard. (No one dared say so, of course.) As for his haircut, it was Basic Training sidewall. Having survived the Korea's Yaloo River retreat fighting the Communist Chinese, the lice and the cold, he swore never to have body hair longer than a millimeter, including the pubic hairs around his crotch. It had become such an obsession with him it broke up his marriage. His wife filed for divorce. She refused to have sex with a bald-headed body.

Yes, and in his hand 1stSgt Persilla carried an object that any NCO worthy of his stripes dare not be without. The clipboard! That, and the elevated boots, were symbolic of military authority and its control over the enlisted man. The clipboard meant power. It dictated every aspect of a soldier's life, not the clipboard itself but that which was attached to the clipboard, namely, The Orders of the Day! And what were a company's Orders of the Day? They were decrees, esoteric ramblings, the lay of the entrails that could make or break a soldier, turn him into a mean-machine or an emotional wreck. Who wrote the Orders of the Day, or from whence did they come? No one knew for sure. The guess was the cartoon desk at Loony Toons. However, when attached to a first sergeant's clipboard, the Orders of the Day were carved in granite. Call it the Ten Commandments. The law of the land. And it was the 1stSgt's job to implement that law with, "ATTENTION!"

Also attached to a first sergeant's clipboard was another sanctimonious enunciation, known as the Duty Roster. Its task was to correlate codes, codes to work details, work details to names, and names back to codes that had no correlation at all except, maybe, semantics. "Hey you! PFC Butts! That your name, huh? Okay, Butts! Bend over and police that butt!"

There was a Duty Roster for this, a Duty Roster for that, on the spot duty, after duty-duty, weekend duty, mandatory duty, beautification duty, flag duty, training duty, police-call duty, drill duty, KP duty, maintenance duty, inspection duty, and, hmm, Howdy Doody! The Duty Roster was everything and anything to keep soldiers soldiering and dutifully dutying.

To the junior enlisted, the clipboard, with it's symbiosis of Orders of the Day and Duty Roster was a marriage made in hell. Its one saving factor was it could penalize the guard as well as the prisoner. Should an NCO, any NCO, lose his clipboard, chances were he would lose his ability to communicate. It happened once to 1stSgt Persilla. The result? He snapped mentally. He was no longer sure who to ball out. For three days he was unable to verbalize a command and took to sucking his thumb. Only when his clipboard was later found and returned to him was he able to command, run, and march the company again.

With a strut, 1stSgt Persilla stepped to his place at the head of the formation, all eyes on him. His gait was measured, suggesting strength, though everyone knew it was the high heels. Head high, nose up, he stretched, it seemed, for that illusive millimeter. He was the image of a leader, a picture of a soldier's soldier, albeit in miniature. It could be said of the 1stSgt he was the best. "COMPANY!" Army proud. "TEEEN-CHUN!" Professional. "ROLL CALL!"

The formation snapped to attention as best it could. The three platoon sergeants about-faced. Taking the body count, the squad leaders passed it forward to the platoon sergeants. Again, the three platoon sergeants about-faced and faced 1st Sgt Persilla. One after another they shouted, "ALL PRESENT AND ACCOUNTED FOR!"

Disappointed, 1st Sergeant Persilla shook his head. "Sloppy, platoon sergeants, sloppy!" The men do not appear to be with it this morning! They respond like basic training 'cruits! We do it again! "COMPANYYY!" he ordered at pitch. "TEEEN-CHUN! ROLL CALL!"

After four practice runs, the formation came to attention with enough vigor, though it lacked the vim, so the 1st Sgt could finally give the order to "STAND AAAT--EASE!" The formation relaxed. WHOOSSH!

"Sergeant Sweechek, was that your Red Skin who jumped out the window as I came out of the barracks?"

"Yes, First Sergeant!" snapped the master sergeant crisply.

"How many times he done that now? Pull that soldier's pass! What's his name?"

"Specialist, SPC-4 Lightpony, First Sergeant!"

"Well, he is now PFC Lightpony." The formation gasped. Lightpony had just been busted one rank. "And he gets 'kitchen police' duty for a week!" Persilla added, making a note on his clipboard. "If he jumps again, confine him to barracks! That clear, Platoon Sergeant?"

"YES! FIRST SERGEANT!"

The effect of the punishment rippled through the ranks with a "Wooosh!" Sympathetic mumbling was even heard from the inebriates. They fluttered blue-vein eyelids in condolence. The term, "Poor bastard" could be heard among the murmurs. Loss of rank and KP duty was bad enough, but to lose one's "off-post" pass was considered a personal calamity. It meant incarceration, no downtown bars, no women, no beer, no riot. Only drill, discipline, and that numbing conformity that is the US Army. SPC-4, now PFC-E3 Jimmy Lightpony the Shoshone, showed no emotion, typical of that Great Plains slab look.

1st Sergeant Persilla flipped a page on his clipboard and looked up. "Men, this has just come down from Brigade Command. It has been reported to the German *polizei* that a man in civilian dress believed to be an American soldier has been sneaking into woman's latrines at the downtown bars and peeping on them, frightening them and... Wa´? Who laughed?" The 1stSgt shot a demonic look into the formation. "I heard someone laugh. Men, this ain't funny! It's serious business! Now, who laughed?" he huffed.

A soldier from the second platoon acknowledged himself. "I did, First Sarge!"

"Drop and give me twenty!" Persilla ordered.

The soldier dropped into the push-up position and began to count out loud doing the push-ups as he did. It was followed by another twenty as 1st Sergeant Persilla continued to brief the company. "According to this report, the peeper spooks women on the toilet. He does a dance then runs out. Now, if any of you men know who the peeper is, it is your responsibility to report him to the Orderly Room immediately. I say immediately!" the 1stSgt stated, his voice raking against the cold morning air.

The soldier doing the pushups had already counted 60, well above the required twenty. "Recover!" ordered First Sergeant Persilla. Trembling from the excess, the soldier got up and stepped back into the ranks, but only when two men took him by the arms.

Specialist Yorit raised his hand and was recognized. "Can't be one of our guys, First Sarge. Signalmen don't peep. They grope!" There was some laughter.

"At ease! At ease!" ordered the 1ˢᵗSgt. "Don't make light of this, men! Central Intelligence Division is on the case. It's that serious! They are running a priority investigation to find out who the sick-o is. As of today they narrowed it down to two outfits: Brigade Service Company here next door and us, the 592ⁿᵈ Signal Company!" With the mention of the 592ⁿᵈ, the 1ˢᵗSgt's voice took on a perceptible edge other then his usual snap of the lash. "If I find out that any of my soldiers is the latrine peeper, I will personally have him busted and shipped back to the Zone and Baumholder's 8ᵗʰ Infantry. That man will be pounding tank tread as a PVT-E1 for the rest of his tour of duty! I will not have anyone embarrass the Army, this company, or our commander, not while I'm first sergeant! Hear?"

A man from the first platoon raised his hand. He was recognized. "How do we know it wasn't a German national who did the peep job, First Sarge?"

"Because Germans don't peep on women. They *'Sieg Heil'* 'em," uttered Robuck from his place in the third platoon. The men around him chuckled.

Lavoss touched his wounded cheek. "Ouch!" A piece of toilet paper detached where he had cut himself while shaving. It fluttered to the ground.

SPC-4 Jonas of the third platoon raised his hand. He was recognized. Jonas was from Alabama and talked like it. One had to listen twice to understand him, especially the soldiers from the North. "First Sarge, how do we know the peeper wasn't one o' them boys from-a, the 6ᵗʰ Infon-try posted at McNair Barracks?"

Considering the point, Persilla rubbed his jaw. A man from the first platoon raised his hand. He was recognized. "It can't be 6ᵗʰ Infantry, First Sarge. The officers over at the 6ᵗʰ don't let the animals out of the cage at night." There were some chuckles at the wise crack

"At ease!"

"Ah, First Sergeant!" It was PFC Kevin Kantwell of the third platoon who raised his hand. He was the new guy in the company. Soldiers called him "Puccini" or "Maestro" because he had studied classical music in civilian life; he could play several instruments, but when he opened his mouth his voice raised eyebrows. His enunciation was a little too correct for military tastes. The light shibboleth that rolled off his tongue hinted of some breeding—or alternate lifestyle—but no one commented on it. "First Sarge, here at Brigade Special Troops we have a bunch of companies: 287 MPs, 42 Engineers, Headquarters Company, 298 Army Band, and the Military Intelligence. The peeper could be from any one of those units too."

"Or a 40th Armored tanker. They're the infantry on treads," interrupted someone from second platoon.

"Tankers ain't peepers. They're warriors!" said another man from second platoon.

"Yeah, yeah," murmured some men from the ranks. Others nodded in agreement. "Tankers are tough guys."

"At ease! AT EASE!" ordered the 1stSgt, raising his voice. "That may be, men, but according to this report, the finger points toward Service Company and Signal. You, soldier, you and your buddy in second platoon there. You both weren't recognized. Drop and give me twenty!"

They dropped in place and began to do pushups the army way. "ONE, First Sergeant! TWO, First Sergeant! THREE…"

"Damn, there goes that finger again," whispered Yorit under his breath from his place in the third platoon.

"What finger is that?" slurred Robuck in the squad next to him. He was still recovering from his hangover.

"That fickle finger. Haven't you ever been fucked by the fickle finger of fate?"

"Yes, when I raised it with my hand to enlist in the Army," Robuck answered.

"Shut up back there!" growled PltSgt Sweechek over the shoulder. The men hushed up.

The 1stSgt looked out over the formation. "Any more questions?"

Rousing himself from under his hangover, Pereski raised his hand; his head was beginning to clear. The 1stSgt recognized him. "Top, you say the peeper did a dance. Could it be he was doing a, whatdoyacallit, *plie*? Did the report say the peeper pointed his toes and danced like a butterfly?"

The men in the third platoon caught the drift of the question. They glanced toward Yorit, the only man at 592nd Signal Company, if not the whole of the Berlin Brigade, with classical dance training in slippers and the only one who could and do *plies*. On occasion, he did them in the barracks hallway, only without the stretch bar.

It should be noted that Yorit did not walk into formation like the rest of the company; he danced into it. He did it for amusement. He thought it a fun thing to do, especially at 0530 reveille when everyone was in a half stupor. It was his way to get a chuckle out of the gloom. It was also his way to let the Army know that he was still an individual—a person, an entity. In the barracks he was once heard to scream, "I am substance, not a nomenclature!" With Pereski's *plie* comment, there arose a suspicion. Could Yorit be the peeper?

In the Army there is a mind set. If a man does not conform, and certainly dancing in the ranks is nonconformist, it can arouse suspicion, like now. And where there's suspicion, according to that mind set, there is guilt.

Standing at ease, hands behind his back, Yorit felt a sense of panic. He knew such an inference, and it was only that, could get him into trouble. He glared back at Pereski, standing in the second squad. "Pfsst! Hey, asshole! Cut the shit!" he hissed.

SPC-4 Pat O'Malley, another 3rd platoon man and the company pool shark (his gorilla-like knuckles and long arms made him ideal for the game) leaned toward Yorit. "Yoyo," he fizzed. "That fickle finger of fate you was talkin' about; well, it looks like Pereski's finger."

"Hush up back there!" rumbled PltSgt Sweechek again over his shoulder.

1st Sgt Persilla focused on the 3rd platoon. "If you're trying to tell me something there, soldier, you see me in the Orderly Room after PT training." He made a note on his clipboard. "Now, let me repeat! We are guests by conquest here in West Berlin. This does not give us the liberty to interfere, I say interfere, with the latrine needs of the German women. Get it?"

"May we interfere with their libido needs?" asked someone from the first platoon.

"What do you mean by that?"

"He means can we fuck'm?" said another soldier; followed by laughter in the ranks.

1stSgt Persilla glared. "Sergeant Oats! It seems we have a couple of smart guys in your platoon. I want their names for my discipline squad." He scribbled another note on his clipboard pad.

PltSgt Oats about faced. "You, PFC Smith! Drop and give the first sergeant forty! Johnson, you too! Now! It was you two made the wise cracks we heard!"

Both men did as they were told, counting out loud. "ONE, First Sergeant! TWO, First Sergeant! THREE..."

1ˢᵗSgt Persilla looked again at the formation. "Any more dumb questions?" There were none. He drew himself to attention. Squinting, he took a breath and puckered as if about to blow into the mouthpiece of an invisible tuba. "Companyyyy! 'TEE-N-CNEN!" he roared, his voice carrying well beyond his five foot one stature. He was about to turn the company back to their PltSgt for the morning's physical training—PT—when he noticed the third platoon. It swooned. The first squad swayed to the right, the second squad to the left, the third rocked back again to the right as if to a soundless waltz. A thin, vaporous methane-looking tint hung languorously just above the ranks; it blurred the motor pool beyond. Persilla recognized it. It was the tell-tale sign of...alcohol breath! Swallowing hard, he felt his blood pressure rise.

"Platoon Sergeant Sweechek, your platoon is not at an attitude of attention," he growled. "Are they trying to test the Southeast Asian domino theory? Look at them swoon!"

PltSgt Sweechek abruptly about-faced. Immediately he saw the problem. "Third platoon, one step backward, HUMPF!" he snap-ordered.

With that, the four squads stepped back in unison, except SPC-4 Bravo and one other man, Hatnoy, also of SPC-4 rank. They hung where they stood, fast asleep, shoulder-to- shoulder, supported by the squads. It was they who caused the third platoon to swoon. With the one step backward the two men lost their shoulder anchors and collapsed, ignobly on the sidewalk and promptly woke up. "Huh... Wah..."

"As long as you men are in the leaning rest position, give me twenty!" ordered PltDgt Sweechek, visibly annoyed at their behavior.

Counting out loud, as they were taught, Hatnoy and Bravo began their pushups: "ONE, Master Sergeant! TWO, Master Sergeant! THREE..." until they reached the number twenty.

"Recover!"

Struggling to stand, both men had to be helped to their feet. They had been to Rosenblum's Hail and Farewell festivity the night before.

"Master Sergeant Sweechek, I want those cat-nappers to report to the Orderly Room after chow for discipline," the first sergeant ordered.

"Yes, First Sergeant!"

Looking over the three platoons and raising his voice decibels, 1ˢᵗSgt Persilla became strenuous, almost operatic. "How many times I gotta tell you men, no napping in the ranks! This ain't Air Force basic training, you know!"

He hated churlish, non-military behavior. It was endemic of those who did not take Army life seriously. Only later, after some degree of maturity, did it occur to a draftee soldier that garrison training prepared him for battle, especially now should the "so-called" Vietnam police action really get serious. The military was a life or death affair. To survive it, a man had best get with the program. No one knew this better then he, 1ˢᵗSgt Luis Persilla, World War II and Korean War veteran with two Purple Hearts and a Bronze Star.

He fixed his company in a stare that was comparable to a collegiate hazing. "Platoon Sergeant Oats take these sad sacks to morning PT. I want them wrung out, hung up and dried before they return to barracks and morning chow. Give them a long run. Make it hurt! Then bring my soldiers back here, sober and combat ready. Is that clear, Platoon Sergeant Oats?"

"YESSIRFIRSTSERGENT!" bawled the platoon leader.

With a salute, PltSgt Oats right faced the whole company, then gave the order to, "Forwaaard! 'ARCH! Yo' lef'! Yo' lef'! Yo lef'… righ'…lef'…two, three, fo'…"

The 93 men of 592ⁿᵈ Signal Company, Berlin Brigade, immediately fell in step behind the guide-arm soldier. PltSgt Oats was now a man with a mission. He was doing the job he loved, that of a leader in the US Army.

The other Platoon Sergeants, Sweechek and Cabul, did the same. Heads high, necks arched, backs ramrod straight, they fell into step next to their platoons like Phoenician overseers guiding their charges to the galleys.

"…Yo' lef'…two…three…fo'…! Cadeeence…CALL!"

"I hear it calling," boasted the three platoons. "Calling for me-e-e, the queen of battle…it must be infantry-y-y…!"

"…two, three, fo'…"

As the company marched, the third platoon swayed, walked, and stumbled in wobbly order from the sidewalk to the curb, from the curb to the street, leaving behind—and much to everyone's relief—the heathen smell of collective beer breath where birds dared not to tread. That spring one did, and dropped dead at the feet of the shocked formation.

"…Yo' lef…righ'…lef…two…three…fo'! Cadeeence!"

"I hear it calling, calling for me-e-e! The king of battle…it must be artillery…"

"…Two, three, fo'…"

The company passed under the majestic linden trees, empty of foliage. The once- bright leaves, what few there were, had been nipped and curled by the November frost. It reflected the soldiers' sullen mood.

"Hey guys, look! The sky!" Kantwell called out, his voice sounding gleeful, the mark of the still uninitiated. A sudden wind churned the clouds. The hangovers rolled their arthritic eyes to the sky and groaned, "Yeah, sure…murmur, murmur…"

The three platoons passed the expanse of motor pool, the rows of vehicles covered with morning dew. They marched sullenly, mournfully, some of the signalmen out of step, unable to march to the cadence, no matter the effort.

"…Yo' lef'! Yo' lef…he…haw! Cadeeence! CALL!" PltSgt Oats bellowed out.

"I hear it calling, calling for more-or-or, the voice of battle…it must be Signal Corps…" cried out the three platoons in unison.

"…two, three, fo', yo' lef'…!"

At the corner of Avenue C, the company passed the ruin of a building; it was the derelict Nazi Waffen SS Barracks, once home to the elite regiment, *Leibwachtstandarte* Adolf Hitler. It stood empty. The windows were broken, the neoclassical facade mottled with decay. Small trees and weeds grew from the gutters and the sills. Though a ruin, the four- story structure was still impressive to look upon. The only reason it had not been torn down was because the Army utilized its cellars for an ammo dump.

The vacant SS barracks was said to be haunted, especially when storms blew up, as they often did, across the vast North German Plain. In the fall season, when the nights came on early, storms were especially robust. The wind and the rain would blow through the broken windows and down the barren hallways and into the eerie empty rooms, turning the building into a giant pipe organ of groans and shrieks.

Once, as the story goes, a man from Finance Company had been caught embezzling soldier allotments into his own bank account. Facing charges and a Dishonorable Discharge and disgrace, he committed suicide in the motor pool yard across from the old barracks. As his corpse was being placed in a body bag by the morgue detail, some of those standing around glanced up at the derelict barracks and saw a lone figure watching from an upper story window. The figure wore a black tunic, open at the collar, the riddle of a smile on his face.

Whether it had to do with the death of the soldier, or a fluke of nature, that night a terrific storm blew up out of the North Sea. The storm pounded the SS barracks with such fury it made the building tremble and shriek as if cheering the death. That next morning three men from Signal Company whose quarters were directly across the street from the vacant barracks put in for a room transfer.

"…Yo' lef'! Yo' lef'! Yo' lef' righ'…"

The old barracks also had a secondary function; it served as the senior officers' wine cellar. The thick walls and constant temperature were ideal for a cache. Ever since 1950, command officers used it to store their collection of Rheinhessen and Mosel wines. The IG (Inspector General) sometimes questioned it—not the stash, but the mixture of champagne, wine, and ordinance (grenades, RPGs and ammo) in the cellars. They let the issue stand.

General Omar ten Uncle, the current commanding general of the Berlin Brigade, was no exception. He was a viticulturist and had himself a substantial hoard. He even possessed several bottles of vintage 1914 Bordeaux from the cellars of Air Marshall Goring's Chateau Karin. On occasion, General ten Uncle would send a driver to the barrack to pick up a bottle or two for the officers' nightly celebrations at the Harnack House, or for poker nights, or for the Woman's Club meetings, or junior's birthday party. Whatever its uses, the suspicious signalmen generally avoided the old SS barracks on Avenue C. The company marched quickly past, giving it only a furtive glance. "…Yo lef'! Yo lef'! Yo…"

The platoons were now more sullen then ever, especially the third platoon. They were faced with a morning of PT physical training exercise made up of the "daily dozen," and the "run," which, taken together, was the equivalent of corporal punishment. It can be said of PT (Physical Training) that it was a discipline invented by the Army to bend a soldier to its indomitable will.

"…He-haw! Cadeeence…CALL!"

"Let it blow…Let it blow…Let the four winds blow…From east to west Alpha Company, Alpha Company is the best…" bellowed the three platoons in unison out loud.

"…Yo lef'… righ'…lef'…Humpf!"

The company marched past the underground rifle range built during the days of the *Kaiser Reich*. It passed the Maintenance Division buildings. Turning off the *Altdorfer Strasse*, it marched up a grassy rise, finally reaching the training area known to the soldiers as Yankee Stadium!

To see Yankee Stadium was to see high school. It had a football field, a track, a shot-put and broad jump pit. There was also a baseball diamond and an outfield. But it was the grandstands that caught the eye. Built from volcanic stone, the grandstands left the impression of a Circus Maximus long disused, waiting for the chariots to appear. The stands were earthen and tiered, and oval in shape. At the 50-yard line a high stone platform had been built. On it stood an altar with four giant, roughly cut, granite pillars that supported three roughly cut granite blocks in "Post and Lentil" construction. It was Stonehenge. Iron rings had been hammered into the granite either to tether horses for Druid worship or to tie female slaves for sacrifice. Where ritual torches once burned, only the metal grips remained. Why Stonehenge was built in the middle of Berlin, and for what purpose no one knew, or if they knew they kept the ritual, a Nazi ritual, to themselves. The soldiers had a name for the altar: "Himmler's Porch," after the infamous SS chief upon whose orders millions were murdered in concentration camps during the Third Reich days. The whole of the setting gave the impression of something alien, heathen, and primitive. Call it "Visigoth Revisited." To stand on Himmler's porch was to invite oneself to flagellate—"ideal for the tumults of morning PT," according to the BrSgtM.

The three platoons reached the quarter mile track. PltSgt Oats raised his arm.

"Compaaany! Double tiiime! 'ARCH!"

The command had the sting of a whiplash. "…hut-n-hut-n-hut…!" Immediately, the sighs and cries went up from the inebriates. They trembled as they ran, a chorus of tormented grunts and strangled groans. After two laps around the track, a man from the second platoon fell out and vomited. He was, no doubt, a boozer. Another quarter mile and another man dropped out. By the lap of four the muffled cries had grown to a crescendo of curses. Reluctant lungs fought for oxygen that did not seem to be there. Each step was more a dash through a knee high pool of Mother's Oats cereal than an open-air track. Another half mile (two times around the track) and three more men fell out, this time from the third platoon. They were sidelined with alcohol-induced emphysema

"I'm going to heave!" Bravo cried from his place in the ranks. The boilermakers from the night before had turned his stomach into an effervescent cocktail. Those running with him looked worried. Would he vomit? Bravo was in the middle of the second squad and there was a breeze.

Running along side of the platoon, PltSgt Sweechek dropped back. The perspiring soldiers marveled at how he could maintain the tempo, a man of his age, pushing forty. What they did not know was the MSgt was suffering as much as they were. Also, he had survived the 90 days of battle defending the Pusan Pocket in Korea, a heroic feat that almost cost him his life. A little workout was not about to put him off. "Stay in step, Hatnoy!" he ordered between the running cadences of "…hut-n-hut-n-hut…"

Near the rear of the platoon, Lavoss staggered more then he ran. Jimmy Lightpony the Shoshone pushed him from behind to keep him from tripping up. With each step, Lavoss drew in great droughts of what he hoped was oxygen, only it tasted of cognac. He spit and spit.

Jonas, the Alabama golden boy, jogged next to him. Jonas was called "Golden Boy," not because he was made of gold, but because the German women loved his southern accent. "Lavoss, you're disgusting," he huffed. "What'd you drink last night? Turpentine?"

Trembling as he ran, Lavoss wiped the spittle from his chin. "You name it, I drank it." Suddenly Lavoss grabbed his heart and called out like Christ on the Cross: "Father, into thy hands I command my spirit!"

"If you do, can I get your tobacco ration?" huffed Yorit who jogged easily nearby. He was thankful he had missed Rosenblum's "Hail and Farewell" party. Double-timing as they ran, everyone around him was sick, or thinking about it. The platoon and some of the company was a picture of misery.

"No talkin' in the ranks!" puffed the PltSgt, pumping his arms vigorously while "hut-huting."

"They're not-a-talkin', Sarge!" Robuck called out. "That's the death rattle you hear!"

The MSgt dropped behind the platoon. He checked the rank; he checked the file; he ran in spurts, forever encouraging, forever haranguing. "You're lagging, ladies!"

"How does he do it?" wondered Robuck, out of breath.

"Request permission to fall out and puke!" shouted a flushed-faced Pereski.

The MSgt rolled up next to him. "Permission denied! Run, damnit! You're a soldier!"

"I can't breathe!" Pereski wheezed."Use your aperture!"

"My aperture, Sarge?"

"Yes, you asshole!" snapped MSgt Sweechek.

By lap seven the three platoons together sounded like a Spike Jones ensemble playing "Tea-for-Two." Every second head took on the cadmium color of red and, like carnival balloons filled with helium, threatened to blow off. 3rd Platoon's Bravo swore off drink, at least for a week, while Robuck, who ran at the front of the squad, was considering life after death. Abruptly he broke from the "hut-hut" rhythm, drawing the squad out of step with him. PltSgt Sweechek quickly saddled up to Robuck and fixed him with a "I-dare-you-to-fuck-up" stare. "Pick up the pace or its five more laps for you when we're done!" the NCO ordered, breathless.

Wailing, Robuck resumed the platoon's pace.

A man from the 2nd Platoon who had boozed the night before on the *Haupt Strasse* (the main street bars) fell out. He took three steps, grabbed his chest and collapsed. The rest of the 2nd Platoon, and behind it, the 3rd, rushed past, around, and over the prostrate body, indifferent to the soldier's condition.

"Maintain tempo!" MSgt Sweechek ordered, looking back at the prostrate soldier.

Concerned, Lavoss shouted, "But, Sarge! That man! It could be a coronary!"

"Then it's too late anyway! Maintain tempo, I say!" Sweechek repeated. "Hut-n-hut-n- hut-n..."

As the 3rd Platoon passed over the prostrate soldier, two men tripped on him. The body didn't move. "Not to worry," panted Bravo. "Next lap we pick'm up and stuff him in a body bag."

The Signal Company formation ran; it struggled; it staggered; it wheezed; it (the soldiers) gagged as they fought their hangovers and the devil to maintain cadence, and why? It had nothing to do with unit pride or unit honor, but with unit fear, fear of a platoon sergeant's wrath and his favorite thumbscrew, that extra lap. Or should that not suffice, the dreaded after duty-duty, and an extra lap. "…hut-n-hut-n-hut-n..."

By lap ten, 2nd Platoon's Sgt Cabul was well out of his stupor and haranguing his soldiers with a fresh eloquence of a man rejuvenated. He tightened up the platoon's rear and picked up his dropouts. 1st Platoon's Sgt Oats, who lost some men, neither cajoled nor harangued the soldiers who had fallen out, but continued running until, out of shame, they rejoined the ranks and tempo with their buddies. The 3rd Platoon already ran as a functioning unit, enough to satisfy PltSgt Sweechek.

Shirts soaked and weaned from the night's bibulous affair, the remaining stragglers rejoined the ranks, even the soldier who was thought to have had a coronary. He rose as if from the dead and took his place back in the 2nd Platoon. What was and had been a besotted mob of stragglers in army fatigues with lolling tongues, was now a force to be dealt with. They were clear thinking U.S. Army soldiers again. "…hut-n-hut-n-hut. Cadaaance...CALL!"

"When my granny was ninety..."
"ONE!"
"She did PT just for fun..."
"TWO!"
"She could do PT better than you..."
"THREE!"
"She got up before dawn to do PT..."
"FOUR!"
"She did PT more and more..."
"FIVE!"
"She did PT to stay alive..."
"SIX!"
"She did PT just for kicks... "
"SEVEN!"
"She up and died and went to heaven."
"SHE!"
"Met St. Peter at the pearly gate..."
"SHE!"
"Said to St. Peter, am I too late..."
"SAINT!"
"Pete said to her with a big wide grin..."
"GET!"
"Down granny and give me ten...!"
"…hut-n-hut-n-hut-n..."

In the Army, things happen that are not to be explained. Its roots have to do with the psychology of the fighting unit. When a company faces tribulation, PT for example, or field combat, the unit either pulls together or disintegrates. However, when good leadership and high morale are part of the equation, a company, more often than not, will pull itself together and carry on. The 592nd Signal Company had both, that high morale and dedicated leadership. The proof? After an all-night binge and only an hour's sleep, soldiers did what soldiers have done since the days of the Hittites; they climbed over the top, or rather, climbed out of their bunks for PT training. It said something of the Company's "Esprit," the sentient call-to-arms. By lap twelve the Esprit had jumped from platoon to platoon, man to man, rejuvenating and igniting the spirit.

Still running, the soldiers began to clap. It became infectious. All three platoons were now hand-clapping to PltSgt Oat's sing-song cadence. Amazingly, all could breathe again, thanks to that pungent Berliner *luft,* or air. The lakes and forests that surround the city were famous for its reinvigorating powers, especially for soldiers. It cleared the heads and lifted the soldiers' moribund spirits. "…hut-n-hut-n-hut-n…Cadeeence!"

"Two ol' ladies were lying in be-ed…"
"One rolled over and she sa-id..."
"I wanna be an Airborne Ranger..."
"Live the life of guts and danger..."
"…hut-n-hut-n…"

In the east, the slate blanket of cloud that had hung for days over central Germany appeared to reach its margin above the Transportation Division garages. A virgin sunbeam broke through and poured flame into the late autumn treetops, setting them on fire. Whether it was the steep angle of the November sun or the heaven's dark backdrop or the light's reflection off the wet granite, the Stonehenge lit up. The Himmler Porch took on a tremulous and ghostly irridescent topaz tint. As the sunlight grew in intensity, the ten-ton pillar blocks appeared to lift themselves. The vision was Wagnerian in magnitude. Hesitating, the soldiers stared. Did it…did it mean the awakening of the Valkrie? The return of Siegfried to the sound of trumpets, or the reappearance of those minions of not so long ago, shouting, "*Sieg Heil*"? Trotting, wide-eyed and staring, the company wondered.

Overwhelmed by the magnanimity of the moment, the signalmen ceased hand-a-clapping. Even PltSgt Oats shut up his "…hut-n-hut-n…" the cadence call masticating. The company now focused on the Druid stones in expectation. Such was the drama of the moment. Then the spell broke.

Out from between the mighty granite pillars, and not quite the deity he should have been, stepped 1stSgt Persilla. "Huh?" The disappointment was tactile. The magic of the moment vanished. The slate of the November cloud retrieved the sun. Without the morning light for leverage, the Druidic Stonehedge stones dropped back to earth with a thud.

Perspiring, and disappointed, the company resumed the pace of, "...hut-n-hut-n-hut..."

"Talk about a wet dream gone bad," puffed one sweaty voice— Yorit's.

"1st Sarge could be God if he wasn't a midget," Bravo called over.

"Maybe God is a midget," huffed O'Malley.

"That would give God a Spic heritage," blubbered Robuck, puffing.

"Hey, if God is a midget, and Spics are midgets, then 1st Sarge must be...no, it can't be, a God?'"

"...hut -n-hut-n-hut-n..."

1stSgt Persella moved to the edge of Himmler's veranda and stood smartly at parade rest. He liked the veranda's dimensions. It was a stage that gave him not only a superb view of his charges but a sense of power, perfect for a short man on elevated combat boots. For once his soldiers had to look up at him, something his short stature did not permit on a level field. Though he knew it was an illusion, it filled him with a nascent sense of rule. It was an adrenaline high as exhilarating as standing outside the safety bars at Niagara Falls, something he once did years ago to prove his "kid courage." For that one stunt he took a slap from his father who had to jerk him back from the Niagara brink. Now, gazing down from the heights, he grasped what Adolf Hitler must have felt at the Nürnberg Rallies. Invincibility! Inhaling, 1stSgt Persilla absorbed the spiritual recharge. His day could now begin.

Below, on the quarter mile track, MSgt Sweechek stumbled, but caught himself. He turned, and running backwards, faced his platoon. "Give the 'Top' a good show, men, and he'll let us go for chow! That I promise you!"

Still double-timeing, the 93 male voices of the company shouted: "Army yeah! Navy no! Signalman, yeah! Air Force yo's-slow! HUMPF!"

From the verandah porch and proud, 1stSgt Persilla watched his soldiers. "Second platoon, tighten up there!" he ordered out as the

Second Platoon passed under his critical eye. It was followed by the Third Platoon. "Looking good, Sergeant Sweechek!" he called out. Two coveted hand claps followed. It was the signal for "Well done!" Sweechek swelled with pride as his men struggled to carry on.

The whole company had been running around Yankee Stadium for a half hour and had about reached its limit when 1ˢᵗSgt Persilla cupped his hands to his mouth and shouted, "Sergeant Oats! CEASE PT!" The platoons did not have to be ordered twice. They immediately slowed to march-step. "Bring the company back to barracks and morning chow!" to which one exhausted soldier raised his hands to heaven and cried out: "Praise the Lord! The midget has been propitiated!" Fresh, awake and energetic, the company began to sing, cadence marching:

"ROUND HER NECK SHE WORE A YELLOW RIBBON...
SHE WORE IT IN THE SPRING TIME IN THE EARLY MONTH OF MAY...
AND IF YOU ASK HER WHY THE HECK SHE WORE IT...
SHE WORE IT FOR HER SOLDIER, WHO IS FAR, FAR AWAY...
FAR AWAY! FAR AWAY-Y...
SHE WORE IT FOR HER SOLDIER, FAR, FAR AWAY..."

Back on *Altdorfer Strasse* in front of the barracks, the 592ⁿᵈ Signal Company of three platoons, four squads each, 93 men stood at attention, wrung out, perspiring, and wide awake. No one was in a body bag. Facing them again was Signal Company's 1ˢᵗSgt Persilla. He smiled for the first time. "My, how fresh my soldiers look. Okay! Chow time! COMPANY TEEENSION! FALL OUT!"

SSgt = staff sergeant = Oberfeldwebel

The Mess Hall

Again in formation and back at the company, the three platoons were now wide awake, motivated and looking forward to chow time, or as they say in civilian life, breakfast, lunch, or dinner. Other than a kind senior NCO, there are two things in the army that can stir a soldier's heart: Mail Call and barracks chow. And what is barracks chow? It is a sobriquet referring to anything nondescript, ill-defined and tasteless.

With the command to FALL OUT! the three hungry platoons broke ranks. They ran, skipped and jumped, wisecracking their way back into the company barracks, the misery of PT, (Physical Training) behind them. They ran down the short flight of stairs; they raced up the dimly lit corridor past the Armory, past the Mail Room, through the swinging green doors, into the brightness of the Mess Hall (the dining room). There, following the principles of physics when an immovable object meets an irresistible force, they braked. Facing them like a mastodon in heat, puffing, was the company Mess Hall staff sergeant—like a stone wall, left tackle ("I'm black and proud of it!")—Cookie Nast, also known as the "Mess Hall Daddy."

Dressed in fatigue pants, tee shirt, white apron, and looking like the commercial character Mr. Clean, SSgt Nast stood, legs apart, his bull arms folded, holding a metal ladle said to be made from a North Korean tank fender. With their path blocked by this pillar of strength, the hungry signalmen soldiers stopped, piling up in front of him.

The line backed up. Back through the swinging green, mess hall doors, back up the dimly lit corridor, past the Mail Room, past the Armory, back up the flight of stairs and out the door of the barracks entrance. There, the chow line ended with rumbling groans and one painful shout of, "Oh, shit, last again!" It was Robert Yorit, picking himself off the ground where he had been knocked down in the rush.

When he recovered, he looked around and saw where he was. "Oh shit, last again!" he whined, snapping his fingers.

"Don't complain," said Robuck, his buddy. "To be last is in the Polak nature."

"What do you mean? You're last too!" Yorit griped, not appreciating the crack about his Polish heritage.

"No, I'm not. I'm second to last. You're last! You're behind me!"

"And you're behind me?" asked Pereski, standing in line in front of both Robuck and Yorit.

"And you're behind me," stated Bravo in his Jersey twang to provoke the other three men.

Grabbing Bravo, they rough-necked him and each other the way boys do who share brotherly adversity—shoving, punching arms, a headlock here, a headlock there.

"Ha ha! And you're all behind me!" It was Lavoss. He joined in the rough necking. Inside, the barracks the hallway was long, the ceiling low, the walls confining. One of the ceiling lamps blinked as if trying to go out. The chow line itself, long and stretched, had already solidified. After the abrupt rush and some rough neck play among the signalmen soldiers, the chow line ceased to move. The hungry men, as always, now had to wait. Standing behind one another they bit nails, picked noses, smoked, and chatted to the tune of stomach growls. Yet, there was a hope, hope that someone, somewhere, somehow would throw the switch, open the green doors of the Mess Hall and get the chow line shoving forward again. It always did, only, like any bureaucracy, it took some time.

"That's the trouble with chow lines," Yorit complained. "No matter where you stand you still got half the company in front of you!"

"Yeah," grunted Robuck, "and I sometimes ask myself where I would be if I wasn't standing in a chow line?"

"Standing in the gutter. Where else?" said Jonas out loud in his southern drawl from further up the chow line.

"Lines ain't so bad," added Pereski. "Back home you'd be standing in line too, only a civilian one. I don't care where you go—the movies, a New York Nicks game, even at a relative's funeral you'd have to stand in line and wait."

"You mean they have chow lines in funeral parlors in New York? " Pereski laughed. "It's why they call NYC 'the Big Apple.' You get to chew on the corpses."

Lavoss touched his wounded chin from a quick shave; it still hurt but was healing. "Quite frankly, I'd prefer to stand in line at a home funeral than an Army chow line. At least the line to a grave is a short one."

"It's even shorter if it's your own grave," said Robuck, thoughtful.

Shifting where he stood, Yorit nodded in agreement. "Yeah, and even if you only had one leg, the Army would still have you stand in line at formation."

"Wrong!" drawled Jonas. "The Army would have you stand on the leg you ain't got." For the soldiers, the hallway air was getting heavy and the groans vocal. "Huff!"

And the chow line moved up one.

"Shit!"

"Damnit!"

"Modderfuck!"

"Say Al, you been in the Army for what, six years? How come you still got the lowly rank of a two stripe E-4 Specialist?" asked Bravo in Jersey, a finger to his chin.

"Don't knock the rank. Don't knock the rank!" Lavoss retorted. "I'll have you know it took me only five months out of AIT (Advance Infantry Training School) to jump from Private E-1 to Specialist E-4, an Uncle Sam record," he said proudly.

"Yeah, and another six years from now you'll still be an E-4 grunt, a second Army record," cajoled Pereski.

"Is it my fault the brass does not recognize talent and genius?"

"They do, but you got to be a college ROTC lieutenant with a degree in elementary education. There they teach B.A. grads to count to four the Army way: `Yo one, a-two, yo-three, a-four," Robuck called out from his place in the line.

In a row, one man behind the other, they leaned against the wall. And they stretched. And they yawned. And they inhaled. The air, stuffy-wet from their PT physical training, they perspired and together, groaned. The groans amplified.

"The way I see it," said Bravo in Jersey tongue, "Army promotions are like this here chow line. FOREVER! None come down from Brigade Headquarters because there ain't none to give out. Just look at us. We of the Third Platoon, or Signal Company, or any company here in the Berlin Brigade have to beg for promotion. You can go from Korea to Germany, Greenland to Turkey, wherever our guys are posted, and it's the same. No promotion! In the U.S. Army, Army rank is another name for stagnation."

Standing in front of Lavoss, Jonas raised his finger. "From what I understand, there's a promotion freeze going on here in today's U.S.Army. Why, I don't know. It's as if we're all locked into this crummy two-stripe E-4 rank stuff."

"It's the same in the officer corp. First lieutenants don't get promoted either. The Army is short on captains from what I hear," added Pereski.

"A real rank freeze," said Bravo.

Stretching, Yorit looked down the long hallway and observed that there was still no forward movement.

No push, no thrust, only the crush of one man behind the other. "Yeah, Frank's got a point there," he said, referring to Bravo. "I knew a guy in Service Company who has been a Spc-4 corporal going on 10 years."

"Why's that?" asked Robuck.

"He was from Nebraska."

"What's Nebraska got to do with it?"

"Its a state where the schools there only teach you basic arithmatic in the 12th grade, so I've been told.. Divide , add and subtract by four."

"Four! Why, that's our Army cadence call. The Nabraska boy would make a perfect non-commission officer."

"But," O'Malley interrupted, "what if a guy from Nebraska wants to learn to count to five?"

"Then he would have to join the Marines."

And the chow line moved up one.

"Mother fu..!"

"Damn-it, man!"

"Shit!"

"Hmmm!"

"There's got to be some way to break this Army promotion freeze we're in," said Pereski, looking around, wishing the chow line would stampede, or at least move a step.

"There is a way," said Yorit. "In the *Stars and Stripes* an article read that if the Army goes to war then we'll all get promoted, like fast. Look at our Heb buddy, Rosenblum. Just because of a little police action out there in Vietnam he got promoted to Sergeant E-5. Like that!" he said, snapping his fingers.

"I thought he got promoted because he re-enlisted for flight gunnery school and helicopters," said Robuck.

"I would never risk my life for an extra stripe," added Pereski, looking again down the hallway, his frustration mounting.

"Me neither," said Bravo.

"Or me," said Lavoss. "That's an invitation to bereavement."

"Bereavement! What's that?" asked Kantwell, the new PFC in the platoon. He also stood in the chow line, only in front of Jonas.

"It's what you feel when NCOs dump on you. It's worth be-reaving about," said Lavos

"Right!" responded Pereski. "Now, let's everyone bereave. All together now, one, two, three—bereave!" and gave a short scream. In the line, Kantwell stepped up and joined him, as did O'Malley. He stood in front of Jonas, who stood in front of Lavoss, who stood in front of Bravo, who stood in front of Pereski, who stood in front of Robuck, who stood in front of "Oh-shit-last-again!" Yorit. Together, they bereaved. The screams echoed and startled the waiting hallway crowd of soldiers.

Such was life at company level in an Army chow line of the 592nd Signal Company, Berlin Brigade.

And the line moved up one.

As the others chatted, Jonas pulled out the Army newspaper, the *Stars and Stripes*. He slapped the front page. "Will you look at this? Back home them Negras are demonstrating again in Selma, Alabam. They's tearin' up the South!"

"What do you mean by 'they's'?" asked Pereski. "Sounds to me like it's the other way around. The South is tearing up the Negras.

"It's why black folks demonstrate," said Bravo, who was from New Jersey and not from the South.

Yorit frowned, not appreciating Jonas' comment. "They got to demonstrate, Cecil. Don't forget those four little girls down South who were murdered—where was it, in Birmingham? And in a church, no less. Kids go to church to worship, not to die. If you ask me, white folks should be out there demonstrating with the black folks."

Jonas looked around at his buddies, sharing the chow line with him. Though they were all from the North, in his opinion, they were ignorant of life in the South. "It's that coon, Martin Luther King," he retorted. "The South was a fine place to live until he come-on down there and started a-stirring things up."

"Maybe it's about time someone stirred things up down South," commented Robuck.

Before Jonas could reply, there was a loud cry. It came from someone in the middle of the shunting and shifting line of hungry soldiers. "Will somebody get this fucking snake a-moving? Pleeease!"

As if an answer to prayer, the chow line wobbled. It swayed. It leaned this way, then that way, then it trembled as if doing the hokey pokey. "You put your right foot in, you put your right foot out, you put your left foot in and turn it all about. You do the hokey pokey and..."

And the line did move up one.

"Grrrr!"

"Damn!"

"Rumble, rumble!"

Yorit punched Pereski in the arm. "Oh, by the way, thanks, Bimbo."

"Ouch! What did I do right for a change?" he said, rubbing his arm.

Yorit pointed at him. "This morning at formation, in front of the whole company, you hinted that I was the peeper, the guy spooking on broads! What are you trying to do? Get me court marshalled? Just because I happen to have had classical dance training and point my toes in the ranks does not mean I `peep´ on women in the downtown bars!"

Pereski laughed. "Not to worry, Yoyo."

"Not to worry?" Yorit fumed. "You know how the Army is; they pick up on a scent and it's guilt by aroma. Just because I happen to have been trained in 'the Dance' back in college, Kent State University, does not mean I'm a Peeping Tom!"

Pereski scratched his chin. "Well, you know what they say, don't you?"

"No, what?"

"If the ballet tutus fit, wear them."

Yorit thought for a moment. He pointed his toes. "Which color?"

Suddenly, abruptly, surprisingly, the soldier chow line shunted. It moved, not sideways but forward. Immediately, the signalmen leaning against the wall jumped in. And the line moved up, this time three.

"What! That all?"

"Fuck it!"

"I give up!"

"Grunt!"

"Groan!"

"Hm!" Lavoss looked around. "Where's Bravo? I hear him breathing, but I can't see him."

"He's standing here in front of you, Bimbo," said Lavoss, patting the shorter man, Bravo, on the head.

"Oh, I thought that was a footstool."

At 5´5" and with an Italian heritage, Bravo possessed Neanderthal size eyebrows and was often the butt of barracks Dago jokes. He was not amused at Robuck's wisecrack. "Being short has its advantages," he snorted.

"And what advantages are those?" asked Robuck.

"When 1st Sarge asks for detail volunteers, he passed me over," he answered with a confident smirk.

O'Malley turned around. "Is that right? At our next company formation, remind me to get on my knees."

The chow line snorted, followed by vocal gargling, then moans and repeats. With hunger pangs thundering, the signalmen soldiers were growing more impatient.

Tired of the wait, Robuck stepped out of the famished line and boldly walked up the hallway corridor toward the swinging green doors of the barracks Mess Hall.

"Hey, fella! You jumpin' the line?" one of soldier from the Second Platoon called out.

"Me jump the line? I wouldn't think of it!" Robuck called back, then moved to make a dash for the chow hall's green doors. He was that hungry.

"Grab him!" someone shouted.

PFC Dandy Benjamin, a first platoon man and one of the few black soldiers in Signal Company, grabbed Robuck by the collar. He jerked him back. Another man grabbed at him, then another, and another. In spite of Robuck'ss protests, he was pushed, shoved, and passed back up the suffering chow line until he was again in his place a-way back at the rear. "Damn it! Last again," he protested

"Not quite. I'm still behind you," said Yorit passively.

And the line did move up one.

Hands on his neck, Pereski stretched. He looked over the shuffling bodies in front of him, all dressed in Army work fatigues. He shook his head. "You know, in high school geometry, I could never grasp the concept of infinity. Funny thing is I do now standing here in Uncle Sam's chow line, I get it. Chow lines are infinity!"

Just than, O'Malley woke up with a start. "Where am I? Where am I?" the big Irishman croaked. Leaning against the wallm he had dozed in place.

"What's a matter with you?" demanded Lavoss.

"I just had a nightmare."

"Tell us about it."

O'Malley rubbed his eyes. "I dreamed I was back in the service and standing in a chow line."

"But…but you are in the service and in the chow line," said Yorit, surprised by the comment.

O'Malley looked around. "You mean it wasn't a dream? This is for real? I'm still on active duty, still in the Army and still in a chow line,?" He began to cry.

It was at that moment that 3rdPltSgt Sweechek came strutting up the hallway corridor, the image of authority. He was frowning when he noticed O'Malley weeping. "What's the matter with you, soldier?" he asked firmly. "Physical training too much for a big Patty boy like you?"

"Not really, Sarge. I dreamed I re-enlisted in the army and they promoted me to Sgt. E-5. Made me an NCO."

"I sympathize," said the 3rdPltSgt. "Well, men, don't just stand there. Someone cut O'Malley's throat and put him out of his misery." Chuckling, he walked proudly away. The men watched their PltSgt saunter to the front of the chow line and go through the Mess Hall's swinging green doors to be served first.

"Of all the neroi-ve!" protested Bravo, talking Jersey. "How-sa come he gets ta go to da head of da chow line and I dun't?"

"Rank, my poor man," drawled Jonas. "You gotta have rank to get somewhere in life, Army life that is."

Frustrated by the long wait and restless, Pereski began hopping on both feet. "What I wouldn't give for a little rank. Hear me, everyone?" he called out loud, hands cupped to his mouth. "What I wouldn't do for a little rank! My net worth for some Army rank, E-5, E-6! Any rank!"

"And just what is your current net worth as a soldier?" asked Yorit, behind him.

Pereski started counting on his fingers. "Let's see. I'm worth one bunk, two bed sheets, and a brown wool blanket with the letters `US´ stamped on it. Yes, and a laundry bag too."

"In other words, you're broke," said Robuck.

"More or less."

"Demote that man!" Lavoss cried out.

And the line moved up one.

Head down and walking in circles like a criminal confined to a cell, Bravo clinched his fists. "It ain't right! What I want to know is what gives our platoon sergeant, Sarge Sweetcheeks, the right to go to the front of the chow line while we, the enlisted men, the front line guys, all have to wait?"

"Wounded in both legs by Chinese incoming," stated a strong voice behind them. The men looked around. It was the First Platoon's Sgt Oats; he had just come down the corridor and overheard Bravo. "His name is Master Sergeant Sweechek. Not Sweetcheeks! Show a little respect for a man who spent two years in Korea when you all were kids bouncing around in the first grade. And for that matter, I'm going to the front of the chow line too."

"You were in Korea, Sarge?" asked Kantwell, the new guy.

The PltSgt nodded. "Three years, till 1953, beginning to end."

Impressed, the men looked at one another. "Step to the head of the chow line, Saff Searge. we respect you. You earned it." said Yorit, with a subservient bow.

"Oh, and which one of us would you like to wait on your table?" Lavoss asked, his tone humble. They watched Sgt. Oats as he walked proudly down the corridor and pass through the swinging green doors and into the company Mess Hall.

"As a kid I was once hit in the head by a BB from my brother's BB gun. Does that permit me to go to the head of the line too?" Robuck wondered.

"Yes, if it was a Chinese BB," said Lavoss.

And the line moved up one.

Warmed from the mix of bodies, the chow line jerked forward, then stalled, then jerked forward again. It was like the shunting of cattle cars. The brackish smell of burnt toast and bacon fat now permeated the length of the company hallway. Unpleasant though the smell was, not one of the hungry signalmen complained. Chow lines, like animal odors and communal showers, were part of barracks life.

One disgruntled 2nd Platoon man threw up his arms. "Lines and gridlock! Lines and gridlock! Why is it in the Army we have to hurry up and wait only to stand in line and gridlock?"

"What are you bitching about, fella? You're close to the front. We're gridlocked here at the back," Jonas shouted up.

"The way this chow line is moving I may as well be standing with you Third Platoon guys at the back!" he retorted.

Folding his arms, Pereski leaned against the wall. "If I was paid a government salary I could tolerate this fucking waiting game."

"You are paid a government salary. $90-a-month. Big bucks for the year 1963. Its a garbage man's wage back home in Minnesota," noted Robuck.

Frustrated, Pereski turned and grabbed Yorit by the throat. He began to shake him. "We stand in line for Mail Call. We stand in line for Pay Call. We stand in line at formation, and stand in line to shit, shower and shave. Whoever invented the Army chow line, I want to strangle him!"

"Well, it wasn't me," Yorit protested, trying to break the grip.

"Blame grade school," said Bravo as he watched the two buddies wrestle and hug.

Pereski let go of Yorit . He looked at Bravo. "Why grade school?"

"Because it is the root of all lines, Army as well as civilian. Think about it. As kids we had to stand in line formation from the first grade to the eighth. I remember my first grade teacher, a Miss Ann; she was like a platoon sergeant, only she had tits, and could she count cadence!"

"With her tits?"

"Don't I wish! No, she used to march us bumbling kids—book bags, lunch pails and all—into the class room. We resembled a bunch of Humpty-Dumpties. Grade school was my first experience with military discipline."

"Was she ever a sergeant in the Army?" asked Kantwell, the new guy.

"The way she drilled us, you'd think so," said Bravo.

"I hate all first grade teachers," said Robuck, punching Yorit in the shoulder.

"Hey, what, what?"

O'Malley took out a pack of gum from his pocket. "What we need here is a little more love and a little less chow line."

Lavoss looked at him. "Love! What's that? I forget."

"It has to do with the opposite sex," answered O'Malley.

"There's an opposite sex? Where do I find one?"

"Not in the company Orderly Room that's for sure," said Yorit.

And again the line moved up one.

"Ugh!"

"Noooo!"

"Growl!"

In the company hallway, the air was growing stale, the moaning and groaning vociferous, discussions voluminous. Then Pereski spoke up. "What I don't like about lines is…"

"Yeah, tell me what you don't like about lines."

"…is standing in the latrine line. On our floor we got three sinks and three mirrors for thirty soldiers. To shave I'm forever looking over someone's shoulder in front of me."

"That's nothing," said Yorit. "This morning there was such a crush in the latrine I found myself shaving the guy in front of me."

Robuck chuckled. "You wouldn't have that problem if Bravo stood in front of you."

Not appreciating the wise crack, Bravo, the shorter man, growled. "I'm taller than the 1st Sarge and twice as mean."

"You can't afford to be mean. Someone might step on you," Robuck chuckled again.

"Back to the short guy jokes are we, Roby?" Bravo said, lunging at him.

Lavoss and Jonas jumped in between the two buddies. They pulled Bravo back. He pointed at Robuck. "Fair warning, Roger. Don't take off them glasses or you won't see my punch coming!"

Robuck laughed. Bravo lunged again, throwing a punch. It hit the wall. "Ouch!" he cried. And the chow line had moved up three, taking Robuck with it.

There were cheers. The company chow line had picked up tempo. It moved forward, as if in a rush. It had reached a milestone—the Armory Room door. There, the momentum died. Groaning, the soldiers leaned against one another again. They leaned against the wall. They stretched. They crouched. They murmured and waited as if for the Dead Sea to part. "My leg fell asleep," said Pereski, slapping his thigh.

"Which leg?" asked Yorit.

"My third!"

"Then you'll have to play with it."

"Game of chess anyone?" asked Kantwell. There were no takers, only plenty of bad humor bitching.

O'Malley called over to Jimmy Lightpony, the Shoshone. He was close to the front of the chow line. "Hey, Chief! Why the hold up?"

Head high, arms folded, Lightpony was a picture of meditative indifference. He turned and answered in the Shoshone language. O'Malley nodded.

"What did he say?" asked Kantwell.

"He said the hens haven't laid the eggs yet, but the pigs are being slaughtered."

Pereski stared at O'Malley, surprised. "What? Irish, you can understand Shoshone?"

"Sure! Strange though it is, the Shoshone and Gaelic language have similar linguistic roots."

"Yes, all one syllable words," quipped Yorit.

The indian, Lightpony, slipped out of the chow line and in his gliding way, ambled up to the swinging green doors of the mess hall. No one said anything. No one dared. Not to Jimmy Lightpony, the Shoshone. He was the company wild man and dangerous when touched. He pushed through the doors and disappeared inside the mess hall to join the company sergeants who had already gone in to be served first.

"Hey, he can't do that!" protested a Second Platoon man near the front.

"If you are as famous as he is, you can." said another.

"Famous for what?"

"Got his head on every nickel in circulation."

Shunting forward, the chow line reached the Mail Room door, the so-called 20 yard line.

"Almost the end zone," Pereski called over.

Robuck looked at Lavoss, then he looked at him again. "Al, why you in the Army anyway? Tell me."

Lavoss thought for a moment. It was a good question. Dare he tell? Being from Illinois, a football scholarship had gotten Lavoss into Northwestern University, but his drinking got him out. In the middle of his junior year he dropped out of college and joined the military rather than be drafted. The recruiting sergeant had assured his parents that the Armed Forces, with its heavy dose of discipline, was just what the young man needed to get his drinking habit under control. Encouraged by his mother, Lavoss enlisted. Six years of active duty later proved the recruiting sergeant right. He could now handle twice the liquor, all German, without staggering.

From the Mess Hall came a turbulent sound of crashing metal trays. Someone yelled. There was a loud scream. An argument ensued. In the corridor the chit-chat ceased. Everyone looked toward the swinging green doors and the commotion within.

"Is there a fight?" Yorit called out.

"No. Someone dropped a pancake."

One of the doors banged open, hitting the wall. It was Sgt Falosco of the First Platoon. He stormed up the hallway, his face in a boil.

"Hey, Sarge, where you going? Chow hall's that-a-way!" Bravo called after him.

"Not for me. I'm going to the snack bar."

"What does the snack bar have that the Mess Hall doesn't?"

"Unpowdered eggs!" Sgt Falosco vanished around the corner.

The men looked at one another. There was a noticeable look of concern. "What did he mean by powered eggs?"

"I don't care," said Pereski. "I'm hungry and need a coffee like a foal needs a tit."

"God, how I wish our chow hall would serve that," sighed Robuck.

"Serve what, a foal?"

"No, Tits!"

And the chow line moved up two.

It jerked, stopped, and jerked again, shunting. It stopped to a sequence of groans and curses and the clatter of distant trays from the soldiers already inside the company Mess Hall.

"What is this, the Siegfried Line?" someone shouted out his patience at an end.

Another man who had peeked through the swinging green doors called up the line of hungry soldiers. "The officers are being served! We're next!"

"Oh, the commanders' morning golf game must be over," said Yorit

"What do you mean?" asked the new guy, Kantwell, not understanding.

"You see, Kevin, for PT, Army officers play golf while we, the grunts, have to do the side-straddle-hop, pushups, situps, and hustle the three-mile run. It's one of the privileges of rank."

"Well, at least we're not their caddies," said Robuck.

Tired of the debilitating wait, one man from the First Platoon left his place in line and followed Sgt Falosco up the corridor, up the steps and out the front entrence. "Enough!" he called after himself.

Jonas looked hopeful. "Now if only the other 85 guys in front of us would do the same, we'd be-a next."

From behind the swinging doors, Mess Sgt Cookie Nast could be heard bawling someone out. There followed a shrill laugh.

"Wonder what's so funny?" asked Pereski, rubbing his stomach.

"Someone tasted the cooking."

Suddenly, and unexpectedly, the chow line quickened. Spirits brightened. As if drawn by a magnet, the clusters of hungry men were thrust forward, past the Amory, past the Mail Room, past the Supply Room too. They had reached the five-yard line. The four! The three! The two! The one! Touchdown! They were through the swinging green doors and into neon glare of the 592nd Signal Company Mess Hall. The soldiers blinked, not believing they were there. They had survived another morning in the Army without starving to death. The hallway waitm with all the griping and complaining, had been only twenty minutes; though it seemed like an hour.

What the enlisted man did not know, but the senior NCOs and officers did know, was that the best way to maintain military discipline—Army, Navy, Air Force, or Marines—is to keep the cattle hungry. That way, for a bowl of Cheerios a soldier would do what he was ordered. It is called discipline. "CHOW TIME, SOLDIERS! LET'S EAT!"

***

The 592nd Signal Company Mess Hall was a large, clean rectangular room with a spit-shined floor, light beige walls and all the warmth of a hospital ward. A white picket fence with floral boxes partitioned the room, separating the lower ranks from the elite—the NCOs. The officers, should they be there, had their own private dining room. They and the senior sergeants ate off porcelain dishes on tables covered with checkered table cloths and decorated with small vases; whereas the simple soldiers ate from metal trays on table tops made of formica. No tablecloth. No flowers. Though it was clear discrimination not unlike India's Hindu cast system, it had been the pecking order of things in the US Army ever since Washington crossed the Delaware. Noncoms and officers just don't mix with the lower orders, period!

The Mess Hall's bright kitchen, with its assortment of pans and pots, some the size of Volkswagens, was separated from the dining area by a long metal counter. Battered aluminum strap-pans were tossed on to the countertops by KP, Kitchen Police servers, and draftee acolyte cooks in fatigue pants, tee shirts and tattoos. They welded lethal looking skimmers (ladles) that looked like machetes. The skimmers' purpose was to slop the contents of the counter strap-pans into soldier trays with all the loving care of a priest suffering hemorrhoids while serving Holy Communion.

"Keep moving! Keep moving! Keep moving!" rat-tat-tatted the four KP servers back and fourth across the counter as they served the signalmen. "Okay, next guy! Grrr! Come on! Move it! Grumble, grumble, grrr! Been up since 0400! Grumble grumble. You there, guy! I'm in no mood! Keep your butt moving!"

Behind the KP servers, frowning, stood the ever watchful company Mess Daddy, SGt Cookie "Stonewall" Nast, the black NCO chef. He shifted his leprous eyes (they were sensitive to peeled onions) while prowling the counter. He strutted back and forth, sniffing the food, checking the servers, scrutinizing the behavior of the hungry soldiers. On occasion he would stretch one well-muscled forearm that would do Popeye proud in order to make a culinary point. Should a soldier question the serving, Nast would advise, "Don't think about it, fella. Just chew!"

SSgt Cookie Nast had been an infantryman during the Korean War. It was where he earned his rank of Staff Sergeant. That was eleven years ago. Today, 1963, it was still his rank. Like everyone else in the modern Army, he was caught in the Pentagon's promotion freeze.

Back in Korea he lost his trigger finger in a skirmish with the Chinese. Rather than force him to discharge, Command allowed him to cross-train. He became a category "92 Golf." A cook! It was the only job the US Army had open for a black man with nine-and-a-half fingers. It was a smart decision. Not only did the Army keep a dedicated NCO, but SSgt Nast developed into a first-rate cook and facility manager, with wall awards to prove it.

Like most career NCOs, MessSgt Nast too had eccentricities, like counting to four in his sleep, swatting at unseen gnats, and scratching his armpits while preparing lunch. But what made the men fearful of him was his short ladle, that so-called kitchen ladle "skimmer." With it in hand he commanded respect.

Made from a North Korean tank fender, the skimmer had the shape of a college fraternity paddle with a scoop at one end. Instead of a the inscription "Phi Kappa Beta" on the handle, it read, 'JERK!' and the names of those soldiers unfortunate enough to be knighted by it. Bonk! He used it to point out the serving counter's dubious choices of scrambled eggs, pancakes, fried spam, and any other unknown substances that may have been conjured up from the Pentagon's selection of voodoo recipes. With Mess Hall Sgt 'Cookie' Nast behind the counter, snorting and waving his much feared skimmer, no one dared refuse the extra helpings he recommend, not even the officers.

Yorit picked up a tray and utensils. Holding up a spoon, he turned it over. He nudged Robuck next to him. "Roger, look at this spoon, will ya? Funky. Here, hold my place in line."

"Why, where you going, Yo?"

"You don't expect me to eat with a dirty spoon? I'm going up to my quarters to fetch my field trenching tool."

"Your trenching tool won't fit in the mouth."

"No, but it's clean:"

Taking Yorit's spoon, Robuck called over to MessGt Nast. "Now Cookie, just looky here. Don't you wash the silverware?"

"Of course we do," grumbled the SSgt.

"Well, next time use soap."

"Smart ass, I see," the MessSgt snapped.

Robuck held up the spoon with its petrified black speck of what had once been ground meat. "Not at all, Sarge. I'm just concerned about your reputation."

MessSgt Nast grabbed the spoon. "Take another one, Grunt!" he snarled.

Further up the line, Bravo tapped at his serving of pancakes with a butter knife the KP server had just dropped into his tray. He nudged Lavoss next to him. "Why do I get the feeling I've been served a piece of shoe leather?"

"Because you have just been served a piece of shoe leather," agreed Lavoss.

"I'm going to put it back. I don't know if my fillings can withstand the pressure of a chew," he said, moving to dump the pancakes back into the strap-pan.

Pereski, who stood next to Bravo, looked over his shoulder. "Keep one pancake, Franky. You can use it to sole your boot."

Overhearing the commentaries, MessSgt Nast reached over the pancake strap-pan with his tank skimmer and tapped Bravo on the shoulder. He shoved the skimmer under Bravo's chin, forcing him to look up. The skimmer raised Bravo to his tiptoes; it was that or lose the only jaw he had. "You disapprove of my cuisine, there-a soldier?"

"Who me, Sarge?" Bravo whined between clenched teeth as he stared into the fierce face of Captain Queequeg.

"It's you I'm talking to, ain't it?" rumbled the Mess Daddy.

"Sure is, Cookie!""You got a problem with Army quisine, Solider?"

"Oh no, Cookie. I respect the chow and the effort you and your KPs put into it," he replied, his teeth clenched. The skimmer was pressing up through his jaw bone.

"I presume you would like an extra helping of pancakes, right, Soldier?"

"Ah, yeah, Cookie. You know me, ha-ha. I love Aunt Jemima's.

Grinning, MessSgt Nast let Bravo down from his tip toes. He nodded to his KP server next to him. "Give'm an extra helping of them flapjacks."

Behind him, Robuck whispered. "Frank, take all you can get. We can use the pancakes later for a game of Frisbee." Bravo held out his tin tray.

Hustling the soldiers along, the KP servers aggressively ladled the contents of the strap-pans into their trays. Most of the company had already collected their breakfast and were chowing down at the tables.

"Say, Cookie, does your MOS permit you to go to the rifle range?" asked Yorit blithely.

"I got to qualify once-a-year like everyone else. Why?"

"Well, since the fried eggs appear solidified, in my opinion they'd make perfect range targets."

MessSgt Nast leveled a scowl at Yorit. "Another cutie wise guy, huh? Soldier, you're on my KP shit list for tomorrow morning! 0400! Be there! What's your name—Ginny or Wap?" he snapped, teeth flashing.

"Neither," said Yorit, putting his hand over his name tag. It's spelled L-A-V-O-S-S, first name is Albert."

"Okay, Specialist Lavoss. Tomorrow at 0400, and don't be late!" grunted the mess sergeant, turning away.

"Did somebody call me?" It was Lavoss; he had rejoined the serving line.

"Yes, Al. Got news for you; you're on KP duty tomorrow at 0400," said Yorit, his voice passive..

"Who says?"

"Mess Daddy Cookie."

"What'd I do wrong?"

"You enlisted."

Quickly and with determination, the rest of the hungry signalmen soldiers moved along the counter, picking and jabbing, trying to identify the contents of the strap-pans. At one strap-pan they stopped. Robuck nudged Pereski, who nudged Jonas, who nudged O'Malley, who nudged Bravo, who nudged Yorit, who nudged Lavoss. Together, they all looked down at the contents in the pan. "What do you suppose that is?" asked Jonas, pointing.

Robuck sniffed at it. "I haven't got a clue."

It was Pereski's turn to sniff. "I'll take an educated guess. Dehydrated slugs?"

"Did I just see one squirm, or am I imagining tha-ings?" asked Jonas in his drawl.

Startled, Robuck backed away. "Quick, get a bayonet! One slug just yawned!"

Pereski poked into the strap-pan with his fork. "Not to worry, guys. It's only fried bacon."

"Yes, but since when does fried bacon yawn?"

"Isn't fried bacon supposed to be flat and crispy and not thick and curly?" asked Robuck, his voice heavy with doubt.

"Guys, I've lost my appetite," said Pereski, now pale.

Listening and annoyed, one KP server, Pvt Boils (the nickname he'd earned because of his acne) leaned over the counter. He waved his ladle as if it was a fencing foil. "Keep moving! Keep moving! We close down the chow line in five minutes. Shit or get off the pot!"

Shocked at the language, the men looked at Boils. "KP, you've just killed my appetite," Yorit charged him.

Bravo looked at Yorit. "You mean your appetite ain't already dead?"

"Don't I wish."

Lavoss looked up at the wall clock above the mess hall doors. "Guys, we don't have much time to chow down. Come on. Let's eat."

KP Boils saw his chance and dumped a scoop of wet fried potatoes into Lavoss' tray.

"Hey, I didn't ask for that!"

"In the Army you don't ask. You get!" It was MessSgt Cookie Nast again. He had returned to the counter.

"Pancakes! Potatoes! All these carbohydrates! It's no wonder I'm constipated," complained O'Malley.

"That's why soldiers grunt!" said the MessSgt, his lips tight.

Further up the chow line, Yorit stared into one of the strap-pans. "Cookie, I'm lost here. What's this?"

Before MessSgt Nast could answer, Pereski stepped up to the strap pan in question. "Fellas, I want you to observe the morning menu is improving. May I introduce you to Caviar soaked in goat milk, a Persian delicacy," he said, pointing to the strap pan. Its contents had been hardly touched by the company.

"Oohs" and "aahs" followed.

"Is this really a Persian delicacy, Cookie?" asked Bravo.

The MessSgt looked from Bravo to Pereski to Robuck to Yorit, unsure of their motives, but his pride at being a first-rate Army chef with numerous awards to prove it tempted him to boast. "Well, not quite a delicacy. Actually the recipe is Betty Crocker's with a little of the Nathan Nast touch. Can't help tampering, you know." And for the first time that morning, if not that month, the MessSgt smiled, barely. "Here we have diced onions mixed with a hamburger meat. And the trick is—yep, that's where professionalism comes in—the trick is the Carnation Milk. It's all in how you pour it. The pan can't be too hot, see, otherwise the milk would curdle. Add a mix of spice and ladle it lightly over buttered toast and you have..."

"...Shit-on-a-Shingle!" It was Jonas. He had stepped over to the group again.

Everyone flinched. "On second thought, I'll just stick with the fried eggs and pancakes," said Yorit, gnashing his teeth.

The large blood vessel at the Mess Daddy's temple began to thump. He eyed the soldiers in front of him. "I should have known!" he thundered, causing the rest of the Mess Hall to stop eating and look up. "I should have known this was a stunt! I want you, you, and you assholes on my KP duty tomorrow at 0400! The request goes up to the 1st Sargeant's desk right now!"

The men panicked. Trays still in hand, they apologized profusely. To placate Sgt Nast, they loaded the trays with extra helpings of everything on the counter: bacon, pancakes, potatoes, and fried eggs, which had begun to turn green in the aluminum pans, though at the pan of SOS they still balked. No one in the Army ever took extra helpings of Shit-on-a-Shingle.

"Cookie, I'll have a helping of that if you don't mind," said Bravo, nodding toward the stuff. For a moment, all activity in the chow line ceased. Even the KP cook, PVT Boils, took on a surprised expression. "Yes, please ladle me out some S.O.S. would you, my good man?" said Bravo in a condescending tone.

"Are you sure, Shorty?" asked MessSgt Nast, uncertain he had heard right. Bravo held out his tray. He nodded to his KP, Pvt. Boils, who promptly dumped in the extra helping.

Yorit stared at his buddy, Bravo. "Frank, now we know why you stopped growing."

"You really going to eat that stuff?" asked a perplexed Robuck near by and watching..

"Not really," declared Bravo. "When I inhale the stuff it helps clear my sinuses."

Startled by the comment, MessSgt Nast promptly conked Bravo on the had with his skimmer. "Soldier, I dub you one honorary jerk!"

Bravo stumbled, barely supporting his tray. Shocked, the soldiers around him could only stare. They had never seen an NCO with rank conk anyone before except in Basic Training. There, every recruit got bopped for something.

"This is worse than hell week back home in college," gasped Yorit.

Lavoss took a deep breath. He knew he was taking a chance of getting himself conked as well, but he felt he had to ask. "Mess Daddy, can I ask you something personal? How'd you get all those awards hanging on the Mess Hall wall there? It can't be the food. The toast is cold, the bacon is burned, the pancakes are shoe leather, and this concoction here we won't discuss," he said, nodding toward the pan of S.O.S.. "So tell us, Sarge, what was it that got you all those awards?"

MessSgt Nast fixed on Lavoss. Squinting, he tapped the palm of his hand with the skimmer. Anticipating another whack with the instrument, O'Malley stepped out of the line and went for bandages, but the MessSgt surprised everyone. His voice turned amiable. "Soldier, hold out your tray would you please?" he said to Lavoss and began filling the one dish on it with a disproportionate helping of S.O.S.. "The secret is, I can break two eggs with one hand."

"That's no big deal. I've seen a mess cook at Fort Bragg break four," said Robuck.

"Yes, but were they powdered?"

The chow line slammed shut. Anyone who came in late to the company chow hall got nothing. The resonant sound of skimmers cracking on strap-pans diminished, then ceased. The stacks of fried eggs, flapjacks, burnt toast, twisted bacon strips, and withered sausage vanished, along with the griping, into the mouths of the hungry signalmen. A soldier's appetite can be voracious. Even the helpings of S.O.S. were consumed.

The Mess Hall was loud with talk, youthful laughter, and the occasional belch that burst like flack off the room's low ceiling. Once, Third Platoon's O'Malley let out a well practiced, high school belch, the kind that resonates like a foghorn in the mist. A Special Troops MSgt who happened to drop by the Signal Company Mess Hall for a quick eat with the signalmen, dropped to the floor in a reflex response. The belch sounded like Communist Chinese incoming. He, too, like many of the senior NCOs in the Brigade, had fought long and hard along the 38th parallel in Korea and never quite recovered from the experience. For his behavioral indiscretion, O'Malley was disciplined and given an extra work detail.

In the company Mess Hall, behind the little white garden fence that sectioned off the NCO tables from the enlisted tables, PltSgt Oats sat alone. Satisfied with his breakfast, he pulled out a white alabaster pipe. It was a handsome object, beautifully carved and highly polished. It had once been a North Korean thigh bone. PltSgt. Oats then took some tobacco from the dried scrotum pouch he carried (he was not sure if it was North Korean or Chinese since Asian scrotums all look alike once they were bleached) and filled his pipe. He lit it and sat back, content. "Has a smooth draw," he was fond of saying to his shocked observers. When asked why a North Korean thigh bone for a pipe, he would answer, "Asian bone is more porous than Caucasian. It has to do with their diet of rice and vegetables. It keeps the pipe cool."

It was during the Korean War that PltSgt Oats discovered the market niche for thighbone pipes and scrotum tobacco pouches. He sold them to different combat units. The scrotums were noted for their velvety touch and colored draw strings. The business thrived until the Army put a stop to it. Some of the bone pipes turned out to be South Korean.

For his questionable entrepreneurship, PltSgt Oats was sent back to the States and Walter Reed Hospital for psychiatric observation. The report's analysis concluded that he suffered from extreme battle fatigue. After his years in Korea and no leave, he was just not himself. Instead of a Court Marshal, he was promoted to the rank of Sergeant First Class (SFC) and reassigned to Fort Sill, Oklahoma where he

DI-ed basic training until the Korean conflict was over. Now, all that remained of what might have been a lucrative Fortune 500 company was one well-polished North Korean thigh bone pipe with a smooth draw, and a Chinese scrotum pouch with a velvety touch..

Their trays piled high with food, the men of the communication squad looked around the Mess Hall for a free table. All were soldier occupied. There were two tables free in the NCO sector where PltSgts Cabul, Sweechek, Oats, and the other company NCOs sat, but that was beyond the pale for the lower orders.

Holding his tray high so as not to bump anyone, Robuck stepped carefully around the seated signalmen. He found a table where the occupants were almost finished with their morning chow. "All right, First Platoon guys, you're done. Buzz off! Third Platoon squad needs the chairs," he snapped at them.

The table conversation abruptly stopped. Spc Blasdale, a *Teufelsberg* (Devil's Mountain) Berlin radio site repairman and a First Platoon soldier, looked up at Robuck. "I'm still drinking my coffee, or are you too blind to notice, Third Platoon fella?"

"Looks to me as if you're already finished," Robuck replied.

"I told you I'm still drinking my coffee," retorted Blasdale, not liking the interruption.

Robuck stepped up to the seated man. "Are you saying 'no' to a person holding a lethal tray of Shit-on-a-Shingle?" He tipped his tray for Blasdale to see.

Standing behind Robuck, Yorit interrupted. "Ah, gentlemen, you had better be careful. My friend here has a hair trigger finger. That tray of S.O.S. could go off any second and, ah, into your lap."

There was a moment of tension, then frowning, Blasdale got up. He considered the trade off: a punch in the mouth for what could be a ruined set of freshly starched work fatigues. The odds did not look favorable for him. "OK, let's go, guys. We're done chowing down anyway," he said to his two table buddies.

"Retreat is the better part of valor, I always say," announced Robuck with a note of sarcasm, taking the empty seat.

One of Blasdale's companions glared down at him. "And my friend has a hair-trigger punch. First platoon is letting you off this time, but I advise you, don't pull this stunt again, Robuck. You have been duly warned."

There was another moment of brief tension, a hard look or two, then it passed. The three First Platoon men walked away, taking their empty chow trays with them.

The men of the Commo Squad sat down to the unsyncopated clatter of utensils. They began to eat like the rest of the chow hall soldiers, hungrily, snorting like a brood of young lions over a downed carcass. Except for the crunching of fried bacon and the occasional grunt, there was little conversation.

"Here, here! Soui, soui! Where did you men learn to eat like that? On a New Jersey pig farm?" It was PltSgt Sweechek. He had come up to the section table.

"I take offense to that, Sarge," said Bravo, who was from the state.

"That suck and pop you hear ain't Bravo, Sarge; its Yorit licking his fingers, and he's from Ohio," said Pereski.

Yorit put down his spoon. "At lease I don't eat cornflakes with a knife and fork, Missouri boy. Bythe way, you got a wet Wheaty flake stuck to your nose."

Pereski looked cross-eyed down his nose. Sure enough, a Wheaty cornflake had stuck and dried there. He flicked it off with his finger.

Sweechek held up his clipboard. Besides being a PltSgt, he was also the communication section NCO. Everyone at the table sensed trouble coming. A SecSgt with clipboard in a chow hall was a bad sign. It hinted of the work details to come. "I want you guys over at Communication Shed in five minutes. We have a briefing."

"But, Sarge, we just sat down!" Pereski protested.

"We was stuck at da end of dat line," whined Bravo, slipping into his Jersey accent.

Robuck slouched in his chair. "Sarge, we won't even have time for a bowel movement, let alone eat and report," he complained, his mouth full of fried egg and toast.

"All right! I'll give you men fifteen minutes to eat and go." That said, the NCO turned and walked away.

The Commo Squad soldiers watched him as he went, vanishing through the swinging green doors of the company Mess Hall. "Yeah, sure, hurry up!" mimed Lavoss. "The same old Army rap of hurry up and wait, hurry up and wait, and for what? For nothing!" he sing-songed.

Picking up two knives, O'Malley began to tap out a beat on the table. "It is always hurry up and wait, hurry up and wait, hurry up and wait, and wait…

Picking up on the rhythm, the men at the table began to snap their fingers to the beat. "Hurry up and wait, wait for parade, hurry up and wait, wait for inspection, hurry up and wait wait for wait to wait, hurry up, hurry up, getty-up to wait. Yahoo!"

Lavoss frowned. "We got fifteen minutes, guys. Let's hurry up!"

In the corner of the Mess Hall was the company coffee machine. It had a boiler that hissed. Assistant cook, PFC Wilber was on his tiptoes, replacing the filter. He poured in a can of Maxwell House Coffee. Standing next to him and waiting was a short line of impatient looking men holding out coffee mugs.

"About ready?" asked one of the men from the Second Platoon. He sounded desperate, his voice rasping.

Cook Wilber closed the boiler's cover. "Coffee has to percolate first." Next to him the Second Platoon coughed out loud. "What's a matter with you?" he asked.

"A piece of bacon. It's wedged in my throat," wheezed the Second Platoon man. "Gotta wash it down."

"Here, wash it down with this," said Cook Wilber, digging out some wet coffee grounds from the filter with a spoon in hand. He plopped the grounds into the man's cup.

"Huh, what?"

"It'll break up the log jam."

"You're kidding," coughed the Second Platoon man.

"Drink and swallow," Wilber encouraged.

"The Second Platoon man followed the advice. It did the trick. He could swallow again. Grateful, he thanked the assistant cook and walked away, but not before swearing off mess hall fried bacon for the rest of his tour.

By now the coffee boiler was percolating. The other men in the line quickly filled their mugs when Yorit stepped up to the coffee boiler and filled his. He swirled the coffee in his mug, not quite sure what to make of the swampy looking liquid. "Say, Cooky, this here coffee looks tinted, or am I just imagining things."

PFC Wilber glanced into Yorit's cup. "You're imagining things."

"Since when does GI coffee have a blue tint? It wasn't that way at Basic. There it was black."

"If that's what the coffee machine pumps out," said Cook Wilber, who was from Arkansas and tended to drag his syllables when talking.

"Oh good," Replied Yorit, not trusting the drink. "You had me worried. I thought the coffee was laced with cider."

"It sometimes is. Say, you got something against Amy java, there-a, Spc- 4?"

"Actually no, but when I find my java tinted with apple cider, yes."

Wilber wiped his hands on his stained apron. "You cath-o-lic or something?"

"What's religion got to do with Army coffee?"

"Blue tint is the Virgin Mary's favorite color."

"The Virgin Mary? I didn't know she drank coffee."

"Look, just pretend the java is black and drink it."

Yorit, sniffed the cup. "I would, only I forgot my fountain pen. What did you use for a coffee filter, an ink pad?"

Cook Wilber looked at Yorit. He sighed. He was tired. He was always questioned about the chow. "Maxwell House filter paper! Now look, Soldier! Me and the crew have been up since 0400 preparing chow for you guys. We put in 14-hour days. That's like every day, six days a week. For that, we get no rank and less respect. I'm beat and in no mood for complaints, as if I don't get enough already. Drink Uncle Sam's java. It'll clear yo' head fo' wha' ever ails ya', as them jamboree darkies used to sing back home."

"I dunno?" questioned Yorit, doubtful.

Wilber stepped up close to him. "Tell me, Soldier, does it smell like coffee?" he asked, pointing to Yorit's mug. Yorit nodded. "Does it taste like coffee?" Again the nod. "Then it must be, what else, but..." Wilber flipped open his hand for the obvious answer, to which Yorit replied, "Terpintine?"

The PFC cook sighed, but decided on one more try to placate the bird brain in front of him. He was determined to make Yorit understand the science of Armed Services coffee and its pedigrees, of which this was one. He brushed back his tensor. (The company had a new barber who gave close hair cut shaves.) "Okay, you leave me no choice. Give me your mug. We'll give the java that Arkansas mud test. Take off your boot!"

"My boot? What for?"

"To drop it in the mug. If the boot floats, it's coffee."

At the table across the chow hall, Lavoss stood up, He signaled Jonas and O'Malley, who sat together at another table. He pointed to his watch. "A briefing at the shop in five minutes," he called over.

They looked at each other. "We just sat down!" O'Malley called back at him.

Lavoss motioned to Jimmy Lightpony, the Shoshone. He sat alone, a bowl of Rice Crispies in his hand; he was eating with his fingers. It was all he ever ate for breakfast, lunch, and dinner. Only in the field did he change his diet. There he ate C-ration spam, all he could get. When asked, "Why spam?" He would answer in Shoshone. "Closest thing to Great Plains buffalo meat." With a nod, Lightpony got up to go.

Bravo looked across the table at Pereski. "Say-a, Paul. What did Rosenblum say to you last night just before he got on the duty train to Bremenhaven?" he asked through a mouthful of toast and eggs. Bravo had a habit of talking with a mouth full while chewing a toothpick; it had to do with his Italo-Jersey upbringing. The question came out sounding Esperanto. "Say-a, Paul, wats-a Rosy-boom there a-say yous lats nit jus' fo' he goes on da toosy train?"

In the Army, to eat and talk with a mouth full is the norm. It is usually followed by a loud unintentional intestinal burp, or scores of burps. It has to do with the Army's all-male environment. It does not make any difference if a man is signalman, tanker, engineer, or infantry, especially infantry, where soldiers end every burp punctuated by the word, "Geronimo!" That, and chewing with a mouthful, along with smoking, drinking, and swearing, dominates a soldier's behavior. Good manners and proper etiquette, habits which were carefully nurtured by loving mothers over the years, are tossed to the wind in an Army Mess Hall environment.

Once, in a rare moment of insight around the company mess hall table, Yorit made a profound statement. With a mouthful of chow he said, "Guys," chump, chump, "you know what is missing today in the Army?" chomp. "It's women. We need more women soldiers in our ranks." Chomp. "Their presences would certainly improve our dining behavior." Chomp, growl, fart.

It was a discerning statement of things to come. In the meantime, in the all-male Armed Services, young men would continue to chew, garble, and burp with their mouths full. Sorry, Mom.

"Rosy asked me if he did the right thing by re-enlisting," answered Pereski.

"Yes, and what was it Rosy was referring to by 'the right thing'?" asked Yorit, considering Bravo's question.

Pereski put down his fork and looked around the table. "He wanted to know if it was a wise decision to re-enlist for combat in Vietnam. I told him, 'no.' That he was being sucked in by our re-enlistment NCO, Sgt Chuckles. In my opinion, Sarge Chuckles pulled a fast one on Rosy," (At the 592nd Signal Company the re-enlistment NCO was called "Sergeant Chuckles" because every time he got a man to re-enlist in the Army, he chuckled.) "As you know, the sarge promised him copter gunnery school, promotion to the rank of sergeant-E5, plus a bonus. It had to do with the Vietnam police action. It was a dangerous package and not worth the risk."

Buttering his toast, Bravo looked up. "Is that all he got?"

"No, to sweeten the deal the Army threw in a free *Barmitzfa*.

Startled, Yorit dropped his spoonful of SOS; it was half way to his mouth. "A free *Barmitzfa*? I thought Jewish kids got that at age thirteen!"

"It was his second."

Suddeny there was a short clang. It was the company alarm bell. At the Mess Hall tables the men looked at one another. It was that minor alert which meant, "Mail Call," that magic word that reminds soldiers of home. Quickly, those still in the Mess Hall chowed down their breakfast meal, jumped up, and ran out of the hall. Robuck, Yorit, Pereski and Bravo jumped up too. Stuffed, satiated and burping, they headed for the Mess Hall's swinging green doors, but were stopped. MessSgt Cookie Nast blocked their way. Robuck ran into Yorit, who ran into Pereski, who bumped into the shorter Bravo, who bounced off the Mess Daddy's mighty chest mass. Only Lavoss refused to be intimidated by the sound of the alarm bell. He remained seated and content, smoking a cigarette.

"Just where do you men think you're going?" MessSgt Nast growled.

Speaking all at once, they shouted, "Mail Call!"

"Are you girls trying to make an ass out of an old time NCO? You know the regulations here. CLEAR YOUR TABLE! AT ONCE!" he barked. When angry, which was often, MessSgt Nast's voice was not unlike a firing squad volley; it was why soldiers tried to avoid him and kitchen police duty. "Get those trays to the wash window on the double or I'll have you men scrubbing my floors with a toothbrush from now till midnight!"

"But it's Mail Call time, Sarge!" Yorit pleaded.

"Me and my sidearm (the skimmer made from a North Korean tank fender) says not till your table's cleared. Like pronto!" he barked, pointing toward the kitchen police room window where the dirty trays were brought and stacked for those on kitchen police duty.

Immediately, the four men ran back to their chow hall table and grabbed the trays. Reaching out, Pereski jerked the cigarette from between Lavoss contemplative lips where he was still seated. He dropped the butt into his coffee cup. "Hey, wha…" In three seconds the table was cleared.

As if breaking from starting blocks, they sprinted past the still frowning Mess Daddy and through the swinging green doors of the Mess Hall and down the length of hallway until they reached the Mail Room door. A line had already formed. And what a line! Three platoons worth. 85 men. The line had grown in multiples and ran the length of the hallway beyond the Mail Room, past the Arms Room, around the corner and up the short flight of steps, and out the front entrance door to *Altdorfer Strasse* where, for the second time that morning Spc-4 Robert Yorit shouted, "Damn it! Last again!"

THE BERLIN BRIGADE

The 592nd, Sig. Co.

3rd Platoon

POLICE PATR

POLICE DEPT.

The Keystone Grunts— All Over Again

that is

Déjà vu – Catch 22 –

They Don't Come Any Tougher
Or Drunker

1963

The Keystone Grunts

Behind the 592nd Signal Company was a motor pool. It was a reservoir for vehicles from the different companies. There were jeeps, semi trucks, five tons, and deuce-and-a-halves, all standing in parallel rows, and all painted the only color in the army that counts. Olive drab! They were the Army's reserve vehicles, parked and waiting for the Battle of Berlin to begin, should it ever. Since 1945 they sat, mostly idle, little used, sometimes shunted from one corner of the motor pool to the other in order to keep them operational. Occasionally they would be pulled from the rows and sent on convoy runs to West Germany or used in field exercises that the Brigade fought once a year against the French and British garrisons, their allies; otherwise, the vehicles stood parked, rust collecting. It was one of the Berlin Brigade's motor pools.

However, there was one corner of the vast motor pool that did buzz with some activity. It was the Communication Area. There, two white-washed concrete buildings stood next to each other, one a MARS station with it's sixty-foot antenna for worldwide communication; the other, a low, nondescript bunker with thick walls and narrow windows. The bunker, or "Commo Shed," as it was called, belonged to the third squad of the third platoon of the 592nd Signal Company, MSgt Humphrey Sweechek, NCOIC, in charge.

The door of the Commo Shed swung open and in stepped three soldiers: Yorit, Lavoss, and Pereski. With them came a swirl of morning moisture into the room. "Shut the damn door!" Jonas called out in southern. They grunted "Hellos!" that mixed with the Squad Room's voice murmurs. Opening their field jackets, the three men took their places on the olive drab painted benches, eighteen layers of it, one for each year the US Army had been in West Berlin. The olive drab benches were set against olive drab painted walls on olive drab painted floors.

The ceiling, the only part of the room not painted olive drab, was once the color of beige but cigarette smoke had long ago turned the ceiling into a greasy mustared color, giving it a tint of, what else, olive drab.

Three large bulletin boards hung on the walls. They were covered with a profusion of radio and vehicle maintenance charts that resembled printouts of Einstein's Theory of Relativity—impossible to read, and if read, never understood. On one wall was a series of photographs; it was the Army's "Chain of Command." It began with a portrait of the President of the United States, than the Secretary of State, than the Secretary of Defense, the officers of the Joint Chiefs of Staff, the Commanding General of 7th Army, the Commanding General of Berlin Brigade and the Brigade Sergeant Major. The photographs of 592nd Signal Company Commander, Captain Mellon and the company's 1st Sergeant, Luis Persilla, brought up the Chain of Command's rear.

Such a Chain of Command could be found hanging in every barracks, in every shop, on every post in the Army, Navy, Air Force, and Marines. Whereever servicemen were posted, be it in the Atlantic or Pacific Theater, in Europe or in Asia, or in the USA itself, the photographs of the "Chain" were there, bound and bolted to olive drab walls to remind servicemen of who was running the show. To drive the point home, soldiers had to memorize the Chain of Command. To know it by heart was a standard "Order-of-the-Day." And why? Because everyone had to know who above them was giving the orders, and to whom soldiers had to report. If a grievance needed to be addressed, such as the one made by Bravo about a 20-hour work detail he had not volunteered for, the grievance had to walk the "Chain," as they say.

The odyssey always began at the bottom in the work section. Then the grievance would pass from squad to platoon level, then to company level and the 1ˢᵗ Sgt. From there, it would be handled by the Company Commander where, if not resolved, would progress to Brigade level, then to Heidelberg Command, or Stuttgart and 7th Army Command. If no resolution was found at that point, the grievance would be passed on up to the Department of the Army and, should it be necessary, to the desk of the Commander and Chief of the Armed Forces, the President of the United States himself.

Bravo's grievance never got that far. It remained at company level, where it died along with all other soldier grievances, on the desk of 1ˢᵗSgt Persilla. He gave Bravo's complaint a quick read and stamped it "Resolved!" before filing it in the wastepaper basket. At the time of his discharge, Bravo was still waiting for a response from the President of the United States.

The members of the Chain of Command never smiled. President John Kennedy hinted at one but gave up because no one else in the row of photographs smiled. In his photo, thin- lipped Vice President Johnson appeared to have swallowed his dentures, which gave him a reason not to smile. Robert McNamara dared not smile; he was after all Secretary of Defense and had to look tough. The State Department's Dean Rusk did not smile because he was loosing his hair, which is no laughing matter. The Secretary of the Army's photo was over exposed from the excess brass, the four stars and chest medals he was wearing. He may have been smiling, but it was doubtful. The commander of the Berlin Brigade, General Omar ten Onkel, also did not smile, nor did the Brigade's Command MSgt. All glowered as if angry at having to sit for the snapshot.

When soldiers stood before the photogenic majesty of the Army Chain of Command they trembled, unsure of what to do. Some chose to genuflect. Others saluted as they stepped past. One man prostrated himself like a church acolyte and worshiped. Some soldiers did all three.

One morning, on paint detail and day-dreaming, Spc-4 Hatnoy unintentionally painted over the Chain of Command, blending the photographs, frames and all, to the olive drab colored wall. It went unnoticed until three months later during the annual I.G. (Inspector General) inspection. When the misbegot was discovered the shit hit the fan, as they say. When the accusations and screams ceased, MSgt Sweechek, as NCOIC of the communication section, was given a verbal reprimand, the Army's equivalent of a high school "Mister Meaner" note. For discipline, the commo squad had to memorize the names of the Chain of Command and daily scream them out loud at the top of their lungs while standing at attention in the motor pool. The ritual took place three times a day and once at night. No amount of argument could reduce the discipline, though the soldiers claimed that whoever had painted over the chain photographs was just following SMP, standard military procedure—that is, IF IT DON'T MOVE, PAINT IT! The photographs did not move. Captain Milton, the company commander, was unsympathetic and the discipline stood. Thus, for ten minutes, three times a day and once at night, at the top of their lungs--scream! An NCO was in charge to record it.

In the barren environment of the squad room the only decoration was a metal lampshade that hung from the ceiling with a 100 watt light bulb stuck into it. The light was on as Pereski looked up. He rubbed his eyes. They still smarted from the party at the Golden Sun Bar the evening before. "Say, Yoyo, you never did tell us where you were from."

Yorit, who sat on the other side of the squad room bench, looked up. "Sure I did. Cleveland, Ohio. Remember?"

"Cleveland? Oh yeah. Isn't that the place where rivers catch fire?"

Yorit gave Pereski a nod. "Ya, that's the Cuyahoga River. You heard about it, then?"

Next to Pereski, O'Malley unzipped his field jacket. "Everyone has heard about the Cuyahoga River. But, gosh, how does a river catch on fire?"

Yorit stretched himself out on the olive drab bench. "It has to do with the methane gas that builds up on the river bed. It comes from the steel mills up stream: Bethlehem Steel, Republic Steel, Jones and Laughten Steel. They dump their refuse into it. The Cuyahoga River is the only river in America where they have to call out the fire department to put out the water."

"It's that polluted?" asked the new guy, Pfc Kantwell,. He sat on the other olive drab bench.

"Sounds like water you don't want to swim in," remarked Jonas, looking at his fingernails.

"Who swims? You walk on it," said Yorit.

"You what?"

"Walk on the water," Yorit repeated. "That's why when you meet someone from Cleveland, Ohio it's like meeting Jesus. Anyone here need a blessing?"

In the middle of the Squad Room a large Biedermeier table dominated the floor. It was the only real piece of furniture. How it got there, no one knew for sure. It was believed that a soldier with an eye for antiques bought it from a German family for a couple of C-ration cartons of cigarettes back in the hungry days of 1946 when the Germans were selling their daughters and furniture for food. When the soldier found he could not ship the Biedermeier table back home to the States, he donated it to the section. The polished cherry wood surface was promptly painted OD--in keeping with army regulations--and placed in the middle of the squad room, where it remained ever since.

Sitting on the edge of the table, Lavoss put out his cigarette. Around him on the OD benches the men chatted with each other. He raised his hand as if to volunteer to clean the latrine. "Guys, I've made my decision."

"Wha's that?" asked Jonas.

"I'm going to re-enlist," Lavoss answered, looking up at the ceiling.

The room, a moment before busy with murmurs and talk, stopped. Yorit turned to Robuck, who sat next to him. "See what an extra helping of Mess Hall SOS can do to you? Brain damage!"

"Now why you wanna do a damn fool thing like that?" asked Pereski, leaning against the bulletin board.

Lavoss rubbed his chin thoughtfully. "Our re-enlistment NCO, Sergeant Chuckles, told me he needed one more man to meet his quota for the month. So I thought I'd help him out."

O'Malley gasped, his voice at the edge of incredulity. "You what? You re-enlisted four more years in the army to help a re-up sergeant meet his quota. Are you nuts?"

Robuck, too, looked skeptical. "That makes about as much sense as setting the house on fire to grill steaks."

"Gosh, that proves it," gulped Yorit. "Mess Hall chow does blow one's mind. I'm swearing off the stuff."

Lavoss held up his hand to calm the controversy. "Now guys, I know it sounds dumb, but after thinking about it I feel I do owe Uncle Sam a favor." The men on the Squad Room benches looked at one another. "It's like this," he continued, the Army's been good to me. It put a roof over my head, put money in my pocket—not much, but enough. It does my entire medical at no cost, and it taught me a profession— communications, should I ever go civilian again. It would be a waste of the taxpayer dollars if I quit."

"The Army does not draft people to be cost effective," noted a skeptical Pereski. "The Army selfishly drafted you for a job no normal person in his right mind would do."

"And what job is that?"

"Peel potatoes on KP, clean the latreen with a toothbrush, shovel snow with a pick ax."

O'Malley shook his head. "Al, you paid your dues. You already did four years service. N,o six years. I mean, don't you want to go out and date chicks, get married, and have kids some day?"

"Sure I do."

"Not while you're in the Army, ya'all won't," warned Jonas in his southern drawl. "There might be an alert or a detail to be done, which means when ya'll make a date with a girl, you can't keep it. Or too, you might be too broke at the end of the month to affo-ord a date."

"And don't forget the permissions," added Yorit. "Just to get off post to meet a girl you have to have Pplatoon sergeant's permission, then the 1stSgt's permission, then the company commander's permission, and last but not least…my permission."

"Why your permission?"

"If the chick's cute, I might want to date her first."

"Then," Pereski interrupted, "should you ever decide to marry a foreign national, you have to get Berlin Brigade's permission."

Robuck held up a finger. "But there is one way you get around such red tape."

"What's that?"

"Let 1st Sarge be the first to screw the bride-to-be."

The discussion, hot and heavy, bounced around the Squad Room, the soldiers questioning the sanity of an Army reenlistment. It was questioned, doubted, feared. "No way, José!" was the usual response.

Pereski popped some chewing gum into his mouth. "Army life is tough on families. I should know. I grew up in one," he said looking out the window at the rows of military vehicles, trucks and jeeps on line in the lot.

"That's right," said Robuck. "Look at the career sergeants we know around here. Half of them are divorced, and the other half got crummy marriages."

"How do you know when a marriage is crummy?" asked Kantwell, the new guy.

"The wives are all overweight."

"Al, you sure you want to re-enlist?" asked Yorit, concerned about his buddy.

With everyone talking at once, Jonas jumped up. "Hey, wait a minute, guys. I smell a can of worms." He fixed on Lavoss. "What else did the re-up sarge promise you?" he drawled.

Still leaning against on the OD colored Biedermeier table, Lavoss looked down at the floor as if embarrassed. "Well, to be honest, he promised me a promotion to sergeant-E5."

The signalmen looked at each other. O'Malley sat back and folded his arms, staring at Lavoss. "No one gets promoted these days. The

Army's got that world wide promotion freeze on. You know that. We talked about it. Only if you put yourself in for combat training like Rosenblum did is there a chance for promotion."

"That's me," responded Lavoss.

"Promotion to sergeant-E5? Hm, now you are in trouble, Al."

"How's that?"

"You'll have to go back to school to learn how to count, the Army way, on your fingers. It's not quite algebra, but close."

"And you'll have to sleep with a clipboard under your pillow," added Robuck.

"And yell out orders with a mouth full of marbles like NCOs do," said Yorit.

"Marbles?"asked Kantwell, naively.

"Yes," O'Malley chuckled. "Call it voice training. In order to count cadence at the proper decibel range. Its why Army sergeants chew marbles."

"For real?" Kantwell had not been in the army long enough to know better.

"They teach you that in PLDC, the NCO school," O'Malley went on. "Sergeants have to stick marbles in their mouths the way classical Greeks used to do, then count out loud. Instead of a sissified, one two three, you get: 'One-a! Do! Trei-o! Fou'! Yo leef-ri-leef! Huh!'"

At that, the room laughed. Immediately, Yorit jumped to his feet. He began to march in place, mimicking the count. "Do! Trei-o! Fou'..." The room laughed again. Then Robuck jumped up and fell in step behind him. Then everyone. The whole squad room was on their feet and marching in place. "Yo leef-ri-lef'...Doe! Trie-o-foe...!"

"All right, guys, funny, funny!" Lavoss called out, not amused. "Calm down and listen to me. Listen to me!" Everyone sat down. "Just look at us. After our years of service, where are we? Like, no where! We're all still low ranked E-4s. A bunch of corporals. Nobodies. Bottom of the totem pole. My pals back home have jobs pulling down big bucks in the factories, going to college, getting laid. And what about me? Us? We're only grunts earning $110 base pay a month as specialists. It's embarrassing."

"Could be worse," said Robuck. "We could all be a Pfcs earning $90 a month. Ain't that right, Maestro?" Kantwell, the section's only Pfc, shrugged. "Maybe."

Lavoss shrugged too. "We're back to the same old story. Is there a life after the service, huh? Yorit, you been in the Army almost four years. What you going to do when your enlistment is up?"

Yorit shook his head. "I don't know."

"And you Paul?"

Pereski gave a blank stare.

"You, Irish?" Lavoss asked O'Malley who answered with an open mouth and said nothing as if his jaw was too heavy to support a response.

"And that goes for the rest of us," added Lavoss. "Don't you see? We're all civilian life dropouts with neither direction nor purpose. Well, here in the military we've been given a purpose. We get to serve our country. Call it a career. Call it an opportunity. Even with all its eccentricities, the Army can be a home if we give it a chance. Me? I'm going to re-enlist. Good chance I'll go to that police action hot spot Vietnam and maybe, who knows, join our Kik-buddy, Rosenblum there." The shock bounced around the room. "Yes, that's right," said Lavoss hastily. "The Army needs guys with our MOS in communication. The re-up sarge told me so. I may get to be part of a helicopter crew. Ride choppers, ya know. It's what Rosy signed up for, right?" Looking around at his surprised buddies, Lavoss could tell by the expression on their faces he had landed an eye opener. "That's right. Ride choppers. Anyone care to reenlist with me?"

Pereski was on his feet. "You mean if I reenlist I get to fly in choppers and don't have to hump field pack radio behind pimple faced 2nd lieutenant officers anymore?"

"Maybe."

"Show me the dotted line and give me a pen."

Standing next to the window, Jonas scratched his head. The sky outside was brightening—cloudy, but brightening. "I don't remember re-up Sarge Chuckles saying anything about chopper jobs or promotion at our last re-enlistment briefing."

Lavoss turned to Jimmy Lightpony the Shoshone sitting by himself in the corner of the Squad Room. "Say, Tonto, you're not saying much. What's your opinion?"

Lightpony glanced up. He did not answer immediately. It was his nature to be meditative. He sat, back straight, on the olive colored bench, hands on his knees, cross-legged, a maintenance manual open in his lap.

"Yeah, Chief, what's the Great Spirit got to say about it?" wondered Robuck.

Lightpony frowned as if trying to collect his thoughts. When he spoke his voice was soft, the dialect was smooth, as if to vocalize the wind and the expanse of the Great Plains from whence he came. He mumbled something.

Sitting close by O'Malley nodded, understanding. He turned to the crew of signalmen sitting around the OD painted walls. "Crazy. He says we're all crazy."

"That proves it!" Robuck snapped.

"Proves what?" asked Yorit.

"That Ireland is really Indian territory."

"You mean Northern Ireland," added Jonas.

O'Malley stood up. "Hey, wait a minute. Just because I happen to understand Shoshone…"

"…means the Shoshone Indians discovered Ireland long before Amerigo Vespuchi discovered America," said Robuck with conviction.

"I disagree," said Pereski out loud. "If that was true, all Shoshone Indians would have freckles, red hair and carry shillelaghs." With that, everyone laughed.

"Did you really re-enlist or are you just thinking about it?" Jonas asked, serious.

Lavoss frowned. "Actually, I'm still thinking about it."

The sighs of relief could be heard around the room. There was a pause. The conversation died. The room fell silent. Robuck lit up a cigarette. Yorit took out a pack of Lucky Strikes The men sitting on the olive drab benches appeared thoughtful. Outside, the morning sun broke the clouds and beamed through the back window. It lit up the room. Suddenly, the door to the Squad Room swung open. It was Bravo. He stood at the entrance. Shivering, he stepped inside and closed the door behind him. He looked around. From the expression on his face, drained, everyone knew 1st Sgt Persilla had given him a dressing down. "Thank you, prick heads!" he burst out, vehement.

"What'd we do wrong?" asked Robuck, not appreciating the comment.

"As if you don't know! At formation this morning you guys let me drop on the sidewalk. No one held me up. 1st Sarge pulled my pass and put me on beautification detail. Not only that, I have to serve two hours in his discipline squad. Thanks again, prick heads!"

"What are you blaming us for? You got yourself in the jam," said Robuck. "You know you ain't supposed to sleep in formation without a pillow."

"Come on, Frank, you're in the army! What'd you expect? You got to stand on your own two knees and learn to bottom feed like the rest of us," stated Lavoss.

Bravo unbuttoned his field jacket and took his place on the olive drab painted bench. "Still, someone could have grabbed me. If the company formation been a swimming pool, I'd have drowned."

"No way," said O'Malley. "With all the liquor you drank last night, you'd have floated."

Pereski looked up from the Dick Tracy comic book he was reading.. He put his fingers to his temple. "Say, Frank, what did you do with the brazzier that chick, Twin Buttes, gave you?"

Bravo cocked his head. "Twin Buttes' what?" (Twin Buttes was the Anita Eckberg of West Berlin who, because of her marvelous chest, soldiers fell in love with and wet-dreamed about.)

"Her bra, Frank. Remember? She took it off and gave it to you."

Bravo sat up. "She did?"

"Yes!"

He scratched his forehead in reflection. "Hm, that right? I did wake up this morning with the love object wrapped around my head, but I didn't know how it got there."

"Remember, there was a bet on," said Pereski. "The bet was you couldn't chug-a-lug suds in three gulps from her size 42 double D cup."

Bravo's eyes lit up. "Wow! Did I?"

"No."

"Damn!"

"But you tried," Pereski grinned.

"It took three of us to help you drain that double D," added Lavoss, his expression lively.

"You mean to drain the suds or drain the boob?"

"Both."

Listening to the discussion, Yorit punched his hand. He regretted having missed the event. "How do you know the brazzier was a size 42 double D?"

"It fit over Bravo's head."

The room howled.

Suddenly Robuck leaned forward on the bench and grabbed his

stomach. Perspiration was forming on his forehead. "Damn, cramps," he grunted, belching.

Yorit looked at him. "How many cups of Mess Hall coffee did you drink?"

"Four."

"You drank four cups of Mess Hall coffee?

"No, one. I polished my boots with other three." Getting up and rubbing his stomach, he stepped over and into the latrine. He didn't feel good.

Suddenly the door to the Command Room flew opened. Startled, everyone looked up. There, standing in the doorway in his starched work fatigues, stood the communication section's NCOIC in charge, MSgt Sweechek. The boss! He was also the company's 3rd Platoon's NCOIC in charge. With clipboard in hand and flashing his six stripe rank, he stepped into the middle of the Squad Room. In his mouth was a half smoked cheroot. The smell hit Robuck. He gagged, got up and dashed for the small latrine next to the section door. From inside, the men in the squad room could hear him vomiting. "What's wrong with him?" inquired the MSgt.

"Another Montazuma's revenge," said Kantwell. "Army chow."

The NCOIC frowned. "You mean Robuck ain't got the army lead belly yet? He'll have to re-enlist."

Like most senior NCOs, MSgt Sweechek rarely smiled, weighed down as he was by the Army's redundant and often superfluous responsibility. In civilian life such responsibility would drive a man to drink, as it did some of the senior enlisted. Watching him, the section soldiers could tell by the expression on his face that he was in one of his mood swings.

"All right, then, men. At ease!" he began, though no one had stood at attention. He had a command habit of "At ease-ing!" every other paragraph. It came from over twenty years of tough soldiering. Simple conversation with the MSgt was almost impossible without an "At ease!" or two slipping in. At home it drove his wife crazy, especially when making love. It almost cost him his second marriage. It did the first, at easing during sex. Sniffing loudly, he pulled at his belt with authority. "Men, the first thing on the program this morning is an award. I want to congratulate our Indian here, Jimmy Lightpony. Since he joined our communication section we've had no radio equipment breakdowns or power failures. He's our top maintenance guy. Let's give'm a hand."

The "Atta-boys" and weak hand claps went around the Squad Room. Unused to praise, Lightpony smiled his flawless white teeth that could open beer bottles and bend nails. The men of the platoon liked him, especially his non-military antics, like jumping out second and third story barracks windows. He was also a good back-up man in the fist fight that, on occasion, broke out in the downtown Schöneberg bars.

Checking his clipboard, M.Sgt Sweechek began with, "It's Wednesday morning again and communication training day."

Bravo suddenly jumped up. "Sarge, watch out! Your cigar! The ash! It's going to burn your lips!"

The cheroot Sweechek was smoking had burned down to a stub and appeared to smoldered to within a millimeter of his lips.

Taking the butt out of his mouth, he turned his heavy lidded eyes on Bravo. "Son, the best part of a cigar is the part that drops behind your teeth. Not to worry. It makes for a good chew."

Pfc Kantwell, the new man who every one called "the Maestro," raised his hand. "Sarge, I have a question. Do we call you Sergeant Sweechek or Sergeant 'Sweet-cheeks'?" he asked with a light sibilant attached. In civilian life he had studied music at the Julliard School of Music in New York, but dropped out because of a failed love affair. To his parents regret, he joined the Army to prove his manhood, and was the only soldier to ever board a troop ship heading for Europe with a cello packed into a duffel bag.

The MSgt fixed on him. "Sweet wa?" he rumbled. "Where'd you hear that, Soldier?"

Suddenly insecure, Kantwell wavered. "I hear the other soldiers call you that."

Sweechek's eyes, usually weighty slits, popped open as the men in the Squad Room searched for a crack in the floor to crawl into. "Sweet-cheeks, you say?"

Kantwell was about to say something more when he caught Pererski's warning stare and subtle shake of the head, meaning, "Hush-up, dummy!" If a knitted brow had been a thrown punch, Pereski's would have knocked Kantwell out. Sensitive to the visual vibes, he did not dare ask any more questions.

The MSgt "Humpfed!" A cascade of cigar ash tumbled down his

fatigue shirt. He brushed it away. Taking a toothpick from his pocket, he jabbed the quarter inch length of unsmoked cheroot, impaling it. It squirmed as he dropped it into the ashtray on the OD painted Biedermeier table. Just then Robuck came out of the latrine, saw it, gagged, and grabbing his stomach, ran back into the latrine.

"Pfc, my name is Master Sergeant Sweechek, ranking NCO with two years of combat in Korea. I am not a Sweetcheeks! Sweatcheeks maybe, but no Sweetcheeks! I'm a senior NCO with rank earned! We NCOs earned rank with sweat, some of it with blood. Is that clear, Soldier?" he scorned, looking directly at Kantwell. "How long you been in the company, son?"

"Two weeks, Sarge."

"And already you're on my shit list!" Kantwell withered. "All right. At ease, now," the SecSgt turned back to the program at hand and looked at his clipboard. Around the room on the olive drab benches the men relaxed. "Like I said, this morning we are scheduled for city training."

Pfc Kantwell raised his hand again, this time tremulously.

"Okay, Maestro, now what is it?"

"Sarge, what do you mean by city training?" he asked, sounding like a mouse looking for a corner.

Sgt Sweechek sighed patiently. Rumbling, he answered. "Our job is to train and maintain communication throughout the city of West Berlin. At our shop here we learn how to prepare for war. At ease!" he scolded, startling his soldiers. "We patrol the different sectors of the West Berlin like Spandau, Wedding, Neu-Köln. There we test our radios communication equipment to be sure our communication is battle ready. Should the commies ever come over the Wall we got to be ready to fight'm and kick ass. Got it?"

"Sure, then beat a retreat back to West Germany," interrupted Lavoss.

"At ease there, Lavoss! You raise your hand when you want to speak. And don't be cute!"

"Sorry, Sarge."

"Say, Sarge." It was Kantwell again. The SecSgt rolled his eyes. "Do we have to train in East Berlin too?" he asked, his youthful good looks as naive as the question.

With that, around the room, every thought, snort, innocuous activity and reflex response ceased: Bravo in the middle of a gum chew, Yorit picking his nose (to the knuckle), Lavoss coughing, half into a drag on a cigarette. Pen knife in hand, Pereski nipped his finger. "Ouch!" O'Malley and Jonas looked dumbly at each other, doubting the new guy's intelligence. Back from the latrine and looking pale, Robuck could care less. He slumped down on the bench. Ever wise and stone faced, Jimmy Lightpony the Shoshone shrugged.

Sgt Sweechek a-humphed! "East Berlin is enemy territory. You don't train in enemy territory unless you got orders to train there."

"Or are looking to get shot at," said O'Malley.

"Or start World War III," added Yorit.

Now the whole Squad Room broke into a babbling discussion of the pros and cons of what might happen if an Army jeep, or a convoy of vehicles missed the *Autobahn* checkpoint and drove into Communist East Germany unannounced. It did happen once. A convoy from 3rd Battalion, 6th Infantry out of McNair Barracks missed a turn-off on the way to West Germany and drove into Magdeburg. Startled, the Soviets went on alert. They thought the six trucks were part of an invasion force. Back in Washington, the Joint Chiefs went skizzo over the error for it caused the Berlin Brigade, the 7th Army, NATO, and SHAPE to all go on alert.

"At ease! At ease!" ordered Sweechek above his babbling section. "Let's have some discipline here. At ease, I say!" The Squad Room calmed down.

Yorit nudged Robuck. "See what a little college can get you? Kantwell's as dumb as you are."

"That can't be. I didn't go to college. That's why I'm smart."

The MSgt looked at Lavoss, a soldier with experience. "You, Specialist Lavoss. Kantwell here needs monitoring. You got the kid today. I assigned him to your vehicle. Train'm."

"Aw, Sarge, do I have to? I don't want the Maestro riding shotgun in my jeep."

"Just get him learned, Specialist! It's why you got the E4 rank To teach! It's what I and the Army wants of you. In our section you got the most radio communication experience. Got to make this Pfc part of the team. Do you roger that, soldier?"

"But sarge..." Sweechek glared. Lavoss stiffened. "Roger that, Master Sarge!"

The SecSgt paused. He lit up a fresh cheroot while looking over the young unlined faces of his soldiers, kids really, all apple-cheeked and bright-eyed like he once was when the Army sent him off to Korea in 1951.

"At ease," he ordered again. "Now, I'm going to tell you men something, and don't anyone in this Squad Room dare forget it. In West Berlin we are cannon fodder, every swinging dick of us." (Most army NCOs were fond of that expression, even the officers. A Pentagon report once noted that the term "swinging dick" was a euphemism denoting latent homosexuality. It had to do with men without women living too long in close quarters. The Pentagon report was squashed.) "We're 110 miles behind the lines and surrounded by 150 Soviet and East German divisions. Should the balloon go up, that'll give us five minutes to defend ourselves before Brigade is overrun with you either dead, captured, or on the run."

Pfc Kantwell looked up. "That's what happened at Thermopylae."

"Who's she?" asked Bravo out loud. He wasn't familiar with the name.

"A Greek chick," said Pereski. Kantwell shook his head.

Yorit then raised his hand. "Sarge, I thought NATO was supposed to come to our rescue."

"How can it when NATO will be retreating to West Germany's Rhine River?" said Pereski.

Lavoss looked at him. "The North Atlantic Treaty Organization wouldn't dare retreat and leave us alone here," he intoned gravely.

"Oh yeah?" responded Robuck, "Ever hear of Corrigador?" He was feeling better after his trip to the latrine.

"Corrigador! Who's she?" asked Bravo again.

Yorit glance at his short buddy. "Frank, didn't they teach you history back in high school?"

"Of course. Neu Jousey history."

MSgt Sweechek looked at the ceiling. "My soldiers," he mumbled, shaking his head. "Now listen to me, men. I've been through a couple of retreats. In Korea. And by the looks of things, a retreat out of West Berlin won't be any different. It could be another Corrigador, like Robuck says. The odds of us coming out of the second 'Battle of Berlin' alive are as good as Hitler's was in the first. Probably less. Keep in mind, we of the Berlin Brigade are political pawns to be sacrificed for a political point of view; namely, the defense of this city and the Federal Republic of Germany.

"What are you trying to tell us, Sarge?" asked O'Malley, not sure if he understood.

"That we are sitting ducks." The MSgt lit his cheroot again. It had gone out. "At ease!" he ordered. "What I'm trying to tell you is that the only way to survive in this environment is to be well-trained, and if you are you just might get out of here with your life." Around the Squad Room the signalmen listened with interest. "Therefore...we train the army way. We train often. We train tight. We train each other, and train the guy next to us, and train the guy behind us. Anyone who rides in our vehicles gets training, even if his name is Howdy Doody. Training! Training! Training! That is the name of the game. Do I make myself clear?"

"Okay, Sarge, if you insist," said Pereski, "I'll go ahead and train with Howdy Doody."

"I'll take Flub-a-Dub as my sidekick," grinned Robuck.

"Give me Princess Summer-Fall-Winter-Spring," giggled Yorit. "Put her in the back seat of my jeep and get me some pussy."

Bravo frowned. "Yorit, you are crude."

"What about Clarabelle and Mr. Bluster?" asked Jonas, thinking over the remaining characters on CBS Television's "Howdy Doody Show."

Mixing and joking, the discussion jumped back and forth and went around the squad room. Then, as if with the snap of the fingers, everyone began to sing the Howdy Doody fight song every kid learned by heart in the 1950s growing up in America. "It's Howdy Doody time... It's Howdy Doody time, Bob Smith and Howdy-do, say Howdy-do to you...!"

"At ease! At ease!" shouted out MSgt Sweechek, stamping his foot on the wood floor like grade school teachers do. The room fell silent. "When are you men going to grow up and act like soldiers?"

O'Malley looked up at him. " Sarge, but why? It's much more fun being a kid."

"Not in the US Army it ain't," came his gruff response.

Robuck raised his hand. "Sarge, I got a question! I got a question!"

"Hopefully not a kid-shit one," the SecSgt groused.

"No, a serious question, Sarge."

MSgt Sweechek sighed a muffled sigh, the heavy kind loaded with a breath that only career NCOs and elementary school teachers sigh when confronted by a fledgling's puerile antics. "Okay, Robuck, state your question, but don't make it too dumb. Pleeease."

"After two years in the Signal Corps, dumb questions are the only ones we know," said Pereski, speaking out of turn.

"So what's the dumb question, Robuck?"

"Does 7th Army have a 'Plan of Battle' for the Berlin Brigade?"

"Of course it does."

"Well, then what kind of plan of battle is it that gives us only five minutes to defend what is obviously an indefensible city: West Berlin?"

The NCO scratched his chin.

"It seems we ain't got much rope, do we, Sarge?" drawled Jonas.

"Don't worry. The Soviets will have enough rope for us all," said Yorit, speaking up.

"Gosh, thinking about it, what if the commies came over the Wall before reveille. We'd have to surrender in our underwear," declared Robuck. "That would be embarrassing!"

Pereski fingered his chin. "I wonder if it's not too late to enlist in the Navy."

Bravo stood up. "Guys, are you ready for this? USAEUR's plan of battle is…there ain't one."

MSgt Sweechek's nod suggested understanding. "You know, Bravo, for a dago gini, you're not so stupid. The fact is, you're probably right."

Speculation, again like silly putty, bounced around the Squad Room, everyone talking at once. Only Jimmy Lightpony the Shoshone sat indifferent, cross-legged on the bench as if at home in the family teepee. He remained silent for he understood; no matter what was said or done, it would not make any difference to the lives of the Shoshone people in the far west. On the reservation, the tribe would still live in poverty.

Jonas stood up. "Guys, I'm going to follow Horace Greeley's advice and, 'Go west young man!' I'm getting the hell out of West Berlin!" He made for the door.

"At ease, Jonas! Get your rebel butt back here! Sit down!" bawled Sweechek, taking the cheroot out of his mouth. "At ease, all of you! You sound like a bunch of old ladies!"

Like well-trained circus seals, the men of the communication squad dutifully fell silent. Jonas took his seat.

MSgt Sweechek raised his clip board. He looked around. "At

ease," he humphed. "Now, let's go to work. You, Lavoss! Since you volunteered to train Kantwell ("I did?") he rides shotgun with you. Show him the ropes, but on this side of the Berlin Wall." The room chuckled. "Here is your SOI (Standard Operating Instructions) and training manual schedule. Your call sign is `Dancer Two,´ as in Santa's reindeer. You drive to Charlottenberg Castle and set up a communication site there."

"Roger that, Sarge!" The two signalmen, Lavoss and Kantwell, got up from the olive drab painted bench.

The MSgt turned to the other men in the squad room. "Bravo, you're with Yorit. Call sign is `Dancer Three.´ Go to Checkpoint Charlie and the Wall. Here's your SOI and schedule."

"Roger, Sarge!"

"Pereski! You're `Dancer Four.´ You and Irish head for Templehof Airport. Spc Robuck, you well enough to drive?" Robuck nodded. "The Chief's your shotgun. Call sign is 'Dancer Five.' You drive to the British sector and the Olympic Stadium. Communicate from there."

Robuck stood up and took the SOI manual. "Roger that, Mas´Sarge! Come, Kim-o-Sabe. Follow me," he ordered Lightpony with a wink.

"I can't," he replied in Shoshoni. "I forgot my tomahawk."

Sweechek continued to tick off the names on his clipboard. " You, Jonas. Your call sign is 'Dancer Five.' You trip alone to Spandau and the Moabit Prison location. Give my greetings to that old Nazi, Rudolf Hess. He's in jail there, ya know. Yes, and stay away from the commie guards there. They're on allied rotation at Spandau this week. We don't want any flaps with those guys."

Bravo raised his hand. "Say, Sarge, did you hear about the tactical radio soldier from 2nd Battalion, 6th Infantry? At the Moabit prison he drove into a guard house with a Soviet commie inside and knocked it over."

"Was there a flap?" asked Pereski.

"There sure was," replied Bravo. "For the fuck up, Brigade sent the poor tac-guy to West Germany and Baumholder for extended driver training.

The soldiers in the squad room gave each other a fearful look. "Baumholder!"

"What's that?" asked Kantwell, who, being a classical trained musician, did not know much German geography.

"Baumholder is a town and army post in West Germany. It's the equivalent of Russia's Siberia and the 'Stations of the Cross' with you on duty carrying the cross during maneuvers," said Pereski, his humor subtle.

Yorit agreed. "Call it the 7th Army's answer to Shades of Hades."

Done handing out the SOI tables and schedule manuals, MSgt Sweechek raised his hand. "At ease! Enough bullshit! Listen up, you men. Now, I want all radio communication to fly hot and fast. Have good radio procedure. Remember, you may be monitored by the Military Intelligence spook boys. That means keep the language clean. No lisping over the net! No drag queens here! Berlin ain't Fire Island, New York!" Sweechek declared, working his cheroot like a baby turd from one corner of his mouth to the other. "The base call sign, that's me, is `Ballroom One.´ Not baseball, tennis ball, or pair-of-balls, but Ballroom One! Got it?" Around the room, the signalmen nodded. "So let's have good 'Round Robin' communication today. Let's show Command we are the best communication outfit in the Army's Berlin Brigade!"

The MSgt's voice took on the timber of a coach at half-time, trying to motivate demoralized players. "We're the best team out here, right, men?" There were mumbles. He tried again. "We're the top commo section in Berlin Brigade, right?" There was one flagging, "Roger Sarge..." and two "Hm's!" and one, "Youbetcha!"—all weak. The section NCO took the cigar out of his mouth and looked sternly around the Squad Room at his soldiers. "At ease! Come on, commo squad. You can do better than that. Are we not the best in the US Army?" he cried out.

On the benches, the men began to sway. Their SecSgt's rap was effusive. Inspired, the new guy Kantwell suddenly jumped up. He cried out, "Rogerm Sarge! That's us!" The other men looked at him with a "What the fu..." expression on their faces. Then Jonas stood up. Being from the South, he let out a rebel yell and pumped his fist.

That did it. It was the spark, the flip of the coin, the crack of the pistol at the starting line. One after another the signalmen soldiers caught fire. "Let's go for it!" O'Malley called out. Yorit was on his feet and moving. Lightpony yelped. Pereski, Jonas, and Bravo all joined in. "That's us! Yeah! Roger!" Only Robuck's cheer fluttered. He still had a bellyache from morning chow.

The MSgt stepped up to him. "Specialist, that attitude might be okay with the Service Company pencil pushers, but not here!" he scolded. "We're front line combat!"

Robuck grunted. "I'm trying, Sarge, but something in me is stuck."

Upon hearing that, Sweechek whacked him hard on the back. Robuck belched, then farted. It was a double discharge that startled the room. It cleared both ends of his digestive tract. With a "Whew!" he blubbered. "I'm ready, Sarge."

"That's the spirit, Robuck!" the MSgt snappped, clapping his hands. "Now let's go, men! Go! Go! Go!"

Up and on their feet, the signalmen broke as if from a game huddle with a sure touchdown play. They charged out the door of the Communication Shed and dashed into the company motor pool and the cool damp of the morning. They cheered as they ran, not because they were inspired by the pep talk, but because they were glad to escape the evil smell of their SecSgt's cheroot, not to mention Robuck's chow hall fart. Exuberant, they ran, skipped and jumped around one another, slapping each other on the back for in front of them, like ponies tethered at the rail, were five moisture-covered M-151 quarter-ton Ford Motor vehicle, saddled and gassed and ready to be driven.

And what is an M151 quarter-ton Ford Motor vehicle? It's an Army jeep. The Army's mean machine. In World War II it carried soldiers into every military campaign, from North Africa to Italy, from Normandy to the Elbe. It was the Ford jeep that played a vital role in getting the soldiers to battle. It was the same in Korea. The Pusan Pocket, Inchon, Chosan, above the 38th Parallel and below, the M151 jeep hauled the American fighting men into combat. It was light, lean, fast. And with its 2-1\2 ton weight and 71 horsepower engine, the M151 could be called "the Jack Dempsey of the automobile industry." It had a four-speed transmission and an independent suspension system that, with a pop of the clutch and the tap of the gas pedal, made it sail over the slick cobblestone streets of West Berlin. It bounded more than it drove. The drivers clocked flight time rather than mileage. The Berlin *Polizei*—should they dare give chase, which was never—could only watch and scratch their heads with envy, knowing their own four-cylinder spinach-colored putt-putt Volkswagen, called "the Beetle," was no match against the zip of the Ford M151. It would have looked like air combat all over again—German *Stukas* against the Air Force P40s. Rat-tat-tat-tat! No match!

The M151 army jeep was a young man's dream. To drive it was

the height of passion that no woman, given her erotica, could match. With the roof down and canvas doors folded, it was pure jetstream and Harley Davidson. In the open air, a beer fart never had a chance.

Each jeep carried two radios: a PRC 25 (you gotta hump'm) field radio with a whip antenna, plus one heavy, all-purpose VCR-10, Vehicle Communication Radio with a single side band. The VCR-10 was the size of Porky Pig and just as squat. It fit snuggly in the back of the jeep and, when necessary, could be used as an extra passenger seat. On rare days, if the atmospheric conditions were right, the VCR-10 could pick up the Grand Ol'Opry out of Memphis, Tennessee; otherwise, its shortwave was confined to the West Berlin area.

With the weight of the two radios and two passengers, the M151 could scoot the West Berlin byways. It rode high on the axles. It was fast, but notoriously unbalanced. It could clip corners, turn on a dime, and sneak up on the Soviet flag sedans that prowled West Berlin outside the Allied compounds, beep the horn and yell, "Boo, Commie!" It could climb steps, do wheelies, and if the bump was right, somersault. Hence, the Ford M151 got its name, the "Keystone Jeep", and the soldiers that drove it, the "Keystone Grunts" in the tradition of the silent film greats like the slapstick comic, Fatty Arbuckle. Wednesday morning training was known as "Keystone Time" That, and the erratic behavior, childish antics of the soldier drivers (on duty or off duty) was to "Keystone it, guys!"

Suddenly, the youthful enthusiasm, so raucous a moment before, came to an abrupt halt. The signalmen stepped to parade rest position in front of their vehicles. The Army ritual. Following them out the Communication Shed, MSgt Sweechek watched, frowning, snorting, mumbling to himself the way senior NCOs do. He looked over his crew then gave the order to, "Check your vehicles, HUMPF!" Up went the jeep hoods for a quick maintenance check—water, oil, and battery—then down came the hoods with a BANG! That done and adrenaline pumping with expectation, the signalmen soldiers swung into the jeep's canvas seats, awaiting orders.

MSgt Sweechek moved closer to the row of metal thoroughbreds. He stretched out his arms, forefingers pointed to the sky as if about to conduct Montavani's 101Strings. Leaning back, he cried out an uncharacteristically non-military: "Gentleman, start your engines!" The five jeeps coughed out cold exhaust, then came to life with a roar, motors gunning. With that, he let his arms drop. It was the signal to go.

Clutches popped, followed by a spray of wet motor pool cinders, pealing tires, and rebel yells. One after another the five M151 Ford Motor jeeps zipped out of the company motor pool. At shotgun, the riders flailed their caps like rodeo cowboys out of the chute. In single file they drove onto Avenue C. They passed the empty Nazi SS barracks, the post theater, the chapel, which most soldiers avoided because they heard the 1st LT preacher there was hinted to be gay. The jeeps passed the quarters of the Pentomic Battalion over from the States, a unit trained to fight while being nuked. They turned onto the post's parade area compound in front of Andrews Barracks. There, the short convoy of jeeps swung past the neo-Roman swimming pool built by the Nazis for the 1936 Olympics. It was a magnificent building with colossal pillars and nude relief sculptures of Germanic athletes that resembled Captain Marvel and Wonder Woman.

At the main gate a lone guard stepped from his guard shack. He looked sharp in his creased uniform: green ascot, bloused boots, white gloves, and his helmet liner pulled low over his eyes. Slowing, the five jeeps approached. The guard snapped a forearm across his chest (the signal to proceed) and the M151s passed under the cast iron arch that was the main gate of Andrews Barracks Army Post, and entered greater West Berlin.

Once out on *Finkenstein Allee*, the street in front of the army post, Lavoss, as lead driver, looked back to checked the line of M151 vehicles to be sure all were there. He turned to Kantwell, riding at shotgun next to him. "This is it, Maestro. From here on out your training begins, so hold on!" Lavoss gave gas. The jeep shot forward. Following him, the other vehicles did the same. Down the *Kadetten Weg* they drove, each man wearing a grin. For the first time in two weeks, the soldiers of the communication section were beyond the grip of Uncle Sam's Army. With the dead hand of the world-by-the-numbers behind them, and the exuberance of unfettered youth in front, they found they could be kids again, and howled out, "Heeee-yah!"

The short convoy passed the Golden Sun *Kneipe*, the soldiers' bar and watering hole. Respectfully, Robuck snapped a salute. Though it was morning, the bar was already open and ready should an off duty soldier drop by.

Yorit and Bravo followed in the next jeep. Reaching back, Bravo flipped on the switch of the VCR-10 radio. He keyed the handset to the single sideband and got Lavoss' tinsel voice over the speaker.

"Does everyone read me?" Lavoss asked as if talking through his nose. All vehicles communicated and reported. "Roger!" Lavoss continued. "Dis-monin' we's-a-gonna play a little foo'ball. You know your positions, so it's on to the Grünewald forest and a game of KEYSTONE GRUNTS!" he called out as his jeep zig-zagged the street. Behind him, the other jeeps did the same.

On the sidewalk, an elderly German man stopped to look. He had never seen Army jeeps do the Boogey Woogey before. Rolling his eyes toward heaven, he mumbled tolerantly, "*Ach, schon wieder die Amerikaner, aber Gottseidank, dass sie da sind, sonst...*" (Oh, the Americans again. But thank God they're here, otherwise...) Like many Germans, he had survived the Allied bombing of Berlin, the Soviet occupation, and eighteen years of G.I. eccentricities. Still, he was grateful. West Berlin was stable and free.

The M151s drove the width of the street, than doodled, then single filed. With Lavoss at quarterback, they were an offensive line that made the on-coming traffic, should there be any, scatter or face the Keystone jeeps head-on. They were a challenge to be avoided.

On Ring Strasse, a large rose bush protruded from behind a cast iron fence. One late blooming yellow rose hung over the sidewalk. It was the last of the season. Yorit saw it and dropped out of the vehicle conga line. His jeep bounced up on the sidewalk, startling a woman carrying a grocery basket. Sitting at shotgun, Bravo gasped. The woman had never confronted an Army jeep head on before. Jumping back, she dropped her basket of groceries just as Yorit stopped. He hopped out and picked up the basket and handed it back to her, apologizing as he did. "*Es tut mir leid, Dame,*" he said in German. (I'm sorry, lady.) Turning, he snapped the yellow rose from the bush and stuck it between his teeth. Bravo thought him nuts but understood; it was the Keystone Grunt thing to do. Be eccentric.

Back on the street, they raced to catch up with the other jeeps. Yorit looked in the rear view mirror at the woman; she was leaning against a tree, her hand over her heart.

Soon, the short convoy of five M151 Army jeeps entered the District of Dahlem, a quiet residential neighborhood of wedding cake like *Grunder Zeit* designed villas. It had once been the home of high Nazi officials, including Joseph Göebbels, Germany's infamous propaganda minister before he shot himself. Since the war, Dahlem had become one of the most coveted West Berlin areas to live in and was now home to the city's over-endowed, overweight, and over-paid politicians who not only governed the country from Bonn but had second jobs on corporate boards. Double incomes.

The District of Dahlem had not been as badly damaged in the war as the rest of the city. Still, there were gaps and gashes in the bucolic symmetry. Some of the ivy-covered villas revealed shot up facades from the fighting eighteen years before. One home the vehicles passed had been completely destroyed. Only two walls were left standing, the result of a wayward British 500 pounder. What had once been a villa was now scattered rubble. At another villa, the second floor was no longer that—a second floor, but a tar-paper roof. The second floor had been blown off. Observing it gave the impression of an elegant garage hiding a Rolls Royce. Noting the tragedy, it led Bravo to comment, "Like a beautiful woman confined to a wheelchair."

The jeeps turned from *Thiel Allee* onto *Gary Strasse,* where the city's only university was located: the "FU" or Free University. It was a gift, built and paid for by the Ford Foundation as an alternative to East Berlin's famous Humboldt University. Being only twenty minutes from Andrews Army Barracks, it was ideal for hungry American soldiers in pursuit of German women. Students could be seen hurrying to their morning classes.

Gary Strasse was crowded with bicycle riders, many of them females. They looked sharp in their wool stocking pants and turtle neck sweaters, the fashion of the day. Some wore short waistcoats that lasciviously accentuated the hips. The celibate soldiers, like priests, could not help but gawk. Over the radio's sideband, Lavoss' nasal voice stuttered, "I see action female at eleven o'clock, over!" The drivers in the other jeeps looked in the direction of eleven o'clock.

"Roger, and wow that!" reported Pereski, his tongue unfolding at the feminine aesthetics.

From their jeeps, the army signalmen glared.

It was she. She strutted on the sidewalk, head high, her briefcase swinging with self- assurance, the image of a woman determined. And soldiers being soldiers, forever lonely, did what soldiers do when confronted by the opposite sex—they hung out the open doors of the jeeps. They waved, whistled and slapped themselves, blowing kisses as they drove past.

"She is just too tantalizing!" reported Bravo over radio sideband.

"I'll take her and all the rest of the broads!" Robuck cried out.

Jonas, in a fit of heat, shouted in tar-paper southern, "Let 'er str-ip tease! Let 'er str-ip tease!"

In his jeep, Lightpony gave a war cry and danced in his seat.

Again, Yorit drove up over the curb, bouncing Bravo at shotgun next to him. "Whoa! Damn man! Riding with you ain't safe anymore!"

They passed two male students who had to step out of the way; it was that or get run over. Yorit braked and stopped just short of the female student carrying a briefcase. Rich blonde hair and pink cheeks, she looked terrific. Startled, she stepped back. Yorit hopped out and with the panache of a musketeer, bowed. He took the yellow rose from between his teeth, the one he had just picked, and presented it to her. Staring as if in shock, she took the rose and pressed it to her chest. She gave a light smile. Yorit fell in love. The two male students who had jumped out of the way when the jeep passed watched. Both frowned disapproval.

"Give our Yoyo three points for that one," reported Lavoss over the radio sideband. "A Keystone Grunt's job well done." The cheering and horn beeps erupted from the other vehicle drivers.

"One unoccupied object at ten o'clock! Will investigate," Robuck reported into the radio handset. He pulled to the opposite side of *Gary Strasse*, just missing an oncoming car. A lone bicycle leaned against a tree. Dropping speed to below cruise, he leaned out the jeep's open door. He bent down and sniffed the bike's seat, his nose grazing it as the vehicle glided past. "Object defined as female! Brunette! Seventeen or eighteen years old, I speculate. Definitely a pink panty type," he called over his communication radio.

"Roger that. I.D. and log it!" ordered Lavoss over sideband. "Give that driver a five pointer."

Impressed by what he just witnessed, the new guy, Pfc Kantwell, turned to Lavoss at the wheel. "It ain`t possible, Al. How could Robuck, driving at 20 miles an hour, define the age, sex, and hair color of a woman by the smell of a bicycle seat?"

Lavoss glanced over at his trainee at shotgun. "Maestro, if you're in the Army and sex starved, you just know."

The convoy neared the *Oscar Heleneheim-Clay Allee* intersection. From his seat, O'Malley jerked his head hungrily from side to side. "A bevy of beautiful German women and I can't touch them. Where have I gone wrong in my life?"

"You were born a Patty," said Pereski, next to him in his shotgun seat.

Behind the wheel, Yorit squinted at a sight. He down-shifted. "Look, Frank. See that girl in front of us at twelve o'clock, the one on the bicycle? Why don't you give her a `buss´ as we pass?"

Bravo glared at his partner, not sure if he heard right. "You mean kiss her?"

"Yes, give here a nick on the cheek. She might enjoy it."

"Kiss her from a moving vehicle? We could collide!"

"If we collide, she'll think its love," said Yorit above the wind stream.

"I'm skeptical."

"So am I, but think of all the points you'll get for the record. You'll be the Keystone Grunt of the month, for sure. A top gun!"

"Really think so?"

"Would I do a buddy wrong?"

Bravo squinted through the windshield. She did look good from behind. "Okay, Yoyo, let's take her!"

Yorit held the handset to his lips and keyed to communication sideband. "One lovely at twelve o'clock. Am going in. Over!"

"Roger that maneuver!" Lavoss reported back, signaling the other jeeps to pull to the outside lane and give Yorit a clear field-of-fire.

"Okay, shotgun, take a firm grip!" yelled Yorit above the engine to Bravo. "The bomb bay doors are open!"

"Just drive the damn vehicle! When it comes to snatch, I know the terrain!" called Bravo as he leaned out the jeep's open door.

With a roar of the engine, Yorit down-shifted. "Stand by, Bombardier!"

"Roger that!" Bravo cried out. Head outside the open door, he turned his fatigue cap around, giving him that Yogi-Berra-from-behind-the-plate look. "Am at the readyyy!"

"Roger that!"

"Dive! Dive!"

"Roger! Roger!" shouted Yorit, dropping the jeep speed further as they approached. They were on a glide. Bravo stretched further out the door of the jeep and into the wind stream when, abruptly, he pulled back inside. He took the wad of gum he was chewing out of this mouth and smacked it with a slap against Yorit's forehead. There it stuck. He grinned "If I don't return from this mission, the gum's yours. Don't forget me."

"Roger that," said Yorit, feeling emotional. "I'll treasure the wad till the day I die."

She was young, blonde, and around twenty. On the bicycle, her rump undulated, an invitation to all things defined as animal, such as an American soldier. Leaning into the cold morning, she pedaled, intent on her destination, unaware that she was the target of some mischief.

Since she had her back to the approaching jeep, Bravo could not see her face. Noting the shape of her rump, the rest of her suggested a knock out of a German girl. Strands of blonde hair peaked out from under her black beret cap; her ears carried a touch of pink from the cold. He called over his shoulder. "This is crazy!"

"Of course it is! We're in the Army!" Yorit yelled back.

Bravo knew he had no choice. He had to do the Keystone thing— that is, be a jerk. It was the commo section rule: the more absurd, the better the action. Gripping the dashboard with his left hand, he leaned a-way out the open door of the jeep's shot gun seat. He smiled to himself, pleased at what he saw. She was an angel, indeed. "Zeroing in on target!" he called back. "Steady as she goes!"

"Roger that!"

It was either the noise of the engine, or that sixth sense of danger. Whatever, it turned the girl student's head just as the jeep passed. With his thick Sicilian lips distended into a pucker, Bravo grazed her cheek. Woosh! It was a bull's eye. It was done before she knew what happened. Startled, she braked her bike in front of the Free University and jumped off. She touched her cheek, unsure of what she had just felt.

"Touchdown!" yelled Jonas over the VCR-10 radio sideband. He was in the jeep behind and saw the body contact. The drivers in the other vehicles pounded their horns and cheered.

"We did it!" Yorit laughed jubilantly. Bravo could only dance in his seat and snap his fingers.

Robuck and Lightpony pulled up alongside in their jeep. Lightpony gave the thumbs up.

Glowing with personal pride at the accomplishment, Bravo grabbed Yorit and popped the wad o' gum from his forehead. "You don't need my good luck charm anymore."

"Too bad! I wanted to frame it." Yorit grinned.

"Welcome to the Keystone Grunt club, Frank!" It was Lavoss'

tinsel voice again over the sideband radio. "You might be short in stature, but as of today you're our top gun. Ten points for body contact! Over and out!"

With a feeling of accomplishment, absurd though it was, Yorit's rejoined the conga line of Army vehicles. "Yeah, Frank, you're top gun."

"No, we are! Both you and me. We're the top gun team!"

"Yes, top team!"

"Roger that!"

As he drove, Yorit glanced back at the buildings of Berlin's Free University and the hustle and bustle of students there. They were between classes, on foot, on bike, in a hurry. It reminded him of the time when he'd been a student back home. He was about to mention it to Bravo when it occurred to him that the Berlin Free University, as a university, had no campus. He thought that odd, and looked back again at the campus that wasn't. All universities in America have campuses, or should have one, or so he thought. In Ohio they do. But this West Berlin school of higher elite education had none. There was only a front yard that ran from the building layout to the street. That was all. By its appearance, the FU was a series of uninspiring structures that resembled large rectangular-shaped domino blocks, suggesting more a barrier to the mind than an invitation to it. No invitation to the "para-pedantic" here. Socrates would have been disappointed. Where were the spires? Yorit asked himself. Where were the Dorian columns, the majestic halls? Was this a university or was it not? Where were the hallowed vistas that were supposed to sweep to the horizon or the panorama that excites the mind? And where were the great elm trees, the sycamores and the oaks that together inflamed young academics toward higher pursuits? Where was the campus? Where? Back home, the Kent State University campus where Yorit went to school was magnet, the buildings Greek, the education most noble. Inspiring! In all its campus and architectual majesty, it could be said of Kent State, it *was* the enlightenment.

Yorit gasped at the thought. How he missed the academic world, especially the campus library. It had a name among students: the Pantheon. It was there under the high ceilings and columned walls where he'd spent many an hour studying. It was there that he, and others like him dreamt to the horizon in pursuit of knowledge. Even to step between the Dorian columns excited the imagination, but here in West Berlin? By its appearance, the FU could only be defined as geometric, "Post and Lentil," checkerboard, the facade a bunker. But then, he questioned himself, what was relevant—the facade or that which was produced inside the facade? "Frank, ever go to college?"

"Nah! You?"

"A couple of years."

"Get anything out of it?"

"I didn't let myself."

"Why's that?"

"I joined the Army."

The mini convoy of Army M-151 jeeps turned onto *Clay Allee Boulevard.*

He was portly and his cheeks were blotched. The nose was swollen and veined, the sure sign of a boozer. Around his ankles he wore two thick rubber bands to keep the cuffs of his trousers from catching on the motor's quick chain. With his brown scarf, synthetic jacket, and Bavarian hat topped by a pigeon feather, he was what Germans classify—and Germans classify everything—a *Spießer,'' 'ein Arbeiter*—a worker, a slob, a low-life, an assembly line guy. He was on his way to a job sight and driving a working class slob's mode of transportation known as a Mopod"— motorbike.

Technically, a Mopod is a cross between a model airplane, a Dutch bicycle and a lawnmower. To the literati, it resembled a V-1 rocket, only with two wheels and no rocket engine. With the motorbike's bug-eyed 15 HP two-stroke cylinder motor pulling the front wheel, it putt-putts along the West Berlin boulevards at a winging speed of 15 miles an hour, fast enough at rush hour to drive the BMW drivers crazy. From a distance, the Mopod was easy to spot. The bike's exhaust laid down a smoke screen not unlike those laid down by destroyers at the Battle of Jutland. Besides its function as a working class slob's transportation, the two-stroke motor could be hooked up to an electric razor for a quick shave. When Bravo first saw a German Mopod, he was not sure what it was, but noted cynically, "And this is the nation that gave the world the Tiger Tank?" To which Yorit replied, "Don't knock it. Ford Motors gave us the Edsel."

From their jeep Pereski and O'Malley looked around. They had not yet pulled off any Keystone Grunt stuff and were looking for an opportunity. Then they saw him: *der Spießer*. That working class slob, by the looks of him. He was on one of those put-put Mopod bikes.

Pereski took the radio handset. He had an idea. "Dancer 2, this is Dancer 4. Gonna check out one UFO Kraut at ten o'clock, over!" he reported over the radio sideband.

"Roger that!" replied Lavoss, giving permission from his vehicle.

Pereski left the conga line of jeeps and drove toward the Mopod. Sitting at shotgun, O'Malley noted the metal basket on the back of the bike; it held a faded brown leather briefcase. "Always wondered what them *Krauts* guys keep in them brown briefcases they all carry."

"I've wondered, too," said Pereski, behind the wheel.

"I see bus drivers with them all the time. Whatdayasay we have us a look?" Both men were feeling mischievous.

Pereski geared down and slowed to the Mopod's putt-putt-burptempo.

The working class slob looked over his shoulder and gave a short petulant look. He gunned the two-stroke motor, discharging an oily plume of exhaust that for a moment blinded the two intruders. Still, the jeep drew up along side the Mopod bike. Imperious, the German stared straight ahead with all the concentration of a Formula One driver.

As they passed the Berlin Brigade Headquarters, the old *Luftwaffe* Command Building, Pereski gave O'Malley the nod. With a deft touch, O'Malley reached out and lifted the German's brown briefcase from the bike's rear basket without the rider being aware. The jeep immediately pulled away.

O'Malley popped the briefcase's two brass buckles and opened the synthetic leather flap. He took out..."A lunch?" It was a sandwich wrapped in waxed paper. O'Malley wrinkled his nose. "I'm disappointed."

Pereski laughed. "What did you expect, the first edition of the German Constitution? Let's see what the wife packed in for him," he said, looking around. The traffic on *Clay Allee* was light.

O'Malley unfolded the waxed paper. "Good God! A pastrami sandwich on pumpernickel bread. The guy's a New York City Jew!"

Still holding the steering wheel with one hand, Pereski reached over and took the sandwich. One corner of waxed paper was open. He took a bite out of the sandwich. "Hey, this ain't pastrami. It tastes like...I don't know what it tastes like."

O'Malley sniffed at a second sandwich. He drew back the top slice of pumpernickel bread. There was pickle and, "Eeee! It's *Blutwurst*! "

"What's that?"

"Blood sausage," said O'Malley. "Who's this guy's butcher, Adolf Eichmann?"

Again, the jeep drove up to the Mopod. This time the German looked over, wondering what the fuss was all about at 15 RPMs. O'Malley looked him square in the eye the way the Irish do before they punch you in the nose, and gave him a big, "Up yours!" wink. Then, with his elbow on the jeep door, he leaned out and took a chomp out of the *Blutwurst* sandwich and chewed. The working class slob, *Spießer-Arbeiter*, had no idea that O'Malley had just taken a bite out of his lunch. Abruptly, the German stiffened and resumed his Formula One posture on the Mopod. Again, the jeep dropped back.

"Repack the sandwich pattie and, oh here, add this." Pereski pulled out a *Playboy Magazine* he kept between the seats. "Tear out Miss October and rap the sandwich in her body. The guy looks like he can use a hard on."

With the sandwich—minus the bite—back in the briefcase, the jeep drew up to the Mopod bike once more. As deftly as before O'Malley dropped the briefcase back into the rear basket. Laughing out loud, Pereski gave the jeep gas and they drove away.

The working class slob pointed to his head the way Germans do, tapping at his temple with his forefinger. He shook his fist, threatening dire retribution should the Mopod ever catch up to the Army jeep. He sensed that he had been made the butt of some esoteric joke, but was not sure what. Mumbling to himself, he fired off his exhaust, blinding a Volkswagen Beetle coming up fast behind him. The traffic along *Clay Allee* was still light.

In the jeep, O'Malley turned to Pereski. "Paul, what do you think he'll say when he finds his lunch wrapped in Miss October's boobs?"

"Don't know, but I'll guarantee you one thing; he'll go to the grave trying to figure it out."

The short convoy of five M151 Army jeeps pulled onto a nameless side street in the direction of the Grünewald Forest. After a short drive, they passed the fenced-in perimeter of Turner Barracks. It was the home of F Company Detachment, 40th Armored. From the road, the signalmen could see several Abram tanks parked in a row, three of them up on blocks in various stages of maintenance. In front of them a platoon stood in formation, at attention, as an officer, neck muscles taught, revved himself up for what appeared to be a disciplinary shout.

"Is that all the tanks we have to defend West Berlin with?" Kantwell asked in his shotgun seat, with Lavoss at the wheel of the jeep.

"No, there's more Abrams in the motor pool. It should be enough to intimidate the Communists," Lavoss answered as they drove past the fenced-in armored company.

Kantwell sat up in his seat. "I count five tanks! Sergeant Sweechek says we're facing 150 Soviet divisions. Can five tanks stop them?"

Lavoss looked at his young buddy, sitting next to him at shotgun. "Maestro, you better hope to Jesus H. Christ they do, otherwise, your ass and mine is grass."

The cobblestone street turned onto a dirt road. On both sides of the road were fir and pine trees that thickened as they drove. The short jeep convoy had just entered the expanse of deep forest.

Known as the Grünewald, the forest surrounded West Berlin and was one of several large forests of the Hansel and Gretel genre. It was part of the North German Plain made up of conifer, fir, pine, spruce, and birch trees that stretched out over the countryside as far as East Prussia and Poland. In places, the Grünewald was so thick it cast deep, damp shadows, perfect for witch huts and snipers. The forest floor was a compost mix of pine needles, dead leaves and sand, the North German Plain having once been covered by an ancient sea and glaciers. The ground's loam was so soft it absorbed all sound. It could muffle the roar of a tank at speed, as well as a pair of lovers in thumping passion. In the Grünewald's density, a jeep's engine was barely a murmur. Nature-loving Germans were often found walking along its rough sandy paths. Even during inter-Allied maneuvers they walked through the Grünewald, though warned to stay away. Nothing could keep the people of West Berliner away from their beloved forests, not even war. An APC semi-tank vehicle could roll up to an individual on a pathway and he would not know the tank was there until he was under the tread. Such was the stillness of the Grünewald Forest

The forests of Berlin were known to be magical. They generated inhabitable oxygen that exhilarated. To inhale the *Berliner Luft*, as the atmosphere was called, cleared the head and regenerated dead tissue. After a tough training day in the field, off-duty soldiers could binge but never get drunk. It had to do with that *Berliner Luft*. The air so invigorated the human body that after five deep breaths and two side-straddle hops, a boozer would get back on his feet and back in the bar, *der Kneipe*, for another round robin of suds.

Also, for the young men driving Army vehicles, the Grünewald forest was a drag racer's dream come true. It was an obstacle course of narrow and rutted paths. There were gullies, pits, sand traps, and obscure open patches. During field exercises, to get lost in it as some 6th Infantry soldiers sometimes did, could be an adventure. Rumor had it that over the years not a few soldiers had gone into the Berlin Grünewald and Havel Forests never to come out or be seen again. But, for the yeoman drivers of the 592nd Signal Company, Communication Section, the forest was all stock car and drag races.

"Give me a single wing!" ordered Lavoss over his radio sideband to the other jeeps. He loved to play New York Giants coach, George Allen, sending out plays to Y.A. Tittle at quarterback. The jeeps shifted position. "Gimme a T-formation!" he called. They maneuvered. "Gimme a shotgun formation!" Again the jeep maneuver. "Okay! An umbrella defense!" Speed shifting, the jeep drivers followed orders. And the Ford M151s bounded over ruts, hopped the pits, down-shifting and up-shifting to the sounds and screams of RPMs. It was launch time.

"Give me a backfield!" Lavoss ordered, his voice sucking in the rich forest air.

Again the signal drivers did as they were told, their shotguns hanging on, rebel-yelling as they drove. "Yau Hee!"

With a quick maneuver, Yorit and Bravo moved their M151 to an offensive position, only without a football. Behind them, and at quarterback, Lavoss and Kantwell drove up in their jeep. Playing the backfield and swerving in and out to avoid colliding with the pine trees danced Pereski and O'Malley in their jeep. Lightpony and Robuck, too, were in theirs. In his vehicle, Jonas as well, all hustling to the down-shifting of transmission gears.

Still at quarterback, Lavoss called for a Keystone Grunt free maneuver. That was what the drivers had been waiting for. It was the signal that let them off the leash. They were now permitted to go mad. No more Army! No more brigade! No more NCOs, 1st Sgt and Company Commander at the controls! Uninhibited, unobserved, and protected by the curtain of forest wall, they were young men in their flying machines. It was their chance to defy gravity, and like the bush pilots of old, they dared reach for the horizon. "Go! Go! Go!" called Lavoss, one hand on the steering wheel, the other gripping the radio's handset as he "Hee-hawed!"

The M151s zigzagged. They figure-eighted. They ran broken field.

They were more in the air then on the ground. The vehicles hit watery ditches and shot out of them in a muddy spray. They banked on trees and cut each other off to the howl of the wind and rebel yells. They broke every rule in the Army's Driver Training Manual and would have been busted and court martial on the spot if caught. But they didn't care. They were the Keystone Grunts.

He was a German, an older man, a gentleman, by his dress. He had silver hair and wore a long leather coat, Continental style, draped at the shoulders. This morning he was smoking a pipe and walking his dog—a cockerspaniel. Like anyone in retirement, he spent most mornings going for a walk, known in Germany as *der Spaziergang*. It was something the people of Berlin loved to do. It was in their nature, and the Grünewald Forest was the perfect place for it; whereas back in the States, to discover nature, American families would hop into the family car and drive to the shopping mall. Germans preferred the forest as their mall, and *der Spaziergang*. With his dog on a leash, the gentleman was no exception. He enjoyed this part of the forest. It muffled the distant city traffic and was not far from where he lived.

As he walked, the cockerspaniel abruptly stiffened,. The gentleman German, too. Turning, he looked down the wide earthen track toward what sounded like growls and snarls. The gentleman squinted, unsure. In the distance he saw what looked like a small herd of hippos rambling about. He felt a sudden fear. "Hippos here?"

The morning mist, though lifting, hung light above the ground, making it difficult to see clearly. With some trepidation, the German gentleman took off his spectacles; he cleaned them with a hanky and put them back on. The hippos appeared to be running wild as they charged up the track in his direction—t him!

The cockerspaniel barked defiantly. The German looked around him. He noticed he was in the open. Sensing panic, he grabbed his dog and sprang toward a pine tree not five meters away. He leaped, just as one of the hippos roared up. It was doing wheelies. Another circled the tree at sharp right-angle turns. The cockerspaniel barked fanatically. The German yelled. He was sure he was about to be trampled to death. The herd passed.

Opening his eyes, he found himself alone, alive, embracing a pine's tree trunk. His glasses hung from one ear. The forest was strangely silent again. As quickly as they had come, the four-wheel hippos had vanished, as if into the forest floor. An illusion? Only the smell of exhaust fumes lingered. The German gentleman looked down. His cockerspaniel had peed on his expensive Continental coat.

Still tremulous from the experience, he picked his hat out of a tire track. Nearby, he found his pipe. It was broken. It was sometime before he reached the *Forester*—the ranger's cottage, and a telephone. He dialed the German equivalent of 911, the *West Berlin Polizei*.

"I wish to lodge a civil complaint against the *Amies*," he said, using the German slang term *Amies* for Americans.

The policeman listened patiently to the irate citizen, *Berger*, and his "near death" experience. With a tolerant sigh, the policeman informed him. "Good citizen, you have no doubt forgot where we are? We are in West Berlin, an occupied city. Politically, we may be part of the Bundesrepublik Deutschland, but militarily we are the property of the United States, the British, and the French Army forces. Here, German jurisprudence has as much influence as parted wind." The policeman further advised the good citizen to, "Shut up! Be a good fellow! Go home and be thankful that the *Amies*, the *Zitronies* (British), and the *Frosch* (French) are here, crazy though they sometimes are. Without them defending our city, West Berlin—your children and mine—would be learning Russian in school, with you in prison for daring to complain." The good *Berger* gentleman dropped his complaint.

At a clearing in the woods, Lavoss drove up and stopped. The other jeeps did the same. In the middle of the clearing was a silver birch tree that grew to the heavens with all the majesty of a Robert Frost poem. Unlike the trees nearby, this one was different; nature gave it an extreme double trunk, unusual for a birch tree. At three feet above ground, the double trunk curved out and around, framing an invisible target in white bark, large enough to sail a large object through. On the ground, six feet in front of the bowl-legged tree trunk, were tire tracks that abruptly ended at a hefty bump on the ground, only to reappear on the other side of the double birch.

Lavoss got out of his jeep, the motor lightly steaming, and walked up to the tree. The other signalmen did the same. He pointed at the two bow-legged shaped tree trunks. "This, my friends, is the ultimate experience. You are looking at the 'Eye of the Needle'. Hop through the `Eye of the Needle´ in one jump without crashing and you earn a star in cement at the Chinese Theater in Hollywood."

Kantwell stuck his head through the bowed space and opened his arms. "Heck, anyone can do that, Frank. Just jump through!"

"Yes, but the trick is to jump through with your vehicle," said Lavoss, his grin mischievous.

O'Malley looked at the target, then at Lavoss. "You're not for real. This space isn't wide enough for an M151 traveling at speed."

"If you shimmy up the tree trunk at speed, you can," said Robuck, guessing.

Lavoss stepped to the large bump on the ground and the tire tracks there. He pointed to it. "It's been been calculated that if you hit this bump here at 60 miles an hour, with a little luck and tail wind you should pass between the two trunks," he said, holding his hand at hip level where the birch opening was widest. "I've seen it done."

"How many Hail Marys you got to say to get through?" asked Robuck, grabbing at a low branch to swing on.

Pereski shook his head. "You're talking about lifting a quarter-ton Army vehicle three feet off the ground. I know Fords can do a lot, but defying gravity isn't one of them."

"That's the reason for the Hail Marys," said Yorit, looking over the dimensions.

Jonas rubbed some dark patches where the bark had been torn away. "What happened here? Someone try and miss?"

Lavoss then told the story. "Well, some guys made it and some guys didn't. There was a corporal, his name was Alvito. This was before your time. He was a Bravo Company, 2nd Battalion soldier out of McNair Barracks. A gutsy type. He tried it. He ran it the Eye of the Needle, hit the bump here, got the vehicle off the ground and hit the tree about here," he said, holding his hand at the dark patch.

"Ouch!"

"Oh my God!"

Yorit thumbed his lip."Wow, that someone dared to dare."

"It was like BAM!" said Lavoss. "Alvito wrecked the jeep and knocked out his shotgun rider. No one knows for sure what happened. The wind may have dropped. Not enough speed. Misjudgment. Who knows?"

"How do you know about this?" asked Robuck.

"I was riding shotgun. It was me who got knocked out."

Lightpony and Pereski walked around the double tree to get a better perspective. "And Alvito? What happened to him?" asked Pereski.

"He was court-marshaled and busted to Pvt-2," said Lavoss sadly. "The last we heard of him, he was humping tank tread back in the Zone at Baumholder. Army won't discharge him until he pays off the jeep he wrecked."

"On a Pvt-2 pay!" Bravo gasped. "He'll be in the Army for the next 30 years." He found the punishment inhumane.

"Call it serving a sentence for your country," said Yorit, thoughtfully.

Lavoss looked around at the commo team—his buddies. "Challenge, anyone? Alvito would love company."

"You have to be crazy to even attempt it," said O'Malley, tossing a stone through the open space between the bow-legged tree trunks.

Bravo glanced over at Jimmy Lightpony, the Great Plains Indian. "Pony, it sounds like your kind of challenge."

Lightpony shrugged a "Yeah, why not?"

Lavoss looked up at the clouded sky. He looked at his watch. "Oh shit! Guys, we're late! Ol' Sarge Sweetcheeks might be spot-checking locations, wondering what the hell happened to his soldiers. Let's hustle!"

Immediately, the signalmen ran back to their jeeps and jumped in. "Change radio frequency to main frequency band," Lavoss called out, over the start up roar of engines.

With that, the five M151 Ford jeeps sped out of the clearing and onto the dirt track. Zigzagging as they went, they headed in the direction of the city.

Checkpoint Charlie

The Checkpoint

Yorit pressed the jeep's gas pedal to the floor. Bravo gripped his field cap; he had to keep the wind eddies from tearing it off. They were late. They had spent too much time in the Grünewald Forest and now had to move fast to get to their location before MSgt Sweechek got suspicious. "You grab-assin' again, Soldier?" he would say. "Sand-baggin', huh? Chasin' *Frauleins* on Army time, huh?" He had been known to drive out and check if a team was in place. If it wasn't, it meant only one thing. GOOF OFF! And when it came to young soldiers, he was usually right, like today.

Yorit zipped in and out of traffic, heading east. Already, they had passed the fashionable Charlottenberg district and the middle class Schöneberg district. Both districts had been bombed during the war and were now in the middle of a building boom.

Scaffolding was going up everywhere. Modern cubey-like buildings sprang up next to gracious bomb-splintered ones that stood next to ruined bombed-out facades that stood next to just dug holes, which themselves were soon to become cubey-like buildings.

Impersonal and formal in style, if not down right ugly, the contempory blockey architectural look was all the trend in West Berlin. It was considered an improvement, though barely, over the grim gutted structures left from the war. One had only to look at *the Amerika Haus* near West Berlins's *Bahnhof Zoo*, the main train station. Visitors mistook the structure for a tourist bureau. It was that nondescript. Or take the restored Schiller Theater on *Kufürsten-Damm Boulevard*. It had the appearance of a department store, only without the merchandice. The Berlin Philharmonic Concert Hall, another Ford Foundation donation, resembled a four-story circus tent in re-enforced concrete with a collapsed roof. It was defined as contemporary-modern in the extreme.

106

At the *Ernst Reuter Platz* (square) where five boulevards converged, much of the new construction had already been completed. During the war, the area had been reduced to rubble, and then reduced again. The piles of rubble led to a world-wide architectural competition, of which Corbusier-tinted architects won all the reconstruction contracts. In place of the destroyed Baroque neo-classical and *Grundelzeit* buildings that once graced the *Ernst Reuter Platz*, ten story geometric tombstones (contemporary-modern) were built and set in a circle, as if in condolence to the lost noble structures. The buildings resembled air-raid bunkers which, upon completion, so shocked the citizens of Berlin it made them wonder if, well, maybe a little rubble was not so bad after all. But rushing past in an Army jeep to get to their position, Yorit and Bravo, barely noticed. Fast driving through the Schöneberg district, they headed east.

In spite of West Berlin's isolation 110 miles behind the lines, districts like Schöneberg and Charlottenberg rejuvenated themselves. They pulsated with a commercial rebirth. It was very noticeable from the bright-light cafes and smart shops that ran along *Kurfürsten Damm Boulevard*. There was one anomaly, however; one area forgotten in the rush to rebuild West Berlin. It was the district known as *Kreuzberg*.

Located near the Berlin Wall, *Kreuzberg* was a working man's neighborhood, and resembled it. It was seedy. It was seedy before the war, seedy during the war, and seedy now. The facades of the buildings there showed it. Not only were they soot covered from brown coal residue (every cold water flat had a coal stove, and there were a thousands of them); many of the apartment buildings were still broken from the fighting. In some places it looked like the Battle of Berlin happened only yesterday: shattered balconies, bullet-riddled walls, empty lots. The closer one got to East Berlin and the "Wall," the more of a no-man's land the district of *Kreuzberg* became. It once prompted Bravo to comment, "Gee, the Bronx!"

Whether it was the lack of money for restoration, or because it was a worker's district (workers politically defined as low-life), or simply because it was located on the edge of western civilization, the *Kreuzberg* district did not get the funds the other Berlin districts did, and looked it.

At *Yorck Strasse*, Yorit turned onto *Mehring*. He drove further to *Hallesche Tor* area and stopped. Here, he turned off the engine.

Bravo looked over at him. "What'd you stop for? We're not at Checkpoint Charlie yet."

"Shh!" Yorit hissed, his finger to his lips. "Tell me, what do you hear, Frank?"

Bravo hesitated. He looked around. "I don' hear not'in'," he answered in Jersey.

"That's just it. You don't hear nothing. It's the hush. It means we're close to the Wall," said Yorit, his head cocked and listening. There was nothing to hear. No traffic. No voices. No shouts. No sirens.

The hush began at the *Hallesche Tor*. The closer to the Wall and East Berlin one came, the greater the hush. It was as if someone had slammed the door on the city's hustle and bustle. The ubiquitous sound of traffic and jackhammers that was everywhere died in the expanse of *Kreuzberg's* moonscape of empty lots and vacant buildings. The silence was impressive. It suggested intrigue, danger, fear. The Cold War.

In the distance, caught between vanishing points, was the horizon. It was a gray parallel line that looked like a rip in the skyline, a partition that separated earth and sky, 63 zig-zagging miles of it. It was the Berlin Wall. On a single morning in August 1961 the governing communist regime had set it up. Its purpose: to prevent East Germans from escaping into West Berlin, as they had done many a-times.

The Wall, not to be compared to the Chinese Wall, had the color of anthracite— sometimes purple, sometimes gray, depending on the mood of the observer, or the time of day, or the season of the year. In winter, the Wall took on a dark slate tonality. In summer, a light slate. Only the guard towers and the half-ruined structures beyond the Wall in East Berlin broke the symmetry.

Restarting the engine, Yorit turned onto *Friedrich Strasse*. "Frank, we're here," he said in a low voice.

"Again? I don't wanna be here," said Bravo, his voice turgid. It had to do with the atmosphere; it was oppressive.

Friedrich Strasse was a short street, paved with cobblestones that made the M151 shutter and bounce. The buildings were a mix of several sleazy looking bars and one hotel; "*Ein Pension*" the Germans called it. The *Strasse* appeared deserted except for the occasional male character or two, with bullet-shaped heads, who stood on the sidewalk in their trench coats. To the observer, the *Friedrich Strasse* did not seem worth the international attention it got, let alone to go to war over. Yet here, two years before, Soviet and American armor faced off and almost did.

Yorit tapped the brakes and brought the jeep to a halt. A barber pole, the barrier that separated the two Berlins, was down. A dirty white strip marked the cobblestone street from curb to curb. It was here that West Berlin and democracy ended and East Berlin and Communism began. It was the border and a no-man's land. Nearby was a large sign written in bold black letters in four languages. The sign read, NOW LEAVING THE AMERICAN SECTOR! They had reached Checkpoint Charlie.

If one did not know what to expect, To see the Checkpoint Charlie Guard House was a minor shock. The newspapers and television left the impression of a large defensive post with plenty of hustle and bustle. In reality, the Guard House had the size of a garden tool shed. It was painted a peachy beige color and was totally incongruous to the frayed grisaille tones of the surrounding buildings. In summer, the checkpoint even supported flower boxes. Inside, MPs worked and processed paperwork for VIPs, Allied diplomats, and Soviet officials passing through, and any spy with a bullet-shaped head wearing a trench coat. Beyond the checkpoint, on the other side of the white demarcation line, was what the Allies defined as, enemy territory. East Berlin! East German police known as *die Volkspolizei* or *Vopos* guarded the enemy territory.

Yorit turned off the jeep's engine. The two soldiers looked at each other. "We're here. What now?"

"Net communication," said Bravo, reaching into the back of the jeep,. He calibrated the VCR-10, heavy-duty radio. The radio buzzed and whizzed. "I hope ol′ Master Sarge was not trying to reach us otherwise, deep shit!"

"In the Army that's par for the course," said Yorit, looking over at the Checkpoint Guard House. "Hm, I don't recognize any of the MPs on duty there. Must be new guys." Just then a British Rover drove up and parked. Inside sat an officer and his driver.

Bravo took the radio's handset. Over the speaker they could hear the voice-coded messages. The communication traffic. "Damn, the radio net is already open." Quickly, he checked the SOI table code for a chance to jump in. A communication break opened and he jumped in with his call sign, "Dancer two. Dancer two. Request permission to enter the net. Over."

MSgt Sweechek's asphalt voice came back with a "Roger that!" and "Where the hell you been, Dancer two? Goofing off? Report to Operations immediately when you return to the motor pool!"

In the jeep, the two signalmen looked at each other. "Deep shit!"

Bravo nervously chewed a knuckle. "You know, the Army could be a nice place if it wasn't staffed with mean senior NCOs. They're always bustin′ butt."

"What would you staff it with?" asked Yorit.

Bravo tilted his head. "Female sergeants. When they bark an order at you, it's a reason to fall in love with them."

Watching the Vopo border guards, Yorit took a stick of Clove gum out of his pocket. "Isn't that what dating is all about, bark and love? Say, Frank, talking about and love, what are the girls like back in Jersey?"

"Chaste. All chaste."

"You poor man."

"Back in Jersey the girls are either Catholic or they're Jewish. Prima donnas, most of them. You know the kind, the ones who think their shit don't stink. You have to be classified a saint, or be a college man to date one."

"Oh, then I can date Jersey ladies," said Yorit, smiling.

"Are you a saint?"

"No, but I'm a college man. A dropout, but a college man."

On the other side of the border a Vopo guard with an assault rifle and fieldglass turned and focused on the Army jeep. Seeing it was no threat, he turned back to his post

"And what are the girls like from Ohio?" wondered Bravo, slouching in his seat, one knee up on the dashboard.

Yorit thought for a moment. "Racey! The problem is the mothers; they're a barrier. They won't let you near their daughters unless you are chaperoned. It can drive a bull to masturbate."

"Are you a bull?"

"Most definitely."

"Well, then, move to Jersey," chuckling Bravo. "There, masturbation is an art form."

Yorit chuckled. "You know, when I enlisted in the Army, the recruiter saw me coming. He sniffed me out. He saw how desperate I was for female companionship. He said if I volunteered to serve Uncle Sam for four years I'd have more pussy than I could handle."

"And?"

"And what?"

"Do you have more pussy now than you could handle?" asked Bravo, curious.

Yorit shook his head. "Don't I wish."

"You mean your Army recruiter, a man you can trust, someone you can believe in, the Army's so called father figure, he lied to you?"

"No, he was being truthful. There is plenty of pussy out here. It's just that the recruiter failed to tell me that as a soldier in the Uncle Sam's Army before you can date a German girl you need permission— permission from the CO, permission from the 1st Sergeant, permission from your Platoon Sergeant, permission from the Section Sergeant. Gee, did I forget anyone?"

"Yes, your state congressman."

"Yes, permission from your state congressman. However, by the time a soldier finally gets all those permissions lined up and documented, in order to get off-post, his date forgets who it was she had a date with. So much for all the pussy you can handle."

The Dancer Two call sign came up on the radio. It was Jimmy Lightpony, the Shoshone. Because Lightpony disdained the language of the white man he spoke his native Shoshone. Bravo picked up the handset and "Rogered!" the Shoshone communication. He placed it back at the radio.

"What'd he say?"

"I don't know."

With the transmission done, Yorit slouched down in his seat, one knee up on the steeringwheel, his field cap down over his eyes. "You know, this is what I like about the Army, five minutes on the job earns you twenty-five minutes of shuteye."

Bravo agreed. "Yeah, and where else can you get a good night's sleep till five o'clock reveille? Only in the Army."

On the East German side of the *Friedrick Strasse* stood a military guard tower. The one guard on it raised his fieldglasses and focused on the American jeep. From his vantage point he could have shot dead both Yorit and Bravo, had he been ordered to. But not being ordered to do so, he only raised his fieldglasses and focused his rifle on his shoulder.

Bravo watched him, curious as to why the Vopo was fixed on them so. Since the jeep had pulled into Checkpoint Charlie he was fixed and fcused on them, never putting down his fieldglasses. Bravo pushed open the jeep's canvas door and returned the hard stare, then, raising his hand, he cocked his thumb and pointed his finger. "Bang!" he called out.

On the tower silhouetted against the sky, the Vopo looked around his fieldglasses. He pointed his finger and returned the simulated fire. Determined, Bravo did the same. "Bang, bang! Ping! Bop! Bang!" Back and forth it went over the demarcation line that separated West Berlin from East Berlin, Communism from Capitalism, a Democratic Republic from a Socialist one. Finger shooting.

Startled by one particularly loud vocal shot, Yorit woke up. He had dozed. "What the..." He sniffed the air. The jeep's cabin smelled of cordite. "Is that small arms fire I hear?"

Bravo held up his forefinger and blew into it, clearing the tip. "You did."

"When we get back to company you better confine that finger of yours to the company Arms Room. It's dangerous," suggested Yorit.

"How can I? The finger is part of my body."

"Then you'll have to confine your body to the company Arms Room."

Except for the metallic squeaks and static voices of the VCR-10 communication radio, there were few further transmissions. *Friedrick Strasse* was quiet. Time slipped by. The British Rover that had stopped earlier picked up a passenger in civilian dress, then drove into East Berlin. It meandered the low S-shaped concrete gauntlet of the East German traffic barriers and stopped at the Russian checkpoint on the other side.

A message came up on the communication radio. "Change position to the Brandenburg Gate, over!" was the order. Hand set in hand, Bravo "Rogered" the command order and gave Yorit a nod. "Let's move."

Yorit was about to start the engine when they heard something that pricked their ears. It had a familiar tinkle, the peep and squeak of something playful. Bravo gasped. "It can't be!"

"Impossible," uttered Yorit, himself startled.

The two soldiers looked at each other. There it was again, that tinkle. It was the unmistakable twitter of, of ..."American female!"

On *Friedrich Strasse*, an absolute dead end street, the voices stood out fresh and fragrant, a crystal innocence, clean and refreshing. The tones were light like the chatter of robins in a springtime fuss, a stark contrast to the *Umlouts* and *Dipthongs* of the German language, which, to the American soldier's ear, tends to sound like a deep throat, ideal for the opera, or for shouting "Achtung!" In a moment of passion, a

German voiced "*Ich liebe Dich*" (I love you) has all the sensuality of a frog that missed the mating season. But this! What Bravo and Yorit heard was pure California feline.

Stiffening, their heads snapped this way and that. Where? What? How? Who? Yorit started crowing. Bravo had difficulty with his tongue. It fell out. For there, standing in the doorway of Checkpoint Charlie Guard House and chatting with the on-duty MPs were two girls. Each wore a Bordeaux-colored baseball jacket with big white UCLA letters on the back. They were twenty, twenty one, wore penny loafers and ankle-length jeans that accentuated their marvelous bulbous rumps. Their hair, lightly bleached from the California sun, was all pony tail that revealed thin, porcelain necks, begging to be stroked. They chewed gum, wads of it, out loud as they talked, while flashing white teeth that dazzled. Occasionally, they released airy globes of Double Bubble that popped like gunshots in the forest. It was they that turned the male heads and had Bravo and Yorit sitting tall with expectation. The girls were a rare ray of sunshine in the barren landscape of Checkpoint Charlie. Even the German near-by *Polizei* and the trench coat clad bullet-head figures on the street turned to look.

"Valley girls!" croaked Yorit.

"Pinch me, I'm dreaming," groaned Bravo, gnawing on his field cap.

"And they're wearing a tan, " Yorit whined, his face in his hands. "I haven't seen a tan in years!"

"And no socks!" Bravo blubbered, tearing at his field cap with his teeth. "Look at them ankles, will ya? Just look at them ankles!"

"Oh, Lord, just let me stoke one of them, please!" begged Yorit, ogling.

Bravo sniffed. "They must think they're still in California by the way they're dressed."

"They are in California," said Yorit, not able to take his eyes off the vision. "They brought the state with them."

Both men quivered. "What I wouldn't give to have the tall one rub her tan off on me," Bravo gusied.

The two co-eds stepped away from the Checkpoint Guard Shack. Passing the parked jeep, both Yorit and Bravo gasped. "Frank, get their attention! Talk to them!"

"You talk to them!"

"They're on your side!"

"Okay, okay!" Bravo leaned out the jeep door. He grinned and began to blubber in a Jersey Esperanto voice.

Both co-eds looked at him and twittered. "Hey, Soldier, your tongue is hanging out!"

Embarrassed, Yorit slid down in his seat. "Frank, you are one big klutz, you know that?"

"What was I supposed to do? Jump out and grab a boob!"

"Yes. Now I have to do it!"

The two muses who had magically dropped from Olympus walked up to the white demarcation line that was the border. They leaned on the barber pole barrier that separated the two Berlins while the two signalmen argued with each other.

"You hustle the short girl. I'll take the big one," said Yorit.

Bravo protested. "Why is it I always get the short chicks?"

"Because she's your size!"

"I want the big blonde!"

"But the other one is prettier," noted Yorit.

"Says you!" Bravo argued. "I never get the big blondes."

"That's because you're swarthy and talk Jersey!"

"Let's let them decide, okay?"

"Okay."

The two signalmen moved to get out of the jeep and hustle the valley girls, but stopped. They stared through the windshield. "Oh, shit! We're in trouble now!" said Yorit, aghast.

While chatting, and indifferent as two shoppers in a Mall, the two co-eds from UCLA stepped around the barber pole barrier and crossed the white demarcation line and into East Berlin. Knowingly or unknowingly, they had just left the Western civilization and entered Zulu country. Communist territory!

From their East German posts, the Vopo guards jerked to a stop. They looked. The guard on the tower, who a moment before had frivolously played finger guns with Bravo, slipped his rifle from his shoulder. No one ever just walked rinky-dink, bimbo-like, into Soviet-controlled territory. There were formalities, procedures, paperwork. Yet the two valley girl co-eds did just that. Rinky-dink!

Inside the Checkpoint Charlie Guard House the two MPs had returned to their desks; one was still grinning from the feminine sunshine bestowed on him when he happened to glance up. He looked, not believing his eyes. His grin faded. Immediately he grabbed for the yellow emergency phone.

The co-eds who were in West Berlin on a student exchange program had unexpectedly thrown themselves into the Cold War spotlight. When they said "Goodbye" to the MP guards, it was assumed they would turn around and go back into city. Instead, they crossed the border into Communist East Berlin, unescorted, unannounced, and without papers or visas. Looking back, they waved their gingerbread fingers and called over their shoulders to the paralyzed soldiers. "Too-do-loo!"

Everyone's chin dropped. The MP phone call went out and alerted Brigade Headquarters Operations. "Emergency! Emergency!" At McNair Barracks the Alpha Company of the 3rd Battalion got orders to immediately send half a platoon—the rest were in training or peeling potatoes—to Checkpoint Charlie. From the Arms Room, they drew their M16 weapons and jumped into vehicles and, with a German *Polizei* escort, rushed in the direction of the *Kreuzberg* district, lights flashing. Their orders: to save the two damsels from California and maybe prevent a war ta-boot. However, in the 20 minutes, the time it took to get there, the East-West, super power confrontation was over. The treat of nuclear annihilation had passed. The co-eds had beaten it back across the border into West Berlin.

What happened was the Valley Girls approached one of the youthful-looking Vopo guards to ask directions. Startled by their scented presence, he stuttered nervously while stroking the stock of his Kalashnikov assault rifle. He was not sure if he should shoot them or make love, when an officer ran out from the walled fortress that was the East Berlin checkpoint. "*Zurück!*" (Go back!), he shouted, punching the air threateningly with his fist as he approached them.

Startled, the two co-ed intruders hesitated, then stepped back, then turned and broke into a run. They dashed, lickity-split, back toward the West, the Vopo officer and one soldier in chase. Bravo, Yorit, the MPs, the bullet heads, the British, the French (Where'd they come from?) and from their green Volkswagen Beetle car parked at the curb, the West Berlin *Polizei* all shouted, "Hurry!" "*Schnell!*" "*Mon du!*" "Blimy!" and, "Get the hell out of there, bitch!" in three languages and Cockney.

Finally, safe on the west side of the demarcation line and in friendly territory, one of the co-eds stopped; she turned, and in a gesture of defiance, took her wad o' Double Bubble she had been chewing and tossed it, more a push, since it had the weight of a shot put, into East

Berlin. The moist glob hit the Vopo officer square in the chest. It stopped him cold. The Double Bubble stuck.

Startled, he looked down at the juicy wad and staggered backwards. He had never seen such a ferocious thing in his life, all pink, gooey and dripping. Chewing gum was an object of western decadence that did not exist in the German Democratic Republic. He tried to brush it off with his hand, but the more he brushed it the more it stuck to his fingers, to his the uniform, in his hair. Hopping around and cursing, the Vopo officer looked like Brear Wolf fighting the tar-paper doll in the film *Song of the South.*

"That *Vop-Kraut* will never scrape off that stuff, not in a million years," said Bravo, feeling sorry for him.

"Oh, yuck!" grunted Yorit. They watched, standing outside their jeep.

From the West Berlin side of the Checkpoint Charlie, the other co-ed yelled out a Valley Girl expletive through cupped hands: "Up yours, asshole!"

"Dear me, such language. Do all Valley Girls talk like that," asked Bravo, feigning shock.

Watching, Yorit found the whole event amusing. "Had that commie officer known who the girls were, I'm sure he'd have followed them over the Wall and married one."

Bravo snapped his fingers. "Hey, idea! That's how we can keep the commies out of West Berlin. Forget barbed wire and tactical defense. Just mine the border with Double Bubble. Gum up their armor, it would."

Yorit considered the point. "But there's a logistical problem, Frank. The Berlin Brigade doesn't have enough soldiers around to chew gum."

"Not a problem. We get the Air Force guys out of Tempelhof to do that. Give them something to do besides fly kites."

Yorit laughed. "Are you asking the Air Force to do their mission and chew gum at the same time? That's like asking them to march in step at parade without skipping."

***

For the most part, no one cared about how the Air Force, Army, or Marines march. But on German Independence Day they did. It was the day that all Germany celebrated the East German uprising against Communism. It was defined as the revolution that failed. To commerate the event, 17 June 1953, the Allied Powers occupying West Berlin celebrated it as the German "Day of Independence." Together, with the British and French, the American Berlin Brigade marched and paraded past the city's nobel *Tiergarten's* and up *Bismark Strasse* in a "display of support" for the people of Germany. Ever grateful, the West Berliners stand ten deep on both sides of the grand boulevard and wave hankies, weep, and cheer to the thump and roll of drums and marshal music as the Allied garrisons marched stuffly. It was called, "Pass-in-Review."

Always first to march by the crowd was the British Brigade, known as "The Army of the Rhein." They were always first to march and "Pass in Review" because the "Brits," as they are known, were super marchers. They would proudly strut, heads high with that graceful cock of their arms that is so British. Dressed proud in their plaid skirt and uniforms, the Scots would play the bagpipes. They always played the bagpipes. Bagpipes inspired and the Berliners applauded.

Then, handsome in their berets, would march the French garrison, a phalanx of proud soldiers doing that special strut which distinguishes them from their British and American Allies. Lining the boulevard, the crowd had no choice but to applaud.

On the high grandstand, the generals and colonels of all three Armies would salute. Next to them, the West Berlin politicians would stand at attention, hands over their hearts with Willi Brandt, the mayor, *Bergermeister* of West Berlin, with them.

Then, bringing up the rear, marched the companies of the American Berlin Brigade. Ten soldiers across and ten deep, they were another phalanx of stiff, chin-high, chest-out young men, marching with pride to the beat of the trumpets and drums of the 298 Army Band playing John Philip Soussa. First came the 6th Infantry soldiers; they stepped smartly past, followed by the Brigade's Special Troops, then the tanks of the 40th Armored. Taken all together, it was a grand display of NATO's commitment to the city and the people of West Berlin.

Like any military parade, someone had to bring up the rear. For the American contingent, it was the Army Air Force out of Templehof. They were placed at the rear of the military parade, and for a reason. The Air Force can't march! They tend to march out of step and hop. To the Brigade commanders, it was an embarrassment. Thus, by the time the Air Force reached the high VIP platform of generals and civilian dignitaries, the platform was half empty, everyone on their way to lunch. But that was not so for the people of West Berlin. They stood their ground in the sun, in the heat or in the rain—if it rained, and waited. They looked forward to the Air Force, *especially* the Air Force. For, when the US Air Force passed in review, out of step, stumbling or hopping, the crowd would break into a cheer, and they cheered wildly. The Berliner women threw bouquets of flowers and waved handkerchiefs as the airmen passed, and not only flowers and handkerchiefs, but they threw kisses too. Young women would run out into the marching formation to kiss the passing airmen. The reason: the people of West Berlin never forgot how, during the Berlin Blockade of 1948, it was the Air Force in their C54s and C47s, and the British airmen in their converted Lancaster bombers that saved the city.

In order to keep the threatened city supplied, it was they who flew in every kind of weather, day and night, 1440 missions, one aircraft after another, landing and taking off every three minutes from Templehof and Tegel Airports. The airmen risked (some lost) their lives for the people of West Berlin. They did this for a whole year, delivering over two million tons of food, coal and CARE packages that kept the population from starving and freezing. In the spring of 1949 it was the Air Force, and only the Air Force, that BROKE the back of the Soviet blockade.

In the eyes of the city's two million civilians, the fly boys could do no wrong. Eighteen years after the event, they were still the most beloved of the occupation forces. No one cared that the airmen couldn't march, that their NCOs couldn't count cadence, that they always seem to need haircuts and that their boots did not shine. The airmen were the city's heroes. Then, now, and forever! One only need ask the women who daily at 17:00 stood outside the gates of Tempelhof Airfield and waited for the airmen to get off duty. Their ambition: marry one.

Fall in love and marry one, whether a mechanic, an administration guy, or a flight crew, someone, anyone, pigeon-toed or not. This 17th of July celebration was the day the people of West Berlin had a chance to cry out, "*Du, Flieger! Danke!*" (Hey, flyboy! Thank you!)

***

Meanwhile, back at Checkpoint Charlie, the UCLA co-eds were immediately surrounded by men in uniform. There was much gesticulating and slapping of foreheads. Two military intelligence,

MI bullet-heads in trench coats on a covert operation came out from one of the hotels. They were spooking on the Communists from an upper-story window and saw and recorded everything. They joined the MP Sergeant-of-the-Guard and two officers, one of them an officer. A major. They all confronted the two Valley Girls, while the German *Polizei*, the French--they were still there--and the British looked on. Not to be left out, one of the street's prostitutes who was hookering stepped up to the group and wanted to see what the commotion was all about. With everyone vigorously gesticulating, the major, who was at the Checkpoint on a mission, gave the young women a tongue lashing. "They could have taken you!" he fumed. "They could have taken you!"

The co-ed began to cry, the one who threw the Double Bubble "stun-gum" that dropped the Vopo officer. The other UCLA co-ed remained defiant. "They wouldn't dare," she said. "My father is a state congressman!"

Meanwhile, the two MP guards standing at rest absorbed their sergeant-of-the-guard's solvent glare, plus the major's vocal lacerations. "You two men are responsible for this!"

At that moment, racing up *Friedrich Strasse* in battle dress, came the truck with Alpha Company, 3rd Battalion soldiers. The 6th Infantry to the rescue! They were escorted by two Berlin *Polizei* squad cars, green Volkswagen Beetles at full siren and flashing blue lights.

In their M151 Ford jeep, Yorit and Bravo watched. "Frank, we're too close to the vortex of this thing. We better get out of here before they blame us for something. That major has already looked over twice," worried Yorit,

"Blame us. What for? We didn't do anything," said Bravo, not quite understanding.

"Oh, no? We're within a ten yard radius of a flap. That's too close to the bull's eye." Yorit started the engine.

Bravo glanced over at the still on-going altercation. The major was indeed observing them, and considering a guilt-by-vicinity charge. In the Army, anything was possible. "Yoyo, you're right. Let's get out of here before we're toilet paper." Turning the jeep, they drove back down the *Friedrich Strasse*, bouncing over the cobblestones as they went.

And what became of the girls from UCLA? Yorit and Bravo were later to find out that their visas were canceled. They were escorted to Templehof Airport, put on the next flight, booked as cargo, and flown to West Germany.

In their M151 jeep, the two signalmen headed in the direction of *Potsdamer Platz*. Along the way, they passed barren fields where mounds of rubble poked above the moonscape acreage of what had once been buildings. It was now an area of scrub—rough and uneven. Except for the occasional bush, the earth seemed almost unwilling to support vegetation. Most of the ruins had been leveled, enabling one to see in all directions, from *Oranien Strasse* to *Linden Strasse*, even as far as *Prinzen Strasse,* a street in the distance. The exposed streets ran at right angles to each other, giving the impression of an out-of-proportion checkerboard. The few ruined buildings that still stood were scarred and derelict. With the open vistas as a backdrop, they looked like broken teeth in a surreal Salvador Dali composition. Beyond them, under a horizon of torn sky and curving away, stood the silent arc of the Berlin Wall and its guard towers. The air smelled of moisture. "Gonna rain," said Bravo.

Yorit stopped the jeep. He looked out of the windshield at the vast expanse of landscape. "What the fuck ever happened to this place?" he asked with a tug of emotion. "What cataclysmic event could level such a majestic city?"

Bravo pushed open the jeep's canvas door. "Would you believe the 8th Army Air Force?"

Yorit sat back. "And Berlin used to be known as the Venice of the North." Shaking his head, he threw the jeep into gear and hit the gas. It jumped. Driving fast, the vehicle bounced up over the curb, over the broken sidewalk, and onto the rough ground of derelict empty ground lots.

"Hey, whadayadoin'? Where we goin'?" shouted Bravo, never used to his partner's sudden crazies.

"See that building over there, the one with the big hole in the wall and earthen ramp? We're driving in!"

"We'll never fit!"

"Let's see!"

Hitting ruts and broken bricks of what was once buildings, the jeep chassis jerked and shuddered. One rut bounced them from their seats. "If we'd have hit that hole with my `54 Chevy we'd have torn out the universal joint!" yelled out Bravo, hanging on to his seat for dear life.

Yorit geared down. Another lurch. "But not with a Ford Motor M151! Not never! It's indestructible! I'm going to buy one when I get home."

As they approached the ruin's ornate facade, they saw it was very badly scared. It had all the marks of combat: bomb splinters, bullet chips, patches of scorch that told of a horrific battle that once was. Several noble arch windows had been chewed away by small-arms fire, one of them blown out. It left a hole large enough to drive a tank through. It was the opening Yorit aimed for. Earth and brush had been bulldozed up to the opening, creating a ramp. In spite of the damage, the building still had the grandeur of what was once Romanesque. Gear-shifting, the jeep reached the ramp and drove up and into the Acropolis. He turned off the engine.

Inside, along the walls, was a vast empty cavern with *Tromp-de-Oel* columns. The high ceiling was amazingly intact. Refuse and earth mounds covered the broken marble floor. At one end of what may have once been a ballroom, two lion's heads supported an enormous mantel above a fireplace; at the other end was a stage big enough for a symphony orchestra to perform. Amazingly, a large glass chandelier still hung from the ceiling; a second one had crashed to the floor and lay there like broken bones, the fist-size crystals scattered like diamonds on the Namibian shore.

Two crows, shiny black things known for scrounging city dumps, sprang from a niche in the wall, apparently their nest. They swooped down, upset at being disturbed. Circling, they screeched a dire warning to the intruders before flying out one of the arched windows.

The two soldiers stepped out of the jeep. They cocked their heads back in wonder, for there, on the tattered and scarred walls of the ruined structure, were gigantic frescos of German knights in medieval armor. They were dressed for battle and carried battle axes and swords. Yorit and Bravo had never seen anything like it before, not in New Jersey, not in Ohio. "This place..." Yorit slapped his hand to his mouth; his voice carried in the cathedral void. He dropped to a whisper. "Wow! This place is philharmonic."

"What do you suppose it once was?" asked Bravo in a hushed voice, sensative to the environment.

"Beats me. The National Socialist Hall of Mirrors, only without the mirrors."

"You mean, like a Versailles?"

Stooping, Yorit picked up one of the chandelier crystals from the floor. It was heavy.

Bravo, stepping over some broken sandbags, held his arms

outstretched to get a feel for the dimensions of the grand chamber. "I got it. I know what this place was. A Fellini movie set. What else?"

"Yeah, perfect for freaks and ghouls," said Yorit, pushing his field cap back with his thumb. "I know a couple of Platoon Sergeants back at company who would be right at home here."

There was a screech and a battering of wings. One of the crows had returned. It flew in and landed on the hanging chandelier's tendril, making it tremble, the crystals tinkling, hollow sounding. The two signalmen watched. "Beware the Ides of March," whispered Yorit furtively.

"Is that an Alfred Hitchcock quote?" asked Bravo, down on one knee to pick up something in the dirt.

"No, Shakespeare. Macbeth."

Bravo stood up. "Bad omen. Crows symbolize death, but whose death? Mine? Yours?"

"Can't be me. I'm superman," said Yorit.

Bravo stepped over to him and opened his hand. He held out a corroded shell casing. There was Cyrillic lettering stamped on it. "It's a Russian slug. Some bad ass fighting must have gone on in here. I say we *do* have to beware of the Ides of November."

Yorit took the brass casing between his fingers. He rubbed it against his field jacket, polishing it. "No, in Macbeth it was the Ides of March. It has to be March."

"But this is November, 1963. Got to be the Ides of November. And you know birds don't lie," Bravo assured him.

Yorit shrugged. "Okay, you win. Beware of the Ides of November, 1963. But what Ides?"

Suddenly the VCR-10 radio crackled from the back of the jeep. "Dancer two! Dancer two! This is Ballroom one! What is your location? Where the hell are you guys? Report! Over!"

"Oh shit, it's our Section Sarge, Sergeant Sweechek. He's after us. Shit!"

Immediately, the two soldiers hopped back into their jeep. Bravo fiddled with the radio as Yorit started the engine. He gave it some gas. They drove out the hole in the wall and down the earthen ramp. At a high speed, the M151 hit the ground and bounced, and bounced again. Avoiding a ditch and driving frantically, they reached the *Prinzen Strasse*. From there they were not far from the *Brandenburg Gate*, the next point for a call-in and communication report. "Damn it! Will Big

Brother never stop watching us?" Yorit yelled out above the engine's roar.

"Big Brother has to watch us!" Bravo yelled back.

"Why's that?"

"Because Bigb rother is the Army! He-yaw! He-yaw!"

The Golden Sun

The Golden Sun *Kneipe* was a bar across the street from the Andrews Barracks Army. Post. It was the first off-post stop in a soldier's "Stations of the Cross" ritual that took them up town to the main street bars of West Berlin. In the evening, off-duty soldiers would cross the street and enter the Golden Sun on their feet and depart, more often than not, on their knees, sometimes their backs. They would crisscross the city by tram, bus, car, and piggy-back if necessary, going from the *Lichtefelde* district to the *Steglitz* district, from *Friedenau* to *Schöneberg* and back, tapping into the liquid seam of *Berliner Kindel* beer and *Schnapps* liquor, drinks that never ran out. They would sniff out every bar in the Berlin districts in an effort to drink them dry before midnight, the time when a soldier's Army pass expired. Girls were met, adventures had, and fights fought. It was the stuff of youthful memories. And it all began at the Golden Sun *Kneipe*.

The name itself was a misnomer. There was no gold, except maybe in the bibulous dreams of those who dropped off to sleep across the tables, and there was no sun since the sun rarely shined in Berlin. (The Germans blamed Hitler for that.) The bar itself was only one step up—or down, depending on one's position to the floor—from a hometown dive. It can be said of the Special Troops brigade soldiers, the Golden Sun bar was a second home, if not a refuge after training and soldiering all day with the U.S. Army.

The Sun itself was made up of two large rooms: one for the bar and tables, the other for dancing. The tables and chairs were funky and mismatched, the floorboards worn. Dull colored lights hung from the ceiling, which gave the bar a backstreet look, suggesting a whore house about to be raided. From the Sun's large front window the patrons had a view of the Andrews´ main gate awash in flood lights. The on-duty gate guards patroled there, billy clubs in hand. And the bar served snacks: Bavarian pretzels (*Prezela*) and sausages (*Bochwurst*) to order with mustard. Thus it can be said of the Golden Sun, it was the ideal port for a quick last shot and a beer before a soldier's good-till-midnight pass expired.

The evening was cold. Outside, it had begun to drizzle the way it does in Berlin, a fine spray rather than raindrops. It was that way when Yorit and Robuck entered the Golden Sun. Pulling back the heavy curtains, they shook themselves and looked around. There were only a few patrons. The evening had not yet begun. Immediately, they stepped up to the bar, smacking their lips to the atmosphere. They ordered two *Berliner Kindels*. Robuck glowed. "At last the tide has come in."

"Pray it never goes out," said Yorit, as they greeted Fritz, the bartender.

Hans Fritz, the owner of the Golden Sun, was also the bar-keep, and the dish washer-keep, and the waiter-keep, and the bouncer, and the anything else a German saloon keeper had to be to survive in a country where national taxes took half the income. He was in his forties, thin, and balding. He had a sinewy neck and well-developed arms that came from loading 88mm shells during the war in North Africa. He tended to grimace when he smiled, making him appear cruel, as if taking pleasure in watching his American guests pass out on the floor. He was fond of saying out loud, *"Trinksen Sie meine friendsen op! Youvs machen me reich!"* With one eye puckered, he slid two perspiring glasses of Berliner Kindel, the beer of choice, toward Robuck and Yorit. Robuck slid two German Marks back. "Fritz, you're a genius."

"I knowvs dat," Fritz agreed, hissingly.

The two soldiers clinked their drinks. "Why do Germans always hiss when they talk English?"

Robuck shrugged. "It's the cobra in their nature. Just don't let one bite you."

"The girls, yes, but the guys, no."

At the edge of the dance floor a juke box glared like a large Christmas ornament. It waited for a coin to bring it to life. The pinball machine next to the door was already up and humming. A soldier in rumpled work fatigues played the flippers, running the numbers. In the crook of his arm he cradled half-aglass of beer. Noting the soldier's arm patch, Robuck nudged Yorit. He was from the 42nd Engineers. They felt sorry for him. The 42nd Engineers was a 24-7 line company where one was forever on duty.

The engineer, a Pfc, seemed full of tension. His anger was pronounced, the kind of anger that comes from having been institutionalized too long. With each pass of the pinball he gnashed his teeth and growled, hitting at the surface of the pinball machine with the palm of his hand in an effort to work unseen knots out of the fermentation of his mind. To accumulate game points was not important; to beat up the pinball machine was. Wack! TILT! "Take that, Sergeant Bender, you asshole!" he barked out loud, not caring who heard him. "Fuck you and shove it, dumb ass NCO!" It was obvious the sergeant was not there; otherwise the Pfc would have been disciplined on the spot. He slapped at the pinball machine again and again. Finally, the backboard lit up. Ding, ding, ding! The engineer smiled at his Pyrrhic victory. It took some of the crimson from his face.

"Who is Sarge Bender, I wonder?" asked Yorit, wiping the beer-foam from his mouth.

"Got to be his section NCO," replied Robuck. "Who else in the Army can piss a man off that much but a Section Sargeant giving orders?"

"Or a spouse giving orders," said Yorit, thinking his retort clever.

Robuck thought for a moment. "You know, when the engineer guy is finished I'm going to get on that pinball machine and do some dumpin' myself."

Yorit drained his glass. "Why? Got a gripe?"

Robuck nodded. "Our Platoon Sarge. He's been getting on my nerves lately."

"What, Sarge Sweetcheeks? He's a good guy," said Yorit in defense of him.

Robuck moaned. "Oh, yeah? Two days ago at reveille he came into my quarters beating a wastepaper basket. You know, Basic Training shit!"

"Did he put the wastebasket over your head and beat it?"

"No."

Yorit shrugged. "Then you got nothing to gripe about."

From one of the tables a man jumped up and spread-eagled himself against the room's tatty wallpaper. He kissed the wall. "Golden Sun, I love you," he uttered. It had been weeks since his 1stSgt—he was from the Service Company—allowed him an off-post pass. This evening was his coming-out party. For him to drink was the jovial equivalent of a first lay. On the wall above his head hung a large canvas-framed painting. It was a Fragonard copy of the "Fountenbleau Forest," a nymphet on a swing in the moonlight, or rather, in the sunlight. Years of nicotine and dust had darkened the painting's surface to a moony fuzz. The Service Company man pressed his lips to the corner of the canvas and kissed the female figure's delicate foot, then he dropped to the floor and began bumping his head in worshipful gratitude, the way Moslems do. "I'm released! I'm released!" he kept repeating. From the bar, Yorit and Robuck watched, sympathetic to his condition.

"By the looks of it, that's the closest that poor bastard's been to sex in months," said Robuck, feeling sorry for him.

"If bumping your head on the floor generates a hard on, go for it, I say," Yorit agreed. Robuck too. He dropped down on his knees.

"What are you doing?"

"I'm going to bump my head on the floor. I can use an erection."

More soldier patrons came into the Golden Sun, two in work fatigues. They were followed by three German girls. Immediately, male heads turned in erotic admiration. The girls' make-up was slick and smooth, giving them that chalky look of store window mannequins, with no facial fissures. Their hair was piled high on their heads in a beehive fashion, Brigitte Bardot style. From the bar, the soldiers ogled them as if honing in with radar. They were not that attractive, but to look at them was a refreshing alternative to Army- olive drab everything. The Service Company man who kissed the Fragonard painting dumbly stared, his mouth open, an invitation for a moth should one want to enter and nest there.

The three women looked around, then waved toward familiar faces. Their dates. They crossed the room like cats marking their territory, throwing off the scent of Old Spice Aftershave as they went. It was the lotion of choice. To all things in and out of uniform, it meant these women were American soldier molls. Their fragrance, Old Spice Aftershave, was a warning code to the Brits and Frenchies. It meant, Allies—Hands off! Hungrily, Yorit and Robuck sniffed after them, as did half the men in the room.

More patrons entered; only a few wore work fatigues. Those dressed in civilian duds wore blazers, jackets, and pleated pants. Their intention was to go uptown later and party.

As fast as the soldiers came up to the bar, Fritz pulled beer *Kindel* from the tap, filling their beer *Krugs*, or glasses. Someone dropped a coin in the jukebox. A Bo Diddly record came on.

Yorit turned and looked. Their buddies—Bravo, Pereski, and Lavoss—stood at the curtain entrance. They had just come in. They saw Yorit and Robuck, who had taken a table. They moved to joined them. The evening was underway.

Behind them a stranger entered the Sun. From his appearance, it was obvious he was not a soldier—no white socks or ankle-length trousers. He wore a black corduroy outfit that made him look like a cowboy: bell bottom pants, waist jacket, a tight vest over a white shirt buttoned to the neck, and a bolo tie. But it was the hat, its wide brim, sombrero like, that gave him the Poncho Villa look. Even more incongruous were the silver buttons—large ones the size of quarters; they were sewn on his pockets, on his jacket, down the front of his corduroy trousers in a square pattern like a sailor's fly. A pocketwatch chain with a dozen silver trinkets hung across the open vest. They tingled and tinkled as he moved toward the bar, his whole demeanor suggesting, "Make way, hombre, or else!" The cowboy's gaze was steady as if measuring up the place for a gun fight. Satisfied, he rolled his shoulders and stepped up to the bar and ordered a drink in gutteral German. Nearby, the tables buzzed with curiosity: "Where did the Texas Ranger come from?"

"Got to be from West Texas," said Lavoss as the big man passed the tables and stepped to the bar. "Seen guys like him when I was at Ft. Hood. Texans dress like that."

"Could be he's the original Lone Ranger," replied Bravo, sitting back in his chair.

"Not a chance," said Yorit. "I don't see Tonto around."

Pereski pressed a contemplative finger to his cheek. "Now what would a cowboy be doing here in West Berlin, Germany? He should be back home on the range with his guitar."

"Maybe West Berlin is the range...and the wild west!" said Lavoss. "Hey, Frank, where you going?"

Bravo had gotten up and moved toward the bar. "Going to take on the big cowboy," he answered back. Hooking his thumbs into his belt, he strutted up to the German with a Gabby Hays swagger.

The German cowboy had his *Bier* glass to his mouth and was deep into a swallow when Bravo introduced himself. "Say, hombre. Howdy-do!"

The big German rolled one eyeball down and looked at Bravo, the short interloper who came up to his chest. "*Brart ya mit mij?*" (You talking with me?) he asked in *Platt* (flat) German.

Bravo cupped his hands to his mouth and called across the room to his buddies' table. "He's from West Texas, all right. I can't understand a word he's saying!" He turned back to the big German. "You a long way from home, ain't ya'all, cowboy? How did you get through communsit territory dressed in this fancy outfit without getting shot? Where's your horse?"

The German's blue eyes narrowed; he was not sure if he was being made fun of. Fritz, the bartender, was filling beer drinks at the tap and overheard. Chuckling, he told the cowboy what Bravo had said. The big man saw the humor and laughed. It was a deep-chested, tuba sort of laugh that made the men standing at the bar turn and look.

"He ist no a cowboys," said Fritz in his broken English. "He *ist ein Tischler*—a wood- maker in yous da English language. He ist from da Oldenburg town in da Friesland. *Das ist Nord Deutschland. Alle Tischlern* dresses likes his. Our da Brotchen bakers-en, they dresses in white and wear, what you say, big *Huten* (hats). *Nordsee* fishermans, they wears blue stripe shirts and *Segelerhuten* (sailing caps). In Deutschland, da cloths tell yous da jobs mans dos. Though he looks like cowboy, ha-ha, he ist really a woodman—a *Tischler*."

Bravo listened with interest. "You mean a carpenter? But from where? Friesland? That near the panhandle?"

One of the soldiers standing at the bar who had just enough to drink to be nervy, stepped up to the big German Tischler (carpenter). "Say, cowboy, what's all them silver bangles and buttons for?"

"I bet he's a gun fighter, a trinket for each man he's shot," said another soldierm dressed in work fatigues. He was leaning against the bar with the others.

Fritz the bartender told the *Tischler* what was beingsaid about him. The big man laughed and nodded. "*Glauben Sie mir. Ich bin nur ein Tischler.*" (Believe me. I'm only a carpenter) he said, this time in high German, and not dialect. He ordered drinks for Bravo and the soldiers at the bar and explained the meaning of the silver buttons. Between pulls on the tap, Fritz translated and called the carpenter a "crapenter."

It was a tradition in Germany that went back to the middle ages, the time when apprentices traveled from town to town. After a job was done, an apprentice would receive a token, a grade, like a report card, from the town mayor. It proved craftsmanship and experience.

Accumulate enough tokens and in three years an apprentice would be promoted to journeyman. The trinkets were his grades.

Back at the table, Bravo explained what Fritz the bartender had told him. "The cowboy is a *crapenter*."

"What the hell is that?"

"Someone who builds homes and shits on the job." Everyone laughed.

Lavoss finished his beer and got up to get another. "If you guys think that fellow is odd, ever see a German chimneysweep? He dresses in black and wears gold buttons on his jacket. Not only that, he wears a silk top hat, and get this, he wears it while cleaning a chimney! Can you imagine that?"

"A silk top hat? I see visions of a Prussian Fred Astaire dancing on a roof," said Pereski.

Yorit nodded. "You know, I'm beginning to like Germany. It's quirky."

The Golden Sun had gotten crowded. All the tables were now occupied. A line stood at the bar. On the floor, two couples danced to the jukebox tunes. At one of the tables a poker game had begun; the pot was a mix of German Marks and dollars. Everyone drank. Everyone smoked. Fritz the bartender grinned. "You boys makes, maken me reich!" he bubbled out loud for the third time.

The pinball machine had changed hands. The Engineer at the flippers had finished thrashing his Sgt and passed the game to the next frustrated player, a HHC headquarters man who was even more animated at the flipper, flipping. He hopped up and down, back and forth to the whistle and whiz of the backboard bells. The game's flippers blurred under his experienced hand and cries of, "Yeah! Yeah!"

A Sgt from the M.I. Company (military intelligence), a big man himself, stepped up to the Oldenberg cowboy and challenged him to armwrestle. He agreed. Over a *Krug* of *Bier* they bumped heads and stared each other down with a "Kick your butt!" look. Instead of a punch in the nose, bets were placed and the battle of the forearms began. The winner got to drink a singular glass of *Schnapps* that was placed on the table just under their death grips. Even the card game table stopped to watch. More bets were placed. Grimacing and grunting, the Sgt from M.I. and the Oldenberg cowboy gripped hands, their skins red-faced from the effort. There was a crash. The back of the Sgt's hand hit the table. He lost. The cowboy got to drink the *Schnapps.* There was some applause, followed by a re-challenge. Another *Schnapps* liquor was placed on the table.

It was then that they came in. The two women. Stepping beyond the curtain that hung in the doorway, the soldiers could see they had style. They were wearing black stockings and short skirts that hid strong thighs. One soldier whistled. Leaving a trail of Old Spice Aftershave after them, they strutted across the smoke-filled room, momentarily blunting male conversation as they passed. The soldiers recognized them. They were the two harlots known as "Sin" and her sister, "Death." Their real names were Monika and Hertha.

They picked up other nicknames too like, "Last of the Mohicans," and an irreverent, "Three Stooges," though there were only two of them. It was a Headquarters Company sobriquet. But the cruelest sobriquet of all were the names, "Sin," and her sister, "Death." It was the label that stuck. It fit them because they were always together. Oddly, the two women liked the degradation. It twittered the Americans. The rude label gave them a kind of celebrity status among the companies at Andrews Army Post. It made soldiers want to "Know Death" and "Commit Sin," as they said. In the barracks, one humorist conjectured: to have sex with one was a sin, and to marry the other was death.

The moment Sin and Death entered the Golden Sun, the men at the bar visually stripped them of their garments and redressed them with a grade of B-. They would have been graded higher had they been younger. Nevertheless, the male attitude was: "Will ya look at them thighs? Will ya?"

"And who are these women?" was the question in the minds of some soldiers. Are they whores? Are they one-night stands? Could they be married and brought home to Mother? To the unwary, such as the younger soldiers, they looked like good pickings. But to the more experienced, those posted in the Berlin Brigade longer than two years, they were just "Army Issue" to be passed from one generation of G.I.s to the next, to be used and re-used, like stock weapons in the Company Arms Room.

Over the years, in their personal search for love, both Sin and Death used to hand out quickies, hoping it would lead to marriage. Now, it was no more. Those were bygone days. After so many disappointments, they had become selective. Though girlfriends of theirs were married off to soldiers, that magic bullet—a G.I. proposal—had eluded them. Currently, they were concentrating on Signal Company soldiers and its store of hot bachelors. What these two B- graded woman were, and what most soldiers in the Golden Sun did not know, nor care to know, was that they were the last of a generation of German women who were teenagers at the end of World War II. They had survived National Socialism, carpet bombing, and the Battle of Berlin. With the arrival of the 82 Airborne Division in 1945 they, and thousands of women like them, wanted only one thing: TO GET THE HELL OUT OF BERLIN, NO MATTER WHAT! The ticket? Marry G.I. Joe! And many did. Some did not—Sin and Death among them. Eighteen years later, they were still trying. They longed to get away from the cold, dreary legacy of the still-wounded city. In spite of all the hype and hustle of the so-called economic miracle, *Wiederaufbau und Wirtshcaftswunder,* of West Germany, their lives had not improved much. They still had to scrape to make ends meet, and still had to live in one-room cold-water flats. A chance at happiness with a German male was doubtful. Most of them walked around uttering under their breath, pondering the meaning of *Das Vaterland* and their identity to it. "How could we have lost the war? We were the master race!"

With the Wall cutting the city in two and adding to the East-West confrontation, Death and Sin (Monika and Hertha) wanted out of the city more than ever. For them, and for other West Berlin women, American soldiers were defined as the "cream of the crop," followed by the British soldiers from their garrison. The British had a pickings number 2. Out of Napoleon Barracks in the district of Wedding, the French Army soldiers finished in third place. It had to do with their lousy pay and garlic breath. For German women in East Germany, the Russian soldiers, no matter the rank, were a definite no-no.

Many of Death and Sin's friends who had married Americans sent back letters, tantalizing letters, about the American dream of shopping centers, of big back yards, of three channel television, of Elvis and Oldsmobile cars. There were Doris Day films to see, neighborhood track homes to live in, and central heating, a heating which was very different from the tubular black coal stoves found in the West Berlin apartments. And there was Hollywood with its California sun, and New York with its big city skyscrapers and so much more. It excited the imagination.

The brides now living in America were happy. It was dreams come true. Who cared if the G.I. husband came from the Ozarks, ate with his mouth open, mixed white wine with red, wore white socks, or had a fat ass. He was the game plan! The big ticket! The free ride! The green card! Hook'm, fuck'm, marry'm, then unload'm! Then go out and land *"Herr Richtig,"* the German term for "Mr. Right guy."

In their pursuit of the American male dream, both Death and Sin seem to have been jinxed. Over the years, no G.I. offered them a proposal, not even the boys from the Ozarks, or the tobacco chewing East Tennesseeans. With each year that passed, Death and Sin's physical grades dropped a degree. As young women in their twenties and attractive, they had been classified "top stuff." That was in 1950. Now, in their late thirties, though rich with maturity and still attractive, in the soldier's eyes they were down-graded to a B-.

In the Golden Sun, Monik (Sin) and Hertha (Death) took their chairs at the Signal soldier table. The men were grateful. They had female company. Sin looked around. "Where are all the good men tonight?" she asked in her delightful German accent. It was the kind of accent that charmed Americans. It made soldiers fall in love, if only for one night. Though Sin was born a German, she spoke good English, with a light banjo twang of someone born south of the Mason-Dixon Line.

"There are a few good men around," said Yorit, "but you have to take off your bra to get them interested. You can begin with me."

"Or me!" chirped Bravo, a little too enthusiastic.

Chuckling, Sin reached over and tickled Bravo under the chin. "Perhaps, Franky, but are you intelligent?"

"He's intelligent, all right," said Lavoss, picking up on the flirt. "Bravo got his high school diploma in the Army. He knows radio nomenclatures by heart."

"Don't knock Army education," grumped Bravo, not appreciating the wisecrack. "I went from the 10th to the 12th grade and got a high school diploma, all in six weeks. Where else can you do that but in Uncle Sam's Army?"

"Try Disneyland," suggested Yorit.

Sin took a cigarette out of a pack lying on the table. It was a Pall Mall. "Give me a light," she uttered huskily. Trembling, Robuck broke two matches trying to light up when the click of a Zippo lighter flashed; it belonged to a HHC Company man from the next table. Sin lit off his Zippo, adding an invitational wink, the kind that makes a man's throat go dry. "I'll be right over, *Schatz* (dear)," she said to him.

Robuck scuffed. "You smoke my cigarettes but light off a stranger's lighter. I'd call that infidelity."

"You, *Liebling* (darling), were too slow to light my flame," Sin cooed.

The table "Wowzered!" her retort and gave her a thumbs up for wit and barb. Sin, herself, was used to rough guy talk, and could give as good as she got. Reparté was the name of the game with G.I.s.

Looking around with that preoccupied air of one who understood men, Sin caught the eye of a soldier in civilian dress standing at the bar. He was known to be a Staff Sergeant. Leaving his drink, he walked over to the Signal table and invited Sin to dance. She had netted her first big fish of the evening—an NCO.

Pereski stood up and looked hard at the interloper. "She's Signal Company terrain, there, Sarge."

Getting up from the table, Sin snipped back defiantly at Pereski. "I am no man's terrain!"

"Or every other man's terrain as long as it's one at a time," interrupted Robuck with a laugh. The table joined him.

Indignant, Sin took the sergeant's arm. "Come, *Schatz*. Let us dance."

Yorit watched. "Paul, she just put you down. It comes from being too long in the service of your country, don't you think? You've forgotten how to talk to women."

"No, that's not the reason. I can talk and hustle German women. The problem is our rank. If I had more rank. One lousy stripe. An E-5 sergeant. Then she'd have jumped on me. Tell me, just what does a guy have to do to make it with ladies around here? Tell me," demanded Pereski, not happy that he had lost Sin for the moment.

"Try saying something romantic," suggested Bravo. "Something that would really turn on the other species."

"Like what?"

"Tell her you're hung!"

The gang at the table broke up. "Yeah!" "Right on!" "Be a stud." "Cool!" Everyone laughed.

Just then, someone turned up the jukebox music. It mixed with the room's dense cigarette smoke, the murmurs, and loud talk. The atmosphere was like a beehive in conflict, and growing. Death, who had been chatting with a girlfriend at another table, returned to the signalmen table and sat down. She crossed her legs and lit a cigarette.

"Robert, have you seen Oats?" she asked in a voice a little too adolescent for a woman her age.

"Oats? You mean Oats as in General Mills oats or our 2nd Platoon Sarge, Sergeant Oats?"

"She means fat-ass, big-butt, loud-mouth, Platoon Sergeant Oats," Bravo broke in.

"Watch your tongue," warned Pereski. "Sarge Oats has been to North Korea in winter, and it wasn't for vacation. Show a little respect for a snowman."

Death asked Yorit again, "Have you seen him? He promised to call me at my workplace, but I hear nothing."

"I see him every morning at reveille," Yorit replied, wondering what she was driving at. "Why? Do you and the Sarge have a thing going?"

"Only friends," she answered, lightly tossing back her jacket, revealing a white wool sweater whose contents jumped out as if to be interviewed. Watching from another table, an Ordinance Division man stood up, lusting. He growled. In the semi-light of the smoke-filled room, Death looked especially desirable. When she arched her back to stretch, her figure took like a mound cake.

This evening, unknown to the boys at the table, Death and Sin had made a pact: no sleeping with the lower rank and file. If their goal was to marry an American male, he had to have at least the rank of Staff Sergeant. The women had enough of mundane E-3s, E-4's and corporals whose only connection with the real world began and ended at the crotch. The two women wanted men who had some of life's scars, who were a little burned out and ready to settle down. "Rank and maturity, no pimples please," was the new name of their dating game.

"Forget Sergeant Oats," said Yorit; "he's a lush and a drunk. The only thing that makes him happy is counting cadence, which means he can only make love by the numbers. 'Huh, two, three, four...' You want that, dear?"

Bravo leaned over toward Death. "Did you know Sergeant Oats smokes a pipe made of human thighbone?" he asked, hoping to shock her.

"Human thighbone?" She was unsure what he meant.

"Yes, and no one knows for sure if it's his ex-wife's thighbone or her boyfriend's." Death's eyes widened in disbelief. "And he carries a dried tobacco pouch with him as well," Bravo added.

"What is wrong with that?"

"The pouch is made from North Korean scrotum."

Death looked puzzled. "What is a schro-toomb?" she pronounced, her English not quite the King's English.

"You don't want to know," said Pereski.

"Maybe she does," said Lavoss.

"Then take out yours and show her." The guys at the table laughed, followed by a bumblebee buzz of conversation.

Feeling mellow from drink, Yorit took Death's hand. Her skin felt chapped. "Let's not talk about Sergeant Oats and his pipes and scrotums. Let's talk about your plumbing, dear."

Death shook her head. "My plumbing? What do you mean?"

"Your orifices, that sort of thing. Tell me how many do you have that are open?"

"I do not know. What you mean by orifice?" she replied not understanding.

Yorit smiled mischievously. "Let me expose you, my dear. We can go to my apartment and explore your plumbing."

Surprised by what Yorit said, Robuck put down his drink. "Now see here, Yoyo. Are you telling us you have an off-post apartment, and you didn't inform us about it?"

Yorit straightened. "Well, not exactly an apartment; I was thinking of the back seat of my M151 Ford jeep."

Death withdrew her hand. "I have no idea what you boys talk about, but I will ask you this. Are you, either of you a Sergeant yet?"

"No, Uncle Sam does not promote these days," said Yorit. "What's rank got to do with your orifice?"

"Nothing," said Death, suddenly aloof, this time lighting her own cigarette.

Yorit waved the smoke away. "How do you like that? Death has become a gold digger. She's only interested in guys with rank who can count to four on their fingers—the worst kind."

Robuck looked skeptical. "I wouldn't exactly call dating an NCO digging for gold. I mean, most of them have to pay child support and are as broke as we are."

Yorit took Death's hand again. "Look, dear. I've been company Soldier-of-the-Month twice, a noble title, and am now up for the Soldier-of-the-Quarter award," he added, hoping to impress her with his military awards.

Unimpressed, Death frowned. Just then another man, a Detachment-A guy, came up to the table where the signalmen sat. He asked Death to dance. Together, they went off to the dance floor. Sitting around the table, the signalmen watched them go. Pereski looked across to Yorit. "Twice, Soldier-of-the-Month, huh? Like big deal. My friend, you'll never discover the female orifice by flashing Army awards."

Pouting, Yorit slouched in his chair. "Yeah, well, shot out of the saddle doesn't mean I can't climb back on the horse. Death loves to dance. I'll just grab her and dance jitterbug, then you guys just watch. That's one thing that the Detach-A character can't do, I'm sure."

Robuck stood up to get another drink. "Come on, guys, let's not spend too much time with those two old-time dames. Death and Sin are both pushing age 40 and sagging. Leave them for the SrSgts, since they're sagging, too."

"I can't help myself," said Yorit as he watched the couples hop to the juke box music. "Since I've been in the Army, besides bad habits like smoking and drinking, I've picked up an Oedipus complex. I've developed the hots for older chicks—German chicks, even if they are tatty around the edges."

Lavoss nodged Yorit. "You better watch out, buddy," he warned. "Them two, Sin and Death, are about to enter menopause."

"Then I'll have to join them."

From across the room, cheers suddenly erupted. The arm-wrestling match was again in progress. This time a man from the 42nd Engineers won the match. He had arm-flattened a medic from the 279 Hospital who had taken up the challenge. With that, the Engineer man grabbed the *Schnapps* glass and downed the shot.. "Next!" he slurred out loud. He was getting drunk from victory. It was his fourth.

Sin returned to the table and sat down just as Little Richard's "Good Golly Miss Molly" came up on the jukebox. She crossed and re-crossed her strong legs, a move that forced up her skirt, revealing milky thighs as ripe as summer peaches about to burst. Sitting next to her, Pereski could not help but notice. He let out a faint cry. Watching, Robuck swallowed hard. Lavoss had to look away. Yorit appeared anguished. The combination of beer, *Schnapps*, and female thighs had a glandular effect that translated into full male, libido impulses, especially for American soldiers forever on the lookout for love.

A man came over to the Signal table from the bar. He chitchatted briefly with Sin, hoping to win favors. She got up to dance with him just as Death returned from the floor when another soldier from Maintenance Company hustled up to her, oblivious of the possessive looking signalmen sitting around. He asked her to dance. She declined politely.

"What is this, make out by-the-numbers?" stated Robuck with obvious disapproval. "I thought Sin and Death were Signal Company's comfort ladies."

"By the looks of things they are also Headquarters, Service, Engineer, and M.I. Company's comfort ladies as well," noted Lavoss, with tonal disapproval..

There was a sudden loud *bang.* It was the sound of wood splitting. Everyone looked. From behind the door of the men's WC (water closet), there was a fight going on. Someone had thrown a punch, missed his target and hit the door, cracking the wood. At the bar, Fritz the bartender dropped what he was doing and grabbed the baseball bat he kept under the counter, a Louisville Slugger. He kept it there for just such an emergency. He rushed the men's room. There was the sound of a "thud'," followed by a "whack." The door flew open and out dashed two frightened men, one in civilian dress, the other in work fatigues, both pursued by Fritz, his Louisville Slugger in hand. He barked threats in that shrill voice of a *Stümbahnfurher*. The two ran for the front door. At the tables some of the crowd applauded.

Satisfied with his triumph, Fritz returned to the bar and replaced the bat. The gaiety resumed, and the Golden Sun returned to its bedlam.

Elvis's "Love Me Tender" crooned on the juke box. "Let us dance, Robert," invited Death, taking his hand. Pleased with the request, Yorit got up and followed her to the floor. Three couples were already dancing cheek-to-cheek.

In his arms, she danced close. Thankful, Yorit sniffed Death. On women, men's Old Spice Aftershave cologne had another scent. It mixed well with the female chemistry. Soldiers loved it. Yorit fixed on Death. "Honey, are you really serious about going steady with that nasty old Sergeant Oats?"

"He is my fiancé, and he is not a nasty old anything," Death replied warmly. She liked Yorit's grace.

"SFC Oats is your fiancée? Since when? The only partner in his life is the Army."

"Yes, and now me too," she said firmly, pressing herself against him, her accented voice like warm milk to his ear.

Yorit studied her face: the large eyes, the fine nose, her style inviting. "Death, are you telling me you're rejecting our society: the Golden Sun, the good times, the best and the brightest of America, me, in order to settle down with an Army Sergeant first class? I'm shocked."

"Yes, and I will be his wife when he asks me."

"Oh!" Surprised, Yorit glanced at the other couples dancing around them. They appeared absorbed in each other. "Do you realize if you marry ol' Sarge Oats, you marry an Army drill instructor? He'll have you up for reveille and standing in morning formation in your nightgown and slippers with your kids. You'll celebrate Thanksgiving in the company Mess Hall. Knowing him as a Platoon Sergeant, he won't make love to you unless our company commander is there to give the order to 'Present Arms!' Besides, he's from a small town in Kansas."

She looked at him quizzically. "What do you mean?"

Yorit shrugged. "In Kansas they consider it an achievement if you finish grade school. He hasn't. Is that the kind of man you want for a husband, someone who hasn't finished grade school?"

"Your President Eisenhower. He came from Kansas too, no?"

"Yes, and he never finished grade school. It's why he's a Republican."

Death loosened her arms from around Yorit's shoulders. She looked at him, he at her. She had neat wrinkles at the corner of her eyes. Age was setting in. Her lips were worn, but suggestive; her hair style, fabulous. "I am a woman, Robert Yorit, and I have seen much, perhaps more than I should have. I know hunger and I know what it is to have nothing. After the war, my mother's flat had only three walls. And my father? Who knows. I have not seen him since 1942. My brother, I know he is dead. Here in West Berlin I am a woman alone like many women, and I am tired of alone. You understand me?"

"I'm sorry," Yorit murmured.

As she talked, her voice seemed to shrink. "Monika and I have fun with you GIs. You make us laugh, but it is not enough. We want families, real homes, the things every woman wishes to have. If Oats says he loves me, if he wants to marry me, the way I feel about him is not important. I shall learn to love him."

Around them, more couples moved to the dance floor. The lights were low, the music, lethargic. Yorit thought for a moment. "But, dear, if you marry him, we are going to have a problem. Who is going to haul soldier ashes?"

"Haul ashes? What do you mean?"

"Forget it," Yorit mumbled, knowing Death would not understand. He liked her.

Swaying in his arms, she continued. "Your Sergeant Oats calls me loving names like darling, sweetheart, and my baby."

Frowning, he looked at her with solemnity as they truned. "Honey, that's what he calls his rifle."

For a moment she appeared hurt, then she smiled, then she laughed. "Oh, you *Amies*! You are never serious."

"Only when we are being shot at." said Yorit, now trying to kiss her.

Death drew away. "You *Amies* just float and bump along like balloons untouched by the real world. Children balloons, baby balloons."

"Yes," he mumbled, nibbling at her neck. She let him. "Yes, balloons." Yorit could taste the flavor of the Old Spice Aftershave lotion on her neck. He never imagined a male scent could taste so erotic. He felt himself heating up.

"You *Amies* all float on the wind, above, in the sky, from woman to woman." she moaned. The soldier passion was beginning to mellow her. Death stretched her neck. "…balloons…on the wind…. Yes."

Flushing with heat, Yorit crushed her to him. She did not resist. She, too, was growing sensual. Just then, at that moment that Chubby Checkers ignited the jukebox, Death pushed him off her. She squealed. "Oh, Come on, G.I.! Let's do the Twist! Let's dance!"

By now the Golden Sun was very busy. Beer consumption had reached a Fort Lauderdale pitch on spring break. The poker game had expanded to seven players and two tables. The pinball machine, ever hot, continued to ring up big scores. Now, with Chubby Checkers' jukebox shouts, the dance floor quickly filled with twisting, wiggling couples.

There was a sudden rush of fresh air. Someone forgot to close the front door. It revived one soldier whose head lay on a table. He sat up. Feeling sick, he got up. He staggered to the men's toilet. There, inside, he collapsed on the floor, one hand against the urinal well. Guests who wanted to pee had to step over him.

Back at the bar, the action, ever lively, the soldiers played the game of "catch up." It was the Golden Sun's game of drink. The idea was for a player to chug-a-lug beer from a three-liter glass boot shaped like a woman's leg, knee to foot. In drinking, if a player was not careful, the laws of gravity would plop the beer trapped in the glass toe, driving it like Big Sur up the length of the boot and into the imbiber's nose, washing over the face. Over the years, more than one soldier needed mouth-to-mouth resuscitation following such a washout.

O'Malley was invited to play. The big Irishman spent most of the evening at the bar. At first he resisted, until the brim-filled feline-shaped glass boot was put into his hands. Assenting, he said a Hail Mary prayer and drank. The evening had grown bibulous

Through the heavy curtains covering the front door, a face peaked in—a black face. It was Davis Jefferson, a man from the 298 Army Band. He hesitated, then, pushing aside the curtains, he entered the evening's riot.

At first no one noticed him, but as he crossed the room to the bar some heads turned, eyebrows arched. For a moment the fast-paced card game stopped, a card hanging in the dealer's finger tips, then he delt it.

The Golden Sun *Kneipe* was known as a white soldiers' bar. It was unusual for a black soldier to enter the Sun, just as it was unusual for white soldiers to hang out at the black soldier bars uptown on the Berlin *Hauptstrasse*, a half-hour tram ride away. Though the army discouraged racism on post, off-post it was another story. There, the races kept to themselves. When Jefferson walked in, he broke the unspoken rule: Colors don't mix!

Hard narrow looks, especially from the Southern boys, followed him as he stepped to the bar. He ordered a beer. Turning, he glanced around the room, hoping to find a friendly face. There was none. The noise in the bar a moment before been so prevalentm but it was now strangely muted, obviously resentful of the black soldier's presence.

"Wa's der Nikker doin' hier!" came a blunt, female voice. It was one of the German girls. She challenged Jefferson's presence. She was at a table with two white soldiers. She was cute, snub-nosed with short light hair that gave her a tough, sportsman look. "*No Nikker ist in diesem Lokal erlaubt,* boy!" (not allowed in here) she said, with a nasty hybrid of English and German mashed together in a tobacco-road drawl. "Now, you goes *hier raus* like a good Nikker-boy, you hear!" she stated out loud for all the bar to hear.

The two soldiers staanding with her at the bar uttered agreement, as did some of those at the tables. With nods of approval, they urged her on. Others in the room, like Robuck and Bravo, cringed with embarrassment, yet no one moved to stop her racism. She was one of those who hated black people but did not know why. She only repeated what bigoted lovers said to her when cursing Dr. Martin Luther King and the Civil Rights movement, which was making the headlines in the newspapers. She stood up. " *Du*, boy! You goes down towns *wo Du* belongs! *Dieses hier ist ein Weißerman Lokal*," she said sharply. (This is a white man's bar.)

Jefferson hesitated. His eyes puckering, he tried to cap his steam of building rage. He was not showing fear, only caution. He knew he was in a white soldier bar, off limits, and outnumbered 50 to 1. Then his rage crested. He threw caution to the wind. In a bound he was in front of his tormentor and gave her the kind of a slap that Moses heard when God parted the Red Sea. CRACK! It spun her head, and she fell back onto the lap of one of the men at the table. Her two soldier friends at the bar, both Southerners, jumped to move on Jefferson and kick his ass. Jefferson backed up. "You hit m' hog, boy!" threatened one of them who was from the 42nd Engineer Company.

"And I'll slug her again!" Jefferson challenged, ready to take on the bar should he have to.

"Your hog deserved it!" It was Lavoss. He had caught the action and came over. He moved to Jefferson's side, "Your bitch insulted a friend of mine." O'Malley, refreshed from chuck-a-lugging the glass boot, also stepped into the breach, Pereski with him. Now there were four of them should any of the Southerners gang-jump Jefferson. Three men from the other tables moved to join the boys from the South. It was developing into a donnybrook, should there be one, when Fritz the bartender stepped between the two groups. He had his Louieville Slugger in hand. "Yous Manner! I cracke yous the skull! I warn!" Fritz gripped the Louisville Slugger in both hands, ready to swing.

In her chair, her eyes teary, one side of her head a healthy red tone from the slap, the girl looked at her defenders. "Isn't ya goin' to do somethin', *Schatz*? Da bastard hit me," she said to her boyfriend in "Ding-lish."

The boyfriend, a 42nd Engineer, held a clinched fist at the ready. He looked at Fritz, at his Louisville Slugger, thought it over and stepped back. "Well, what the hell, honey? You did insult 'm."

Now angry, the so-called "soldier's hog" let out a barrage of insults in German that no one understood except Fritz and the Oldenberg cowboy. Both were surprised at her language. The boyfriend threatened to give her a wallop if she didn't shut up. "Fikky you!" she shot back. Grabbing her coat, she stormed past the curtains and out the front door of the Golden Sun.

The 42nd Engineer turned to Jefferson "You'll get yours, black boy. I don't forget!" And he followed his German girlfriend out the door.

The tension broken, Lavoss invited Jefferson to join them at the Signal Company table. "Whew, that was a close one. What are you doing in our neck of the woods, fella?" he asked, pushing a shot glass into Jefferson's hand to calm him down. His adrenaline was still pumping.

"I was supposed to meet someone outside, but he didn't show up. It's cold, so I came in to wait."

"That was taking a chance. You know this is a white guy bar, don't you?" said Robuck.

"Not any more," added Bravo. "We need some color around here," and shook Jefferson's hand in welcome, as did the others around the table.

In the rough atmosphere of the bar, Sin was becoming tipsy. The soldiers kept buying her favorite drink, *Sekt*, a kind of German champagne. Each man hoped to be the lucky one and net Sin's body for the evening. Still, she remained aloof, waiting for the right male chemistry, Staff Sergeant and above, to come along. They could afford sex. If no one showed, the Corporals and PFCs hoped she would pick one of them for a tumble between the covers.

With their hot bodies, the soldiers worked the woman as territory, but they had to be quick about it. The goal was to get laid before their company pass—that damnable company pass, that document, that stamp of limitation, intimidation, control and enforcement pass—expired. At 2400 hours, twelve o'clock midnight in civilian life, most soldiers had to be back on post, back at company and in the bunk or be charged with AWOL. If AWOL (Absent Without Leave) happened more than three times, a soldier would be penalized and shipped out to the snow-covered hills of Baumholder in West Germany, the infantry's no-no land.

Struggling against the male-female ratio of 8 to 1, a man had to be quick with his cool; otherwise, all available women would be picked off. It was now or never to get one into bed, or into a bush, or into the back seat of a Volkswagen Beetle, the few soldiers who owned one. Berlin women were in demand!

Taking a chance, Pereski threw his hat into the ring again. "Sin, you danced with several guys tonight, all second rate. Now it's our turn."

She fixed on him. "Our? How many GIs are you, Paul?" she asked with a twinkle.

"Actually, I was just thinking of me."

She looked teasingly into his eyes. "You are so young, *meine Liebe*." (my darling)

Pereski grinned. "Tell you what. I'll even sweeten the deal and add a kiss or two."

Sin teased further, her mouth suggestive. "I should let you, but you have no beard."

"I don't need a beard to pucker up."

"But I like the feel of a man on my cheek," she soothed, lightly touching his chin.

Bravo, who was of Italian heritage and wore a permanent five o'clock shadow, offered to take Pereski's place. Pereski glared at him. "How can I make out with her if you interrupt, Dago?"

Bravo shrugged. "Who is interrupting? I'm only running interference. Its the Dago tradition."

"I don't need a downfield blocker. I can hustle pussy myself," Pereski insisted. He turned back to Sin.

She glared at him, one eyebrow arched with just enough contempt to suggest offense. She had overheard Pereski's demeaning remark. "I am not `pussy,'" she uttered scornfully in dagger tones. He tried to reply, but she had already grabbed Bravo. "Hey, *Du Kleine. Komm! Wir tanzen*!" (You, shorty. Come! Let's dance!)

At the table, Yorit, Pereski, Lavoss, Jefferson and Robuck watched like bidders at a horse auction who saw the prize mare go to the competition. "Well, if there is no Sin, there's always Death," said Yorit, looking Death's way. She was now at the bar surrounded by other soldiers.

"Or life," Lavoss proposed.

"No," insisted Robuck. "After Army soldiering 24 hours a day, give me the erotic; no, the exotic with a full bare chest. Give me Death!"

"You're too young to die, man."

"Not in a woman's arms, I ain't."

Smoking, a drink in hand, Pereski watched Bravo and Sin, dance together. "How can a man that short and homely dance with a woman that tall and attractive?"

"Facial hair," said Jefferson, the Army band man. "German women love men with facial hair."

Lavoss laughed. "Only if it's in pubic places."

Robuck popped a chewing gum into his mouth. "Take note, gentlemen. It has to do with that mother instinct all women have. See how Sin holds Bravo against her? It's that feeling for things short and chubby."

"If that's so, make me short and chubby and put me in a diaper," mocked Yorit, above the juke box music.

Robuck sighed. "Oh, why couldn't I have been born short with a five o'clock shadow?"

"What?" asked Pereski. "And be called a 'Wap' the rest of your life. No way!"

A few more women came into the Golden Sun as others departed with their soldier pickups. One of them, Helga, had the unusual sobriquet. She was called "Sweettalkin'marge" by the soldiers because of her loose language. She had dark hair, dressed stylish, and looked tough. She was known to be sassy, if not downright dirty. She stepped up to the bar and the men standing there. "Well, which of you is going to buy me a fucking drink?" The men who did not know her were shocked; those who did were not. They laughed. "Yo, Kevin!" she called to O'Malley, a soldier she once mated with. "How's it hanging?" O'Malley cringed. "Anyone want to get screwed tonight?" she called out loud. Three hands went up. "Well, then, line up, boys!"

That was "Sweettalkin'marge." It was women like her who gave the Golden Sun *Kneipe* bar its character, and to the soldiers of the Berlin Brigade their fondest memories.

So it went throughout the evening. The women, seated and standing, laughing and chatting, charmed the soldiers as the soldiers plied them with drink and return conversation, but always with one eye on the clock and that magic moment: 2400 hours. It was when most off-post passes expired and soldiers turned into pumpkins.

A fight broke out on the other side of the room, but was quickly put down by Fritz and his trusty Louisville Slugger. One of the pinball players cursed the machine and tried to pick it up and throw it. He failed. It was screwed to the floor.

Lavoss, in a fit of inspiration (he had by now too much to drink) got up on one table and with an unexpected panache delivered Mark Anthony's eulogy to Julius Caesar. "Friends, Romans, countrymen, lend me your ears. I've come to praise Caesar not to bury him. For the evil that men do..." Only Death, an audience of one, gave him applause. Hearing enough of Anthony's speech, someone dropped a coin into the jukebox. He preferred the Beatle's "Long Day's Night" to Mark Anthony's eulogy.

"Where'd you learn that?" Jefferson asked Lavoss when he stepped down from the table.

"Boot camp. Guard duty. You know the guard is a great place to memorize Shakespeare. It keeps a Grunt cultural."

After her dance with Bravo, Sin returned to the table and sat down. She shoo-shooed one soldier away; his pay grade was too low, Pvt-2. She was determined to meet only senior staff as long as he stayed sober and could converse. "*Keine flüchtige Beziehung mehr*," she insisted. (No more nickel and dime relationships.)

Pereski saw his chance. Taking the chair next to her, he made a last valiant effort to get her to sleep with him. Refilling her glass with *Sekt*, her sixth of the evening, he offered her the world. "I promise you love and wealth—and an American green card if you have sex with me tonight."

"That is not enough, Soldier Boy," Sin replied, shaking her head no.

Bravo held up a finger. "Sin 1! Pereski 0!" The men laughed.

"Can't you guys disappear for five minutes?" Pereski protested.

"No!" came the multiple responses.

He turned back to Sin. She was too exotic to resist, in spite of her age. He began to beg. "What is it about you German women that can turn a guy on?"

"The hair on their legs," quipped Robuck. They laughed again.

Another coin was fed into the jukebox. Little Richard popped up. Excited by the music, Death came back from the bar and grabbed Yorit. "*Lass uns tanzen!*" (Let's dance.)

Though 15 years separated their age, Yorit and Death danced like candidates on Dick Clark's "American Bandstand." Out on the floor, the other dancers stopped and formed a circle around them. Following a couple of inspiration calls of "Go man, go!" Yorit swung Death into a turn. He lightly tapdanced, dazzling the audience, some of whom had come over from the bar to watch.

Still at the table, Sin finished her glass of *Sekt*. Now, floating as if on a bed of bubbles, she felt warm and cozy all over. She glanced at the despondent Pereski. Feeling sorry for him, she grabbed him. She had been playing hard ball, but now she had what the neighborhood back home called "The hots!" She pulled him out of his chair. She kissed him lightly, then heavily. He sighed in sentient gratitude. They smothered each other and petted. "Let's go!" he rasped, his tongue in a tight handshake around hers. "Yesth!" she answered back with a sigh and a lisp. Locked in an embrace, her pelvis met his. It was too much. They headed for the bar room door. A that moment the whistle blew. It screached, startling them.

It was an MP from the 287 MP Company in full battle dress and helmet. He stood at the curtain entrance of the Golden Sun, legs apart, arms akimbo on his hips; he wore a side arm holster and webbing. He blew the whistle again. "ALERT!" he shouted out. "Every man to his unit! IMMEDIATELY!"

It was like someone slammed on the brakes. All activity in the Sun came to an abrupt halt. Every movement, vibrant and tender, stiffened. A look of disbelief flashed across the faces of the stunned soldiers. "An alert?" "Oh, no!" "That can't be!" came the retorts and cries that reverberated off the walls of the bar's two rooms. "That can't be! It's... it's Saturday night!"

Military alerts in West Berlin were often enough, two three times a month, mostly for training affairs, but some alerts were real superpower confrontations. It was like a soccer game played with colored penalty cards. A stalled Soviet sedan in Steglitz district could initiate an alert. A stranger with a camera who looked Russian could cause one. An East German Vopo *Polizist* giving the finger to a visiting US Senator from Rhode Island was an excuse to have an alert. It happened once. Blocking the East German Autobahn, delaying army duty trains, or suspicious military maneuvers too close to the city's border, demarkation line were reasons to blow the whistle for a Brigade alert. But it never, never happened on a Saturday night! That was the night NATO, if not the Warsaw Pact itself, took a day off. It was the weekend. Time to take a break from the Cold War mania. In London, weekends were bingo nights. In Paris, soirees were all the rage. In Washington there were festivities. In the Army, most soldiers were off duty. Military alerts were supposed to wait until Monday morning, at the latest. It was the Cold War's unspoken rule unless—and it was a *big* unless— the Communists were about to...Honest-to-god! Ya-better-believe-it! .come over the Wall.

"ALERT!" shouted the MP again, blowing his whistle for the third time.

That did it. There followed a mad rush for the door. It was a stampede. In the rush, the door curtain tore down. Where before there were shouts and quaffs of beer-filled tankards to the calls of "Hail, thou good fellow, well!" now, chairs overturned. Beer glasses dropped and broke. Poker cards scattered.

Holding tight to Sin's hand, Pereski took on the appearance of petrified wood. He could not believe what he was hearing. He wanted to weep. Dashing past him, Robuck and O'Malley grabbed Pereski, knocking him off his feet. They rushed him out the front door of the Golden Sun the way the Gypsy horsemen did to Ingrid Bergman in the Hemmingway film, "For Whom the Bell Tolls"—head first, feet up and back, arms outstretched, weeping and pleading. In desperation, Pereski cried out, "Please God! Not tonight! I'm about to get laid!" But it was too late. He and the rest of the Brigade's soldiers were sucked into the night's dark orifice and vanished. The Golden Sun *Kneipe* had emptied.

A large crowd had formed at the front gate of Andrews Barracks Army Post. The NCOs from Tread Towers—the family quarters on Sundgauer Strasse—raced up Finkenstein Allee in a convoy of cars, the officers too. The whole Army complex became alive with bodies, equipment and vehicles, a centrifuge that resembled a mob more than a disciplined organization.

At company level, M15 rifles were drawn. Battle gear strapped on: field jackets, helmets, webbing and ammo pouches. They ran outside for a quick formation body count. Troop carrier vehicles roared up and out of the motor pool, along with the M151 jeeps and ammo trucks. They loaded up. At 40th Armored, M-60 tanks revved their cold engines. The soldiers from 94th Field Artillery had already left their barracks and deployed. 6th Infantry had too. It was the same with the British and the French garrisons in their Berlin sectors. According to the Plan-of-Battle, all systems (personnel and equipment) moved to prearranged locations throughout the city, ready to throw back any and all invaders. It was 11,000 Allied soldiers versus the Warsaw Pact's of one-and-a-half million strong force, half of which was mechanized. A fair match?

7th Army's Plan-of-Battle had already been laid out. When push came to shove, the Allied forces in West Berlin were to show resolution, then make a statement backed up by force. The British, French, and American garrisons would stand and defend the city against Communism's tyranny and not to be driven out without a fight. West Berlin, with its two million inhabitants, was the line drawn in the sand. An attack by the Warsaw Pact on the city would mobilize NATO in Western Europe and, according to the Plan-of-Battle, NATO would come charging to the rescue like the Cavalry of old.

But there was a problem. There was no Cavalry. There was no Patton, no Montgomery to lead the charge. There would be no cannons blazing to the so-called fanfare and flag rescue of the city. Unbeknownst to the men of the Berlin Brigade, NATO's Plan-of-Battle was a "contingency" Plan-of-Battle, and kept top secret. It read: NATO forces were to give ground, back up, and retreat to the Rhine River. There, NATO forces were to regroup, and *then* counterattack. For the Allied garrisons posted in West Berlin, including the 592nd Signal Company, it would mean not 110 miles behind the lines, but 550 miles behind the lines.

In the scheme of things, the Berlin Brigade's role was to hold up the Soviet and East German armies as long as possible. (It was calculated to take five minutes at the most before West Berlin was overrun.) The Brigade was expected to be, though no one would admit it, the meatgrinder, the pawn, a "Corrigador" used to buy time. Given the massive force mounted against the Allies, the question was this: would a five-minute goal-line stand be enough to delay the mighty Soviet juggernaut? It led one senior officer to say with some sagacity, "When the second Battle of Berlin begins, forget General Auliff and the 'Fighting Bastards of Bastogne'. This is going to be General MacArthur and 'Back to Bataan!'"

With the soldier boys gone, the Golden Sun *Kneipe* looked spooked. Almost all the tables were empty. Unfinished mugs of beer and drink stood abandoned. Lit cigarettes smouldered in ashtrays. Furniture was knocked about. The Oldenberg cowboy snored in one corner where he had dropped off to sleep from too much drink. Though it had no player, the corner pinball machine still rung up numbers, then eventually ceased. Fritz the bartender, his face without expression, polished a beer glass and grumbled. Tonight the Army wasn't going to make him rich.

It had taken 20 seconds to empty the place of American servicemen.

In shock and feeling stranded, the women of West Berlin stood around with a "What now?" look on their faces. Static, they half sat, some stood, a Frans Hals composition all. They stared at the black hole that was the front door into which their soldier boys had vanished. Whereas before there had been a room full of warm, male, responding bodies, now there was only a broken curtain frame and the rush of cold draft. "*Schließ die verdammte Tür!*" (Close the damn door) snapped one of the women angrily.

Someone dropped a coin into the jukebox. It lit up. The song, "A Thousand Miles Away," caught the melancholy of the moment. As if seeking solace from a catastrophic loss, the women gravitated toward one another and began to dance in the uneven light. They held, consoled, and rocked each other, disturbed that their game had been interrupted, the fun turned void, the love emptied.

These were the woman of West Berlin. They were the GI molls who wore hard makeup, smelled of Old Spice. They talked the dialect of the *Sudeten*, the *Schlesien* and the *Pommern* Germans. Some were *Sachsen* immigrants from the East. No one in West Berlin was from West Berlin; they were from everywhere but West Berlin. They lived in cold water flats, had mundane jobs, most with bleak futures. Their one saving grace was their incredible passion for life. They drank a lot and laughed little while dutifully and selflessly bedding the American soldier along the way. They lullabied him, pacified him, kept him quiescent while taking the rage out of his soul with their sex. They got no medals for it. They got no praise. Their birthdays were often forgotten. Rudely treated, they were tagged with names like "Thumper" and "Hog" and passed around like tire retreads from unit to unit, GI to GI. But they were tough and took it on the chin. In return, they gave unrequited love; they forgot and forgave. For some, that endurance paid off. They married their soldier boy. With him, they picked up the magical green card and the promise of a Little House on the Prairie, or in Brooklyn, or down on the Delta. The commanders of the Berlin Brigade never acknowledged it, but the women of West Berlin were as vital to the smooth function of the US Army as any military training.

On the dance floor Sin and Death held each other close. They danced cheek-to-cheek, languorous in the room's half shadows, while outside the M35 trucks roared out the of Andrews Barracks main gate with their cargo of love objects—the soldier boys.

"*Wo ist die große Liebe?*" Hertha (Sin) asked her friend. (Where is the big love?)

Sad, her voice a whisper, Monika (Death) replied, "*Liebe? Was ist das? Es gibt kein Liebe.*" (Love? What is love? It does not exist.)

The next day

"Hey, Sarge Oats. Your girl friend, Death, she was looking for you last night."

"She was?"

"Yeah! She says you and she are gonna get married. That right?"

"I'm already married."

"Does she know that?"

"No!"

"You gonna tell her."

"What for?"

Gestapo

Gestapo

The drizzle had stopped. The morning was overcast. In the seat of his M151 jeep Yorit slouched as he looked out the window, one foot against the dashboard. Behind him, the high frequency VCR-10 fat radio buzzed with voice transmissions. Call-signs and messages crisscrossed the net. He hardly noticed. It was mostly inter-allied stuff—the French garrison from their sector, the British garrison from theirs. Except for one message of little significance, none passed his site. It was going to be another slow day in the US Army, West Berlin.

Outside, Checkpoint Charlie was quiet . It was always quiet at Checkpoint Charlie. No matter what time of day, morning, afternoon or evening, it was quiet. It had to do with the *Friedrich Strasse* location. It was a dead end street. Not only that, it was the border. The end of the road. The Wall! The zones—American, British, French and Soviet— ended and started here, depending on which way one was going. It was the reason for the oppressive quiet. What was prevalent were the Army guards: East German, West German, American. One did not see the Russians. Were they hiding?

The guards were typical of gate border guards anywhere. Bored. They sauntered, strolled, and yawned, waiting for the order to "Open fire!" should anyone attempt to across the No Man's Land of barbed wire and brick that separated Communism from capitalism, democracy from dictatorship or, should the order be given, to fist fight and punch out the opponent. Here, anything was possible.

At Checkpoint Charlie there was some activity, like the occasional exchange of military flag sedans. They were vehicles that carried tiny national flags on the front fenders. Near Yorit's jeep a Czech made two-door Skoda cross the demarcation line and stop at Checkpoint Charlie for a document check. From inside the sedan four Russian officers sat and looked out. They were grim-faced and had a reason to be. They had to sit for the next three to four hours cramped in the sedan's small space, windows up, doors locked, all the while holding their bladders as the flag sedan cruised the American sector to spook.

The same happened in the opposite direction. The American four-door Chevrolet flag sedans, olive drab in color, also drove into the Soviet sector. The Chevys usually carried two Berlin Brigade officers. Their job was also to spook.

This morning the two-flag sedans stood, parked across from each other, Checkpoint Charlie between them. The occupants—enemies—eyeballed each other menacingly, daring the other to say something crude like, "Come on, motherfucker! Just try it! Just try it!" Try what? No one knew for sure. It was just that. After so many years of Cold War bluff playing, the state antagonists were expected to hate each other. That was the mindset.

One of the officers in the American-flag sedan flashed the finger to the occupants of the Russian-flag sedan. Indignant, the Soviet officer inside flashed it back the Russian way, with a fisted hand across the arm. On German soil such behavior was a serious confrontation. Bobbing and weaving, feigning, the two social systems stood, about to clash. The two "Fuck yous!" in international speak could be defined as "Round one!" But then the two-flag sedans departed and drove off into each other's sector, and the barrage of fist and finger flashing ceased and the smoke cleared. There was no round two.

The cross-border exchange of military flag sedans was a daily ritual, one of many agreed upon by the Potsdam Accords of 1945. Though the flashing the finger was not part of the protocol, it was the soldier's way, the only way, to communicate with the enemy. No one smiled. No one waved. Not a shot fired. Everyone just stared. All was quiet on the western, Friedrich Strasse front. Been that way since 1945.

It was another Wednesday morning and a training day. The weather, crummy. Yorit and Bravo had to drive to different locations in West Berlin to test out radio equipment and communication frequencies to see if all worked well in the bad weather. Checkpoint Charlie was, as usual, one of the locations and the reason the two signalmen happen to be sitting near the Wall in their jeep, observing the two enemy flag sedans confront each other and play that game of "Frown and Comfront." The two signalmen thought it silly. But what was not silly in Cold War Berlin was where two ideologies met headon trying, to make a point. "Hey you! Punk-o! My system is better than your system. If you don't believe me, I'll nuke you to prove it. So there!"

Observing the two military flag sedans, Bravo could only shake his head. "You know, Robert, this stuff is really kid shit."

"What's kid shit?" mumbled Yorit, flipping through the SOI code book for the next change in the radio transmission code.

"I mean those two flag sedans there, ours and the Russian, challenging each other. Why don't the drivers just get out and have a fist fight? That or shake hands."

Yorit put his finger on the code book number. He looked up. "Because no one ordered them to, that's why. You can't get into a fist fight or wage nuclear war without command orders."

Bravo shrugged. He raised the field glasses (binoculars) he had brought with him; he wanted to observe the east side of the *Friedrich Strasse* and the *Volkspolize'* (Vopo) guards there. He had borrowed the fieldglass piece from MSgt Sweechek in order to, just once, see the enemy up close. "After all," he told his section sergeant, "if I'm going to shoot a Commie I should know what he looks like."

From the east side of the Berlin Wall, the Vopos moseyed back and forth, the way guards do. Sluggish. Their uniforms were handsome, real tin soldier stuff. They wore creased riding pants, jackboots, jackets belted at the waist, ribbons and flashy medals. *Impressive*, Bravo thought. It was as if the *Volks Polizei* guards were waiting for the parade to begin. Only their weapons, the Kalashnikov rifles, gave them away for what they were: a bunch of kids waiting for the order to "OPEN FIRE!"

"Gee, except for their uniforms those Commies look just like us. They can't be all that bad," guessed Bravo, slouched in his seat.

"Yes they can if they look like us," said Yorit as he made notes in his code pad.

Bravo raised the fieldglass piece again and scanned the so-called death strip zone into East Berlin territory. He looked to the right, then to the left, then up the middle of *Friedrich Strasse* at the half-restored buildings there, some covered in scaffolding. He focused on the flat clapboard structure of the Soviet-East German border post. "Yes sir, they look just like us."

Yorit closed the army SOI code book. "Like us? Frank, that can't be,. They're the enemy. We are suppose to hate them."

"Think so? I'll have to ask my senator," said Bravo, taking an apple out of his pocket that he had taken from the mess hall.

"Ask him what?"

"Ask him why we have to hate the Commies."

"I know why," said Yorit.

"Why?"

"We have to hate the Commies because, ahm hm…we have to hate the Commies."

Bravo thought for a moment. "That makes sense."

"It does?"

"Yes," Braavo replied. "It's like you said, because we have to hate the Commies. I mean, we eyeball each other day after day across the Berlin Wall and sometimes, ya know, IT DRIVES ME NUTS!" he burst out suddenly, scolding the windshield. He took a bite out of his apple.

Yorit fumbled with his lip, finger playing, unsure of his logic. "That makes sense."

Now it was Bravo's turn to ask, "It does?"

Yorit took off his field cap and scratched his head. "On the other hand, if the Commies, I mean them East German Vopos and Russians there are like us and we are the good guys, than it reasons that the Vopos and Russians are good guys too. And if that is so, then there really is no reason to reason for this just because."

Bravo glanced at him. "Are you saying there is no reason to hate them just because?"

"Yes! Whoever is telling us to hate the Commies `just because' has got `the becauses' all wrong."

Bravo nodded. "I like that rationale. You know, I think I will write my senator."

"Send him my regards."

While talking, the two signalmen watched as an East German guard walked toward the concrete barriers and tank traps that made *Friedrick Strasse* the deadly obstacle course that it was. Twenty feet away, he stopped. Hands on his hips, he looked over and watched his opponents on the west side of the Berlin Wall, the border M.P.s at the Checkpoint Charlie guard shack.

The M.P.s were typical big guys, broad shouldered and tall. The Brigade command did not send anyone under 6′1″ to staff Checkpoint Charlie. It was the image thing. Though they looked tough, the M.P. Military Police only carried sidearm weapons and nightsticks, no match for the Kalashnikov rifles the Vopo guards carried. Also, the side arms were not loaded. It was a Cold War secret the Communists never knew about. Had they known, they would have hopped over the Berlin Wall and invaded the city long ago.

On the East German side of the Wall stood a 30-foot watch tower. From there, a Vopo guard raised his fieldglass to focus on Check Point Charlie and the American jeep below. Bravo noticed him. Taking his fieldglasses from his lap, he pushed open the jeep's canvas door and focused on the Vopo. Again, it was the unspoken game between enemies. Silent and visual though it was, it was the one way to communicate, should one want to. Tongue in cheek, it was often played in a friendly confrontation that Command did not know about.

The two adversaries, Bravo and the Vopo, glared at each other. One minute passed, two minutes passed. Back and forth went the two fixed stares. Bravo ground his teeth, snorted, and uttered epithets. The Vopo the same. It was that or gunfire. Finally, having grown tired of the game, the Vopo guard turned away and focused in another direction.

"I won!" Bravo cried out. "I won one for the West!"

Behind the steering wheel, Yorit sat up. "Won what?"

"The statement!"

Yorit yawned. "Well, that should bring down the Berlin Wall."

"See what a little determination can do? The Commie guy backed off," Bravo boasted, proud of his effort.

Yorit stretched. "If you're right, I can see the Russians voting for Kennedy in `64,"

Bravo punched his partner in the shoulder. "And what have you done for your country lately besides occupy space?"

Yorit rubbed his cheek thoughtfully and gave himself a "Hm, well, I guess you might say I'm prepared to take your place on the field of battle should that Vopo guard there whip you in the next round of focus-on-the-enemy. Say, Frank, look! That Vopo whose butt you just kicked; he's challenging you again."

Bravo glanced up. The East German guard had his fieldglasses trained on their M151 jeep. "Ah, ha! The bastard ain't had enough. I'm gonna have to work him over a second time."

Stepping out of the jeep, Bravo took his fieldglasses and menacingly fired back a leer so determined it fogged the enemy's binoculars. On the tower, the Vopo guard stopped back to check his fieldpiece. He took out a handkerchief to clean the lenses. They had fogged up. The two signalmen cried out in triumph.

"Now Frank, this is getting ridiculous," Yorit called from his side of the jeep. "Come on, let's drive. We got other locations to radio transmit from."

Gripping the fieldglasses firmly in one hand, Bravo looked back at the tower guard. "Not just yet! The asshole is still challenging me. Got to whip'm first." Bravo gave the guard the finger.

Yorit started the engine. "Say 'bang-bang.' We're moving!"

"Got the Vopo fixed in my cross wires! We don't wanna lose, do we?"

"Lose what?"

"The Cold War statement!"

"Frank, give me a break, please!"

"Don't you know it takes minor pitched battles like this to win against totalitarianism?"

"I didn't know you were married."

"That Commie Kraut gotta drop first! It's a battle to the death!" Bravo insisted.

Yorit stepped out of the jeep and walked over to the shotgun side. "Or until one of you goes blind."

Bravo looked at his partner. "Wha´ ya doin´?" he asked the Jersey way.

"Giving that Commie guard the finger too. Two fuck fingers are better then one, I say."

Tired of the adolescent antics, the Vopo guard dropped his fieldglasses to his chest. Turning, he walked to the other side of the tower, there to focus on something more definitive.

"He gave up! I won!" Bravo cried out.

"No, we won!" Yorit boasted, also jubilant.

"See what an extra middle finger can do?" Bravo grinned. "Tell me that two fingers ain't better than one."

"You're right, Frank. What better way to defend West Berlin than flashing the stink finger."

Pleased with themselves, the two signalmen soldiers jumped back into their jeep. Inside the Checkpoint Charlie shack and watching them drive off, one of the M.P.s touched his head with a finger. "Must be 592nd Signal Company guys. You always see them dancing around their vehicles."

Inside their jeep, Yorit turned down *Zimmer Strasse*, that claustrophobic street parallel to the Berlin Wall. It had been that way ever since the Wall went up in 1961, leaving the isolated shops there to face the ten-foot brick and mortar construction. To walk the *Zimmer Strasse* was like stepping into a Chiracio painting, a void accompanied by shadows. Vehicle traffic, if any, had to drive half on the sidewalk, half on the street to avoid scraping the cinder-blocks in the middle of the street. A U-turn was impossible. The shops, what few there were, were derelict. Dirty plate glass windows and faded signs told of what was once a bakery, a tobacco store, a jeweler. All were cut off from the neighborhood when the Wall went up. Now, instead of a street located in the middle of a city rebuilding itself, *Zimmer Strasse* was a street on the confrontational edge of a city cut in half. It was the front line, a front line that zigzagged 63 miles, north to south, through and around Berlin, breaking the city, the community, the neighborhoods, block by block, in half. The Wall sliced off door entrances, partitioned buildings, separated families.

One family, according to the newspaper, *Tages Zeitung*, lost its backyard toilet. The living room was in the West, the outside toilet in the East, the Wall in the middle. To use the toilet, the family had to scale the wall, negotiate the barbed wire, and take a chance on getting shot when they went potty. Then back! Understanding the danger, the city built the family a new bathroom—one in the west, but against the Wall.

It was a short drive to the corner of *Wilhelm Strasse* and the open space there, the buildings around having been destroyed during the war. There were empty lots in every direction. Where once majestic neoclassical, baroque and *Grunderzeit* buildings stood, there were now only empty lots and dead silence. A serrated moonscape. The only salient features left were a mound of bulldozed rubble piled near half-ruined structures with cracked walls. Standing alone, they resembled a lone outcrop, groaning above the noble earth. Eighteen years earlier it had barely escaped Bomber Harris and the wrath of the British Royal Air Force.

"What's that?" asked Yorit, pointing beyond the Wall into the east at a massive structure with an odd convex roof.

Bravo looked up from where he was checking the timetable for the next radio transmission. "Robuck told me it was once Hermann Göring's Air Ministry. Supposed to be one of the largest buildings in

Berlin, like our Pentagon. Would you believe it has a roof made of concrete?"

"Concrete? What for?"

"To bounce bombs;" said Bravo. "It's bomb proof. It was built that way so Allied bombs would just bounce off it. They did, and blew up the buildings next door. Hey, Yoyo, where are you going?"

Yorit had opened the canvas door of the jeep and stepped out. "Got to find me a latrine. Gotta pee. Frank, call Operations and tell them we've reached our checkpoint position, though not quite."

Bravo took the radio's handset. "Make me do all the dirty work, huh?" Bavo called over.

"Not really. I have to hold my own pecker," said Yorit, closing the canvas door.

Walking across the rough ground covered with broken brick and small potholes, he found he had to walk carefully.　Not far away there was an open pit. He made for it. At the pit's edge a flight of stone stairs led down to what looked like a cellar wall covered with white tiles. There were several similar dug-up pits that looked like archeological sites. It was as if whoever was excavating had been digging for clues. What clues was anyone's guess. Yorit descended the steps.

Meditatively standing at the cellar's tiled wall, he opened his fly and looked around, the way men do in nature. He checked the sky; it was still overcast. He checked the environment around him, all ruin. He checked his penis; it was still there. Urinating, Yorit rested his free hand against the wall tiles. Though the tiles appeared smooth, he noticed the surface of one of them. It was rough and scratchy. He looked closer. A script had been etched into the tile's hard surface. It was crudely written script, as if done by a pen knife or a nail. It was barely discernible. There was a date, Okt 44. Under the date were the initials, "PvB" and a words, '*Lieber Gott, bitte rette mich*!' (Dear God, please save me!) It was an appeal.

With one hand still on his crotch, Yorit ran his fingers over another tile. He felt another initial, then another and another. The white tiled wall was full of such scribblings, mostly initials. Putting himself away and closing his field pants he asked himself, "But why?" Along the wall, he saw and touched other worn and weathered initals. *Who wrote this stuff?* he pondered. Why so much scribbling? Who was PvB? He ran his fingers over the white tiles again, then understood. This pit must have once been a prison cell, and the scribbling was the names of the cell's many prisoners. Were the men who penned these signatures about to die, to vanish into the concentration camps? To be gassed? He would never know. A shiver ran down his back. It was too disturbing to comprehend. Touched by the discovery, Yorit leaned his forehead against the cellar's tiles and whispered in prayer, "I hear you. I hear you." He pressed his fingertips over the scratchy penmanship again.

He remembered once reading a newspaper article about Alcatraz and the California state prisoners there. They used to etch their names on the cell walls; the reason was not to be forgotten. It was the same in London's Bedlam, the mad house, and the Bastille in the days of the French Revolution. Back home at West Tech High School it happened to him. He was once disciplined and had to sit on Mr. Brown's, the assistant principal, bench,. To sit on Mr. Brown's bench was a penalty of the first magnitude. Three hours on that sturdy old oak block was to a ninth grader's unblemished mind comparable to the black hole of Calcutta, or Christ on the Cross. One never failed to walk away without butt blisters. Not to be forgotten, Yorit scratched his initials in the hard oak of the assistant principal's bench. Perhaps it was the same here in Berlin. Not wanting to be forgotten, the jail cell's authors scribbled their initials on the wall tiles. It was West Tech and Mr. Brown's bench all over again.

Fascinated by what he had just discovered, Yorit continued to run his fingers back and forth over the wall script as if trying to sense PvB's voice, the "it" and the "who."

Yorit looked up into the heavens and the clouds fulmination there. Was this the reason why the skies above Berlin were always in perpetual turbulence, why the sun rarely shined? Had it to do with PvB's lost voice and the millions of other lost voices that perished under Germany's National Socialist rule? Yorit felt a sense of burden.

"Nieyaaa!" came the cry. It was sudden, broken, a banshee cry. It came from above and beyond. Or was other-worldly?

Startled, Yorit stepped back from the cellar wall. He looked up and gasped. Hazel, the Wicked Witch of the North, was standing at the edge of the pit, glaring down—green face, hook nose, warts and all—and she wasn't in Kansas! Her hair was strung out wild, like a cornered cat's. She wore a shabby, dark wool coat with a scarf drawn tight at the shoulders. She stared down at him, full of accusation.

"*Junge, was machst Du da?*" (Boy, what are you doing?) It was not so much what she said, but the way she said it—demonic! Frightened, Yorit scrambled up the steps. At the top, she confronted him. *"Weisst Du nicht, wo Du bist?"* she cried. (Do you know where you are?)

Yorit wanted to run, but he hesitated. Fascinated by this entity, he asked in broken German, "Ah, no lady. Where am I?" He could understand simple German, especially when it was yelled at him, which was most of the time, a German habit when talking to foreigners.

"Hier ist die Gestapo Hauptquartier! Die Topografie des Terrors! Ohne ein Erlaubnes ist es hier streng verboten!" (Here is Gestapo Headquarters! The topography of terror! Without a permit it is forbidden to stand here!) Than Hazel the Witch's voice dropped, conspiratorial. "It is all around you, the evil that is *Deutschland*," she whispered in a strange, accented German as she stamped the sodden soil. "It is buried here in this ground."

Yorit was not sure how to respond. He never heard a woman scream and whisper at the same time. Only Army sergeants did that.

She pointed. Yorit followed her finger. *"Da druben ist das SS Hauptquartier, die Prinz Albert Palee!"* (Over there is the SS Headquarters, Prince Albert Palace!). What she pointed at in the distance was a pile of rubble. *"Hier ist die Hölle los! Raus hier, Junge! Raus hier bevor es zu spät ist! Raus!"* (Here is the hell! Get out before it is to late! Get out!) she threatened, again raising her voice to a screeching pitch.

Startled by her revelation—SS Headquarters—Yorit felt his fingers begin to burn. It was as if he was standing on the edge of Dante's Inferno, looking into a chamber where misery was once home. Now he understood and felt the meaning of the initials on the tiled walls. They were cells.

"Alles ruinen! Alles tot!" she threatened aloud, going from desperation to outrage, to silence, to laughter, and back. Then, drawing up her ankle-length skirt, she squatted and defecated at the edge of the pit.

Yorit took off running. He stumbled as he ran and did not stop until he reached *Wilhelm Strasse*. Breathing hard, he turned to look back.

"That, young man, is mad Helle," said a voice in the Queen's English behind him.

Yorit spun around with a "Huh?" He appeared to be a gentleman, older and dressed in a gray leather trench coat. He stood on the sidewalk, smoking a pipe, one hand in the trench coat pocket, the thumb out. He had been watching the witch confront Yorit at the pit. "The woman talking with you was once an official. She worked for the Gestapo, she did. One of those who was responsible for the orders, you might say."

"What orders?" asked Yorit, wondering why the stranger was talking to him.

"Death orders. You see, she was part of the apparatus of death, that apparatus that sent a million Jews and others to the camps. I'm sure you heard about it. The whole world has," he stated his tone noble. "Did she mention the Topography of Terror? Well, this is it, here. Most amusing, no?" His pipe in hand as if it was a wand, he pointed the stem over the ruined landscape.

Still breathing hard from the dash, Yorit looked closely at the stranger; he had a nasty scar on one cheek, a wound common among older Germans of that generation. "What's amusing about death?"

"Oh, that there are people in government whose job it was to murder. It has to do with the bureaucratic mindset we Germans have," he said, his English enunciation perfect. By his appearance he could have once been a diplomat, or maybe still was.

"I never thought about that," said Yorit, still wondering why the stranger was talking with him.

"Mad Helle is an interesting case in point. At her job she had to type up lists, lists of people to be picked up for Gestapo interrogation. When it was rumored such people were transported to camps and put to death, it broke her. She dared protest to her superiors. At the time it was considered very un-German. Incorrect."

"You mean she complained to her bosses?"

"Yes, you may say that," replied the stranger plaintively, without emotion. "She was arrested and sent to Bergan Belsen camp. Her husband too, I believe." Here, the gentleman in the trench coat paused. He took out a match, and in the cold relit his pipe. It had gone out. "Lost her mind, she did," he said as he puffed.

In the distance, "Helle the Witch" began to poke the ground with a stick.

"Why does she poke the ground?" Yorit asked, observing her. He felt sorry for the woman.

"Revenge," the man answered. "She comes here every other day to defecate on Nazi soil. Wait a moment and you will see. She will howl like a wolf. Just wait."

"How come you know so much about her?"

The gentleman puffed on his pipe. "I was her supervisor. I am mad, too." And he walked away, his trench coat open.

Back at the jeep, Bravo looked up from the *Playboy* magazine he was reading; it was a back issue, the month of May. Soldiers never threw away their *Playboys*. "What was that all about?" he asked as Yorit slid into the driver's seat.

Yorit shook his head. "This city of West Berlin certainly has its share of lunatics."

Bravo chuckled cynically. "You mean we in the Army ain't alone?".

Yorit started the jeep's engine and pulled away from the curb. He looked back across the broken Kreuzberg landscape where the dark figure of Mad Helle roamed alone among the open cell pits. As she walked, she brushed her shoulders vigorously as if plagued by dandruff. She stopped and began to slap at the air around her.

Both soldiers watched and looked, unsure. In the air churning around Mad Helle there appeared to be a presence of gauzy furies. Was it the morning mist playing tricks on their eyes? Suddenly she howled, and howled again. Her supervisor was right; she did sound like a wolf.

Yorit reached over and took the radio handset; he called into it. "Round house one, round house one. This is round house three. Do you read me? Over!"

The receiver crackled. "Roger! Roger! We read you. What is your location? Over!"

"The madhouse," Yorit answered back. And the army, M151 Ford jeep sped away.

Radio Room

It was hot, always hot. No matter if you were stripped to the waist or wore fatigues, it was hot. But there was no question of stripping. The operators, all 592nd signalmen, had to wear fatigues on the job or be charged with "Out-of-Uniform." It had to do with the three floor-to-ceiling General Electric Mega-Radio transmitter-receivers. They whirred, burped, and slurred 24 hours a day, 365 days a year, generating a jet engine heat that divested itself into an enclosed space the size of a broom closet. It was the Berlin Brigade Radio Room.

Instead of installing the big-tube radios above ground for which they were designed, the Army placed them under Brigade Headquarters on Clay Allee, several stories down, inside a bomb-proof bunker. The cellar! The problem was someone forgot to put in ventilation. So, for eight or twelve hours a day, the period of a shift, the heat left the radio operators awash in their own sweat as they faced the demon breath of the GE mega transmitter-receivers. Fat guys lost weight; thin guys dehydrated. The on-duty operators griped and complained about it through the Army's Chain-of-Command, but no one seemed able to do anything about it. Pereski, one of the operators, likened Radio Room duty to "walking over hot coals with the whites of your eyes."

The operators used every excuse in the book to get out of Radio Room duty. O'Malley once took it to an extreme and dropped a typewriter on his toe, claiming a battlefield injury. He was given crutches, a pep talk, and returned to his shift with his toe in a cast. MSgt Sweechek told him and Jonas, his partner on shift, "At the 592nd Signal Company, the wounded stay on the line!" dramatically adding, "Radio Room duty is vital to the survival of West Berlin and democracy. If we fail to communicate from this broom closet, Berlin Brigade will be cut off from the Free World, with us trapped 110 miles behind the lines. You want that?"

165

Startled by the revelation, the two operators, O'Malley and Jonas, yelled out, "Negative, Master Sergeant!" and put on their sweatbands and sunglasses and continued their sweat-stained mission.

One transmitter-receiver was hooked up to 7th Army Headquarters in West Germany. Another was hooked to the French and British garrisons in their sectors of West Berlin. A third, besides being used to boil water for coffee, was the communication workhorse within the Brigade itself. It dealt with internal defense and supply on a daily basis. It allowed brigade operations to communicate with the recon-vehicles that patrolled along the Wall, the Potsdam station, troop trains, and the vehicle supply convoys that drove through Communist territory to West Germany. With such heavy responsibility, the Radio Room was in the middle of every communication vital to the Brigade and thus, the city's survival. Down in the bowels of Brigade Headquarters, in the Radio Room, on the wall a pin board sign read, "World peace don't get no deeper than this!"

Outside, at the BBHQ gate, an MP guard checked soldier IDs as they passed the gate. He matched the faces to the ID cards, followed by an affirmative nod of the head: permission to pass. A grave-looking Yorit and Jimmy Lightpony the Shoshone entered the compound. Tonight they were on duty. In one of the gray buildings they entered and descended the circular metal staircase that led to the lower levels. The further down they went the warmer it got. At the third deck, Yorit stopped and took a deep breath. "All I did was walk in the door and already I'm wet under the arms."

Lightpony gave an understanding nod. Under the hard glare of the ceiling's neon light they turned a corner. They entered the Radio Room.

The room that MSgt Sweechek defined as a pigeonhole was a narrow space. It was large enough for a pot of coffee, a work table and two operators in chairs. The three floor-to- ceiling mega radio transmitter-receivers dominated like boilers in the hold of a tramp steamer. Hillbilly music played on AFN, the Armed Forces Network radio. Above, a ceiling fan turned with aging effort.

"Your relief team," Yorit grunted in a flat voice, taking a handkerchief out of his fatigue shirt pocket to wipe the sweat from his forehead. "Whew! I'm sweating already."

Robuck and Kantwell looked up. Both were pale and dehydrated from their twelve- hour vigil. The room's bright light had caused their eyes to be bloodshot and was the reason everyone on shift wore sun glasses.

"Welcome to the Louisiana Bayou," said Robuck.

"Anything exciting happen on your watch?" asked Lightpony. (With his company buddies he would sometimes speak English, but only sometimes. However, around army officers and NCOs, he spoke in his native tongue, Shoshone. It was his way to keep the command confused.)

"Same old bore," answered Robuck, signing off on the log book, indicating the end of his team's shift. He turned the log over to Yorit, who signed his team on. "Tracking communication," said Robuck. "We have one train stuck in Potsdam just over the border, and a convoy on the 'Autobahn' at the Charlie-Delta checkpoint; that's the Leipzig turnoff. No delay problems there, thank God."

Yorit turned back to the log. "What's with the train stuck at commie Potsdam?"

Robuck pointed to the wall map next to the pin board; a thin ribbon of pins marked the Army duty train and the East German Autobahn checkpoints. "The Vopos found a man riding the rails. He was hiding under a wagon, trying to escape. They pulled him out and rife-butted him on the platform for all to see. Took him away, they did. Commie bastards! It's all here in the log book," said Robuck.

"Who reported it?"

"Bravo did. He's the radio operator on the duty train tonight. He saw everything from his compartment window. He told the train commander and communicated the report."

"I feel sorry for the runaway," said Lightpony.

"You should," said Kantwell. "The escapee was reported to be a Navaho soldier from 6th Infantry." No one laughed at the bad joke. Radio Room duty was too uncomfortable for humor.

"The Russians are pissed about the East German escapee," Robuck added. "They're holding up the Army duty train until the situation is clarified."

"How did he get on our moving train anyway?" asked Yorit.

"Don't know. Had to jump it, I guess," said Robuck, reaching for his field jacket. "Brigade's got an officer down there now to help get our train moving again. A Major Dimwitty, according to Bravo. He's negotiating with the Soviets. But that's his problem, and yours. Me and the Maestro, we're outta here. Hoorah! Right, Kevin? When we get back to barracks, we're going straight to the Golden Sun and soak our pores in suds."

"Right on," answered Kantwell, taking his jacket and field cap from the hook. The two signalmen left the Radio Room.

Suddenly Yorit felt weak. The shift had not yet begun and already the heat was getting to him. Lightpony turned up AFN, Arms Forces Radio, as they both settled into their chairs.

Yorit wiggled. The vinyl seat was still warm from Robuck's butt. The seat had the feel of an enlarged campfire marshmallow. "If this cushion gets any hotter we could substitute it for the electric chair," he grunted uncomfortably, glancing at Lightpony who was, surprisingly, already asleep. Yorit shook him. "Hey, Pony Man, that ain't fair. We didn't toss a coin to see who crashes first."

"I did and you lost," Lightpony puffed, returning to his meditative breathing. The late shift had begun.

Yorit stared at the GE transmitter's bank of dials and twitching needles. In the background, the hum and chatter of the Morse Code and voice transmissions could be heard; it was gobbled and meshed in an erratic chatter that was both annoying and tranquil. The chatter danced over the airwaves like the buzz inside a Cleveland Light and Power substation at lunch time back home. As a civilian, Yorit once worked for Muni Light, as it was called. At lunch time the gruff linemen would eat, drink beer, and play poker to the sound of such twitching needles and transmitter hums. They would wisecrack and pound the table to champion a winning hand. Sitting uncomfortably in the heat of the Radio Room, Yorit missed the Muni Light camaraderie.

With a sigh he looked at his watch, then at the GE mega transmitters, the needles twitching up on the plate. The wall the clock read 0015. The shift had just begun, and already he felt bored. "Ho-hum," he breathed. It would be a long night, 0015 until 1200 tomorrow morning. Reaching out, he took the table microphone in front of him. It was time to call Bravo's duty train. He pressed the hand key. "Farmhouse 2, this is Farmhouse 1. What is your present location? Over!"

"Dis is Farmhouse 2. Over!" Bravo's Jersey accent answered back.

"Is the duty train still stalled? Over!" Yorit inquired.

"Roger that. Over!" Bravo answered back through the call's static. "East German escapee problem has been resolved. The Vopos are clearing the track now. Hope to proceed to Marienborn check point shortly. Over!" his voice crackled over the radio receiver.

"Roger that. Out!" Yorit made a note in the log. Next, he called the truck convoy somewhere on the East German Autobahn. "Farmhouse

3, this is Farmhouse 1; your location. Over." He recognized Robuck's nasal midwestern accent. Was the accent Pennsylvanian or Iowan, he asked himself? "All is well. Over," was his communication reply. Yorit recorded it in the log book and returned to his slouch.

Leaning back in his hot seat, he opened his fatigue shirt. It was just too hot. "The hell with regulations," he quarreled with himself. Biting a fingernail, he took off his shirt, then he looked at the wall. He looked at the ceiling. He looked at his partner, Jimmy Lightpony the Shoshone, seated in his chair and wondered, how Lightpony could sleep in that position: head back, legs crossed on the seat, hands open on his lap as if waiting for someone to drop him a dime. *Did the North American Indians study Buddhism?* Yorit wondered.

He checked the wall clock again. Barely a half hour into their shift and the room's claustrophobic atmosphere was already getting to him. Yorit felt he would never get used to Radio Room duty. "No, never!" he called out loud to himself.

From a shelf, he took down one of several Army manuals; it was the one marked "Emergency Procedures." The manuals were forever being changed and updated. All radio operators were required to familiarize themselves with the nomenclatures and other mumbo- jumbo which no one understood but nevertheless had to read. Talking to himself, he flipped the pages when something caught his eye. He turned back to the book cover to be sure he had the correct SOP manual. He did. Under the chapter heading "Attack Mode," the paragraph read: "In case of a Soviet attack, radio operators are instructed to maintain communication at all costs until NATO relief forces arrive. Should there be a threat to classified documentation, operators are ordered to shred all documentation, Confidential to Top Secret, beginning with Top Secret. Should there be an equipment failure, operators are instructed to immediately eat, chew, and swallow all classified data-documentation, Confidential to Top Secret, beginning with Top Secret. Suggested procedure is: 1. carefully tear out the page; 2. roll it into a ball; 3. chew and swallow. A drink of water and, or coffee can help facilitate the swallowing procedure."

Yorit read the instruction again. "Is somebody nuts?" he asked himself out loud. "Who wrote this? The Department of Defense or Clarabelle the Clown? This is ridiculous." Reaching over, he tapped his duty partner, Lightpony, on the shoulder. "Hey, Tonto, wake up."

A light sleeper, Lightpony awoke with a start and began to swing.

Yorit jumped up and pulled his chair against his chest. "Hey, back off, Tonto! I only tapped your shoulder."

"Oh, sorry, Yo," said Lightpony, a little embarrassed. "Dreamed I was back in Wyoming hunting buffalo."

"Or taking scalps. Wyoming must be a dangerous place if you react like that to a tap on the shoulder." Yorit put the chair down and took his seat.

Lightpony chuckled. "We only take scalps on Saturday nights."

Yorit laughed. "I understand. Saturday nights are dangerous everywhere, even in Cleveland, Ohio." He showed Lightpony the regulation on eating classified documentation, starting with the Top Secret pages. "Did you know about this Army regulation?"

Lightpony read the paragraph. "Oh, is that what we're supposed to do? Okay!" and ripped out the page from the SOP book and began to chew it.

Aghast, Yorit grabbed him by the throat. "Jimmy, stop! What are you doing? Stop chewing! You only eat the docs' if we're being attacked and the commies are outside the door, knocking! It's gotta be an emergency!"

With a gage, Lightpony pulled the chewed up page out of his mouth. He handed it back to his partner. "Sorry Yo."

Muttering to himself, Yorit carefully took the half-chewed page and flattened it out on the table with his hand, then laid it back in the Army manual. "What a ridiculous regulation."

After several minutes, the two signalmen slipped back into their lethargy, Yorit with his head nodding, Lightpony in the lotus position. It was then a call came in from an Army flag car, one of several that the Brigade sent daily into East Berlin. The flag car's job was reconnaissance. The Army wanted to be sure the Soviets complied with the Allied Occupation Agreements and not try a sneak attack. The Russians did the same with their flag vehicles, as well as the British; and the French with theirs. The Radio Room's assignments were to track the American flag cars to be sure they did not get lost or kidnapped in the East. It was the Cold War game known as "Snoop-and-Go-Seek." Back in grade school, kids called it "Hide-and-Go-Seek."

Lightpony took the call from the army flag car. He answered in his Shoshone. The officers who drove flag car returned the communication with a " Farm house 4. Roger that. Over!"

Yorit sat up. "Hey, wha´? Chief, that officer you just talked with understood you. How?"

"Yes, and he didn't even know it." Lightpony answered proudly.

"Is he one of your own people?"

"I doubt if he is Shoshone."

"Irish than, like O'Malley?"

"Robert, my friend, you must understand, the Shoshone language is a spiritual language, just like Hindu or Buddhism. It can be understood easily, although people don't realize it."

Yorit looked at him, a little confused. "You're joking,"

"No, I'm not joking." Lightpony tapped at the table to make his point. "Listen, the language of the Plains Indian belongs to Nature, and therefore to all mankind. You only have to be open for it. Let it flow into you like a pond soaking into the soil. That's why I understand the Cheyenne, the Ute, the Shawnee, and they me. It is because Shoshone is Mother Nature's tongue. When you hear it, you don't even know it. It is in the wind, the rustle of leaves in the forest, a sunset."

"Could it be a heartbeat?"

"A heartbeat too," he affirmed.

Reflective, Yorit nodded. "I can't believe that. Sorry."

Lightpony looked at the wall clock. "Bravo should be calling in about now. When he does, I will answer him in the language of the Plains Indian. You watch. He'll reply and won't even know I talked to him in Shoshone," he said in soft voice, suggesting tolerance of the ignorant.

"No way," said Yorit with a shake of his head. "Bravo's a Sicilian. A Dago. Not only that, he's from New Jersey. He can hardly speak English let alone your language."

"I'll call him and we shall see." Lightpony took the table microphone and drew it to him. He keyed. "Flagstaff 2! This is Flagstaff 1. Do you read me? Over!" he said in Shoshone. Both men looked up at the loudspeaker on the GE mega transmitter-receiver and waited. They did not have long to wait.

"Roger that, Flagstaff 1. Read you loud and clear. Over." communicated Bravo from the duty train.

"Roger Flagstaff 2. What is your situation? Over." repeated Lightpony, again in the Shoshone language.

"Roger, Flagstaff 1! Track has been cleared. Duty train is pulling out now. Proceeding to next checkpoint. Over." came the metallic tone of Bravo's voice over the mega radio's receiver.

Bravo had clearly understood Shoshone. It convinced Yorit. "I heard it, but I don't believe. I heard it. Or maybe you got to be from Jersey and a Dago where people talk like 'dat-n-dis'."

"Roger, out!" said Lightpony, pushing the table microphone away. He noted the transmission in the log book, then turned to Yorit. "Bravo's spirit was open to nature. You're spirit is not."

"It is, but I have to be drunk."

Satisfied with his experiment, the Indian Jimmy Lightpony crocked his legs into the Sitting Bull position and nodded off. Yorit watched him and tried the lotus position. He found himself getting drowsy, more to do with the hot air circulation than the lotus position. Still...

Time passed. The radio Room's heat continued to weigh on the two signalmen like blankets in a sauna. The rotating ceiling fan tried, but did little to circulate the hot air. That, and the constant buzz of the three GE transmitters-receivers, compelled the operators' heads to droop. Though they resisted—it was against regulations to sleep on the job— their heads still drooped. At times the occasional radio transmission from the field would jolt them upright in their chairs like a slap in the face. Swollen-eyed, one of them would take the table microphone and reply, log in, yawn, and return to slumber. Eyes still closed, Lightpony hummed drowsily, arms behind his head. "I once had a girlfriend," he said, breaking the silence.

"Good for you," mumbled Yorit, eyes half shut.

"Yes, a German girl."

Yorit yawned as he took up the *Stars and Stripes* newspaper from the table to read. The morning shift had left it there. "Was it one of the camp followers from the Golden Sun bar?"

"What are camp followers?" asked Lightpony.

"Oh, you know. It's women like Death and Sin, or Sweettalkin' marge, or Hedda the Hussy, or Dagmar the Ditch. They follow the Army. Date only Army guys. Twin Butts, too. You know her, the big boobed girl? She hangs out with the 287 MP guys. She's one of their camp followers."

"Don't know her," said Lightpony. "This girl, she was not like any one of those. This girl was respectable. She was a student nurse, twenty-one years old, and pretty."

Sensing his partner wanted to get something off his chest, Yorit put down the newspaper and looked at him. "A twenty-one year old student? I'm pleasantly surprised. German mothers usually keep their daughters locked up and away from us soldiers, unless their daughters are approaching menopause."

Perspiring under the room's dull light, Lightpony chuckled. "She found me at Bahnhof Zoo, main train station near the *Kufürsten Damm*. I was drunk at the time and, you know, in that condition you do crazy things."

"Tell me about it. I'm an expert when it comes to crazies," said Yorit, curious as he listened.

"It was one of those days. I had my Army pass and nothing to do, so I went down town and bar-hopped. Got drunk. I ended up on a train platform at Bahnhof Zoo. Don't ask me why I was there. As a train pulled in, I began to chant and did my tribes' 'the Dance of the Forest.' It's a spirit dance. Germans getting off the train stopped to watch me. A few tossed some *Pfennig* change, enough for a drink. But there was this one girl; she wasn't amused. Instead of throwing me a coin, she took me by the arm and led me, staggering, outside. She put me in a taxi and brought me back to the barracks. Paid for it, too! Can you imagine that? By than I was sober enough to ask if I could see her again. I guess you can say we kind of liked each other. That was last summer," said Lightpony, wiping the perspiration from his face with his t-shirt.

Yorit put his feet up on the communication table, hands behind his head. "Say, was that about the time you stopped jumping out of windows at company morning formation?"

"Yes," Lightpony answered. "I didn't want my pass pulled for `behavior unbecoming´ and all that. I even started making my bunk properly for inspections."

"That proves it!" snapped Yorit, sitting up. "The right girl can make a difference in a soldier's life if he sings on a train platform. I got to try it."

"She was wonderful."

"If I remember correctly you made Soldier-of-the-Month. First Sarge congratulated our Platoon sarge out in front of the company about it. But wait, you started jumping out of windows again. What happened? Get a 'Dear John' letter?"

Lightpony stood up and stretched. There was a hint of melancholy in his voice. "She dumped me. I loved her and she dumped me, or I should say her mother dumped me."

"You were fucking her mother?"

Lightpony looked up into the neon glare of the ceiling light as if seeking an illusive thought hiding there. "No, her mother didn't approve of my skin."

"What's a matter with your skin? Does it flake?"

"It's the color."

"The color? You look a little greasy, but so do the Latinos, and they make out with the German chicks all the time."

"It's not the grease; it's what happens to my skin in the sun." Yorit was not sure what Lightpony was talking about. "Remember how hot it was for a while last summer? How the sun shined every day for a couple of weeks? Remember the week before President Kennedy arrived in West Berlin? How we were doing all kinds of extra duty: cleaning vehicles, shaping up the motor pool, the company area, the whole post compound, painting everything that didn't move, including the lawn. Remember?" Yorit nodded. "Well, in the afternoon sun you white guys tan. The Plains Indian people ripen. We have another pigment. In the summer sun we take on the look of grapes in a vineyard."

"Do Indians turn blue?"

"No, purple."

"Doesn't suntan lotion help?"

"I wish it did," said Lightpony. "I kept getting more purple by the day, just like the Arizona Navahoes in summer. It just so happened I was invited one Sunday for lunch to meet my girlfriend's parents. They wanted to get to know the American soldier who was dating their daughter."

Yorit sat up. "So what happened?"

"When the mother opened the door, she screamed. She took me for the wild man of Borneo."

Yorit laughed. "Knowing you, she was close. You're the wild man of 592nd Signal Company, Berlin Brigade. Ha,ha!"

"That maybe, but that's only when I want to behave that way," he said softly. "Playing crazy in the Army is only an expression of frustration; otherwise, I'm a proper gentleman."

"Is that with or without your tomahawk?" Yorit smirked, fascinated by the story.

Lightpony sighed and slipped again in the lotus position, but with one leg under the chair. Being an Indian, he was used to the wisecracks from the guys. "Robert, please shut up and let me finish." Yorit apologized and his partner continued. "The mother forbade her daughter to see me again. She thought I was wearing makeup. She didn't want her blue-eyed, blonde-haired angel going out with a crayon. I was deeply offended. Really got me down, it did. The old bitch! So I put a curse on the mom."

"You what?" Yorit cried out in astonishment. "I didn't know it was possible to put a curse on anyone."

"Yes. I trapped a bird, killed it, and hung it on the front door of the mother's house."

"Did it work?"

"I think so. The mother's got a bipolar problem today, or so I've been told."

"But most Germans have that problem," said Yorit.

Just than Pereski's voice came up over the mega radio transmitter-receiver. He reported his convoy's position. Sweating, Lightpony logged it. There was a transmission from 7th Army, Stuttgart. He took the message and passed it to the Operations Center down the hall. Around 0200 hours radio traffic fell off and the two operators sank back into their silent Radio Room lethargy. Yorit stretched to stay awake but kept dozing off. He shook himself and got up. Reaching out, he took the coffeepot off the top of transmitter 3, the hot one. It was empty. "Pony Boy, I'm going down the hall to the Operations Center and see if they got some coffee brewing there. I need a cup desperately."

Back in the corridor, Yorit took a deep breath. It was so much cooler. He sighed, grateful for the relief. The further away he got from the steam heat of the Radio Room, the more the temperature dropped. It was refreshing. He passed several doors marked G1, G2, G3, Provost Marshall. All were locked. They were open only during military alerts and field exercises. Other doors read G4, Staff Quarters, Senior Officer Quarters, and Conference Room. Yorit read them as he passed. Then came the MP Quarters. He passed it. It read, "Concubine Quarters." "Huh?" He stopped and backed up. He re-read the sign on the door. Indeed, the title stenciled in capital letters read "Concubine Quarters." He studied it for a moment, contemplated it, and scratched his head quizzically. "Now what the hell is that supposed to mean?"

It should be noted that after 1700 hours, following the end of the day's bugle call of "Retreat," all senior officers go home to families or back to their quarters to prepare for the evening's events, like bowling and bridge club. There were also cocktail parties to attend and diplomatic parties, West Berlin being what it is, an international city situated in the middle of Cold War Europe. It was also the time when the Brigade's daily command was transferred from above-ground headquarters to the below-ground Operations Center. It was a room located in the cellar, deep under the Brigade headquarters. Above ground, when all activity ceased, the underground Ops Room became operational. The Operations Room itself was a large single room with a battery of phones, desks, maps and one coffee machine. Two senior NCOs always had to be on standby there in case of an emergency. If nothing happened, they would dither over crossword puzzles, football pools and comic books. It was here that Yorit poked his head in the door. He coughed out loud to be recognized.

SFC George Pellon looked up from his desk, where an army manual lay open; he was studying nomenclature math. In grade school they call it arithmetic. Two desks down, another NCO, SSgt Wallace bent over a funny book.

"Say, Sarge," Yorit called in from the doorway.

Sgt Pellon appeared to be mouthing something while counting on his fingers. He looked up and stopped what he was doing. He shook his head, annoyed at the interruption. Now he would have to count on his fingers all over again. "I'll master these multiplication tables yet," he muttered to himself, with obvious frustration. "Who are you, Soldier?" he demanded.

"Specialist Yorit from Radio Room personnel section, Sarge. We're down the hall."

Sergeant Pellon, over 40, balding with a sinister head scar from a wound in Korea, studied the Spc-4 standing in the doorway. "Oh yeah, I know. You're one of the guys from the sweat box communication. I sometimes forget we're not alone down here. Whadayawant?"

"We've run out of coffee, Sarge."

"You got a problem."

Yorit nodded toward the small coffee machine on the other side of the Ops Room. "I see you got a whole pot brewing there, Sarge. May I fill my pot from yours?" he asked politely.

"You got a Top Secret clearance, Soldier?" Sgt Pellon inquired.

Yorit stepped back, surprised by the NCO's reply. "You got to have a Top Secret clearance to get a cup of coffee? What are you brewing there, Sarge? Rocket fuel?"

"Don't be cute with me, Soldier! You got the clearance or not?"

"Got a Secret Clearance. Is that enough for a cup of coffee?" he answered, expecting that to be enough and moved to step into the Operations Room.

Suddenly, the SFC appeared to slip into that controlled rage mode, well practiced from his years as a sergeant in the Army. "You, Soldier, step back into the hall, HUMPF!" he snap ordered.

Startled, Yorit jumped back. The other NCO in the Ops Room , a SSgt Wallace looked up from the comic book he was reading. It was a Captain Marvel comic..

"Don't you dare come in here without a proper clearance or I'll call upstairs to security!" the SFC barked. "This room is a top security area, which means everything here is highly classified, including coffee!"

"Okay, Sarge. You win," Yorit gasped, pulling back. "Tell me what do I got to do to get a cup of coffee out of a highly classified security area?"

"I told you, get a proper clearance," Pellon answered.

"But Sarge, that will take a month, and we in the Radio Room down the hall would like to have a cup of coffee, like now," Yorit pleaded.

"Too bad, Soldier. Next time, you best submit a request before you go on duty."

Feeling his blood begin to boil, Yorit frowned. He tried another tactic. "Look, Sarge, tell me, is the coffee itself classified?"

SFC Pellon's thick hand scratched the back of his neck. He turned to his partner. "Say, Nathan, are Army coffee beans classified?"

The staff sergeant looked up from his Captain Marvel comic book. He took off his too-small army issue, plastic-rimmed glasses. It made him look like he had a case of incipient hydrocephalus. "Nn-noo…" he said after much rubbing of the chin with his thumb. The question perplexed him. "How can brewed coffee be classified? There is nothing secret about the beans. Or is there?"

Sergeant Pellon rubbed his chin. "I never thought of that."

"That is good news," said Yorit, about to step into the Operations Room and fill his pot. He was getting desperate.

"Ah, where do you think you're going, soldier?"

"Sarge, you just agreed that coffee beans are not classified; therefore, if coffee beans are not classified, then a cup of coffee is not classified, right?"

The SFC scratched his head. "For sure. Ah, what are you trying to say, Spc-4?"

"Then I do have a big problem, Sarge" said Yorit, breathily.

"Which is?" asked SSgt. Wallace from over at his desk.

Yorit sighed. "How do I get unclassified coffee out of a classified area?"

"You submit a request, like I tol' ya," said Pellon. He was getting annoyed and wanted to go back to his arithmetic.

"Ya, sure, sarge, but to whom do I submit a request. You, Sarge?"

"No, to Brigade!"

Yorit felt a light "Ping!" of disagreeable pressure at the back of his head. It always happened when he met a dimwit in authority. He gnashed his teeth. With clarity of thought he had not known since his college days, Yorit grasped a fundamental that had always puzzled him about the Army: Why are NCOs and officers with 10 years time and grade incapable of responding to simple questions? Now it dawned on him. It had to be that book on Sgt Pellon's desk. It was the book on Army Regulations, those eternal vague and incomprehensible rules and codes that read like medical journals and paralyze original thought.

Decreed from the Pentagon, Army Regulations manuals cover every contingency and deny every deviation. In the course of their careers, all officers and sergeants are programmed to follow and enforce those regulations, no matter how absurd. Should a question fall outside the "regs," as they were called, like Yorit's request to fill his coffeepot with unclassified coffee from a classified area without the proper clearance, they—the officers and NCOs—choke up. The request didn't fit the mold! It was an anomaly! The request fell between the cracks! No ruling or contingency ruling had yet to be written to cover the need to get a cup of coffee from a security zone. For SFC Pellon a simple, "Yes, Soldier, go get your coffee then get the hell outta here," was inconceivable. Given the times and the Cold War mentality, with the enemy at the gates and heavily armed ta-boot, Yorit's request for coffee smacked of treason, made more sinister by his lack of a proper security clearance. All the sergeant could do was what the manuals didn't teach: bluster and obfuscate until the opposition withdraws. But Yorit, being a Polak kid from Cleveland, Ohio, showed backbone. It was something he learned from the nuns at St. Vincent de Paul Grade School, from the brothers at St. Edwards High School, and shop class at West Tech. "When the going gets tough, wimp'm!"

"Sarge, tell me something. You were there, weren't you? In Korea I mean."

"Yeah, and…"

"Well, how did you hold the line against the Chinese?"

"Bold initiative!" was his proud reply."

"Right!" said Yorit, stepping through the doorway and into the inner sanctum of the Operations Room. He crossed to the coffee machine, filled his pot, turned, and carried it back out the door and into the hallway.

Both NCOs, Pellon and Wallace, were on their feet, Pellon's face changing color.

Yorit looked back and disarmed them both. "Sarge, you're a buddy. Thanks for an old Sarge's advice about initiative. I feel inspired. Oh, and by the way, does the Srmy permit concubines down here at Brigade Operations Headquarters? If so, put my name on the list."

SFC Pellon's expression abruptly changed. "Concubi... Where'd you get that notion?"

"It's written on the door next to the Senior Officer Quarters."

"Oh, that sign still up? I thought it was taken down after last week's field exercise." Pellon turned to Wallace. "Nathan, put in a request to Maintenance Division and tell them to get down here first thing in the morning. If General ten Onkel sees his concubine sign is still up, he'll have a fit."

"Yes, and so will his wife," said Yorit, walking away.

Back in the heat of the Radio Room, he dropped into the hot seat of his chair and fell immediately into a half-slumber. Next to him, Lightpony droused. In the quiet and the hum of the GE Mega transmitters he thought again about the Army as a career. Was it worth all the Mickey Mouse crap one has to put up with, like a secret clearance just to get a cup of coffee? Would he end up like Sgt Pellon, a regulations man and a bit daffy? Yorit shook his head. It was that kind of hassle that made him consider taking a discharge when his four-year enlistment was up. He reached over and tapped Lightpony on the shoulder, lightly this time, not wishing to startle him. "Tonto, did you ever consider re-enlisting?"

"Why should I?" he mumbled, eyes still shut.

Yorit poured himself a cup of Ops Room coffee. "Thanks for your opinion." And the tedium of the shift continued.

It was the the transmission voice; it startled him. It came from the mega transmitter-receiver. The voice was Pereski's. He was guiding another Army convoy over the East German Autobahn. He called in to give his checkpoint location: the Elba River. From the train, Bravo did the same. He reported his location. Only the Army flag car, the one behind enemy lines, so to speak, did not call in. Unusual. Every half hour, flag cars in East Berlin had to call in and give their location. Concerned, Yorit looked up at the wall clock. Late. He logged the late time and called the flag car. It answered. He logged it. Relieved, and with no further communication, Yorit joined Lightpony in the reverie and closed his eyes and began to nod off.

Suddenly, he was jerked awake. He looked around. What made him jump? With a grunt, he drew the log book to him. He checked over the day's transmissions. Then he saw it. There, in the log book, was second "on duty" Army flag car in East Berlin with the call sign, "Flagstaff 5." The vehicle had not called in since he and Lightpony had come on shift and he had not noticed it. It was a breach of responsibility. It was that which jerked Yorit's conscience. That sense that something was wrong. "Uh-oh!" he said to himself.

Yorit slapped Lightpony on the shoulder for the third time. He jumped up but did not throw a punch. "Pleeese, Tonto. Must you jump? I only touched your shoulder, for God's sake. Here, take a look at the log book. One of the two Brigade flag cars in East Berlin has not called in for quite a while. He missed four call-in times, and we didn't pick it up."

"Let me see that," said Lightpony, glancing at the log book. "Say, you're right."

Yorit tapped the empty spaces on the log sheet. "He should have called here and here. The question is, did the staff car cross back into West Berlin without calling in to inform us, or has it been delayed by the commies?"

"Or kidnapped? It's happened before," said Lightpony, concerned and drawing the table microphone to him. "Only one way to find out." He keyed and called, "Flagstaff 5, this is Flagstaff 1. Do you read me? Over?" he said in Shoshone. There was no reply. He called again.

Yorit put his hand over the microphone's mouthpiece. "So much for your theories on the spiritual quintessence of the Great Plains Indian. Talk English, will ya please?"

"Flagstaff 5, this is Flagstaff 1, do you read me? Over." reported Lightpony, this time in English. Still no reply. "He could have stopped for a pizza."

"They ain't got pizza parlors or McDonald's in Communist East Berlin, I don't think," Yorit speculated.

"I'll call the MPs at Checkpoint Charlie and see if the flag car had crossed back over to the west; maybe it already did."

Both signalmen were now very concerned. To lose communication with a Brigade staff car on their watch could get them into a lot of trouble. At an inquiry, it would be judged as "failure to track US property in enemy territory," or "neglect of duty while on duty," or some such thing. Yorit stared at the silent Mega transmitter-receiver. "I think we may have a flap on our hands, Jimmy, my boy. We better call Sergeant Pellon over at Operations. Could be the Vopos have bushwhacked our flag car. Operations have to be informed."

"A couple more tries," Lightpony suggested. Drawing the microphone to him. He made four more calls.

Yorit got up. "Ya, know, ever since Khrushchev threatened to sign a peace treaty with the East Germans, the commies have been pulling this Mickey Mouse shit. In the East, they slashed our flag car tires, broke off antennas, held up convoys. On the Army duty train steam engines they sometimes try to plant the DDR flag. Mickey Mouse shit! This could be one of them shit stunts."

"But isn't that what the Cold War is all about? Mickey Mouse?" asked Lightpony. "Did you know they once blocked one of our staff cars in East German territory? Lavoss told me about it. He had Radio Room duty at the time. Brigade was shitting bricks. Brigade pulled every string in the book, including a threat to send in 40th Armored, to get those guys out. Can you imagine sending in 40th Armored? You may as well send in go-carts for all the good ten charging tanks can do against a Soviet army division."

"Did we get our staff car back?" asked Yorit.

"Yes, and the flap was called off."

"That proves it."

"Proves what?"

"When the going gets tough, send in the go-carts."

At that moment, there was a flash of static from the mega transmitter-receiver. It was Flagstaff 5, the missing army flag car. It had returned to the radio net. The operator stated his location, someplace called *Prenzelberg*. Flagstaff 5 was not kidnapped after all. The driver code-spelled the vehicle's position.

Yorit and Lightpony were relieved. Both operators would not have to stand before an inquiry board and relate how they lost a vehicle. Rogering the call, they logged the transmission and relaxed,

Fanning themselves, they returned to their laid back *Mox Nix* posture, *Mox Nix* could also be said, *"Das macht nichts, "* the soldierized expression for, "It don't mean shit!" Both Yorit and Lightpony fell into a light snooze as time passed.

"Oh, *Schaaatze*," (Oh, sweetheart) sing-songed the light, feline voice over the GE mega transmitter-receiver. It startled Lightpony. It was like a slap in the face with a wet towel. His eyes popped, as did Yorit's. It had the snap of the bugle call at morning reveille. Both men were now wide awake and "What-whating?" and "Who-whoing?"

"What was that?" gasped Lightpony in Shoshoni.

For the first time, Yorit understood the languaage. "That can't be!"

"Oh, Kapi-ta-ain," the feline voice sing-songed again.

"That's a woman's breath!" snapped Lightpony, gasping.

At once, both soldiers jumped to the table microphone. Yorit grabbed it first. He keyed it. "Unknown transmission! This is Flagstaff 1! Identify yourself! Over!" he vocally transmitted. They knew this call was a serious violation of Army regulations. A female, a foreigner no less, calling over a classified communication line. Outrageous! They waited. The return response was a flutter. There was a tingle of laughter. Most unsoldiery.

The two perspiring Radio Room operators stared, transfixed at the wire mesh of the Mega radio speaker, not believing what they heard.

"Impossible," uttered Yorit.

"Unbelievable," croaked Lightpony in Shoshone.

"Incredible!" cried Yorit

"Incomprehensible!" screamed Lightpony, again in Shoshone.

The voice sounded like the old Tokio Rose broadcasts in the Pacific during World War II. It tantalized island-hopping Marines to try to get them to desert. In the heat of the Radio Room, confined in a narrow space and helpless, the two signalmen looked at each other. The voice was erotic, lascivious, licentious.Tormenting!

Perspiring from the GE machine's heat and squirming in the unbreathable space, Yorit and Lightpony could only stare at the radio receiver where the dish size speaker was mounted. Now, the feline voice, forever erotic, began to groan. Lightpony and Yorit felt like monastery monks taking lashes for contrition. The voice purred agonizingly on.

"Oh, you naughty mans! Stoppen yous das!" (Her accent was heavenly.) "Hmmm, squeezes you dieses ones, toos."

Lightpony began to salivate. Yorit wanted to shout obscenities. His throat was parched. Trying, he could only manage an amphibian croak.

"Now, sucken yous dis hier," said the lush feminine voice, breathily, followed by "Oos" and "aahs!"

Yorit cried out. "In this heat she got to say that?"

Lightpony grabbed the microphone and squeaked. "Unauthorized transmission, this is Flagstaff 1! What is your phone number? I repeat! What is..." this time in English.

"*Lieber Gott, Kap-i-tan, es ist uuum, so gross!*" (Mein Gott, Kap-i-tan! It is so biiig!).

Yorit bit his fingers. Lightpony howled. The sensuous voice now swelled with joy. It jerked. It whimpered. Weak cries told of a short, thrusting love gone passionate. For the two signalmen-operators sitting in the overheated Radio Room, mouths open, it was like being tied to an ant hill with the ants wearing head feathers. There followed the gentle sound of slapping flesh.

"What are they doing?" cried Lightpony in Shoshone, Cree and Navaho.

Yorit, now spiritually atune, answered in Cree. "Well, they ain't beating pancakes with a tablespoon, I can tell you that!"

"You mean they're fucking?"

Yorit could not take it any more. With the sweat pouring into his eyes, he climbed up on the table and grabbed the GE Mega radio transmitter-receiver. Lovingly, he embraced it, rubbing and kissing the speakers metal mesh facade.

Lightpony jumped up. "Yoyo, have you gone crazy?"

"What else! I gotta pop!" Yorit cried out.

Lightpony began to tear at his shirt and howl like a Wyoming prairie dog. The erotic groans and sighs of the communication transmission grew more intense. Yorit jumped up and down on the table, scattering the log books. He bumped the shelf of Army manuals. They crashed to the floor.

Dropping to the floor himself and with barely enough wits about him, Lightpony grabbed a pen and the log book. It was on the floor. He wanted to log the passionate transmission when the mega radio transmission-receiver screamed. The two operators screamed...and so did SFC Pellon. "Attention!" he ordered. The two radio operators stiffened.

"What in God's name are you two men doing? Just what the hell is going on in here? Get down from that table, Soldier!" Pellon barked at Yorit. "You, Comanche, off your knees and off the floor! Have you two guys gone nuts? You got the bunker river fever or what? We can hear your screams at Operations, all the way down the hall!"

Yorit broke with his embrace from GE mega transmitter-receiver. Lightpony jumped up from the floor. Both men began to talk at once, Lightpony in Shoshone, Yorit in Apache.

"Slow down! Slow down! What the hell you two babbling about?" demanded the NCO.

"It's the radio, Sarge!" Yorit exclaimed. "There was a woman's voice on the operations radio, and she's fucking somebody over the army net! Just listen!"

The three men turned to the receiver's speakers. Pellon tilted his head. "I don't hear nothin'!"

Yorit and Lightpony looked at each other. Except for the "whirr" of air-wave static and the twitching of the gauge needles, the Mega radio-receiver was silent.

"Sarge, we logged the transmission!" cried Lightpony in desperation, this time in English. "Here, it's all here in the log book, and the log book don't lie!"

The Operations NCO looked at the log book. He turned it back to this two soldiers. "Are you guys kiddin' me? You look!"

Lightpony took the log book. Following a series of neat entries and communication times, there followed an abrupt, incoherent scribbling of a hand out of control at the bottom of the page. He could only stare at the scribbling. He looked back at Yorit. "I tried."

"I'm NCOIC in command down here, and I'm putting both your asses on report! Such childish behavior in the line of duty is disgraceful!" Noting their name tags, SFC Pellon turned and walked out of the Radio Room.

Lightpony looked at Yorit. "Well, what you got to say about that?"

"Plenty! Sergeant Pellon killed my erection."

"Mine, too! And just when I was taking a liking to the GE commo radio," said Lightpony, frustrated.

Yorit "Tsh, tshed," him. "Chief, we're now up shit creek, you know that?"

"I know. I've been there before."

The two signalmen cleaned up the floor, put the manuals back on the shelf and straightened the chairs. Taking their seats again, and with nothing to do, they returned to their former attitude of *Mox Nix*, then they slouched in their chairs.

Lightpony took a towel out of his gym bag and wiped his face. "The sarge didn't believe us, did he?"

"I don't believe it myself," said Yorit, pouring a cup of coffee. "Here, Chief. It's still hot."

"Thanks, I could use one."

Suddenly the radio's receiver gauge needle jumped. Again, the erotic feline voice came on. "Hey, you boys," it purred. "I vants to suck-a-yoos off, too. *Ende!*"

The following week, the two E-4 Specialists, Robert Yorit and Jimmy Lightpony the Shoshone, stood before the Signal Company Commander, Cpt Mellon. They were to be disciplined. A hearing had been ordered. It was set up in the Orderly Room and presided over by their PltSgt, MSgt Sweechek, FSgt Persilla, and a JAG officer sent over from Brigade Headquarters. Both soldiers knew they could be charged with negligence, according to the Uniform Code of Military Justice. It was that serious. If charged, they would receive serious discipline. But lady luck was on their side. The CID-513 MI (spook) division had been monitoring the cross-border frequency and picked up the whole erotic transmission. They logged it. The JAG officer presented it as a defense. Upon further study, the hearing concluded that the women's voice did come from the Brigade flag car, the vehicle code named "Flagstaff 5." The officers on duty, a lieutenant and a captain, were having sex with two East German women, a serious breach of security.

Further investigation into the psychology of the officers found that they both had graduated from their ROTC university programs. The result was both were unable to differentiate between Srmy barracks life and the fraternity house. For some time they had been making it in Army flag cars with East German girls, promising them escape to the West for sex. On that particular evening, with Yorit and Lightpony on duty in the Brigade Radio Room, the officers had mistakenly left the vehicle's radio keyed, sending the whole erotic event over a classified military frequency, a most serious violation. In the claustrophobia of the Radio Room, the two signalmen responded to the hot transmission the only way the Army's lower orders knew how. They howled. Like hounds on all fours and howling, they hugged the one ton G.E. communication equipment. What else can a soldier do in the heat of an Army Radio Room? It was therefore accepted.

The charges against the two signalmen were dropped. Lightpony, though, did get a verbal reprimand for seeking the German woman's telephone number.

The two officers, the captain and the lieutenant, were charged and found guilty of security violations and behavior "unbecoming an officer and a gentleman," plus a whole list of in-the-line-of-duty violations, including the world's first telephone sex charade. In war, it would have earned them a firing squad. But at their Special Court Martial, they were only busted one grade and shipped back to the West German Zone and the Army's equivalent of purgatory, *Baumholder*. It was the boonies, where the sun never shines.

Three days later, the communication team of Yorit and Lightpony were back on duty, perspiring and suffering in the heat of the Radio Room. They were halfway through their shift, and dozing. Low grade radio signals buzzed in the background; country music played on AFN radio. There had been several transmission calls from the troop train at Marienborn, and one from an Army convoy that had just passed the town of Magdeburg. There followed a low, unfamiliar rhythmic tic-tic, tic-tic. It caused Lightpony to raise an eyelid. The gauge needle on one receiver, the one used only for emergencies indicated that an incoming, encrypted message was about to follow. He punched Yorit, who was between snores. "Wake up, Yo! We got some incoming!" he burst out in the Shoshone language. Startled, Yorit jumped up. He gasped; he understood the Shoshoni! "It's in code!" rapped Lightpony. "I think its something serious. The commies must be up to something."

They watched the G.E. receiver's snapping needle. "Oh shit," said Yorit; "it's the alert signal. Quick, take the message, Jimmy. I'll call Operations to get them up on line for a standby."

Fearful, Lightpony flipped the receiver switch and wrote down the coded message. Yorit began to dial up Operations Command. Lightpony stared at the message. "I don't believe it."

"Don't believe what?" asked Yorit, fearful.

"The message."

"Who is it from? What does it state?"

Lightpony hesitated. "Ah, it's from our G.E. transmitter-receiver. It wants to be stroked again."

Kennedy

Kennedy

It was another "Ho-hum" November evening, a boring evening in the Brigade Radio Room with Yorit and his partner, Jimmy Lightpony the Shoshone, on shift. As always, they sat, stripped to their tee-shirts and losing weight. It had to do with the heat from the GE mega-radio transmitters set in a room the size of three telephone booths where the only ventilation was the hallway door and one's own breath. Yorit could not help but yawn. Lightpony too, and then some.

The evening's communication was infrequent. The Radio Room received coded messages from 7th Army Headquarters, as well as several check-point calls from the Army duty train, Robuck transmitting. Yorit "Rogered!" his calls. On the East German Autobahn, it was the same. Every half hour Pereski, in the convoy's lead jeep, would call in his location. Perspiring, Lightpony took the calls and "Rogered!" in Shoshoni. A 2nd battalion unit radioed in from the field. It was logged. There were no transmissions from the Potsdam mission, or the US flag sedans. Yorit and Lightpony were thankful for that.

It was all done with call signs, transmissions, and a Morse Code, "Ditty-dum-dum-ditty!" and repeat. It was the routine. It had to be the routine because that was how the Army functioned: routine. Some call it a rut. Others call it ennui. Call it what you will, it was the Army way. Routine! And no one knew the routine better than the signalmen soldiers who worked shift in the Brigade Radio Room.

It was on that 9 to 9 shift when the transmission came down from 7th Army. It was a coded message. *That's strange*, thought Yorit in his slumber-like stupor, taking the message. He noted the code and translated it for the log book. Then his eyes popped open—wide open. He requested a communication repeat of, "Ditty-dum-dum-ditty!" Reaching over, he punched Lightpony in the shoulder. "Hey, Tonto."

189

"Yeah, what?" droned the Indian. He always spoke English to his partner.

"President Kennedy has been shot."

Lightpony sat up. His eyes popped. He grabbed the log book and read the decoded message they had just received.

"What do we do now?" asked Yorit, feeling—he did not know what he felt. Numb.

Lightpony sucked in his breath. "We do what we were trained to do. Pass the message on to Brigade Operations and pray to God it didn't happen," he said in Shoshone. Yorit understood him.

Several hours later, a second transmission followed: "The President is dead."

On the night of 22 November 1963 the order went out from Berlin Brigade Headquarters for an Army Stand-By alert. It was a world-wide Stand-By alert, not only for 7th Army Europe, but for 8th Army Korea patrolling along the 38th parallel. The Strategic Air Command, SAC, ordered B52 bombers into the air. On the North Atlantic, the US Navy had attack submarines pursue their Soviet counterparts, only a little closer than usual, just in case. Throughout the Armed Forces, a crisis situation had gone into force. There was deep concern. For a few hours no one had their finger on the button. The President was dead!

According to Armed Forces Radio, President Kennedy was in Dallas, Texas, for a speaking engagement. He and his wife, Jackie, along with Texas Governor John Connally, were in a motorcade that took them through downtown Dallas. They passed a building called the Book Depository. Rifle shots were fired. Both the governor and the president were hit. They were rushed to the nearby Parkland Hospital. There, President Kennedy died from his wounds. Governor Connally survived. The news of Kennedy's death flashed around the world, and the world listened, unable to believe, or to comprehend.

The magnitude and shock of what had happened did not hit home until that evening. On television, with millions of Americans watching, CBS News anchorman, Walter Cronkite, grunted. Perspiring, temples throbbing, eyes blinking, jaws working, his mouth opening and closing in front of the cameras, he choked. Walter Cronkite could only say… absolutely nothing. Television's top anchorman was unable to deliver. The world would never be the same again.

Outside, on *Clay Allee*, in front of Berlin Brigade Headquarters, the night felt weighty. There was little activity except for the idling engine of the Army shuttle bus. It waited for the soldiers on shift to come up from the bunkers below-ground. They were to board the shuttle bus for the trip back to the barracks. The driver, a Service Company man, sat, arms folded and lost in thought. He had a handkerchief in his hand and sometimes blew his nose into it.

Soon, one after another, the soldiers on shift emerged from the lower sanctums of the headquarters building and got on the shuttle bus. Usually jocular and vocal, tonight they were subdued. No one talked, or if they talked it was with hushed voices, as if fearful of being overheard.

With the news of President Kennedy's death, there was an awareness, a sense that some universal consciousness had been disturbed. No one could put his finger on it. It was like an itch in the middle of the back, out of reach, annoying. The question, the one that knotted the brow of every soldier on the bus aching to be answered was, "Why?"

As the shuttle bus pulled away, SSgt Wallace of Operations stood up in the aisle. He tried to talk. Gripping the back of a seat, he began. "Ah, men, as you know...ah-hum!" He cleared his throat. "Ah, men, several hours ago..., I mean...ah... He coughed into his hand. The magnitude of the event, the president's death, was too much for him and he sat down.

Outside on Clay Allee there was almost no traffic, unusual for a busy boulevard this time of the evening. The Germans, too, had been flashed the word; they were home, glued to their radios and television sets for the latest news about President Kennedy.

"Madam Nu's revenge," said one of the men from the back of the bus. He was referring to the wife of Vietnam's former president, Ngo Dinh Diem, who had been assassinated a few weeks earlier. It was suggested in the media that President Kennedy had given the order for Diem's elimination. "Will no one rid me of the meddlesome priest?" (King Henry II to his knights about Thomas Becket.) "I'm sure it was Madam Nu who ordered this," the same someone said again.

"I'd say Fidel Castro," speculated another voice. "Who else could it be but Castro? After all, if anyone had an ax to grind against the President, it was him." Again, the shuttle bus fell silent.

Some of the soldiers struggled with "in throat" knots. Others coughed into their hands. Others stared pensively out the windows at the November night, or at the ceiling, or at the floor, unsettled, rattled, all wondering, "What now?"

In Moscow; Politburo Secretary Nikita Khrushchev went to church.

It was the first time he had gone to church since boyhood. His concern was that CIA misinformation might blame the Kremlin. Someone in the Pentagon might think the assassination was a Soviet plot and push the button for "MISSILES TO LAUNCH!" Khrushchev ordered the Soviet armed forces to stand-by alert. Like the Cuban missile confrontation of 1962, the world again seemed vulnerable. It was a reason to go to church.

Up on the West Berlin's *Haupt Strasse*, the main street bars were empty of soldiers. The bartenders read newspapers. The women danced by themselves. For the 287 MPs on evening patrol in the Schöneberg District, it was boring duty. There were no drunken soldiers to write up or heads to conk. So, instead of being on the lookout for trouble, they sat in their jeeps and listened to Armed Forces Radio Network for the latest news from Dallas.

It was no different at the Golden Sun *Kneipe*, the soldiers' bar. The mood was melancholy. There were few patrons. The few who were there sat at the bar and drank their beer as if they were sipping hot tea, their conversation muted. Even the pinball machine was silent; it was the first time since 1945. The jukebox, too. It had been turned off. No dancing with the *Mädels* tonight. The Berlin women, dressed and scented and ready for the evening's festivities, sat around in hushed pairs, talking and wiping their noses with tiny handkerchiefs. With little to do, Fritz the bartender polished and repolished the same beer glass. "*Wie ist es möglich?*" (How is it possible?) he kept uttering to himself.

Across the street at Andrews Barracks Berlin Brigade main gate, the guards on duty sat in their shacks. They waited—for what, they did not know. War? With all companies now on stand-by alert, there was little or no vehicle traffic. The girlfriends, the ones who usually waited outside the Post's main gate for their *Schatzie* boyfriends, they were not there. It was the same at curbside. The taxis parked there hoped for fares that weren't, not tonight anyway. Bored, the drivers slouched in their seats, collars up, as the evening's condensation collected on the hoods of their cabs. On *Finkenstein Allee*, except for an isolated candle that appeared here and there in the windows of some Berlin homes, all was strangely silent.

The Army shuttle bus lumbered up to the Post's main gate and stopped. It let off the soldiers inside, Yorit and Lightpony among them. Most of the men walked through the gate and headed for their companies. A few decided to go across the street to the Golden Sun *Kneipe* for a quick nightcap before turning in. SSgt Wallace took one of the waiting taxis to the Tread Towers building, the NCO married quarters on the *Sundgauer Strasse*. He was in a hurry to be with his family. He wanted to pick up on on the CBS evening news and comments, should the mummified Walter Cronkite speak.

The Army bus drove away. At curbside, Yorit waited. Instead of going back to the company, he joined the few soldiers walking toward the Golden Sun *Kneipe* for a nightcap. They were about to enter when they stopped. From inside the bar there came the grappling sound of groans, then moans, then voices—rough male voices. They were humming, now singing. It was a sober singing, not the usual blubbering of John Barleycorn that took place when soldiers drank. Though off key and the pitch wide of the plate, the voices had a depth that reached out and grabbed the heart. Yorit recognized the tune. It was the "Battle Hymn of the Republic." He hadn't heard it in years. One of the voices, a tenor, stood out, the stanzas above the humming.

"Mine eyes have seen the glo-ry of the com-ing of the Lord

He is tramp-ling out the vin-tage where the grapes of wrath are stored

He hath loosed the fate-ful light-ning of His ter-ri-ble swift sword: His truth is marching on.... Glo-ry, glo-ry, hal-le-lu-jah!"

Outside, on the steps, the soldiers listened. Across the street at Andrews Post main gate, the guards stepped out of their guard shacks to listen. The German cabbies parked at the curb and rolled down their windows. The singing carried on the night.

Yorit felt emotional. He sighed and zipped up his field jacket, tucking in his wool scarf, the one Lightpony had given him for the evening. He was glad he had borrowed it, for the night was nippy. Looking up, he saw that the November stars were out. *Strange*, he thought, *the stars do not sparkle*. Turning, he walked away as the other soldiers entered the Golden Sun for their nightcap. He did not want to go in, nor did he want to go back to the company barracks, not yet, anyway. He felt a need to be alone.

As he walked away, a defective overhead streetlight flickered and buzzed. It echoed Yorit's mood. He stopped at a fence in front of a German home. In one window a lone candle burned. Contemplative, he considered it. *A candle? But tonight is not Christmas.* Taking a deep breath, he continued to walk. He noticed another candle burning in the window of a Berlin family home. It gave off a mellow glow, a comfort against the night's chill. It made him think of a scripture, the light on the hill. In the window of another home it was the same— a single lit candle in the window. Further up the block, on the other side of the street, another candle glowed. Here, there, again and again. Candles. Somber, they glowed on windowsills as they burned into the night. *Most odd*, Yorit thought.

Cap down and field jacket tight at the shoulders, he continued to walk. On the corner of *Baseler Strasse* he stopped and lit a cigarette. It tasted stale. In the chill of the evening he muttered to himself, "Whatever happened to June?"

***

It was the month of June—June 1963. It was hot and the sun shone, unusual for northern Europe. President Kennedy was expected to come to West Berlin to view the Wall for himself. His purpose? To show Russia's Nikita Khrushchev and the Warsaw Pact powers that NATO and the United States of America would never give up the Allied rights to the city. Khrushchev had threatened to sign a separate peace treaty with East Germany, which would have meant war, but Kennedy stood up to the threat. For his tough stand on West Berlin, the Germans loved him. He was their hero. They never forgot how on 20 August 1961, when everyone was fearful of a repeat of the 1948 blockade, if not war, he ordered the 1st Army Battle Group, 18th Infantry, some 1500 men and officers (with bulldozers), to drive the 110 miles up the East German Autobahn from the West German town of Helmstadt. It was a statement, a show of force, an "I-dare-you-Nikita" ploy which, given the fifty Soviet and East German divisions that surrounded West Berlin, quite pointless. Nevertheless, because of what he did, the second blockade of Berlin never materialized. There was no separate peace treaty, and the Soviet Army, in spite of an overwhelming presence, stayed put on their side of the Berlin Wall. Now, two years later, Kennedy was coming to West Berlin to see for himself. It was to be the event of the year.

The whole of Army's Berlin Brigade prepared for the event. It was a top priority, a "blue alert," the Army Command called it. It was spit-and-polish everything from head to toe. The Order-of-the-Day was the standard, "If it don't move, polish it! If it don't breathe, paint it!" For support companies like 592nd Signal, the order was taken literally. Equipment was cleaned, weapons were cleaned, rooms were cleaned, floors were cleaned, scrubbed and waxed, all ready for inspection should the President of the United States happen to drop by the company barracks to check for dust.

And dust! It was that ubiquitous enemy every inspecting officer and non-commisson-officer scouted out with a vengeance. In the Army it was a must. "Dust has to be decapitated!" The NCOs had their soldiers on the knees working the cracks in the floor with brushes and cotton Q-tips, dusting out their quarters, the latrines, the hallways and every nook and cranny. Personal appearance, too, came under the Platoon Sergeant's microscope.

Because it was high summer, the uniform of the day was khaki dress, creased and starched. Every soldier had to get a Marine Corps sidewall haircut, something not seen since Basic Training days. As the curls fell to the barber clippers, there was much weeping and gnashing of teeth.

The few days that President Kennedy was to be in West Berlin, the KP or kitchen police duty would be on duty around the clock, just in case some government VIP should drop by the company Mess Hall for a piece of toast at 0700 in the morning. None did. And miraculously— and much to the delight of the soldiers—the Army chow improved.

MessSgt Cookie Nast stopped mixing C-ration spam with hamburger meat. With a vocal "Hurrah!" from the signalmen, the delicacy known as S.O.S. (Shit-on-a-Shingle) vanished from the breakfast-chow menu, and with it the plague of diarrhea the men sometimes suffered.

Outside the Signal Company barracks, the hedges were trimmed and the lawns cut, snipped and re-cut. Had there been fresh cement within reach, all vegetation would have been paved over for the sake of geometry. In the motor pool, the orders called for all vehicles to be washed: deuce-and-a-halves, trucks, vans, jeeps. All! Every Brigade company commander ordered that their vehicles be checked for rust and painted over should there be any, twice if necessary. Even Army truck tires had to be painted. It was done with a can of roofing pitch for its high gloss content. It was done just in case the president came by to kick a tire for an inspection, and no company would dare allow the President of the United States to kick a dirty tire.

The whole of Andrews Barracks, McNair Barracks, Turner Barracks, Brigade Headquarters, and Army Hospital had to be policed, primed and manicured down to the soldiers' cuticles. And that was only the morning schedule.

In the afternoons the program changed. The afternoon regimen was, "Draw your weapons!" The order was not only for Signal Company, but for all the companies of the Berlin Brigade. "Parade and Drill!" Nobody could escape or hide from the drill, not even the pencil-pushing clerk typists from Service Company, soldiers who had not handled a rifle since their basic training days. Everyone was on the roster for Parade and Drill. The moment a soldier got off regular duty, even if he had just returned from the field or duty shift, he had to draw his weapon from the Arms Room and take his place on the Brigade parade ground for extra training.

"Right shoulder...ARMS! Left shoulder...ARMS! Present... ARMS!" Barrel level with the eyes, fingers placed so, shoulders so, chin so. Snap and repeat. "Right shoulder-ARMS! Left shoulder... ARMS! Present...ARMS!" "Wha'? Sloppy that! You, Soldier! Do it again!" And again. And again. Then, "Forwaaard! Maaaarsch! Humph! Yo' lef'! Yo' lef'!" And so it went for two weeks in the heat of the cloudless and unusually hot June. The mind numbed and the esprit waned until the day President Kennedy arrived in the city. Then all the "Mickey Mouse" stuff, honed to the so-called razor's edge, ceased.

The day before the visit, Major Dimwitty watched the companies do their "Pass in Review!" practice run at Yankee Stadium field. As the companies marched in parade around the track to the thump of the 298nd Army Band, Signal Company drew the Major's attention. He called the company "Spiffy!" The accolade left company commander, Captain Mellon, ecstatic. It made his day. His company, the 592nd Signal company, had looked good. As a reward to the soldiery, he had Cookie Nast pass out extra C-Ration cigarettes, vintage 1952, the kind that turn the fingers brown and give the mouth that hen-house taste of French *Gauloises*.

With the training behind them, the companies of the Berlin Brigade were now ready for the arrival of their Commander-in-chief, President John F. Kennedy.

The June sky was clear, blue, and sunshine rich.. The Germans had a name for it: *Kaiserwetter,* after Emperor Kaiser Wilhelm I. It meant the day was perfect for kings and emperors, or any president who happened to be coming to town.

In their enthusiasm to see the President of the United States, the whole population of West Berlin took the day off. They converged and gathered at *Schöneberger Rathaus,* the town hall, to welcome him.

There, in the middle of the afternoon, over 50,000 Germans packed into the town square and down the boulevards—*Belzig Strasse, Dominicus Damm, Martin Luther Strasse*, and *Stein Strasse*—all cheering their hero to the cry of, "Ken-ne-dy! Ken-ne-dy!"

Above the crowd, in front of the high portico of the *Rathau'* town hall stood the president. With him was the mayor of the city, Willie Brandt, and German Chancellor Konrad Adenauer. They were there to be sure Kennedy wouldn't annex West Berlin. The crowd with all their cheering appeared to want him to. "Ken-ne-dy! –Ken-ne-dy!" they harranged. He was their emperor. And the Emperor wore clothes!

President Kennedy gave a short speech. Whether it was inspirational or not, it mesmerized the multitudes, for they swayed, and they surged, a mass of wedged humanity wild with emotion, all chanting rhapsodically, "Ken-ne-dy! Ken-ne-dy!" They chanted it over and over, as if the magic of the name alone would be enough to bring down the hated Wall, vanquish Communism, or if howled loud and long enough, raise Lazarus. Some said that had he ordered the people of West Berlin to march on the Wall and storm it, they would have in lock step, so great was the enthusiasm of the hour.

At times President Kennedy looked up into the sun and flashed his marvelous teeth. That, and his boyish good looks, energized the crowd. "Ken-ne-dy! Ken-ne-dy!"

Though vocal, his short speech was nothing special. A few platitudes. At the end, he called out to the German people proclaiming, "All free men are Berliners!" Light applause. "Let them (the world) come to Berlin!" More light applause. Then, he ended his speech with the statement, "Ich bin ein Berliner!" (I am a Berliner!) Although the President of the United States had just proclaimed himself a donut. In Germany, *ein Berliner* is a pastry. The crowd, all 100,000 of them, exploded. They went mad. They swayed. They cheered and cheered, "Ken-ne-dy! Ken-ne-dy! Kennedy! Kennedy! Kennedy!" echoing his name to the city's foundations

By the afternoon, the atmosphere was more sober. At Berlin Brigade Army Headquarters everyone stood around, waiting under the hot sun. Military flags, the color guard, the companies, the officers, the diplomats, the 298th Army Band, they all waited expectantly for President Kennedy and his motorcade.

Senior officers were everywhere. Some had even come up from 7th Army and 5th Corps just to get their pictures taken with the president.

There were so many officers in dress uniform their brass competed with the bright afternoon sunlight. Some of the officers' wives complained of the glare, saying it made their makeup run.

In the mean time, the Brigade Companies stood in military formation and at rest along the length of *Clay Allee Boulevard,* the 592nd Signal Company among them. In the afternoon heat they waited, stiffly wishing they could scratch at that spot where the sweat ran down the middle of the back.

The whole morning had been the old Army ritual of "Hurry Up and Wait!" On *Clay Allee,* soldiers and NCOs alike had been hurried off the buses and hustled into position. They stood, company by company, platoon by platoon, ten men across, rank-and-file, three or four squads deep, dressed in cardboard-like creased kaki uniforms, their black polish spit-shined boots, twelve laborious coats of it, and melting, reflecting the sun. For two hours they stood that way on *Clay Allee* while the president and his entourage of senior officers and diplomats ate lunch. Their desert was strawberries and ice cream. In Germany it was the *Erdbeern*— strawberry season.

Across from the company formations, on a wide grassy strip that ran down the middle of *Clay Allee,* a large crowd of Berliners had gathered. It was an estimated crowd of some 5000. They had been there for hours, waiting behind wood police barriers from where they hoped to get a glimpse of their hero. They were in a carnival mood, ambient and relaxed.

Many couples walked hand-in-hand. Others brought picnics and spread blankets on the grass. They ate sandwiches and drank Pepsi, as if waiting for the Central Park concert to begin. The German men stood around in pleated trousers with open-necked shirts, dressed as if for a golf match. In their floral cotton dresses cut deep at the neck, the women looked especially voluptuous, while on the street, not ten yards distant and facing them, the Berlin Brigade soldiers stood shoulder-to-shoulder, watching them from the position of parade rest. Lascivious groaning and utterances could be heard coming from the Army ranks.

"Hey, Yo," hissed Robuck out of the corner of his mouth. "Check out the broad in the red blouse and shorts, will ya?"

"Can't! I'm after the chick at the police barrier to the right," Yorit hissed back out of the corner of his mouth, also standing at parade rest.

In the crowd, moving among them and carrying accordions, were several street musicians. They had come to see President Kennedy as well, and maybe earn a Mark or two.

One musician caught the eye of the children. He played his accordion, with a monkey's head puppet on one hand. The other hand was a metal hook. The hook danced as nimbly as five fingers over the keyboard of the accordion. The original hand had been left on some distant battlefield.

In the white light of the hot afternoon, the Berlin Brigade soldiers watched, wishing they could traverse the couple of yards that separated them from the crowd, the picnics, the pink lemonade, and the girls there who "strutted their stuff" teasingly in front of them. But the soldiers had to stand, rifles at the side, sun in their faces while the sweat trickled down the middle of their backs.

Then, from down the *Clay Allee* the 298 Brigade Army Band struck up the music. Heads turned. It was the anthem, "Hail to the Chief!" President Kennedy was coming—finally, and none too soon. Suffering from heat hydration, two men from Signal Company had already dropped out of the ranks, as did a few from the other companies. Disapproving this, 1stSgt Persilla had them sit in the shade under a tree while he made a note of their names on his clipboard.

1st Sergeant Persilla wore extra thick shoe soles so he would not look too short as President Kennedy drove past. He didn't want to give the president a reason to call out, "Hey, you, Shorty! Outathere!"

Out in front of the company, commander Captain Mellon turned and faced the street and the crowd. He nodded to his first sergeant to stand-by. Immediately, 1stSgt Persilla about-faced and called the company from parade rest to attention. He looked over the three platoons and glowered, as if to say, "Dare you to fuck up on this one!" Satisfied that they were sufficiently intimidated, he returned the company to parade rest position and himself about-face, taking his place behind the company commander.

Along the whole of *Clay Allee*, the Brigade companies stiffened. In a sudden rush, the Berliners moved to the police barriers. Anticipation was in the air. Everyone looked down the *Allee* boulevard toward the distant activity that was brewing there. On their tiptoes, people strained to see over each other's head, jerking their bodies this way and that for a better look.

Only one little girl, a child of about five or six years, did not bother about the expectant activity around her. With her nose just above the police barrier, her interest was straight ahead in front of her at the soldiers in formation. They looked like big shiny toys in their green helmet liners and polished black boots. It was something to wonder about. In the white light of the afternoon sunshine they could be angels, only without wings. She had never seen American soldiers before. The *Bundeswehr*, the German National Army, was never seen in Berlin, nor in any of the towns of West Germany. Having lost two World Wars, they were kept on their compounds behind chain link fences away from the public, in disgrace. So, for the little girl to see real soldiers, or angels, or toys, it was total fascination. She watched them, while behind her her father gripped her shoulders, his own interest directed toward the bustle of activity developing further down *Clay Allee*.

Standing in the first squad, Yorit watched her watch him. He glanced out of the corner of his eye toward 1ˢᵗSgt Persilla, his back was to the company. He glanced at PltSgt Sweechek. The same. Then back at the little girl whose eyes were the size of saucers. From under his helmet and arching an eyebrow, he fired off an exaggerated wink at her she could not miss, followed by a toothy grin. Delighted, she smiled back and waved. That soldier, an angel or a toy, was for real.

In the distance came the sound of cannon firem a 21-gun salute. It was the signal that the president had finished with lunch. "Companyyy, teeen-CHEN!" bellowed Captain Mellon. The other Brigade companies did the same, echoing up Clay Allee. "Companyyy, teeen-CHEN! Companyyy, teeen-CHEN! Companyyy… Companyyy…" one after another.

The motorcade of limousines began to move. It passed the Brigade formations. In the distance, like rolling thunder, one after another, the company commanders called out, "Preseeent…ARMS!" followed by the unified slap of the rifle butts and the rifle salute. It was what the companies had been practicing for two weeks. It was the moment. It was now. "Companny! Preseeent…ARMS!" Slap! It happened one company after another as the president's motorcade limousine passed by. "Compaaany! Preseeent…ARMS!" Slap! "Preseent…ARMS!" Slap! "Prerseent…" And so it went. "Preeesent…ARMS!" "… Preeesent…ARMS!" until it was the turn of the 592ⁿᵈ Signal Company. Captain Mellon snapped the order over his shoulder. "Compannnyyyy! Preseeent…ARMS!" Slam dunk!

Then something happened. Whether it was the threat of 1ˢᵗSergeant Persilla's glower or the charisma of the President of the United States, or all the weeks of training, or the drama of the moment, or perhaps a mishmash of it all, the Brigade's Signal Company, a support company, a *Mox Nix* company, a behind-the-lines company, a bozo company compared to the tough line outfits over at 6th Infantry. Together, the three platoons hit the stocks of their rifles as one. It was something that never quite worked in training. It resembled the grace and perfection of the Radio City Music Hall Rockettes. The soldiers did the sharpest present arms in the history of Brigade. SA—LAP!

Across the street, her blue eyes still the size of saucers, the little German girl watched. She was now convinced the soldiers were not angels, but tin men like her brothers' toys. Above her, one hand waving, the other hand resting on her shoulder, the little girl's father cried out with the roar of the crowd. "Ken-ne-dy! Ken-ne-dy!" The presidential motorcade drove past.

In the motorcade, the West Berlin *Polizei* in white leather jackets, with black pistol belts tight at the waist, were first. Berliners call them, "*die Weisse Mäuse Politzei*." They drove by on heavy BMW motorcycles in a flying wedge formation, gunning the big motors threateningly as they drove slowly. "Not Harleys by the sound of 'em, but I'll take one anyway," one of the soldiers said later. Several black Mercedes limousines, all open convertibles, followed. In the first one, high up, as if on a throne but without a scepter, stood President Kennedy. His face was richly tanned and a bit too wrinkled for a man of some 40 years. A coat hanger appeared wedged at the shoulders of his shiny shark suit, giving him a hatchet-like appearance. With the sun behind him and silhouetted against the sky, he looked as if made of granite, his profile as rigid as the Karl Marx headstone. He looked down and squinted at Signal Company as he passed. No nod of recognition. No smile. No wave. Yet, it was a moment of spiritual quintessence. Here was the enlightenment! The revelation! And zip, the revelation was past.

Two more Mercedes drove past with dignitaries in them, their faces blurred. City Major Willi Brandt? Another followed. It was the media. They were riding in, on, and hanging off of what looked like a bus jalopy. Press photographers leaned out the doors and out the windows; a camera team was on the roof of one with a tripod, film rolling like a scene out of the silent movies. Bringing up the rear came a second wedgie of *Weisse Mäuse Polizei* on BMW motorcycles.

And the cheering? The cheering began as a distant rumble. Gradually, it moved along the crowded barricades of Berliners as the president's motorcade approached. At first it was indistinct, like cheers from a baseball's outfield bleachers. Then it became more focused.

Then   vocal. Then loud. And finally hysterical! "Ken-ne-dy! Ken-ne-dy!" the crowd screamed as the motorcade passed. The people of Berlin cheered, and cheered, and cheered some more. The soldiers, rifle barrels touching the tips of their noses, wanted to cheer too. They wanted to jump up and down like the German crowd in front of them and wave their helmet, but at the enforced position of present arms, they dared not. It was not in the regulations on what to do when saluting the President of the United States.

En mass, the Berliners pushed against the barricades for a glimpse of their prince, President John F. Kennedy, the man who had stood by them when the Wall went up, the man who had stood up to Khrushchev's threats of conquest,. They screamed, yelled, howled, until the crescendo, like rolling thunder, reached its apogee in front of the 592nd Signal Company soldiers. There, across the street from the company, a man held up his baby for absolution. One woman passed out. Others gasped. In the crowd, several people wept. Still others crushed their knuckles to their mouths. Everywhere, little white hankies fluttered above heads. All stood with their arms outstretched, desperate to touch the palpable air of that Kennedy charisma. The earth shook and the curtain rent asunder, the whole atmosphere electric. It was the *Wehrmacht* marching through the Brandenburg Gate, Fredrick Ebert on the balcony announcing the creation of a German Republic, Kaiser Wilhelm from his palace to the crowd on the eve of World War I. It was Babe Ruth hitting his 60th homer. Bob Feller throwing another no hit game. Berlin cheered! Germany cheered! "*Sieg Heil!*" Only the little girl, the one with saucer-like eyes remained unimpressed. She just wanted to take home a tin soldier.

That day, and the days that followed, Americans in uniform could do no wrong. German women came up to them and in broken English invited them on dates. Strangers hailed them on the street. In the *Kneipen and Lokalen* bars it was drinks on the house and "*Prost!*" "Toast!" to President Kennedy and the United States of America—all of America. Even the Prostitute's Trade Union, *die Puffgerwerkschaft*, made a contribution; they had the girls drop prices for any soldier looking for a quickie, and American soldiers were always looking for a quickie.

Of those lilting summer days, being in the US Army had never been so exhilarating. It was a young bachelor's bacchanalian dream come true. In the aftermath of the president's visit and satiated as they were from beer and women, Army re-enlistments surged. It seemed everyone was ready to sign up for an extra four-year hitch in the Army. Only later would it prove calamitous. Many of those re-enlistments went to Viet Nam, some never to come back.

***

Yorit awoke as if from a dream. It was still the month of November. He looked around. The streets were still empty. No traffic. No Germans. Where was everybody? He continued to walk and reflect. He decided to walk up to the U-Bahn subway station at Oscar Helenaheim and from there take an Omnibus, the double-decker bus, back to Andrews Barracks Berlin Brigade and the company.

He was on his way when, from out of the darkness, a stranger approached him, his collar up. He stepped in front of Yorit, bringing his face close to his. "*Es tut mir leid*," (I'm sorry) he said, his voice a mere utter. Then, turning as if embarrassed, he walked away.

Yorit thought that odd. What was he sorry about? He shrugged and continued to walk toward the station, lost in thought. He passed two more homes, again both with singular candles in the front windows. Then it happened. A man in a long leather coat was about to pass him on the street when he stopped abruptly. He gripped Yorit by the sleeve of his Army field jacket. In the shadow of the night his face looked ghoulish, his mouth devoid of lips; where his nose should have been, a hole. The walking dead? He hissed something that Yorit could not understand. Letting go of his sleeve, the walking dead quickly stepped away, leaving Yorit standing there, a gasp in his throat.

On *Thiel Allee* a woman walked up to him in a quick gait as if to say hello. She looked at him and put her hand to her mouth. Turning, she rushed away. Yorit watched her pass in and out of the streetlight like a phantom and disappear into the dark. It was then he heard the call, the kind that carries on the quiet, that makes one stop to ponder. It was distant, yet sharp, a melancholy call like an echo from the other side of a valley. It caught in the skeletal limbs of the leafless, November trees. The cry hung there. "*Der Kennedy ist tooot!*" (Kennedy is deeead!) Yorit hesitated. "*Der Kennedy ist tooot!*" the phantom voice cried out again.

On the other side of the street, fleeting figures passed under a streetlights, warped and shapeless figures as if out of an August Macke painting,. The y appeared to be in a hurry. One of them detached itself from the group. It was an older woman. She crossed the street and came toward Yorit. "Wie loves ihm," she said, her English unsure.

"Who?" he asked.

"*Ihm!*"

Yorit looked at her, then at a nearby house. He pointed at it. "Ma'am, tell me. That candle in the window there. What does it mean?"

She looked toward the house. "*Das? Das bedeutet, ein Sohn ist gefallen.*" (It means a son has fallen in battle.) she answered with a shiver. And hurried back across the street to catch up with her companions.

Now Yorit understood. The president's death was not only a shock to Americans, but a shock to the Berliners as well, to all the Germans. John Kennedy was their president too. His death was the reason for the window candles. It was their way, the German way, to say farewell to a son who had fallen in battle. By touching him, Robert Yorit, the simple soldier, the kid from Cleveland, the Germans could touch Kennedy, touch his wounds, touch his coffin. Touch! In Yorit, they could come to grips with the magnitude of the tragedy. He was their American touchstone for a good cry in the sanctuary, unusual for Prussians who were innured on being tough.

Nearby, the lights of a church glowed dull from the arched windows. One of the doors was open to the street. Inside, lights from unseen devotional candles flickered on a barren wall. A lone figure lingered in the doorway. The figure then stepped inside, throwing a large shadow of itself up against the barren wall. Gliding away, the shadow diminished, then vanished. Yorit moved on.

On *Gary Strasse* several people walked quickly up the street. They seemed to be in a hurry, all going in one direction, toward the U-Bahn subway station at Oskar Heleneheim.

Two women passed him, university students by their appearance. One of them stopped. She turned and gave Yorit an understanding smile the way the bereaved do in search of solace. Under the street light he could see that she was attractive, the kind of woman a man would crawl after on all fours, especially soldiers. "*Kommen Sie mit uns,*" (Come with us.) she invited.

Surprised at the request, Yorit looked around. "Who me?"

"*Kommen Sie mit uns.* You come, yes?" she repeated, solemn and without explanation. He could not think of a reason to say no. Though still in Army work fatigues, he was off duty. He would not be missed back at company, not yet, anyway. The other women joined them. Yorit smiled. This was getting interesting. She told him her name was Sonja, a law student at the FU, the Free University. There was an event that was taking place at *Schöneberger Rathaus*, the West Berlin city hall. "*Kommen Sie mit.*"

On the Omnibus, they talked in low voices. She knew some English. As they talked, Yorit looked around. Some of the bus passengers stared at him, not the way Germans usually do at strangers, down their noses, but with sympathy, a concern, as if sharing a loss of something universal. It was the reason the Omnibus was almost full at this hour; everyone was going to the same destination, wherever that was. "*Wir sind bald da.* We are soon there," Sonja said, her voice tired.

Yorit looked out the window. The bus were somewhere on the *Rhein Strassee* in the Steglitz district. He could see the bars were where off duty soldiers usually hung out were dark. He never knew them to close up. West Berlin was an open city. The *Kneipen* bars were always open till the last drunk ordered breakfast. But tonight the bars were closed. The prostitutes who usually hung out on street corners were not around either. As for the *Polizei*, they were nowhere to be seen. It was as if the whole world was in mourning. *Unusual*, he thought, but then again, the whole day was unusual.

At each stop, a few people got on the bus, some of them carrying unlit *Fackeln*, (hand torches). He asked Sonja what the torches were for. "You shall see," she said softly, her voice suggestive. He looked at her. It was the wrong time, the wrong place; nevertheless, he found himself feeling romantic. He touched her knee with his. She did not move hers.

Of the passengers, no one spoke. They just stood there, rocking lightly with the movement of the Omnibus, listening to the whine of the motors, the wheels on the pavement, the whole atmosphere a Max Beckman composition. The only American, a soldier, on a bus full of Germans, Yorit felt himself getting spooked. "Sonja, would you please tell me where we are going?" She smiled and took his hand in hers. He relaxed.

At *Innsbruck Strasse* in the District of Schöneberg, the Omnibus stopped. The passengers got off. Outside, a large crowd had already gathered. The side streets were blocked off. The Berlin *Polizei* were everywhere. A massive procession was already in progress, with many people carrying lit torches, the *Fackeln*. Some cars tried to get through the crowd but the drivers, giving up, got out and joined the procession.

Getting off the Omnibus, Yorit stepped into the street and followed the push of the crowd. He looked around. Sonja was gone. "Uh,oh! Now what?" he asked himself. Not knowing what to do or where he was, he climbed up on the base of a nearby metal utility pole, hoping to spot her; instead, he caught an unexpected sight. In every direction, as far as the eye could see, was a vast undulating procession. Germans, several thousand of them, were walking the width and length of the boulevard, many carrying torches that bobbed up and down as they walked. There were no cheers, no calling out. There was only the sound of shuffling footsteps on the pavement—or was it the rush of sand pebbles tumbling on the shore? Where were they going, and what for? In many apartment building windows, singular candles flickered, pinpoint beacons that glowed out against the clear cold of the November night. It was then Yorit recalled what the woman had said to him earlier, "*Ein Sohn ist gefallen.*" The people of West Berlin were demonstrating the loss of *their* son, President John F. Kennedy. He was, after all, "*Ein Berliner.*"

Yorit stepped down from the street pole and joined the torch light procession. Seeing the American soldier, Germans drew up to him, walked with him. Some shook his hand. A few embraced him. They touched him, rubbed his shoulder, one woman kissed him on the cheek. Someone handed him a lit torch, the fire flickering. Next to him, the people locked their arms in his and together they marched down the *Kolonnon Strasse* toward the *Schöneberger Rathaus* and city hall. On *Rathaus Platz* the torch light procession came to a stop. They had reached City Hall. A large crowd had already assembled.

On the city hall portico, where six months before President Kennedy had given his famous Berlin speech, stood the mayor of the city, *Burgermeister* Willy Brandt. He stood alone against the dark facade of the majestic building. He was in the middle of a eulogy. The crowd listened in silence, faces lifted, the lighted torches snapping in the night. Yorit felt a hand slide under his arm. It was Sonja. She gave him a smile. He was glad.

Suddenly, from somewhere beyond the throng, two spotlights snapped on—air raid lights by the looks of them. It startled the crowd. They were hard lights, like the ones used during World War II to pick out the B-17 bombers from the night sky as they flew over the Berlin to bomb drop. The hard beam of the lights flashed over the heads of the crowd. On the other side of Rathaus Square they lit up two apartment buildings. Then, moving slowly, the beams climbed the walls of the two apartment buildings and stopped. There, ten stories up and standing on the edge of the apartment roofs as if about to leap off were two U.S. Army buglers from the 298 Army Band. They were in their dress blues and gold and standing at attention, trumpets under their arms. In the beams of the air raid lights they faced each other. Below them stood the crowd. Instantly, as if on command, the two buglers snapped the trumpets to their lips. Yorit, the only soldier in the mass below, felt hands grip his arms and shoulders. Against the night sky, with the hard air raid beams focused on the two buglers, they began to play the Army's military taps, the mourning taps for the dead. First one bugler played, then the other, back and forth across the space of the Rathaus Square. Languid and spiritual, the bugle echoes carried on the night, out and over the masses below, as if calling for the divided city to unite.

Of the multitude, no one moved, no one spoke, a thousand pin-prick torch lights flickering in silence. Like the peeling back of an onion, emotions surfaced and strong men wept. West Berlin mourned. *Ein Sohn ist gefallen.*

West Berlin in Mourning, Thousands Pay Homage

THE BERLIN OBSERVER

VOL. 19, NO. 48 ★ ★ ★ Edition   BERLIN BRIGADE   ★ ★ ★ Edition   FRIDAY, 29 NOVEMBER 1963

JFK's Death Stuns Outpost Residents

One week after the death of John F. Kennedy, the city which gave him the warmest welcome in its history continues to mourn his passing.

Many Americans here in the Divided City feel that the grief of the people of West Berlin may very well be unequalled anywhere outside the United States.

For three days following the shooting of the American President forty-thousand Berliners made their way to U.S. Headquarters on Clayallee to sign a condolence book. It represented their effort "to show the people of America how sorry we are to hear of his death" said one woman waiting to sign her name. The crowd became so great that instead of closing the doors as scheduled the American Headquarters remained open day and night to accommodate mourners.

"These people really cared a lot for the man" said a Berlin Brigade Honor Guard member who volunteered to remain on duty for 15 hours a day to assist elderly people in placing flowers at the base of a large picture of the deceased President set up in the main hall of the building. "After they sign the book they often won't move", said Private First Class Alfred Galloway.

"They just stare at the picture and sometimes mutter to themselves. It's as if he were one of their kin."

Another focal point of the Berlin demonstration of common grief was Schoeneberg Rathaus, West Berlin City Hall. At midnight on November 22, four hours after news of the President's death reached Berlin, 30,000 grieving people stood silently in front of the city hall to hear Governing Mayor Willy Brandt tell them with tears streaming down his face "America has lost a president; Berlin has lost a friend".

The following evening 60,000 Berlin youths bearing lighted candles and torches walked in dead silence from the Airlift Memorial near Tempelhof Airport to the square in front of city hall. Even the military bus bringing U.S. servicemen from Tempelhof had difficulty getting through the crowd.

The marchers followed the same route that Kennedy took on his visit to the city five months previous, almost to the day. In windows from where they had cheered the American President last June the Berliners placed lighted candles symbolizing their loss. There was hardly a habitable

(Continued on page 8)

General Polk Leads American Community in Memorial Service

Major General James H. Polk, U.S. Commander, Berlin spoke to Americans at a special service held in the Sports Center Gymnasium Monday morning concerning the death of President John F. Kennedy. The General said:

Today at this hour all over Europe, men of the United States Armed Forces together with our friends, are gathered to honor the memory of John Fitzgerald Kennedy, our late President and Commander-in-Chief.

It is difficult indeed for us to comprehend the real loss at his untimely death, the brutality, the savagery, the utter needlessness of this tragic occurrence. The whole world recoils at the event. And it is best not to dwell on the fact. Rather we must accept and mourn his passing. But better still we can recall — most of us here at first hand — the tremendous personal impact President Kennedy had on this city. We are indeed fortunate that we are able to remember our own President on this occasion, in the setting of last June 26th — at the spontaneous enthusiasm, the joy, the love that was showered on him by the citizens of Berlin, and of his unstinted response to their tributes on that memorable day. It was a day none of us shall ever forget. And you will recall some of his words to the American Garrison on that occasion, "You are on a sense the nerve-head of a long line of your colleagues in arms who stand guard and watch in dozens of countries around the globe,

and a wall to let them know what you are doing."

John F. Kennedy was our Commander-in-Chief to the most literal sense of the word. Not only in his broad direction of the armed forces, but more particularly in his understanding and upholding support for the Berlin garrison by which he demonstrated to the world on every occasion his determination to maintain Berlin as a free and viable city. His commitment to Berlin was total — he stood solidly behind us in every crisis just at spell his successor — and we could ask for no more.

To his devoted wife and family, we can only say that we share their grief, and we admire their courage in this adversity, and we send them our deepest sympathy.

It is most difficult for me to try to express our collective feelings at this moment. Therefore, with your indulgence, I will quote a brief statement dispatched to us by the acting Secretary of State as most appropriate for this occasion.

"A great President is tragically dead. At a critical moment in history, he evoked from his own nation and from men who cherish human freedom and peace everywhere, the confidence and the faith to move forward.

In his person there were courage, grace, and an understanding of the responsibility that power carries with it. There was also a compassionate sense of the meaning of poverty, fear, and in-

We are proud of you and we appreciate justice — and a will to lift them

In those years he set a course, at home and on the world scene, which visibly saved the hopes of men that freedom could triumph without war and that free men could, by their own devices, despite their lives and those of their children.

He does for his strength on the deepest traditions of our nation. As we grief we face the future, we draw from the living memory of his dedication to those endeavors — and from his unforgettable courage — the will to carry on.

Mayor Albertz Renames Square

Dear American Friends, Dear Berliners,

This place of enthusiasm has today become a place of sorrow and of tears. The radiant sun of June 26 has gone down. It has become very still in this hour of parting from this good and just, this vigilant and wise, this young and proud man whose name was John F. Kennedy, and who was President of the United States of America — this man who was powerful yet so heavily burdened by his office; this man who looked toward the future yet was by no means understood by all — not by all Germans. Now this man I saw in

this city for years; the bond that ties the most powerful nation of the free world to the rich it is bearing together with us Berliners and the proud recognition that the Berliners themselves are accomplishing so much that the President considered it an honor to say "Ich bin ein Berliner" — "I am a Berliner".

All this cannot, all this must not be at an end with the death of John F. Kennedy. I have seen enough dead people, and I know what death is, especially such a death, a death by the hand of a murderer, a violent death as the

A Carton of Cigarettes

Yorit looked up from the letter he was writing. "No!" he said.

"Yo, old buddy, come on. I need the favor," persisted Cecil Jonas, standing next to the desk in Yorit's quarters.

"Cecil, if you need help, it is still no. But, if you need a favor, then I might consider it."

"There's ten bucks in the deal for you," said Jonas, drawing the money out of his pocket.

"Ten dollars! Why didn't you say that to begin with? What kind of a favor is it you want?"

Jonas waved the ten dollar bill under Yorit's nose. "Make a cigarette run for me. I got six cartons of Camels that have to be delivered to a German client of mine."

"Black market cige-boos, huh?"

"Is there any another kind?"

Yorit thought for a moment. "Hm, ten bucks?" Jonas nodded. "All right, Cecil. give me the address. Say, wait a minute. What if the guard at the main gate stops me? This is a black market deal, and you know how the Army feels about that," said Yorit, running a finger across his throat.

"Do you want to earn the ten smackers or don't you?"

Yorit got up from his desk. "I'm broke, otherwise I wouldn't do it."

"You'll do it then?"

"Pay me and I'm gone."

Grinning, Jonas handed Yorit the money and the gym bag containing the cigarette contraband.

"Oh, one question though, Jonas buddy. How come you don't run the black market cigarettes yourself?"

Jonas shrugged. "Me? What if I get caught?"

Outside, at the Post Main Gate Yorit hesitated, then stepped up the guard's shack. Two other soldiers joined him. All three flashed their Army off-post passes. The gate guard, a Headquarters Company man, waved them through, Yorit included. He did not bother to check Yorit's gym bag with the contraband inside, something he should have done as a post gate guard. It was the regulations. Like most Army pencil-pushing cabinet filers, the HHC man was indifferent to guard duty control. A 6th Infantryman guard would have had him field strip his gym bag. Yorit was relieved. He did not have to bribe the guard with the back issue of the *Playboy Magazine* he carried, just in case. In the gym bag, it was open to centerfold on top of the six cartons. For some soldiers, the *Playboy* centerfold was the closest they come to sex while in the army.

It was early evening when Yorit stepped off the streetcar. It was the *Elbe Strasse*. The address he was looking for was not far away. Checking the adress, he looked around. He found it. It was an apartment building with a noble entrance, typical of many *Grundelzeit* structures in the near city. He stepped up to the *Jugendstil* door, an art object in itself, and pushed it open. On the hallway wall was a row of polished wood mailboxes with the names of the building's occupants etched on white ceramic tabs in old *Sütterlin* letters. One name read "Familie Schmitz, 2D." It was the family Yorit was looking for.

He climbed an elegant staircase that looked like a grand piece of stage scenery. On the second floor he found apartment D. There was no bell, only a brass knocker in the middle of a door. He knocked. A minute and another knock later the door opened, but only a crack. The moist eye of an elderly woman looked out. She was obviously suspicious of any stranger knocking at this time of day. After 12 years of Nazi rule, then Communism, then Berlin local government politics, such suspicious behavior was understood. *"Ja, bitte?"* she asked.

"Genädige Frau," (Gracious lady, a title of respect for elderlywomen) "I have the cigarettes you ordered," Yorit stated kindly.

The woman opened the door wider. She was dressed simply, with a shawl over her shoulders. Her white hair was tied back in a bun. She looked at him with large eyes. She cocked her head, unsure as if trying to place his accent. *"Sind Sie Amerikaner?"*

"Yes, madam. I'm the American you are expecting. I have the cigarettes you wanted." he answered in his broken German.

"Moment, *bitte*," she said lightly, closing the door.

Yorit wondered if Jonas had given him the correct address when the door opened again. This time it was an elderly man—her husband, he guessed. He wore a dark wool sweater and old trousers held up by suspenders. His right hand revealed knurled stubs that had once been fingers. Yorit noticed it immediately. *"Sind Sie Amerikaner?"* he asked with some hesitation.

"Yes, I'm an American. Mr. Jonas, your soldier friend, asked me to contact you. The cigarettes, you know." Yorit hoped his broken German was clear enough to be understood.

"Moment, *bitte*," said old man, closing the door again.

What's all the mystery about? Yorit wondered. He considered leaving, but he didn't. A couple cartons of cigarettes were big money; besides, Jonas had already paid him ten dollars for the job. After several minutes the door opened, this time wide open. *"Bitte, kommen Sie herein!"* the old man invited, with a gesture of his knurled hand.

The apartment's hallway was dark, with several closed doors. At one door they stopped. The old man pushed it open. It was the living room. Yorit followed him in.

The room was heavy and airless, the furniture well worn. No suggestion of wealth here. The old *Frau* stood stiffly at the dining table in front of a bay window. She held a tray in front of her, with a bottle of wine and three glasses. She trembled as if excited about something. In the silence of the room the glasses tinkled against each other. Behind her, sunlight glowed through the thin curtains, giving her the appearance of a tired angel. The husband immediately stepped to his wife's side. *"Hertzliche willkommen in unserem Haus!"* (Welcome to our home) he announced, a little too loudly. The invitation startled Yorit.

Carefully, the old *Frau* set the trembling tray on the table. Her husband proceeded to uncork the bottle, nodding for Yorit to join them at the table. He set the gym bag down on the floor as the old man filled the three glasses with white wine. He handed one glass to his guest.

"My wife and I want to thank you for your kindness," he said in German. Yorit nodded, not sure if he understood. After two years as a soldier in West Berlin, he could understand enough of the German language to get by. "We—my wife and I," the old man continued, "are most grateful for this moment. Never have we had the opportunity to thank you for what you and America have done for us until...until now."

Yorit smiled, unsure. "Oh, really? Well, it was nothing. It's in my nature to be helpful when I can. Ah, what exactly did I do? Oh, you mean the cigarettes! I almost forgot about them. Here!" he said, picking up the gym bag from the floor and setting it on the edge of the table. He took out the cellophane-wrapped cartons of Camel cigarettes, taking care not to reveal the *Playboy* to the couple. It was still open to the nude centrefold. This was not the moment to flash Miss January's boobs.

The old man stared at the carton, a puzzled expression on his face. "Zigaretten?"

"Yes, it is what you ordered," said Yorit in his broken German.

The *Frau* looked at her husband, surprised. He sucked in his breath and looked back at her; both seemed bewildered. Reaching over, he picked up one cigarette carton and ran his knurled fingers over it.

Her pale eyes wide open, the woman smiled at Yorit. "The reason we invited you into our home, young man, was because we wished to thank you, to thank you for the CARE *Paketen* Amerika sent to us those years after the war."

"CARE *Paketen*?' You mean packages, as in Care packages?" Yorit guessed, unsure of what they were taking about.

"*Yawohl*!" (Yes!)," replied the old Frau. "We always wanted to thank *Amerika* for the C.A.R.E. *Paketen* we received. We, my husband and I, never had the chance until, well, this moment when you knocked at our door."

The old husband nodded. "You must know, those years after the war were terrible years for many families in Berlin, in all of Germany."

The old *Frau* interrupted, her voice tremulous. "We were a starving people. We had so little to eat, only a some potatos, if that. Then you—Amerika—came to Berlin and brought us the cartons marked, "C.A.R.E!" *Es war unglaublish!* (It was unbelievable!) After the war, in 1946" she went on, "the *Paketen* arrived here, not once, but so many times. In them were cans of fruits and cans of vegetables and meat in cans. We shall never forget."

"*Und Schkolade!*" noted the old man, referring to the bars of chocolate he had often unpacked.

"And the shoes," she said gleefully. "It fit our son. We had no shoes for him to wear. Many children had no shoes. Such gifts brought only joy on those dark winter days in 1946. *Oh, Gott sägnet Amerika!*" (God bless America), she uttered, her voice lush with gratitude. "We are so thankful."

With moisture in her eyes, the old woman stepped around the table and up to Yorit. She looked deep into his eyes. He gave her a nod and a half-smile, not knowing what to expect. She grabbed him by the shoulders and embraced him and kissed him on the cheek. Thenm turning away, she took a handkerchief from her pocket and dabbed at the moisture in her eyes. The husband, also with gratitude, reached out and shook Yorit's hand,.

Yorit looked appreciatvely at the two Berlin Germans in front of him. He thought for a moment, than he remembered when he was six years old and a kid back home in Cleveland, Ohio. He and and his brother Russell would stand at the kitchen table with Mom and help her pack cans of food and sweets and toys into boxes, those boxes marked in bold black letters, "C.A.R.E.".

Once every few months Mom would pack a C.A.R.E.package box with canned goods for the European needy. "We got to help the old country," she used to say as she put in coffee, Cambell Soup cans, and General Mills products like Mother's Oats cereals. There were homemade preserves from the garden too, personally canned. There was also canned Spam known to the Germans as *Hackfleish*. It was the most popular meat product among the starving people, though as kids, Yorit and Russell were glad to see it go. Yorit nodded reflectively, "Oh, yeah, the C.A.R.E. packages."

Yorit's mother would fill the C.A.R.E. package while he and his brother, Russell, put in some old play things for the German kids "Over There," as families used to say. They would add a box of crayons, a coloring book, and an old yoyo or two, not to forget the occasional bag of marshmallows and candy. Dad would take the C.A.R.E. packages to the post office on West 130th Street and Lorraine Avenue and drop it off. Being six years old at the time, his brother Russ age eleven, they did not know that some place called Europe, a far- away place, was in ruins and the people there desperate and starving .

It was under the Truman Administration, back in 1946, that the C.A.R.E. package program was set up. It was to help the people of Europe whose homes and jobs had been destroyed in the war. In America, it became a family project, not for one family, but for thousands of American families, tens of thousands of families, throughout the United States. The families would fill up the C.A.R.E. packages, bring them to the post offices from where they were send off to war-torn Europe. Now, here, facing this German family, the Kid from Cleveland, Robert Yorit, a soldier in the US Army, understood; he understood now why his father used to get angry when he or Russell would leave food on their dinner plates. "Eat!" he would scold. "The people of Europe are starving!"

Looking at the German couple in front of him, Yorit understood indeed, for these two old folks were once the starving people of Europe. In thanking him, a soldier in the U.S. Army's Berlin Brigade, they were thanking America and showing gratitude for that great humanitarian program called C.A.R.E..

With a light bow, Yorit could only say, "Ma'am, you are most welcome," and reaching out, he shook hands with the old man, but he cringed as he did. He had never shaken hands with knurled knuckles before. The old man had lost his fingers at the Front.

"All right now, down to business. Sir, this is what you ordered," he said, picking up one of the Camel cartons on the table. The couple stared at Yorit and the carton of cigarettes as if they were bars of gold.

"Mr. Soldier, this is too much," said the old husband, his voice shaky. I have not smoked *Amerikanishe Zigaretten* in years. They are impossible to buy, and expensive. How can we ever thank you?

Yorit wanted to say, "Sir, you can start first by paying me," but didn't. He sensed something was amiss here.

"*So ein Geschenk*! (What a present) We are overwhelmed," giggled the old *Frau*. "*Amerika* is so good to us Germans."

Yorit gasped, not sure if he understood right. " *Ein Geschenk*? You mean *ein Geschenk* as in, as in...a present? But *Frau* Schmitz, this is..."

"Oh, you have *Zigaretten* for *die Familie Schmitz* too? They live above us, on the next floor," said the old husband.

"Mr. Soldier, how can we ever pay you for this *Geschenk*? We have so little money," said the old *Frau*, her smile perpetual.

"*Geschenk*?" Yorit squeeked weakly.

"Ah, just one moment," said the old husband, holding up a finger from his good hand. "*Liebling, bringst Du mir zwei Flaschen Rheinhessen*." (Dear, bring me two bottles of Rhinehessen wine.)

The old *Frau* quickly stepped into the kitchen. She returned not only with the bottles of wine, but a half a fruitcake, *ein Lebkuchen*, wrapped in tin foil. Home made! She had baked it herself. Paralyzed, Yorit stood, unable to speak.

"Here, take this," she said, with a heartfelt smile as she carefully set the fruitcake with the two wine bottles in his gym bag. She pretended not see the *Playboy* magazine open to Miss January. "It is not much, but it is something for your kindness."

Yorit looked at the Camel cartons neatly set out on the white table cloth, a small fortune. "But...but..."

"We are so fortunate to have *Amerika* as a friend," said the old *Frau*.

The husband's smile creaked with gratitude. " *Vielen, vielen danke.* (Thank you oh, so much.) Now, please, another glass of wine before you go."

Back at the Signal Company barracks, a jovial Jonas bounced into Yorit's room quarters. "Hey, Yoyo, you're back already? Cool! How did the deal go? Got my-yy money, honey? Ha,ha!" he asked in Southern, emphasizing the word, "money"

Yorit lay on his bunk, one empty bottle of Rhinehessen white wine on the floor, the other just broken open. It stood on his foot locker. Slowly, he sat up. "Ah, Jonesie, buddy," he slurred. "Sit down and have a glass of wine with me, will ya? Here's some homemade fruitcake too. So, you're from Louisiana, are ya? Is it true what they say about Southern hospitality?"

The Brits

The army M151 jeep passed by the *Berlin Funkturm*, a radio tower similar to the Eiffel Tower, but without the majesty. It turned on to *Mauern Allee* and there entered the British Army Sector of West Berlin. It was Friday evening and the traffic was heavy. A light rain fell as the Army jeep passed the neo-classical structure of exhibition halls built during the Third Reich. The architecture, monumental in appearance, was a contrast to the Lego-looking building block structures of contemporary Berlin.

Looking out, Bravo turned away from the window. He was in the jeep's front seat next to Lavoss, who was driving. "I still say it's not the right thing to do."

Lavoss stopped for a red light. "Why not?"

Bravo glanced over his shoulder at Yorit and Pereski. They were sitting in the back of the jeep, on the wheel housings, the squat VCR-10 communication-radio, its Porky Pig dimensions between them. "Because we were not invited," said Bravo.

Lavoss flipped on the windshield wipers. It was starting to rain. "Look, Frank, the Limey Sergeant invited me to the British NCO club for a couple beers. So I bring along a buddy or two. What's wrong with that?"

"That's just it. He just invited you, not us."

The streetlight changed to green. The jeep moved with the traffic. Lavoss glanced at Bravo. "Frank, we're all here in Berlin as Allies, ain't we? Besides, the Brits are a hospitable bunch of guys. They wouldn't mind if we walked into their pub to soak up some suds. It gives us a reason to invite them to our post."

"But it just ain't done," Bravo insisted.

Lavoss looked to the right, then to the left to be sure where he was in traffic. "We're not far now."

"It just ain't done."

"You said that."

"Don't make a big deal out of it, Frank," Pereski interrupted from the back of the jeep. "Back home at Penn State where I studied, the Delta Gammas would invite one guy from my fraternity, the Phi Kappa Sigmas, and half the fraternity would show up for the booze-out."

"Delta Gamma?"

"That's a woman sorority."

"Yes, and all physical education majors," added Yorit. "I know the sorority. At my school, Kent State, the babes there are known to be testosterone types. They drink, play volleyball, and arm wrestle like us men."

Lavoss switched on the headlights. "Let's see, what was that Limey guy's name again? Sergeant Sidney, I think he said. Yes, Sarge Sidney."

The jeep lurched, throwing Pereski and Yorit against the vehicle's canvas wall. Yorit grabbed the metal staves supporting the roof. "Easy on those turns, there, Al. We're sliding around like a game of 'slip-the-soap' in the Army showers." (It was the soldier joke because they all showered together.)

It was a Friday evening. Lavoss had sequestered an Army jeep from the motor pool and found himself and his buddies in the British Sector of West Berlin, stuck in a traffic jam behind a line of cars. Impatient, and typical of youth, he turned the steering wheel abruptly and jumped the line, cutting off a green Mercedes. The driver rebuked him with a long blast on the boat horn Mercedes cars are known to have. "Up yours, Kraut!" he yelled out, as if the other driver could hear him.

Yorit looked out the plastic back window of the cabin. "I wouldn't argue with that German. He's driving a Mercedes 230 and it outweighs us. We'd never win in a game of 'chicken' against him."

"He would have to catch us first;" grumped Lavoss over his shoulder, down-shifting and popping the clutch as he spoke. The M151 Ford jeep snorted and rose up on its axle the way jeeps are trained to do and jumped the white mid-stripe that separates traffic. The oncoming cars scattered. Drivers braked. Other swerved. They shouted epithets and waved fists.

Lavoss, the quintessential marksman with a rifle, was the best shot in the company. He fired expert both with the M-15 and the M-1, and drove expert with the Ford M151 jeep.. Behind the wheel he could knock dust off any passing car in traffic. He did just that in driving past the BMW. It made all three of his passengers, Bravo, Yorit, and Pereski, gasp.

"We lost that Mercedes," shouted Yorit, thankful they did not hit anyone, "but now we got a BMW chasing us!" The driver was waving his fist and pointing to his head the way Germans do when angry.

"Let him chase!" Lavoss shouted above the engine. Down-shifting for RPMs, he continued to zigzag the traffic. He lost the BMW and anyone else who dared to give chase.

From a Berlin squad car, the German *Polizei*, the police, watched the jeep's antics as it passed his parked vehicle.

The squad car was the typical VW Beetle, painted shrill green with a little blue light on the middle of the roof. It had a four-cylinder engine that did not match the horsepower of a M151. The *Polizist* driver could only shrug and watch. They did, however, grab the BMW driver and ticketed him for reckless driving. "Why ticket me and not the *Amies*?" he protested in German.

"Because you interfered with the Allied occupation forces defending our city," the *Polizist* scolded. The M151 jeep was long gone.

At an intersection, the stoplight signal turned yellow, slowing the traffic. Lavoss drove through as if there was no stoplight at all. There followed a mighty WOOSH! of air brakes, followed by the stutter of heavy metal and the blast of a truck horn.

Bravo sucked in his breath and gripped the dashboard. "What was that, a freight train?"

Unconcerned that he and his three passengers were almost flattened by a semi five-ton truck, Lavoss continued merrily on his way.

Bravo dabbed his lip where he had bitten it. He looked back at Yorit and Pereski. They were wide-eyed from the shock at almost being crushed to death. "Would anyone care to change places with me?"

"What for?"

"I wet myself."

On *Heer Strasse*, the jeep bounced and jumped the curb, landing half on, half off the sidewalk. They were there. The British Army Club.

Yorit reached over and grabbed Lavoss by the collar of his field jacket. "You almost got us killed, birdbrain! That was just plain dumb-ass reckless driving. Not cool at all."

"You're still alive, ain't ya?"

"Yes, but just barely!"

Trembling from the ride, the four men got out and looked around.

The British Club was a post-war building, non-descript,. The ground floor had once been a car dealership for Izeta and Messerschmitt autos, according to a worn sign taped to the plate glass window. Now empty, the dealership looked like an off-track betting office. A brass plate at the side entrance read "British NCO & Enlisted Service Club."

"This is it," said Lavoss, folding the piece of paper with the address and putting it in his pocket.

He pulled the entrance door open. Inside, the large circular staircase was well lit. From the floor above, voices could be heard. Feeling like intruders, they hesitated. They did not know what to expect, for they, as Americans, had never met the British before, not really. Only on duty for formal ceremonies or during military field exercises did the two armies run across each other; otherwise, never. According to the newspapers, the British did have great credentials as a people: Winston Churchill, Noel Coward, Arthur Conan Doyle, Scotland Yard, Waterloo Bridge, fog, Lawrence of Arabia, Berthrend Russell, Charles Dickens, David Niven, and of late, the Beatles, not to mention that upstart rock-n-roll group called the Rolling Stones.

The four signalmen mounted the circular staircase with some trepidation. Here was the great unknown. The unspoken question was, who were the British anyway? Above a large door at the top of the stairway hung two crossed regimental flags and a German Mauser rifle, symbols of conquest.

Bravo scratched his nose in thought. "I wonder, do the British speak like us?"

"No, the Brits don't talk like us; they talk like you!" said Yorit. "They colonized New Jersey."

Bravo lightened up. "You mean they talk in Joy-zay? I like'm already."

Carefully, Pereski pushed open the door and looked in. "Hey, wait a minute, wait a minute. I'm not going in there. Some of them Limey-Brit guys are wearing skirts."

Lavoss looked through the door with him. "Those are not skirts, dummy; they're Scottish kilts."

"I don't care what the name is, I'm not going in there. What if the Scottish kilt guy asks me to dance?"

"You curtsy and say thank you, the way you were taught back at basic training. What else."

Bravo and Yorit looked in too. "They're only soldiers wearing their traditional regimental dress."

Bravo pointed at the Sporran bag that hung at the waist of one of the men at the bar. "Yeah, and since when is wearing a woman's purse regimental dress? And them socks! Up to the knees. Argyles! I'm not going to dance with him."

Pereski pulled Bravo around. "Hold on, Frank. You got something against the English?"

"Not really. It's just that if someone wears a skirt and a purse around his waist, you don't expect him to have a mustache."

Pushing the reluctant Bravo in front of them and laughing, the three Americans entered the foreign territory—the British NCO Club.

The club was well lit. Unit flags and insignias hung from yard arms that covered light-painted walls. There were two trophy cases with tarnished cups; one had a soccer ball with the date written on it in big letters: 1957. In the middle of the room were simple tables and straightback chairs. Several were occupied by soldiers dressed in the standard wool uniforms of the British Army of the Rhein. The soldiers sitting there talked over foamy pints of beer. At the back of the club was a long bar and an enormous mirror that reflected a wide selection of colored whiskeys and gins. The Americans stared. They had never seen such quantities of liquor in one place before. The bottles twinkled from the backdrop lights. Pereski's broad smile told them what he was thinking. "Fellas, we just found the candy store."

One man, wearing a tartan kilt, which Bravo took to be a skirt, straightened up. He was a large broad-shouldered man with big hands. He was the first to see the Americans enter. Standing at the bar, he put down his pint of beer and wiped his handlebar mustache with a slow, menacing motion. He checked over the new arrivals, not quite sure how to respond to strangers in foreign-looking Army work fatigues. Were they the French or were they Russian?

From an alcove, a dart game was in progress. It stopped when the strangers entered. Its four players, two of them in regimental kilts, turned and watched, as did several men seated at the tables. No one moved. They all checked out the strangers as if they had just climbed out of a Petri dish.

"Where's your Sergeant Sidney?" Yorit asked Lavoss.

Lavoss looked around. "He ain't here."

"What now?"

Bravo glanced at Pereski. "I don't like this, Paul."

"Neither do I."

"I smell trouble," Yorit whispered

Sniffing out loud to brush away the uncertainty, Lavoss slapped himself on the chest. "Well, when in doubt begin with salutations, they say back home," He stepped forward with his arm raised the way Captain John Smith did when he met Chief Powhatan, the father of Pocahontas. "Hoow! I come in peace, rape, and pillage."

The men in the club eyed him suspiciously. "Blamey! 'e speakin' 'nglish, 'e is," said one soldier.

"Can it be they're Yanks?" asked another man.

"Gentlemen," Lavoss continued, "a contingent of the 592nd Signal Company, Berlin Brigade, the American sector, has come to inform you that we are on a beer and whiskey mission. Bartender, set up the house, if you please!" he said, slapping a 20 Mark note on the bar top. At 50 Pfennig-a-pint, that was big money. "I propose round one in honor of her Majesty the Queen and her Army of the Rheine...cough-cough!"

"Well said!" applauded one of the British soldiers, an NCO by the wide chevrons on his waist jacket sleeve.

" 'e sounds like a dri'k'n chap to me-e, Mates" said another.

The bartender, wearing sleeve garters and a bow tie, proceeded to pull at the large tap from the bar's fountain head, drawing Whitney's White Cape Ale into pint glasses. "Come up 'ere, mates! Let's be 'ospi'able now," he encouraged. The ice was broken.

The Army of the Rhine soldiers jumped to the bar with a wind gale force of seven. They did not need to be asked twice. "Yanks are ya?" said one. "I'll drink to that."

Most of the club was now up at the oak bar, including the dart players. There was banter and there was talk, and there was the cuffing of the pints, between shouts of "Cheers!" and "Bottoms up!" and "Here's ta ya." All being soldiers, though from different countries, they exchanged names and units with each other, asking, "Where you from, mate?" If it was not love, it was instant friendship. It was typical of the Anglo-American cultures when confronting each other on foreign soil. It came from sharing generations of war in the battlefields of Europe, North Africa, Korea and the Pacific.

The bartender pulled long draughts into the pint glasses and slid them over the well polished, but dented surface of the bar-top. "Tis a relic, this bar," said one English NCO. "Pinched from Hitler's Ch'ncery, it was." Standing at the relic, leaning against it, the soldiers mingled, asked questions and drank, the atmosphere bonhomie.

Yorit put down his pint. "Al, you're right. The Limies are a friendly bunch, though they talk funny. Not a Sir Lawrence Oliver among them."

Following one soldier's battle cry of "Cheers!" and a quick draining of their pints, another round of drink followed, then another. The next round was bought by the big Scot Sergeant that Bravo suspected might ask him to dance.

"About time you Yanks got 'ere," said one of the Brits. ""Wha' took you so long? We been holden the line agin' the commies 'ere since 1945!"

Yorit stood up to him. "Yeah, well, since you British pulled up stakes East of Suez, we been busy saving the rest of the world from Communism."

"We 'ad to leave you Yanks somethin' to play wit'," said the man in army woolens.

"And what do the Limies do in their sector?" asked Pereski.

"Patrol! Just don't you Yanks get in the way of our patrols, 'ear me? You could get 'urt, ya know," he warned.

"Oh? Where are your patrols?"

"Alon' the Wall."

"Which side, east or west?" Everyone laughed.

"Neither! It's the wall between our sectors," said another man.

"But there ain't no wall there," said Bravo, guardedly.

"There is now!" And everyone laughed again.

A corporal with a mean scar on his head stepped up to the conversation. "And 'ere we thought we was alone keepin' the commies back. We 'ad company all the time. The Yanks!"

"Don't you Limies ever read the newspapers?" asked Pereski. "In 1961, President Kennedy sent in the US Army with bulldozers to rescue this Fort Apache."

"Didn't know we was sharing the property," mumbled a corporal.

"Bulldozers! What bulldozers? Ain't seen no Yank bulldozers since I been 'ere in Berlin," replied one soldier from the English midlands.

Listening, Pereski spoke up. "Didn't have to use them. The American presence was enough to scare Khrushchev and make the commies back down."

"So let's defend the property together," said a Scotsman, dressed in Tartans.

"Of course! We're Allies, aren't we?" said Yorit, with a vocal air of appeasement.

"Ri't-so!" said a Brit.

"We drinks to that," said another.

"Me too!"

"Ri't-so!"

"Cheers!"

"Bottoms up!"

Another soldier dressed in British Army wools, a corporal, pushed himself between Lavoss and Pereski. He drank thirstily.

"Where you from?" Lavoss asked him, making space at the bar.

"Llwynpia, where God dwells," he said with a gargle and a hint of pride in his voice.

Nearby, another NCO who said he was from Yorkshire put down his drink. "You 'ave to pardon me mate 'ere. 'e is a-Welshman, you know, an' is a-given to b-musen the fairies."

There was laughter.

"And damn proud of it, Mate, as long as they're Welsh fairies," he replied with lilting reverence.

Lavoss tried to pronounce the "Ll" gargel of "Llwynpia," the way the Welsh corporal did, with a gargle, but failed, making a fool of himself. No one seemed to mind, least of all, the Welshman.

"I never heard of your town, Ll...ia." Yorit stumbled.

"Every American kid knows where Wales is, but Li... I give up. Too tough to pronounce," said Lavoss respectfully There were grins around of appreciation for his effort.

Another Brit, a SSgt according to the stripes on his arm, banged his pint on the oak relic bar, adding a dent to the 10,000 already marked there. "Wa! Do ya n'ver 'ear of Llwynpia? Surely you've 'eared of the Pontypridd, or the Taff Vale?"

The Americans grew humble. Bravo shrugged. "I'm sorry, no."

Disappointed at their ignorance of the Welsh countryside, the Welsh Sergeant tried again. "The Rhondda Hills, than?"

This time all four Americans shook their heads, for the conversation now centered on them and the two Welshmen—the Sgt and the Cpl. "Then, lads, you ain't been born yet. You never 'eard a whip'rwill call'n in the mornin' or wiff-a-smit of the wind in the Spring?" said the Welsh Sergeant.

"Sure I have," said Yorit.

"Than you've been to the Rhondda, my boy."

"I have?"

"Yes, coal country! Where the colliers go into the pits a-sungen, and comin' out the pits with the *sung* still on their lips, they done," he said with a swagger.

"That is *sung* as in dung," said one of the dartboard players from the English Midlands. "Spitting coal dust is all they can do, them Welsh." he added a vocal "Har-har!"

Sounding Churchillian, the Welshman from Llwynpia pressed his point. "We sung in the 'ills, and we sung in the valleys, and we sung in the pits and in the pubs, and died in 'em too, we did. It's the Welsh way!"

"Right on, Mate. You Welsh go sing to the hills and leave the fuckin' to the English." Everyone laughed. He was a corporal from Blackpool.

The man from Wales waved him away. "Ri't crude, you are too, Sam. Make no m'stake 'bout it. A *sung* to us is a-liken coal dust in the blood," he touted, raising his pint, his fifth for the evening. Then, taking hold of the edge of the oak bar relic for support, he began to sing in a Gaelic tenor that for the moment plugged all talk. It was a lilting voice, gentle yet rich. It carried the room. When the Welshman finished, the room hailed him. The four Americans gave him a "Yeah-cool, and right-ons!" and drank.

"Now, don't let this Charlie-boy, 'ere pull your twit. That valley 'hey come from is a flea's second choice on the back of the Brecon Beacons, it is." It was the another Welsh NCO. He was from the town of Swansee. He got up from a table and joined the bar. "Give this a listen, lads." he said, coughing to clear his throat. He placed one hand to his chest and began to sing. The club fell silent. Every man—the four Americans, the Scots, the Welsh, the English, the Northern Irish, and the bartender—all slipped under the spell of his lilting "*Lied.*" The other Welshman, the one from the Rhondda Valley, had to dry his eyes. He felt only emotion that to anyone un-Welsh could never know. The song was about life in the coal pits and the woman who waited, and about the men who never came out, and when they did, died young. In it was "John Henry" all over again, only a Welsh one.

With the song done there was a pause, then a cheer, and a shake-of-hands to cries of, "Good show!" They drank.

Encouraged, and arms over each others shoulder, the two men, the one from the Welsh valley, the other from the hills, gave their pints a clubby knock and sang a duet about love and the home country. Another round of Whitney Ale followed.

The Americans, too, were encouraged to sing. They were at first embarrassed, but after some cajoling and a brief discussion, together they realized they all knew "Go Tell It On the Mountain." Bravo, who was once a choir boy, raised his arm, the little finger pointing as if about to clean his ear. Without meaning to, together they fell into a barber shop harmony, with Lavoss the deep bass. The harmony was off, way off, but the melody was enough to recognize the old Negro spiritual.

The British were ebullient. There was applause, in spite of Bravo's discordant belch, twice, during the chorus. (It had to do with the ale.) The hosts hummed along.

The singing done, the bar again became chattery, the atmosphere chummy. Foot on the rail, Yorit leaned on the bar. He smacked his lips. Next to him, one of the Englishmen talked about his hometown: Cheltenham. Yorit listened politely, still smacking his lips. He told him about where he came from: Cleveland, Ohio. Then Pereski came up to them. "Say, Yo, what has no head and is flat-chested?"

"Don't know. Eskimo women?" Yorit answered.

"Wrong! United Kingdom beer." They both laughed. "Look at my pint. No foam head. Limey beer is flat-chested. Hopefully the women arn't that way."

Overhearing, the Cheltenham Englishman turned to the bartender. "Blimy, Sarge-e, will you put an ear to `hat. This Yank `ere just insulted 'oly water and our women! Give the Yank 'ere a *Stout* and dare let me 'ear 'im say that ag'in," he said, raising his chin threateningly, staring at Pereski. He called over to one of his mates, the soldier from Blackpool. He joined him.

A glass filled with what looked like pancake syrup was set on the bar top, the dark liquid of which was three-quarters of the glass. The rest was foam. Pereski and Yorit had never seen such a thick head of brown suds, not even on German beer.

The Cheltenham soldier raised an eyebrow at Pereski and pointed at the ale, . "Now tell me, mate, 'bout our ale 'ere bein' flat and all tha'." Both he and the Blackpool man put their arms over Pereski's shoulder and handed him the English glass of *Stout* beer. "Drink up, mate!"

Tremulous, Pereski took the glass, sniffed, and tasted, then rolled the malty liquid around his mouth, and swallowed. The two English brawlers, bare-knuckle types both, by the shape of their noses, observed him keenly, anxious for a response.

"Buxom!" Pereski replied, pleasantly surprised at the taste. "Very buxom, for sure. If English woman are anything like English Stout, I'll change citizenship."

The two guardsmen laughed. "Said like a real Yank!"

"Better than a punch in the nose," said the soldier from Blackpool, dropping his arm.

Yorit took a taste of the pint. "Yeah!" he gleamed. "Hey, bartender, let's have a round of Stout for the mates here!"

Having grown ripe from the evening's consumption, one of the Scottish soldiers raised his glass. He had his beret under the epaulette of his jacket, and began to sing "Aud lang Syne." Everyone joined in, the British and the Americans together. Everyone in the club stood at the bar now, all in an effervescent mood. Anglo-American relations could not have been better.

As they sang, Lavoss slipped up to Pereski. "I caught that. You almost got yourself bopped by those two Limies. Don't piss these guys off. We're outnumbered, and by the looks of some of them they could have crewed with Long John Silver."

Growing tipsy, Pereski gave his friend a blink. "Oh, that may be. But a few of them here are wearing skirts and carrying purses trimmed with feathers. It sends another message."

"Still, just be careful of the wise cracks," Lavoss warned. "We don't want to wear out our welcome, at least not until we've emptied the beer taps."

At one of the tables Yorit sat down with two of the British Sergeants. "What does that mean?" he asked, indicating a metal insignia pinned to one man's epaulet.

"It means 'her Majesty's Grenadiers'," he answered with pride.

Yorit looked surprised. "Grenadiers? What do you fight with in your sector of Berlin, pike and mace?"

"If it'll keep the commies on their side of the Wall, why not?" came the scrappy reply.

Bravo chewed gum as he drank. He popped the gum between swigs of drink and conversation. One of the dart players, a Scotsman wearing a kilt, turned to him with an eyebrow cocked. "If you Yanks chewed gum with your mouth closed Berlin would be a quieter place to serve in."

Bravo had just enough drink to be testy. He stood up to the bigger man. "Gum kills beer breath, pal. Want some?" He blew a large pink bubble from the wad of Double Bubble he was chewing. His critic refused to budge as it expanded. The Double Bubble grew to the size of a cantaloupe, then burst on the dart player's chin, and Bravo, being shorter,on the tip of his nose. They stood that way, glaring at each other. The Scotsman was the first to respond. "You've made your point. Now, how do we become unstuck?"

"I don't know. We may have to go to reveille together. The question is, will it be your reveille or mine?" Both soldiers laughed.

Pereski and the NCO barman were in a heated discussion. The barman had been one of the NATO umpires at the last field exercise. In all exercises the British umpires were expected to be neutral, whereas the French Garrison played the enemy; the Berlin Brigade the good guys. The barman claimed the Brigade had been poorly officered, having lost almost all of 40 Armor tanks and most of the 3rd Battalion from clever French maneuvers. Pereski defended the Brigade's position.

"We lost because as umpires you Brits were biased. You supported the Frenchy Frogs!"

"I beg your pardon?" said the barman, sounding offended.

Pereski pointed at him. "I'm in a communication company, see? We monitor stuff, see? We hear what's going on in field exercises, see? Brigade shot shit out of the Frogs, but you Limy umpires didn't mark it. You were too busy keeping out of the rain."

The barman looked over to one of the NCO Grenadiers nearby. "Gregory, the Yank 'ere says we didn't umpire fair-n-square in the exercise we 'ad. Wha´ you say 'bout 'at?"

Gregory came over from his place at the end of the bar. "Who said that?"

"The Yank `ere."

He leaned toward Pereski. His breath stank and his English was difficult to understand. "I was one o' them umpires, and you're sayin' I don't ump by the rules? Is that what ya sayin' there, Yank?"

Pereski refused to be intimidated. "No, I'm saying you favored the other side, that's all, Brit," he replied coolly.

"And I would say the Commanding Officer of yours—what's his name?"

"You mean our Colonel Blowhardus?"

"Yes, your Colonel Blowhardus. He `ad shit for tactics!"

The atmosphere now took on an edge. The jovial coterie that had been so much of the evening wobbled. The talk had turned from friendly tolerance to competitive innuendo. That was, until Bravo burped out loud. He burped a burp that had the vibrations of a bassoon, drawing their attention. He looked into his glass and said out loud, "By god, there's enough gas in this here Whitney Ale to refloat the Titanic. I love it!"

"Then 'ave another an' float 'er up, chap-ee," cracked a man from the Midlands. At that, everyone in the bar room laughed and the tension subsided.

Bravo looked up at a big Glasgow Sergeant whose eyes had a jaunty glaze. He mixed his drinks—a whiskey—between beers. "What's the matter, Laddy; ain't never seen a man drink before?" asked the Scot.

"Just between you and me, aren't you a little big to be wearing a skirt?" provoked Bravo.

"Aren't you a little short to be askin'?"

"Do all Scots run around like that?"

"Like what?"

"In skirts!"

Straightening, the Glasgow Sergeant gave him an indignant look, picked Bravo up by the shoulders and set him on the bar top. Everyone looked over with an, "Uh-uh, here we go again!"

"You're a wee bit short to be cole-cocked, ain't ja laddy," said the big Scot NCO.

"Don't know what you mean?"

"Because you are ignorant of great cultures, that's what."

His legs dangling over the edge of the bar top, Bravo looked at the big Scot. From the top of the bar, they were eye-to-eye. "So teach me your culture. Like, why do you carry a knife in a plaid colored sock?"

"That's to skin the sheep," the Scot NCO answered, with a hint of scorn.

"I didn't know the British Army had sheep to skin in their sector of West Berlin."

The Scot NCO reached down to withdraw the knife. "We don't. Only the occasional Yank."

With that, Bravo jumped off the bar and moved quickly away. "Better to be safe than sorry."

One of the British soldiers who had been playing darts when the Americans came in drained his pint and set the glass on the bar. He picked up his three darts lying there. "Well, Jim, back to the game, I say. The tide's gone out," he joked to his partner.

"You're on, Robin of Locksly," Jim, his partner replied, taking darts out of his chest pocket.

Yorit, who stood nearby, a pint cradled in his arm, picked up the sobriquet. "Robin of Locksly! You mean, like, you're Robin Hood? Like for real?"

The Englishman, with a toss of dark hair and sleepy eyes, held up one of his darts and winked. "You got it right there, Mate. Call me Robin of Lacksly, they do. These are me arrows, they are. Can knock an apple off the top of a man's head, if I 'ad a mind to. Right, Jim?"

On the bar were three dishes: one filled with peanuts, one with hard-boiled eggs, and the third one with two green apples. Watching, Lavoss grabbed one of the green apples and held it to Yorit's head. "Hey, Robin! Five dollars says you can't hit this here apple in one toss of the dart."

"Challenge!" responded the man known as Robin Hood.

The man known as Robert Yorit, gasped. "Hey, wait a minute!" Before he could protest further, bets were placed; a mix of British Pounds, American Dollars, and German Marks now lay on the bar top.

With everyone talking at once, they moved—Lavoss, Pereski and Bravo3from the bar toward the alcove and the dartboard hanging on the wall, pushing Yorit with them. All were half drunk. Yorit, half drunk himself, tried to resist. "Now wait minute, guys. Come on! I thought we were buddies."

"Until now," said Bravo.

"Robert, we have a chance to make a pound or two for us," said Lavoss, his arm around Yorit's shoulder and pushing.

"Odds are in our favor," added Pereski.

"How's that?"

"He hits the apple…we collect and drink another round for free."

Yorit stared at his friends in disbelief. "Yes, and if he misses I got a sucking head wound puncture. Not my kind of a game. I'm out of here."

Both Lavoss and Bravo grabbed him. "You can't run off, Yo. The Brits will think we're sissies."

"I am!" said Yorit, shaking their grip.

Pereski stepped up to him. "Robert Yorit, you can't cut and run. Think of Anglo-American relations. You run and the word will get out: we Americans are a bunch of cowards. It'll give Brigade a bad name."

"Yeah, and if he misses it'll give me a bad hole in the head!"

"You're assuming Robin Hood ain't a crack shot," said Bravo. "Scotty there reassured me; he never misses."

"But he hasn't reassured me!" protested Yorit.

Pereski shook his head, trying to calm him. "Now, not to worry. Should Robin miss, it ain't the end of the world."

"Not your world, but definitely mine. I'll be dead!"

Again, Pereski put his arm around Yorit's shoulder. "Look, we're not talking about a sucking chest wound here. We're talking about a Polak forehead, the thickest part of the Polish skull. The dart could never penetrate."

Yorit looked at his buddy, unsure if he was serious or putting him on. "Ha-ha! Okay fellas, gag's up. Funny while it lasted. Now I'd like to sit down and finish my pint."

"Would you please stand againt the board there, Yank? I got to get me range," Robin called over.

Pereski turned to Yorit. "Robert, you can't let us down. America's reputation is riding on your skull."

"America's repu... What's the USA got to do with my temple? I can't believe you all. My drinking buddies! You're asking me to commit suicide?"

"Be a sport," Bravo encouraged. "You're getting a piece of the action, and you don't even have to bet."

"Piece of the action? I *am* the action!"

"No, the apple is," said Pereski, pushing him back into the alcove.

Commenting to his mates over his shoulder, the soldier known as Robin Hood stepped up to the white line marked on the floor. Dart in hand, he stood six feet from his target—Yorit!

Yorit continued to protest. "What are you guys trying to do?"

"Trying to win a bet," stated Lavoss.

"Not with my head, you don't!" Defiant; Yorit began to plead, when one of the Englishman, the one who said he was from Yorkshire, came up to him. "Settle down, Chappy. Not to worry, mate. Robin 'ere is a champ, 'e is. Never known 'im to miss a toss."

"Yes, well, tonight might be his night to miss. I want out!" Lavoss and Bravo let go. Yorit stepped briskly away.

There was a quick discussion among the British soldiers. They looked back at the American soldiers in their work fatigues. "Got a solution," the Irishman from Londonderry called out. "Pvt. John Smit 'ere has volun'eered to stand at the target wi' a cigar be'ween 'is teet'." (Private Smith, a small man minding his own business, sat at a table reading a paperback book. He had not been involved in any of the antics.) "Huh?" He looked up at the mention of his name. "If Robin hits Smit's cigar that should be proof 'nough Robin can zero in on the apple, aeh?"

"Sounds fair to me,"said Bravo.

"Our man agrees!" added Lavoss.

Yorit, back at the bar, pint in hand, glared at them. "I did?"

Frowning, Pereski stepped up to him and gave Yorit a cuff on the jaw. "Come on, be a sport, Yoyo. Where's the fight in you? If the Limey here can hit that little ol' cigar, you know what that means?"

"Yes, he can hit me between the eyes."

Fixing on Yorit, Lavoss snorted. "Listen here, Robert Yorit. Since when does one of 592nd Signal Company's finest—you—say no to a challenge? Have you forgotten what you are?"

"Al, don't say it."

"You're a Keystone Grunt-jock, and the Keystone Grunt-jocks don't say no to the rough and tumble."

"What about Bravo? He's a Keystone guy too."

"I can't," said Bravo! "My head and green apples don't match."

Yorit looked around. "Any red apples in the house?"

"You got to go through with this, Robert," added Pereski. "The mittens are off."

"Well, put'm back on!"

Lavoss raised a finger. "I know it's crazy, irrational, inexplicable, inexcusable and insane, but hey, we're in the Army, where everything is crazy, irrational, inexplicable, inexcusable, and insane. It's what we soldiers do. Otherwise, why enlist? Why be drafted? Think of this way; it's for the defense of our country." Yorit wanted to cry. "It's like training exercise, like back at Ft. Campbell where you had to crawl in the mud under the wire. You did't ask why. You did it! Besides, the dart thing is already bigger than both of us."

Now Bravo spoke up. "Just think of it, Yo. You do the deed; we tell the CO. He'll be proud for sure. You know him. Why, I bet he'll even recommend you for bravery under fire."

"Or a Purple Heart." Yorit sighed in resignation. The arguments were too overwhelming.

Lavoss looked his buddy square in the eye. "Remember ol' Joe DiMaggio of the Yankees?"

"The DiMag? Sure, he's one of my heroes."

"Mine, too! There was once a ball game, Yanks against the Red

Sox. The DiMag had pulled a muscle in his back and was in great pain. Could hardly walk. He told manager, Casey Stengel not to put him in the line-up that day. And do you know what Stengel says?" Yorit shook his head. "He says, 'Joe, if you don't get out there on that field and play ball, you ain't got a hair on your ass.' And do you know what the DiMag did?"

Yorit shook his head again. "I'm afraid to ask."

"On all fours and in pain, the DiMag crawls out of the dugout. There, on the field, he straightens up. He throws his shoulders back and plays one hell of a ball game—all nine innings! He hit two home runs and a double that day. That's what he did. The Yankees won."

"The Cleveland Indians could have used him." Sighing, Yorit squinted at his Signal Company buddy. "So what are you telling me? DiMaggio played ball with a bad back and in pain to prove to Casey Stengel he had hair on his ass? Is that what you're trying to tell me?"

"Yep! Now, if you don't get out there and stand up against that dart board like a real signalman, than you ain't got a hair on your ass."

Yorit paused. Then he snarled. "Okay, I'll do it. No one can accuse me of not having a hair on my ass, but Al, only under one condition."

"What's dat?"

"I get to keep the apple."

"Deal!"

"And if the Robin misses?" asked Bravo, standing next to him.

Pereski slapped Yorit on the back. "We'll mount Yoyo's head in the Company Orderly Room."

Yorit frowned, then smiled, then laughed. "Why do I get the feeling I'm about to be crowned with thorns?"

"Not really. Only one thorn."

The Grenadier soldier named Private John Smith—he happen to be the lowest ranking man in club this evening—was taken forward, kicking, into the alcove. He bucked and tried to run but was pushed against the dartboard target. There was no escape. The Belfast Irishman stuck a thick cigar into his mouth. Someone lit it. "Now, John, not to worry," Robin called over. "Just give me a profile. I promise you the cigar won't feel a thing."

"I don't think John's worried about the cigar," whispered Bravo as he watched.

Robin took a dart between his fingers and leaned forward, shaking his wrist as he did. The room fell silent, the Americans off to one side, the British behind their player. Squinting, Robin took a breath, aimed, and tossed. There was a thud, followed by a gasp. The cigar squirmed. It was impaled. Robin had hit the target! There was immediate applause. A moment before kicking and screaming, Private Smith now held up the impaled cigar proudly. Yorit watched and groaned. It was now his turn.

Gingerly, full of apprehension, he stepped up to the dartboard. He looked toward his friends, his eyes begging restitution. There was none. Lavoss placed the green apple on his head. "Don't forget the DiMag," he whispered into his ear.

"And don't forget the forehead is the thickest part of the skull, should he miss," added Pereski.

"Thanks. I'll remember that when they pull the dart out, if it comes out, that is," said Yorit, trying not to shake.

Bravo cupped his hands to his mouth. "Play ball!"

Yorit looked over and saw the pitcher, Robin of Locksly; he was chug-a-lugging a pint of beer. It unsettled him. "I'm out of here," he said and moved to go. Lavoss and Pereski tackled him and pushed him back, and held him there. "Did you see that?" Yorit cried out. "Did you see him down that pint? In one gulp! He's gotta be drunk!"

"Na, no' to worry, there, Yank!" Robin called over. "A couple of pints 'elps me to focus."

"How many did you say you drank tonight?" Yorit shot back.

"Enough! And please stop wiggling." Robin's face instantly fell into a concentration mode. Squinting, he held the missile lightly and leaned forward. Again, the room fell silent. He aimed. Yorit shut his eyes tight. There was a soft sound of a *Thauk!* near his ear. The dart hit the board next to his head. The apple rolled off Yorit's head and fell to the floor.

Yorit immediately grabbed at his head. He felt all over it looking for blood; then he noticed the dart stuck in the target a quarter inch from his ear. The mighty Robin Hood had missed! Yorit screamed and tried to run, but was held fast by Pereski and Lavoss. Bravo stormed up to the Englishman, ready to square off. "What's the meaning of this?"

"Just wanted to get me range. Not to worry, chappy," he retorted.

Bravo stepped over to Yorit at the dartboard. "He says not to worry."

Yorit's eyes rolled. "Phew! Am I glad to hear that. It's exactly what I needed... Now let me the hell out of here!" he screamed, trying to push his way past his buddies.

Pereski and Lavoss gripped him, Bravo too. "Hey, remember who you are!"

"Who am I?"

"The kid from Cleveland! Larry Doby! Bobby Feller!"

Yorit stiffened. "Okay, okay!" he said, brushing himself off. "Why couldn't I be the kid from somewhere else, like Akron?"

Again, the apple was placed on his head. Again, everyone got out of the way. "Hey, guys!" Yorit called out. "Anyone for a quick Hail Mary?"

"What do you think we been doing for the last ten minutes?" said Pereski, his fingers crossed.

One of the Welshman handed Robin his fifth pint of the evening. He took a quick swig, never taking his eyes from the apple, or Yorit's head, as he drank. "Take a deep breath, Yank, and hold it! Don't want me dart to prick you in the nose."

Yorit groaned.

"He just had to say that," Bravo moaned.

Leaning forward, with all the concentration of a bowler aiming for the wicket to bring him the game and victory, Robin raised his missile. He threw. It was a soft toss, an arch of a toss. It took only a flick of the wrist and *Ping*! it was over. Yorit felt nothing, heard nothing, only the plop of something weighty hitting the toe of his boot. He looked down. It was the apple, impaled.

Everyone cheered. Bravo jumped and picked it up. The dart had penetrated the apple up to the hilt. He held it up for all to see. With clamorous celebration—and with the dart sticking out of it—the apple was ceremoniously carried over to the trophy case and placed inside next to the soccer ball. An inscription was quickly scribbled on a *Bierdeckel* (beer card). It read "17 November 64. One bull's eye off the head of one Yank!"

Still standing against the target, Yorit continued to feel his head for the hole that wasn't. Relieved, he stepped away and collapsed into Pereski's arms.

The camaraderie of the evening continued with each Army buying the other Army drinks. It took a while, but after a number of toasts and regaling, the Americans came to understand the different dialects of their British companions. Only one man, the Irish corporal from Londonderry (a Derryman), could not communicate well with the Americans. He mumbled and laughed and talked to himself as if he was his own best friend. Even the Glasgow Scot, who himself had an odd accent, had to bend to understand the Irishman.

It was at that moment, while taking change for the beer, that the Derryman dropped a half penny ('eypenny in British) on the floor. It rolled under a table and lodged in a crack between the floorboards. He got down on his hands and knees and crawled under a table to retrieve it.

"Watch this," said Bravo, with a mischievous glint to his eye. "A stunt my uncle told me about when he was stationed in England." He took a dollar bill out of his pocket and lit it with his Zippo lighter, then, dropping to the floor, he joined the Derryman under the table. He was scratching between the floorboards for the coin with a penknife. "Can I help you find your 'eypenny'?" Bravo asked kindly.

The table exploded. Both men were on their feet, with Bravo stumbling backward. He had taken a punch in the nose.

Yorit sprang from the bar and hit the Derryman with a waist tackle that took both men across the room and over a chair. One of the Brits jumped in, then Pereski, then one of the Grenadiers, and Lavoss. And the donnybrook began. It was the third fight that week at the British NCO and Enlisted Man's Club. The dart-game players were about to jump in if only to get in a few licks, but the big Glasgow NCO stopped them. "Now lads, let's keep the odds fair 'ere. They're our guests, you kno'." It was a veiled warning. There were four Signalmen against four Guardsman, and all seemed to be holding their own, with no knock-downs counted.

It was not a vicious donnybrook. It was not a kick'm while they're down kind of altercation, but an old fashion fight of the fists. Punches thrown, punches missed, grunts of effort, cries of "Ouch!" between curses, all to the meaty sound of, *Pop! Thud! Bop!* At the bar, the fans yelped encouragement. The swirl lasted less then a minute, but to the fist fighters it had the feel of a 10-round bout. The furniture, stable stuff, absorbed the punishment. None broke.

With a nod from the barman, the big Glasgow Scotsman stepped in. They felt the melee had gone far enough. The big NCO grabbed both Bravo and a Yorkshire man by the back of their necks and lifted them like a timpani player about to clash the symbols when there came a shout of, "Ten--tion!" Everyone in the room stiffened.

It was the Captain of the British Guard with his MP escort. The Captain was tall, patrician looking, the picture of a young Montgomery in his army woolens. Because the NCO and Enlisted Man's Club had a reputation as a punchy spot, the captain dropped by to see how things were going. "Just what the hell is going on here?" he demanded in public school English. "Put those two men down, Sergeant!" The Scotsman dropped them.

The fight had ceased. The disheveled, combatants stood, more or less, swaying as they regained their balance and licked their wounds. Yorit, with one swollen eye, helped the Derryman off the floor and apologized. Bravo's nose was buried in a bloody handkerchief. Lavoss' head was the color of a red balloon, as was the Welshman's. They had pummeled each other. The British were no less marked, with one crying, "Me tooth is gone! Me tooth is gone!" It was a piece of a dental bridge he had lost to a Pereski jab. Both men were on the floor, looking for it.

"You are a disgrace to her majesty's uniform, you men!" said the Captain of the Guard vehemently, with a scowl. "This is the third altercation at this club this week! Sergeant Morrison, unless you have an explanation, and you too Sergeant MacDuff, you both are on report! I'll not turn an eye this time!"

Sergeant Morrision, who tended the bar, stepped out from behind it. "We was makin´ a point to the Yanks `ere, sir, and the point got out of 'and, you might saay," he said in a reassuring voice.

"What? Yanks? In our sector? I say!" The Captain of the Guard looked over the roughed up signalmen dressed in work fatigues. Feeling exposed, they drew together. "By Jove, they are Yanks, are they not?" He looked back at his two Sergeants, the Scotsman, MacDuff and Morrison. "Well then I say, who won?"

"A draw, sir," said Sergeant MacDuff, as he gently brushed off Bravo with one paw. "We was careful not to `urt `im, Sir. Wouldn't be polite, yo' kno'."

The Captain of the Guard scowled. "Sergeant, is this any way to treat guests in our sector? Allied guests at that! To dot them! Just look at this poor chap, here. I say, are you hurt, Yankee?" he asked Yorit, noting his swollen eye.

"No, sir. Only a bump. I walked into the door."

"The Yanks put up a good show, Sir," added the bartender, Sergeant Morrison.

The Captain of the Guard nodded tolerantly. "Yes, well, Morrison, don't just stand there. have the men put back the room...and let's find that this soldier's tooth, shall we?" he said, with the dispassion of a prince to his courtiers.

"Yes Sir!" And the men in the pub began to replace the furniture.

"I say, I believe we owe our American Ally friends here an apology. I presume we all agree to that, don't we, Sergeants?" he asked, looking straight at his two NCOs. Appearing contrite, both Sergeants MacDuff and Morrision nodded, "Yes, Sir!" "I suggest we have them as our guests for the rest of the evening. I say, where are you men from, anyway?" the Captain of the Guard asked, turning to the roughed up Lavoss.

"592nd Signal Company, Berlin Brigade, Sir," he answered smartly.

"Yes, well, I say today you may drink at the expense of Her Majesty's 24th Grenadiers. Right, Sergeants?"

"Yessir!" the two British NCOs both snapped.

"We can't allow our American Allies to report to their company commander that we, the soldiers of Her Majesty's Regiment, are not sportsmen, now can we, Sergeants?"

"No Sir!" the two NCOs reported out loud.

"Set them up!"

"Yes Sir!" snapped Sergeant Morrison, jumping behind the bar. He began to pull on the taps.

Pereski nudged Yorit. "See? Whatd I tell you? The Brits are okay guys."

Yorit nodded. "My black eye tells me different."

There were handshakes around and the pint glasses of Whitney Ale refilled, this time on the house. The dart game resumed. The Captain looked over the men gathered at the bar top. "By the way, what was the reason for the punch-up?" he asked

Bravo, his nose bulbous and a little bent, was the first to reply. "Well, you see, Captain, there was this penny..."

Convoy

The door opened. Inside, the room was dark. The CQ runner stepped into the soldier quarters, a flashlight in hand. He went from bunk to bunk, checking faces. At the fourth bunk he stopped and shook the sleeping figure lying there.

Yorit opened one glazed eye into the flashlight's glare. "Hey, mo'fu'. Turn th' thing off," he slurred, not sure if he was dreaming.

"The roster says to wake you. You got convoy duty this morning," said the CQ runner in a low voice, not wanting to disturb the other bunk sleepers in the barracks room.

The CQ runner had been busy. He had just picked up Hatnoy from the MP holding pen at Andrews Post main gate. He had been arrested and dumped there for fighting and drinking at one of the *Haupt Strasse*, downtown bars. After bringing Hatnoy back to the company, the CQ runner crossed the hall to Yorit's quarters. He was in no mood for sleepy back talk and woke him with a jerk. "Staff Duty says to get your ass out of the rack, like, pssst! Now!" he hissed.

"What time is it?" Yorit mumbled, both eyes blinking open and staring into the flashlight's glare.

"0430!"

The door of the Communication Shed banged open It echoed through the empty Squad Room. A light came out from the shed's Command Room. Stepping up to the open door, Yorit looked inside. A sloe-eyed MSgt Sweechek sat at his desk, shuffling papers. He looked tired. He had bags under his eyes, a stubble beard, and a dead cheroot stuck between his lips. He looked up and saw Yorit, his soldier. With a nod to enter, Yorit stepped into the NCO Command Room. MSgt Sweechek grunted, noting Yorit's dress: field jacket, parka, Mickey Mouse boots, a ski cap pulled to the eyebrows under his field cap. "It ain't that cold outside, Soldier. What you got under your parka? A hot water bottle? You look fat."

Embarrassed, Yorit tapped at the parka jacket he was wearing. "How'd you know, Sarge?"

"I just know it. Drivers always try to hide hot water bottles on cold water runs. Come on, Yorit, you're only scheduled for convoy duty to West Germany, not a North Korean fox hole."

"Jeeps are drafty, Sarge," said Yorit, his voice still languorous for sleep.

"Put it on the desk. Come on, put it on the desk," Sweechek ordered. Yorit did as he was told and took out the hot water bottle from under his parka. He dropped it onto the the NCO's desk. "That's better, Soldier. You don't want the Russians to think the Army's a bunch of sissies, do you?"

"No way, Sarge," Yorit answered, noting his SSgt's own dress. He wore a bathrobe. "Hey, wait a minute, there. I might be carrying a hot water bottle under my parka, but you're in a bath robe and pajamas. Dear me, what would the Russians think?"

"It's my day off, Soldier, and I'm not convoy duty to Helmstedt," he said, emphasizing *day off*. "Because of you guys, I have to be here at 0400 to be sure you're all processed properly. Had to climb out of a nice warm sack with the wife to do it, too."

"That's what the Army's all about, Sarge Dedication to the job and not the wife." Yorit yawned, wishing he was back in his fart sack.

The SSgt continued to grumble. "Company regs require us NCOs to get the team up and squared away, no matter the time. For you, that means I gotta be here to pass out documentation: SOIs, call signs, and confidential frequencies that ain't so confidential since the commies already spooked it." Leaning forward in his chai. He, the MSgt, the SSgt , the PltSgt—all his titles—rubbed his nose vigorously, as if trying to wash away the tired mood. "Enough bullshit now! Here, Specialist. Sign this doc-transfer slip." He pushed the clipboard with the convoy guide documents across his desk to Yorit. "Your convoy number is 211. Destination Helmstedt, West Germany. 37 Tactical Transportation Company vehicles out of K-town, Kaiserslautern are waiting for you. They got twelve five-tonners in transit. Go pick them up."

"Same place as always, Sarge?" asked Yorit.

"Yep, on the Autobahn side-spur at Checkpoint Bravo," the MSgt answered with a snort, yawning. "And be careful, Yorit. Heard the

TAC's got a new convoy lieutenant, an ROTC officer just out of college. He's known to strutt his low rank and academic pimples."

"As long as he doesn't ask me to squeeze one of `m, we'll get along just fine," replied Yorit, liking his SSgt's humor.

"He may be the convoy OIC—Officer in Command—on this convoy run, but don't forget, you and your MP sidekick are in command once convoy touches asphalt. East German asphalt, that is. Should the green LT order you to do something stupid, question it and call Brigade Operations," he warned.

"Sarge, are you saying we got to cover his ass if he fucks up?"

"And yours. And mine. Do whatever it takes to get the convoy safely to Helmstedt, West Germany. Got it?"

"Roger that, Mas' Sarge!"

Dropping his pencil, MSgt Sweechek leaned back in his chair. "I don't like these ROTC jocks. They're always so damn Gung-ho. When they fuck up, we senior NCO's got to bail them out. For the life of me, I don't know why we have university ROTC graduates on sensitive missions they ain't trained for."

"Maybe the mission is the training," said Yorit, growing restless. He wanted to get out of the Command Room, not chat.

Sweechek shook his head. "Back than, in Korea, we had tough officers. Came up through the ranks, they did. No college cuties. Blood and guts officers who could lead a platoon out of a battle jam."

"Sure," said Yorit, wondering if his NCO had something personal against the convoy lieutenant.

Sweechek re-lit his cheroot. "Oh, yeah, and for G'sod sake watch out for that tricky Leipzig turnoff. We don't want another Hasselhof flap."

"Hasselhof flap, Sarge?"

"Yeah, the Hasselhof flap. Named after Sergeant E5 Norman Hasselhof until he was busted. He was a 6th infantry man. As driver of the guide vehicle on a convoy run, he missed the fork in the road on the Autobahn. The result was a US Army convoy of ten five-ton trucks rumbling into Leipzig. The Soviets thought it was an invasion. Did that caused a flap! The commies drew weapons and threw up road blocks. That tripped 7th Army and put NATO on yellow alert."

"NATO went on yellow alert over a convoy? What was the convoy carrying? Toilet paper?"

"You heard about it?"

"No."

"Well, just don't give NATO an excuse to go on alert."

"Did the Soviets release the convoy?"

"Yes, but they kept the toilet paper. Lemme tell you, give the commies a role of 3-ply and they will grab the whole cargo. That was the Hasselhof Flap."

"Whatever happened to Sergeant Hasselhof?"

"He was busted to corporal and sentenced to the Army's Baumholder post for the rest of his tour. Once in Baumholder you'll be lucky to ever see the sun again." The thought frightened Yorit. Fixing on his soldier, Sweechek leaned across his desk, "And take off that parka, soldier. You look like you're gonna do the Rolley Polley. You got to look tough when you face them commies at the border!"

"Sarge, it's almost zero temperature out there on the Autobahn and the jeep heaters don't pump all that much heat. Can I have the hot water bottle back?" asked Yorit, his voice still drowsy from the morning wake-up.

MSgt Sweechek raised an eyebrow and fixed his gaze on his soldier. "You call this cold?   No! You don't know what cold is until you been to North Korea in winter."

"If that will be all, Master Sarge, I'll go." Yorit did not want to hear another Korean War story.

"Hold it! Is your vehicle gassed up? Got your MP shield screwed up on the jeep's hood? Got extra radio batteries and a box of C-rats in case of an emergency?"

Suddenly Yorit stiffened and snapped. "That's an affirmative, Master Sargeant!" He stiffly handed back the clipboard back with the signed transfer slip. He was about to turn to go, but stopped. "In case of an emergency. What do you mean?"

The MSgt, SSgt, PltSgt took the dead cigar butt out of his mouth. It had gone dead between his lips in spite of lighting it twice. "I mean, should the commies choose to block the Autobahn while you are on it, don't expect the Cavalry or 7th Army to come to the rescue," he said, taking the clipboard.

"I'd be satisfied with a train ticket back to West Germany."

"And don't expect the Communists to lay out a table of Black Sea caviar. They ain't gonna feed you. If you get blocked by their vehicles— it's happened before—you better have a case of the C-rats to nibble on and couple of canteens of water. It's that or famish!"

Yorit frowned. "Hm, I prefer the Black Sea caviar. Say, Sarge, did you ever notice the dates stamped on those army C-ration cartons we carry? The 1950s! 1950, 1953, 1956. Jonas once opened a C-ration can of pineapples dated 1945."

"You got something against vintage?"

"Wine, no. Perishables, yes."

"Not to worry. C-rations ain't food anyway."

"It ain't? Then what is it we're eating out there in the field?"

"Dehydrated nourishment. Besides, 1953 was a great year—a vintage year for army C-rats."

"How's that, Sarge?"

Sweechek looked straight at his soldier. "That was the year the cease fire in Korea kicked in and we were able to go home. Happiest day of my life. Say, enough bullshit. Now get the hell out of here and pick up your MP sidekick."

"Roger, roger, Mas'Sarge!"

Outside, the motor pool had the look of a hoary frost. It was a ghostly gray under the tower lights. Along the fence, at the perimeter, two figures walked, hunched against the cold, rifles on their backs; they were the German security guards on fence patrol.

In his jeep, Yorit pulled in front of the 287 MP Company barracks. He beeped the horn. Except for a dim window light here and there, the barracks was dark. He beeped again. The barracks door swung open. A lone figure stepped out. He walked stiffly, as if supporting a bad back; in one hand he carried a gym bag. The figure pulled open the canvas door of the M151 jeep. There was a rush of cold air. Yorit looked over. He recognized the MP. It was Sgt Jose Gonzales, a Mexican. Everyone called him "Brill Cream José" because his skin had a sheen that reflected light just like in the Brill Cream ads. "Oh, no. I got a Brill Creamer as my shotgun again? And I just washed my hair!"

"Oh, no!" Gonzales answered back. "I got a Polak in the driver's seat?"

"Who else should sit in the driver's seat but a Polak! I can read maps."

Gonzales tossed his gym bag in the back of the jeep on top of the VCR-10 communication radio. "Why I always gotta get a Polak on my convoy runs?"

"Your good fortune. You finally get some education."

"I'll ride your shotgun, Polak, but you got to promise me one thing."

"What's that, Brill Cream?"

"You don't drive backwards to West Germany."

"What is wrong with driving backwards as long as it gets us there?"

"Yes, but remember," said Gonzales, wanting to make a point, "when you drive, use all four gears. When you stop, use the break pedal and don't drag your foot. I'll read the traffic signs for you if it will help."

"Not to worry, Brill Cream. It'll get us there the Polish way—forwards, backwards, or sideways, should it be necessary."

Yorit the Signalman and Gonzales the Military Policeman looked at each other, then both laughed. They had teamed together several times and were game for racist wisecracks. On the road it was never boring.

Gonzales closed the canvas door on the passenger's side. "Look, Polak, if you want me to ride shotgun with you, we cut Hispanic joke shit. Tonight, I'm not in the mood. I still got a hangover from last night."

Yorit nodded. "Sure, Brill Cream, as long as you don't leave any grease stains on the passenger seat."

Gonzales frowned. "My name is José, or have you forgotten? I'm a third generation Mexican from LA, not a Castro Florida Cuban. They're the ones who shed grease."

"If it will make you feel any better, I'm third generation Polak and can't speak the language, yet my heritage is still the butt of every goddamn joke this side of the East River. How many Polaks does it take to unscrew a light bulb?"

"I heard that one," said MP Gonzales.

"How about this one? Why do Polaks always look at the bottom of a pop bottle before opening it?"

"Tell me."

Because on the bottom of the bottle the sticker reads 'drink from other end'." Gonzales laughed. "Want to hear another Polak joke at 0500 in the morning? Here's one..."

"No, here's a Latin one," interrupted Gonzales. "Why can't LA police read a Mexican's fingerprints?"

Yorit thought for a moment. "Ah, too much grease?"

Gonzales the MP slouched in his seat. "I think we'll get along just fine, Robert."

"We always do, José. We're a team. Let's go." And the jeep pulled away from the curb.

At the main barracks gate, the guard on duty was surprised to see traffic this early in the morning. He stepped out from the unheated guard shack and held up his hand to stop them. Yorit did not recognize him. A new guy. He looked cold in his silk ascot, dress greens, bloused pants, and dandy white gloves—the guard uniform. Yorit opened the door and held up his clipboard to show they were on a convoy run and not stealing the jeep. The guard saluted them through. Outside the gate, they turned onto *Finkenstein Allee* and headed west toward the *Avus Autobahn* and the barbed wire barriers of East Germany, what the soldiers called "Oklahoma Territory."

In the night, the Zehlendorf district appeared frostbitten. It was cold. There was no wind and the moon looked like iron. A thin mist lingered. It threaded out of the surrounding forest and onto the streets and roads, making them icy , *as* the Germans called it. It was hazardous for driving, except if the driver was 24 years old and measured all life experience as a dare. Behind the wheel and confident, Yorit was just that. He gave gas. The Ford M151 jeep shot forward, moving like a tap dancer, lightly riding, barely touching the tops of the cobblestone streets. Should the vehicle skid, all the more fun. The MP, José Gonzales, 25 years old, encouraged him, "Whoop it, baby!" he encouraged. The mist thickened the closer the jeep got to the *Avus Autobahn* and the border. Inside the cabin, the two soldiers talked little, confined as they were like characters in a space capsule, hurling toward a distant planet, the planet known as Communist East Germany.

Thirty minutes later two red points poked out of the darkness against the forest. A bug? Gradually the two red points became more pronounced, then recognizable. They were taillights—convoy truck taillights. The ten-wheeled five tonners. Elephantine and hulking, they appeared to perspire in the jeep's headlights. It was the 37th Tactical Transportation convoy out of Kaiserslautern.

The trucks sat on the shoulder of the road like beached humpback whales waiting for the tide to rise. Nearby, standing in the cold, was a small cluster of men. They were the drivers. They talked and smoked as the Signal-MP jeep passed them. Yorit blinked the headlights and pulled his M151 jeep to the front of the convoy's twelve vehicles. Another jeep was parked there. One man wearing a parka coat got out and walked quickly over to them. He carried a clipboard and appeared to be mad about something. Both Gonzales and Yorit stepped out of their vehicle and saluted. "Special Troops, Military Police escort reporting for duty, sir!" snapped Gonzales.

"You our guide?" demanded the 2ndLt. He was the new ROTC-LT that Sweechek had talked about. He had a weightless voice. He was clean, too clean, unheard of in the 37th Trans Company where the drivers all resembled Brooklyn stevedores in battle dress. Yorit and Gonzales glanced at each other. They knew instantly what he was: an Ivy League cadet. He was age twenty-three and fresh out of college. Sgt Sweechek was right. The 2nd Lt did have pimples on his cheeks.

"Yessir! We're your convoy guide all the way to Helmstedt Detachment, Sir!" Gonzales responded, his words breathy in the near-zero temperature with that elite arrogance the Army MPs are noted for.

The ROTC Lt gave his two convoy guides a warning look as if they were apprentices on the job for the first time. "All right, men," he squeaked, "this is no sightseeing tour. I want a tight ship all the way down this East German Autobahn, hear? By the way, what is the Helmstedt Detachment?"

Again, Yorit and Gonzales looked at each other. "Our convoy's destination, Sir," answered Yorit in a tone tolerant of the Lt's ignorance. "Helmstedt Detachment is named after the town of Helmstedt, just over the border inside West Germany."

"Don't get cute with me, Soldier! I know where West Germany is. It's west!"

"Just want to be helpful, Sir," said Yorit, nodding respectfully as he had been taught to do back at basic training.

"I was just testing your knowledge," said the ROTC Lt, his voice raising not quite beyond puberty.

"Of course, Sir," replied Gonzales, sniffing with irony, certain that this was, no doubt, the pimply Lt's first command to anywhere.

"I want a close formation. I want your vehicle tight on my convoy like two tits in a bra. That close. Got it?" he scorned, pinching two fingers in the jeep's headlight for effect.

The two Special Troops soldiers nodded. "287 MP Company hasn't lost a convoy yet, Sir. Not a one," said Gonzales with his soldier's confidence.

"Better not! Especially mine! Are your radios up on net?"

"Yessir!" Yorit snapped. "Half way into East Germany we will be in constant radio communication with Brigade Operations Radio Room; when out of range, then with Helmstedt communications operations."

"That's in West Germany, Sir." Gonzales repeated with a snip of humor.

The lt raised an eyebrow, but let the wise crackpass. He took a cigar from his field jacket pocket and lit it. It was the size of a senior officer's cigar—thick and weighty, the kind used to intimidate the enlisted man. It was supposed to indicate authority, tough guy-macho, but because of his weightless voice, the convoy Lt could not quite bring it off. His pimples got in the way. He coughed as he puffed.

"All right then. I want you two men to give my drivers a smooth ride. Keep the tempo at 30 miles-per-hour, not 29, not 31. 30 miles! Is that clear?"

Growing numb at being talked at, the two soldiers, Sp E-4 Yorit and Sgt E-5 Gonzales nodded mindlessly. "Don't get too far out in front of my convoy. If we hit a fog bank, I want to be able to see you. I want those taillights in my face, in my face at all times," he said, pointing with two fingers at his eyes. "That clear, Driver?"

"Like two tits in a bra," said Yorit. He could not figure out why the ROTC Lt kept raising his thin voice.

From the other side of the road, the Tac-drivers watched, sympathetic; they knew their 2ndLt was a green, wet-behind-the-ears fellow, trying to make a statement. "Is that clear, you two?" he repeated.

"YESSIR!" Yorit and Gonzales snapped together.

The ROTC Lt held up his clip board to the jeep's head lights. "If you haven't been briefed, there are three convoy runs today: Brigade's 2nd battalion, the 6th is in front of us, and behind us, a French unit. We have to keep a tight schedule, got to run like clockwork." He took a deep breath. "Calibrate your watches, now!" he ordered as if announcing the invasion of D-Day. Yorit and Gonzales checked their watches in the headlights. "It's 0520. We jump off in ten minutes. 0530!"

Back inside the jeep's cabin, Gonzales kicked the floor heater. "What a crock of shit! Where does that pansy pants of a lieutenant think he is—Bastogne? The nerve! Him telling us professionals how to do our job. I'll tell you what, Yo, pimple face is scared shitless, that's what! Hides his insecurity complex behind tough talk! Saw it all the time at one of my postings." Yorit listened as Gonzales mimed. "He needs us to apron-string him all the way up the East German Autobahn. `Keep your tail lights in my face´!" he mimicked It made Yorit laugh. "Who is Lt trying to impress, the Vopos? Shit, with the experience I have here I could get this convoy through a Soviet cannon barrage the whole 110 miles up the commie Autobahn, yes, and with one wheel tied behind the bumper and a Polak behind the wheel."

"Daa, sure!" blubbered Yorit, playing the imbecile and laughing.

Gonzales slapped at the jeep's door handle. "I'm so pissed off. I think I'll give that wet-behind-the-ears second lieutenant a tongue lashing he won't forget, officer or no officer!"

Just then the jeep's canvas door popped open. It was the ROTC Lt. "Did I hear you call me, MP?"

"No Sir," said Gonzales, his tone down-shifting from heated to neutral.

When he had gone, Yorit looked at him. "Gosh, José, did you stand up to that officer? That's what I call a real tongue lashing. Those marshmallows you threw at him must have hurt."

"Yeah, and may he never forget it!"

Outside, on the road, the Convoy Lt walked toward the headlights of the lead truck. Blowing a whistle, he pumped his arms. It was the truckers´signal. The cluster of drivers immediately dropped their cigarettes and scattered. Running to their lined-up vehicles, they climbed in. Spinning his arms, the convoy Lt gave the order out loud: "Start engines!" It was 0530.

There was a whine, then one throaty sputter after another, followed with a cough of exhaust. The GM diesel engines caught, then roared. Headlights flipped on. Now, awakened from their slumber, the Army five-tonners awoke and blinked, their profiles like Corsairs on a flattop ready for take off. The 37th Tactical Transportation convoy out of Kaiserslautern was on the move.

And what was the 37th Tac-Trans, as it was called? It was the lifeline. The outfit. The Red Ball Express. Its drivers, roughnecks all, slept 6 hours and drove 18, every day between Bremenhaven and the Fulda Gap, and from Giessen to Stuttgart, and all places east of the Saar River. They were the machinery and the grease, the blood and stuff that had kept Patton's tanks on the roll during the war, and 7th Army USAEUR supplied and ready in case of war. That was the 37th Tac-Trans out of Kaiserslaughtern.

On the running board of the lead truck, the ROTC Lt leaned back and watched the other 10-wheelers, one after another, lumber onto the road. When he was sure his brood was on line, he jumped off and dramatically dropped to one knee, pointing west with one arm while pumping the other. The trucks rumbled past him, one after another, shredding the morning mist like the Corsairs once did on take-off and into the wild blue yonder in the Pacific Theater.

"Dramatic stuff!" said Yorit, watching above the thunder.

"Yeah," said Gonzales. "It gives you the goose bumps, doesn't it? Let's take up our position."

Yorit started the jeep engine and gave gas. The M151 pulled up in front of the convoy of heavy trucks. At a tempo of 10 miles per hour, the convoy moved forward, gathering speed. Looking out in the distance, they saw the horizon. It glowed, but it was not the morning sun; the sun never shines in the winter in Germany. What the drivers saw was neither the sun coming up nor the moon setting, but the neon and *klieg* lights of the East German frontier.

As they drove, the convoy approached what looked like a massive stone block—a pedestal. On it rested a Russian T42 battle tank, a lone monument to the fierce and horrific Battle of Berlin. The monument was off to the left. Though now silent, the Russian tank's enormous gun barrel pointed menacingly toward the city as if to say "We shall return!"

Above the dashboard lights, Gonzales looked out the window. "Oklahoma Territory, here we come. From here on in we keep our *Schwanzes* (peckers) in the pants."

Borit grinned. "You know, José, for an LA Spic, you're an okay guy."

Gonzales answered him in Spanish.

"I thought you couldn't speak Spanish. What'd you say?"

"You don't wanna know."

With the Russian T42 tank behind them, all concentration was now on the road. The four-lane highway became two. Then, some meters distant, it came up at them, abruptly, on all sides. It was a corridor of concrete topped by barbed wire. The Wall! It was as if someone had pulled a lever and "Pop!" there it was. It was not a singular wall structure that the newspapers depicted, but a series of stone walls pushed together, surreal in the floodlights like a Chirico painting. There were rolls of concertina wire, alarm boxes, barbed wire, guard towers, dog runs, booby traps, trip wires—several rows of them, all designed to discourage one thing: Escape! Beyond that, and almost as formidable, was the damp darkness of the bitter North German forest.

At this point the road narrowed further. The speed limit dropped. Around the convoy, floodlights turned the night into day. Guard towers paralleled both sides of the road. On the ground, dower-looking border guards watched, some carrying machine pistols, fists on hips as the army's 37th Trans vehicles passed. 500 yards further into East German territory the convoy reached the edge of what looked like a shopping mall parking lot. It was a vast open space of uneven concrete slabs, perfect for field-of-fire. Instead of finding a JC Penny and the May Company store anchoring the mall's retail stores, there were only several flat prefabricated structures with rows of open parking bays. A few bays were occupied by long-haul trailers with their cargoes off-loaded and on the ground, custom officials inspecting.

One large watch tower dominated the road. It intimidated the traffic, what little of it there was. Above, on the cat walk and watching with keen interest, were two Vopo guards One had a pair of fieldglasses and appeared to be counting as the convoy approached. Next to him, the other guard scribbled notes. Gonzales watched them. "Uh-oh. It looks like the commies could be tough bunch to beat in a fight."

Yorit squinted through the windshield. "How's that?"

"They're carrying clipboards."

"Clipboards? That is scary," said Yorit, knowing how clipboards dominated everything military.

"It sure is," said Gonzales. "Clipboards are dangerous enough in the hands of senior army NCOs. Think of how dangerous they can be in the hands of the Communists."

The convoy passed the watch tower and reached the first barrier, a pole painted black and white. It was one of several barriers constructed to block access into East Germany. Cradling his machine pistol, a sullen Vopo guard raised the barrier, allowing the convoy to pass. At the next barrier, a guard stood on the side of the roadway, his hand on the lever of an incline plane supporting an enormous block of concrete. It was set on what looked like a Cyclopsian roller skate. Only a heavy metal chain kept the roller skate from thundering onto the road, blocking it. The Vopo waited for the order to release it. There was none. Not yet.

At the next barrier, a raised piece of railroad track with finger-length spikes hung ominously over the roadway at a 45-degree angle, ready to drop. And so it went, one barrier after another, until the American Army convoy was deep into the mall's parking lot and totally cut off. To escape now was impossible. Yorit glanced at the VCR-10 radio in the back of the jeep. It was the convoy's only line of communication to the outside world.

The convoy slowed further. It passed two lines of vehicles—one line for civilian cars, the other for heavy trucks, all waiting to be processed; some had been there for hours. A few German cars were in the control bays. With trunks and hoods open, suitcases open and on the ground, the Vopo security guards inspected. The cars had been selected for closer inspection. Tiny shovel mirrors, the ones on double wheels, poked under the car chassis. The security guards looked into every nook and cranny. They even looked behind the dashboards in search of that illusive, double compartment that might hide an East German rocket scientist wanting to escape. None was ever found. Drained from the experience, the West German drivers could only stand by in the cold and tremble, fearful of getting frostbite, or of being taken away for some minor traffic infraction. One was never sure.

Away from the civilian traffic, the Army convoy slid into a spur. There, Russian soldiers in long brown overcoats and fur hats waited in defensive positions, weapons at the ready. One stood in the middle of the spur. He held up a gloved hand—the signal to stop. Behind him, another Russian dropped the striped barrier pole. Easing the jeep forward, Yorit braked just short of the Russian soldier's legs.

"Cut the bastard off at the kneecaps," whispered Gonzales threateningly.

The guard, a Mongolian judging by his face, didn't move, but glared and dared, his Kalashnikov assault rife at the ready.

Behind the Signal-MP jeep, the convoy of twelve transportation trucks stopped. They had reached Babelsberg, the East German checkpoint, without incident.

An olive drab Mercury sedan from the American mission was parked nearby; it was an Army flag sedan. As the convoy pulled in, the door opened and out stepped an Army senior officer, Major Dimwitty from G4, Berlin Brigade. He wore a field jacket with a web belt and holster tight around the waist, the image of a tough don't-mess-with-me character out of a John Wayne western. The two jeep soldiers could just see the handle of a .45 caliber weapon. "What's the major doing here?" wondered Yorit out loud. It happened that Major Dimwitty had nothing to do on that morning (majors don't do PT, fall out for reveille, or stand for inspection), so he scheduled himself for convoy control in order to observe how the new green ROTC Lt as transport officer handled the processing and documentation procedure.

Major Dimwitty walked briskly up to the lieutenant's jeep behind Jorit's. Stepping out, the ROTC Lt snapped a salute. They exchanged a few words. The two officers then walked toward the small Russian processing shack nearby. Surprised at Major Dimwitty's quick pace, the Lt had to skip to keep up with him. A Russian officer met them at the door. They saluted each other. A few perfunctory words passed. No one smiled. Together, they entered the shack.

Outside, in the morning chill, the drivers sat in their vehicles and watched. Around them were a half dozen Caucasian and Asian-looking Soviet guards. They were young and beardless, and looked small in their great coats that reached down to their ankles. They stared and ogled the Americans as if they were aliens which, in this part of the world, they were. The Americans ogled the Russians back. The impression was that they too were aliens.

A true son of Genghis Khan, the Mongolian guard in front of the Signal-MP jeep had a face that was round and moony, his eyes mere slits, suggesting a need for sleep. The other guard, the Caucasian one, looked as if he had been issued a uniform two sizes too big, with the cap two sizes too small. Their appearance suggested unmenacing teenagers at school with slingshots and not Kalashnikov rifles. The two Soviet guards watched, observing the officers.

When the officers vanished into the processing shack, the Mongolian guard turned back to the Signal-MP jeep. It was time for business. He reached into his great coat and drew out what looked like a gray wool parade cap with a large red star on the visor. With his back to the shack, he pressed it against his chest for the Americans to see. He wiggled his trigger finger.

Yorit and Gonzales watched him. "That's the sign I been waiting for," said Yorit. "See? He wants to trade the cap for a cigarette lighter. I bought a couple of PX-Zippos for just such a deal. Makes an otherwise pointless trip profitable."

"I don't trust Genghis," said Gonzales wearily.

"You can trust him, José. He's not a NYC Spic carrying a knife in his pocket," said Yorit, smirking. Gonzales did not like the comment. "I'm just getting back at you for calling me your 'Polak' driver."

"But you are, aren't you?"

Yorit stuck the Zippo in the palm of his hand and pressed it to the jeep's windshield. The Mongolian guard took a quick look back toward the processing shack to be sure the officers had not yet come out, then he sprang to the jeep door. Pulling it open, he threw in the cap. Yorit slipped him the PX-Zippo. The Mongolian guard quickly returned to his place in front of the jeep and resumed the static position of a no-

nonsense Russian soldier, his moon face still as formless as Budda's.

7th Army regulations forbade all unauthorized fraternization with Soviet Army personnel. The Soviet Command did the same on their side. "No fraternization!" It was the official policy. To be caught was a breach of discipline and meant serious punishment, especially for the Russian draftees, yet the conscripts from both sides of the Iron Curtain took the chance to trade. The pull of market forces was that great.

Now it was the Caucasian Russian's turn. He moved into view in front of the jeep. He shifted his cap, which was too small for his head, and shouldered his weapon, then, cupping his hands to his chest, he made a sign.

"Boobs?" said Yorit.

"Yeah, boobs," said Gonzales in a low voice. "He wants a *Playboy* Magazine. I was hoping someone would ask. On another run, one of our guys picked up a Soviet officer's dress uniform for a couple of *Playboys*."

"No kidding! Did the uniform fit?" asked Yorit, watching the Russian guard.

"No, but it's in the trophy case back at the company. Look, Ivan is signaling again." The Russian cupped his hands and squeezed. "Definitely boobs," said the MP, taking his gym bag from the back of the jeep. He opened it and took out several back issues of *Playboy Magazine*. "Ivan will throw in the family jewels and grandmother for these," he said, grinning.

Yorit picked up one issue. He opened to the centerfold. "I never read the 'Miss July' issue before. Wow! Say, Miss July is a knockout. José, if I throw you my grandmother can I keep this issue of *Playboy*?"

"You'll have to talk with my commie business partner first, the one carrying the Kalashnikov rifle." Yorit dropped the idea.

With the motor of the jeep still idling, they waited to see what the Caucasian guard had to offer. Outside, the guard looked around. Still no officers. From under his coat, he withdrew the handle of what looked like a pistol.

"What? He wants to trade a weapon?" said Yorit, startled at the possibility of such a deal.

"I'll take that," said Gonzales, quickly pressing "Miss July" centerfold to the jeep's windshield. The guard's eyes popped. The Mongolian guard came over and joined him, both of their eyes popping. A few words passed between them. The Caucasian guard flashed three fingers, indicating three issues. "Damn, that guy wants my whole sex trade."

"Must be Jewish," mused Yorit.

"It's obvious he's not a Polak. They'd give it all away." Gonzales held up two fingers, indicating two *Playboy* magazines for trade.

The guard glanced back toward the shack. The coast was still clear—no officers. He drew out the rest of the hand pistol. It was a vintage piece, more a collector's item with a long barrel; the cartridge clip was mounted in front of the trigger-housing.

Yorit sat up. "Look at that, will ya?"

"That I gotta have!" said the MP. He showed the Russian three fingers and gave the nod for a trade. The exchange took half of a half of a split second. The jeep door popped open and the Russian dropped the pistol into Gonzales' lap. The weight of the weapon caused him to grunt. He handed out all three *Playboys*: July, February, and the October issues. October had a stain on the front page.

It was the same all around the Army convoy out of Kaiserslautern. American and Russian soldiers were in business. Surreptitious deals were confirmed with a nod and a wink. Fur hats were traded for Woolworth ball pens, hammer-and-sickle belt buckles for packs of Lucky Strike cigarettes. Tunics, medals, and ashtrays traded for Zippo lighters, comic books, and girlie magazines and any other Made-in-the-West knickknack. In one trade, a Tac driver even got a throw rug with Lenin's heavy jawed face woven into it.

From their side of the road the East German guards could only watch and envy. They could not trade. Cold War politics had cut them off, made them into Hindu untouchables to the Americans. The United States and NATO countries did not recognize the state of East Germany as an entity, which meant their soldiers did not exist as living objects, which meant they were not to be approached, talked to, or dealt with in any way since they weren't there. The Russian soldiers had the American business all for themselves, and they prospered from it.

For ten minutes the trade by barter ran hot and heavy when, all at once, it ceased. The officers had come out of the processing shack.

Gonzales shoved the vintage pistol under the seat. The cross-border communication that defied Cold War animosities switched off. As for the Mongolian and the Caucasian guards, they returned to patrol and a state of antipathy and blank stares.

Carrying a shelf of documents attached to his clipboard, the

Russian officer walked quickly past the Signal-MP jeep where Yorit and Gonzales sat. He was followed by Major Dimwitty and the convoy's ROTC commander, the 2ndLt. He still skipped. They hustled with a business-like air. Two Russian guards followed them, their rifles shouldered.

"Something's wrong out there," observed Gonzales, watching them from the side view mirror.

Moving from truck to truck, the Russian officer appeared to be counting wheels. He checked under the truck carriages while correlating vehicle numbers with the manifest documents in hand. At one truck, the Russian officer pointed to something. Major Dimwitty protested. The Russian officer turned and walked back up the line of Army trucks and began the count again. Under the parking mall's stadium lights that turned night into day and made white faces pale, Major Dimwitty's complexion went crimson. He fingered his holster nervously.

Again, the Russian officer checked the wheels. He checked the carriages and correlated vehicle numbers with the documents in hand. For the second time he stopped and pointed at something. There was an exchange of words. The Russian officer pushed Maj Dimwitty aside and gave one of his men an order. The guard stepped forward and climbed onto the carriage of the truck in question. Major Dimwitty grabbed him and pulled him off. Words exchanged between the two senior officers. The guard was ordered to try again, but this time Major Dimwitty grabbed him and with a punch jerked him and knocked him off. The other guard immediately slipped his weapon from his shoulder and aimed it at the Major, waiting for orders to shoot. The ROTC Lt tried to intervene by flapping his arms the way they taught him back at college. For several seconds it was a stand off. Then the tension broke.

The Russian officer called his men off. Abruptly, he turned and walked back to the Documents Shed and went inside. A moment later he came out. With him was a short, square, senior-looking officer with heavy shoulder epaulettes; he wore a great coat to the ankles. He did not smile, but walked up to Major Dimwitty. He glared at him nose-to-nose. Still glaring, he barked out orders to his soldiers in Russian. His foghorn voice woke Yorit, who had dozed behind the wheel. The Caucasian guard standing in front of the jeep, the one with the *Playboy* magazines under his field coat, reached up for the barrier pole; it had been raised, anticipating their departure. He dropped it. Behind the last convoy truck another barrier, a section of railroad track with spiked nails, was slid into place under the double tires. Army convoy number 211 out of Kaiserslautern was now in a state of blockade.

The Soviet officer with the big epaulettes turned away from Major Dimwitty. There was nothing but scorn on his face. He shrugged a hapless "Tjh!" and walked back to the Processing Shed. His officer followed. Yorit and Gonzales watched them, as did the convoy drivers. "Uh-oh!" said Gonzales.   A very disturbed Maj Dimwitty quickly walked over to the jeep and pulled open the canvas door. "Soldier! Get me the Brigade Operations immediately!"

"Yessir!" answered Yorit, smartly.

The Major took the handset from him. "Hello, Command Operations! This is Major Dimwitty!"

There was some static, then the voice of the Radio Room communicant. Yorit recognized it as Robuck's. "Sir," interrupted Yorit, "your radio procedure is incorrect. You got to use the SOI code and proper communication procedure, Sir."

"Operator!" snapped the major, disregarding the comment, his mouth all over the hand set, "This is Major Dimwitty! We..."

"Unknown entity, this is Flagstaff 1! Please identify yourself with correct call sign and radio procedure. Over," interrupted Robuck briskly from the Radio Communication Room.

"Listen here, Operator! This is Major Dimwitty of convoy command! We are being detained at..."

"Unknown entity, this is Flagstaff 1. Please identify yourself with proper radio procedure. Over!"

Turning purple, Major Dimwitty shouted into the handset. "Operator, this is an emergency! Operator..."

"Unknown entity, this is Flagstaff 1. Call sign is incorrect. Out!"

Mouth opening and closing, adrenaline pulsating, the Major stared at the handset.

Yorit struggled to keep from laughing. "May I try to communicate with Operations, Sir?" he asked kindly, not wanting to ruffle the senior officer's feathers further. Major dimwitty tossed Yorit the handset.

"Flagstaff 1, this is Farmhouse 2. Convoy number 2ll is in a state of blockade. A red flag! I repeat: a red flag! Do you read me? Over!" he stated in voice code.

"Flagstaff 1. Read you loud and clear. Roger! Roger! Out!"

"What's that suppose to mean?" demanded Major Dimwitty.

"Sir, it means the Cavalry is on the way."

Two stories under the Berlin Brigade Headquarters, SFC George Pellon and his partner, SSgt Charles Wallace were about to go off duty. It had been a quiet night at the Operation Center. No flaps. There were no East German hooligans trying to plant red flags on the duty train, something they did on occasion to celebrate Communism. No kid escapee trying to ride the rails into West Germany for a better life, as sometimes happened. When caught, the escapee was either arrested or shot on the spot. No Vopos, bored with guard duty, lobbing smoke grenades into Steinstucken, a West Berlin enclave surrounded by barbed wire inside East Germany. Such was the stuff that set off alerts. No, tonight all was quiet on the Eastern Front.

Sitting at his desk and yawning, SFC Pellon crossed the "T's" and dotted the "I's" of the operations log. Another half hour and he and his partner could close out the shift and go off duty.

An old time NCO, SFC Pellon liked the night work. It was cushy. There was little or no pressure, and no officers. It was a feet-up-on the-table and hands-behind-the-head kind of a job. Only when there was a flap, such as a politically motivated kidnapping or the shutting down of the border barge traffic or some such thing, did command break up their card games and drop their office putters to go down to Brigade Operations Room to see what the rumpus was all about. If the flap was serious, an alert would be called. In such a situation, upon entering the Ops-Room, a senior officer's first question always was, "Is the coffee hot?"

So sat SFC Pellon, feet up on the table. He detested excitement. He'd had his share in the Korean War, two years of it. It was, perhaps, too much. He had once attacked a Chinese machine gun emplacement with a grenade that did not go off. He ended up having to shoot his way out of a bad situation with his trusty M-1 rifle. It almost cost him his life. The shoot-out left three Chinese dead and two captured, and him with a hole in his chest where the bone deflected a round. Though he got a Silver Star for throwing his life on the line, the experience left SFC Pellon gun shy. He had developed a stutter. Under stress it came to the fore. Army psychiatrists had a name for the behavior, "Avoidance Linkage Syndrome" (ALS). In military vernacular it was known as the "Hide Me Blues," a front line disease. (In civilian life it has also been known to manifest itself following a divorce.) It was the reason the soon-to-retire NCO was put on graveyard shift in the Brigade Operations Room. Very little ever happened on night shift worth stuttering about. The duty suited him just fine, thank you.

The Operations Room had three telephones, all on SFC Pellon's desk: a black one for routine calls, a yellow one for internal urgent communications and alerts, and a red one. The red phone was the one for big emergencies. It almost never rang. To pick up the red phone required a really big flap, like the Berlin Blockade of 1948, or when the Wall went up in 1961. The last time the red phone rang was for the Cuban Missile Crisis. The alert brought SAC out of the hangars and onto the flight line. If the red phone rang, both the 7th Army Europe and the 8th Army Korea would have to draw ordinance. It was that serious. This morning no one expected the red phone to jingle, least of all, SFC Pellon, not in the half hour he still had to go while on duty shift.

Sipping his cup of coffee, he opened the envelope in front of him. It was stamped "Confidential." He took out a photograph of a house in Florida, a retirement home in a retirement community. "Say, Charlie, take a look at this dream place, will ya?" he said, handing his partner, SSgt Wallace, the photos. "What do you think? Swimming pool, patio, garden, and a boat dock. Impressive, huh?"

The SSgt turned in his swivel chair and took the brochure. He looked it over. "Hm, sure makes me want to give up the ol' farm back in Watts."

"You from Watts? Where's that?" asked Pellon.

"By San Francisco," answered Wallace lazily. He was tired from the twelve-hour shift.

"What do you do in Watts? Harvest grapes, strawberries?"

"No, we just harvest soul music."

Pellon laughed. He liked his partner and his subtle humor. He would miss him when he retired. "Come on along, Charlie. Bring the family and retire to coastal Florida. There are houses to buy. You only got, what, two years before you retire out of the Army?"

SSgt Wallace, round faced and a little heavy, shook his head. "White folks wouldn't let me move into a community like that," he said, tapping the brochure with his finger.

Pellon chuckled. "Come on, man; this is modern America. The 1960s. You're free to go where you want, live and do what you please."

"Not in Jim Crow country it ain't. No siree! Not even Reverend Martin Luther King could homestead down there. And he's Moses!"

"Now, Charlie, really!"

SSgt Wallace looked at his partner. "Remember Selma, Alabama?

What about Macon, Georgia, where Miss Sally Parks challenged the system. She sat in front of the bus, remember? George, you is talking about the South! And you can't get more south than Florida."

"It's different today. The NAACP is opening up the country."

SAgt Wallace handed back the brochure. "Not quite, George. If I move into that there town—what it is called?" he turned over the brochure, "Seven Acres. The property value would drop and a cross would be burning in my front yard in no time. It's what happens when you put a black folk in white folks' country. Nope, just give me the ol' farm and my front porch back in Watts, California."

SFC Pellon took the brochure. He pointed to one picture. "I already put a down payment on this property here. Another few months and I'll have my 22 years in service, then me and the wife and kids will head out there. Come and look me up. You'll find me on a hammock, tequila in hand, contemplating the sunset." Pellen grinned.

"And the mosquitoes?" asked the SSgt.

"What mosquitoes?"

"The ones from the Canal," said SSgt Wallace. "I hear the South Florida mosquitoes are as big as horse flies with straight razors. Doesn't it say that in the brochure?" Pellon gave a doubtful look. "Tell me, George, how close is the Canal to your property?"

"Very close."

"Well then, you got to watch for alligators too."

SFC Pellon sat up. "Alligators?"

"As big as a boat dock, I hear," said the SSgt. "When you retire to your dream house, better take an Army trenchin' tool shovel with you for protection. You may need it."

Suddenly Pellon began to have doubts about his investment. He put the brochure— dream included—back into the envelope when the black phone rang on his desk. "Tell you what, Charlie, when you come to visit me in Paradise, we go swimming with the alligators, then we'll see." The phone rang again. Pellon picked it up. He got the dial tone. "Say, which one of these phones is ringing anyway?"

Wallace yawned. "Might be Brigade. Who else would call this early in the morning? Maybe General ten Onkel's wife needs her bath water drawn. Ha ha."

Chuckling, SFC Pellon picked up the yellow phone, the one for internal emergencies and alerts. Again the dial tone. His mouth dropped. Wallace stood up. Both stared at the only telephone on the desk untouched: the red phone, the emergency phone, the Call-to-Arms phone. It had rung only four times in the history of the Berlin Brigade and if it rang now, it could only mean—war. R-R-RING! It thundered in its phone bed.

Pellon's stomach turned. He broke out into a cold sweat. He began to stutter. "S-shit-t!" and popped two antacids into his mouth. His "Avoidance Linkage Syndrome" was pulsating. He had that sick feeling of being in a fox hole again and under fire. He glanced at the wall clock. In twenty-five minutes his shift would end. Dare he let the red phone ring that long? He found himself trembling. His breath came heard. To his mind, the sound of the phone ringing was incoming. "Yaaaain't! Wap! Yaaaain't! Wap!" with clumps of earth falling all around.

"George, for God's sake pick up the phone," begged SSgt Wallace.

"Y-y- you p-pick it up!" came the clumsy reply.

"But it's on your desk, George. You have to pick it up." insisted Wallace

"I'll t-t-transfer the c-call to your d-d-desk. Y-you to p-p-ick it up!" Pellon stuttered.

"But you're the NCOIC in charge. George, you got to pick it up!" stated Wallace, sharply this time.

With the syndrome thundering in Pellon's ears, both men stared at the red receiver trembling in its bed. Neither NCO could believe it was actually ringing and ringing on their shift. "Maybe it's the wr-wrong number," said SFC. Pellon, hopeful but doubtful.

"Can't be a wrong number," replied SSgt Wallace. "We got the only crisis telephone in town, and that number is top secret. It's definitely an emergency."

Pellon took out a handkerchief and wiped his mouth and forehead. "W-w-well, I'm not g-going to p-pick it up, not when I'm th-this close t-to retirement."

"The commies could be coming over the Wall, George!" Wallace, himself was now wide-eyed and concerned.

"Then let th-the commies come and pi-pick up the ph-phone!"

"George, Brigade has to be warned!" The two senior NCOs stared at each other, the red telephone's "aain't-aaain'ts" ringing getting angrier.

In the Army, when it comes to emergencies, the stakes are high. For an Operations NCO to pick up the red telephone means he must call down through the whole Chain-of- Command. He must begin with General ten Onkel, the Commanding General of Berlin Brigade; then the second in command, Colonial Blowhardus; then he must call Brigade's G2, G3, G4, and the Brigade's CSSgt, followed by the garrison commanders, including the Air Force at Tempelhof. It was a big responsibility. Then the call goes out to the Allies: the British Army at Tegel, and the French garrison in their sector of Berlin Wedding. The Berlin *Polizei* must be informed, as well as the mayor's office at *Schöneberg Rathaus.* When the Wall went up in 1961, the Mayor of the city, *Bergermeister* Willi Brandt, wore an Army helmet for three days. When a person picks up the emergency telephone an alarm button is automatically activated. It signals all Special Troops units at Andrews Barracks, and the 6th Infantry companies at McNair Barracks, and 279 Field Hospital, and 40th Armor's F Company and the 94th Artillery, C Battery, and 7th Army in West Germany. Everyone had to move out of their compounds and into defensive positions around West Berlin. If it was a true red alert, a command order would follow. The order states, "Draw live, ball ammunition and proceed to World War III." Should some field commander fail to get the message, or should some unit locate to the wrong co-ordnance, it followed that there had to be someone to blame. According to the Army's Chain-of-Command, the one who would be blamed would be the fellow who dared to pick up the red emergency telephone. In this case, that was SFC George Pellen. Call it the "kill-the-messenger" dictate. For Pellon, it could mean a bad mark in his private 201 personal file, and maybe an extension of military service at—where else— Baumholder. Yeiks!

SFC Pellon shivered at the thought. With less than fifteen minutes left on duty and a short time till his Army retirement, he was not about to take that chance by picking up the red phone that hadn't rung in four years. To pick it up now would be like volunteering for combat duty. Crazy! In a state of paralysis, the two Operation Sergeants could only look at each other as the emergency phone hemorrhaged in its cradle.

"One of us-es got to p-pick it up! W-why it g-got to ring on our wa-watch?" Pellen stuttered. "Damn it!"

Trying to appear cool, SSgt Wallace trembled. "George, we got to pick up that phone or be charged with neglect-of-duty. It's that choice between a stone and a hard spot."

Pellon knocked over his coffee. "Oh shit! C-Charlie, I got an idea, let's p-pick up the phone t-t-together. You take the m-mouthpiece and I'll h-hold the receiver; I'll tell you what's s-said so y-you can sp-speak back. Ok-k-kay?"

Feeling feeble, the SSgt too was beginning to stutter. "I d-don't knows!" he replied, wiping the perspiration from his forehead.

Just then Specialist Robuck rushed into the Operations Center from the Radio Room down the hall. He was out of breath after the 30-meter dash. "Sarge! 7th Army, Heidelberg can't get through to Brigade Operations! Is there something wrong with communications here? The Russians have blockaded one of our convoys at Bablesberg checkpoint! They're threatening to shut down the whole East German Autobahn! It could be 1948 blockade all over again!" Robuck blubbered out.

The two senior NCOs looked at each other. They looked at Robuck. They looked at the red alert phone, still bouncing in its bed. They could not believe their good luck. It was a celestial answer to prayer. Grinning, then frowning, SFC Pellon scolded, "Is that right, Soldier? Well, don't just stand there. Pick up the goddamn red phone!"

It was now 0700 hours in the morning, and Colonel Blowhardus had just stepped out of his pajamas and was about to shave when he got the phone call. He still looked gray from the bottle of Scotch he had drunk at the Harnack House, the officers club, the evening before. He had the phone cradled between his shoulder and chin. "What do you mean, the East German Autobahn is closed? What for?" he demanded. "You say a what? A Red Alert?" He changed ears. Shaving cream clung to the telephone's receiver. "All right, who screwed up? 7th Army? The Pentagon? Huh! Wait, who am I talking to here? Specialist E-4 who? Specialist Robuck! What's your function at Brigade Operations, Soldier? What? You're a Radio Room operator? Where is the senior staff? I'll be right over."

At 0700 in the morning, Command Headquarters Berlin Brigade is usually a somnolent complex with two armed MPs guarding the main gate entrance. This morning it was different. This morning outside it was a-buzz of camouflage vehicles and men in battle dress. Inside, everyone seemed to be giving orders to everyone else. It was the same down in the Operations Room bunker, now called the "Situation Room." It was filled with senior officers of every rank. They smoked cigars and swaggered with importance, their thumbs jammed into their web belts. They studied wall charts, asked questions while pinpointing East Germany's Babelsberg checkpoint where the Brigade's convoy was held. Command discussed and raged over it on the secure telephones scattered around the Situation Room while giving orders to the NCOs and the lower enlisted who scooted among the officers, carrying little pieces of colored paper like footmen at the palace ball. The Berlin Brigade was in a state of preparation.

It was 0810 when Bird Colonel Blowhardus and his driver walked into the Situation Room. He took it all in at a glance. Every square foot of space was humming with activity. "TENSION!" someone shouted.

"At ease! Carry on!" said the Colonel, looking around. "Now, who the hell gave the order to alert and draw live-ball ammunition?" he boomed. The room fell silent. All activity ceased except for two telephones that continued to ring. "Someone grab those damn phones!" he ordered. "I ask again, who was the dumb ass who gave the order to red alert and draw live- ball ammunition?" No one answered. "Somebody must have given the order!" The junior officers tried to hide behind the senior officers, who tried to hide behind their NCOs, who tried to hide behind the junior enlisted. Captain Michaels of G-4 logistics stepped up to him. Colonel Blowhardus turned and faced him. "Well, Captain?"

At first, Captain Michaels hesitated. The papers he held trembled visibly. "Well, Dir, ah, no one gave the orders, ah, Sir."

"Impossible!" shouted Colonel Blowhardus, his voice stentorian, hands on hips, daring a response to happen. Everyone shrank back. "Is someone here trying to start a war with the Soviet Union? One shot fired from a bird brain's rifle and the Warsaw Pact will be over the Wall! Now, I want to know who the damn fool was that gave the order! Now! Was it you Captain Michaels?"

Captain Michaels stammered, "Well, Sir. It was...more or less, ah..."

"More or less, what? Out with it, Man! Who gave the dumb command?"

"Well...ah, if you'll beg my pardon, Sir. You did," he said, relieved that it was now out.

"ME?" The Colonel's voice took on the tenor of a bowling ball passing through the lane's ten pins. "Me? What the hell are you talking about, Captain?"

His voice cracking, the officer's voice slipped into alto. "Well, sir, it is standard crisis procedure, Brigade Regulation number 451M drawn up and signed by you and General ten Onkel two years ago, Sir." Reaching behind him the captain picked up the Brigade operations manual from a desk. He opened it to regulation 425M. The room watched and listened, fascinated by the revelation. "If I may quote the regulations, Sir." Michaels coughed into his hand. "In case of a `red` alert crisis--as opposed to a green alert, or a yellow, emergency alert—all units of the Berlin Brigade will draw 'live' ball ammunition and report to designated field position for offensive/defensive action." That said, the Captain held out the manual for Colonel Blowhardus to see. "Note your signature, Sir," he announced, pointing to it.

Bird Colonel Blowhardus, the second in command of Berlin Brigade, with thirty years of service, stared at the page, his mouth half open, mind fumbling. He remembered now. It was an order that had come down from 7th Army back than. "Oh! Well, I guess it's all right. Ha ha. Can't very well challenge my own regulation now, can I? Ha ha," he stumbled, sounding sheepish.

Relieved, the room sighed breathily, rippling the wall maps. "Goddamn Greek!" someone muttered, audible enough for Colonel Blowardus to hear.

He turned around. "Who said that? I want to know who said that!" he demanded, glancing from face to face, hoping to pick out the shifty eye. "No one leaves the Situation Room until I have the man who called me a goddamn Greek. It's an insult to my heritage and rank!"

"Who said what, James?" It was General ten Onkel, the Berlin Brigade Commanding General. He had just come in and caught the, "Who said that?"

"Brigade 'TENSION!'" yelled an aid. Everyone snapped to.

General Ten Onkel wore tennis shoes and white tennis shorts under an army field jacket. On his head was a Bavarian mountain cap with a brush feather and tiny medals, the kind that tinkle when you walk. They were awards he had received from the German community's walkathons, a hobby of his. The General smiled kindly. "At ease, gentlemen," he said, fingering the racket ball he took out of his pocket.

Just who was Brigadier General Walter ten Onkel? He was a highly decorated senior officer and a West Point graduate. During World War II his unit was one of the first to hit Utah Beach. He saw action in France and Germany and shook hands with the Russians on the Elba River. During the Korean War, following the Inchon Invasion, he and his battalion played a pivotal role in the Pusan Pocket breakout. His battalion surrounded and captured a whole North Korean tank brigade, or rather decimated one on the drive north. Also, he was the one senior officer who, in the winter of 1951, kept his command functioning and in tact during the "Big Bug Out," the Army retreat from the Yalu River. It earned him a promotion with honors to the rank of General. Later, he became an aid to ComGen Matthew Ridgeway, helping him to oversee the rebuilding of the 8th Army in Korea. Like General Ridgeway, he rode in an open jeep in winter, suffering the cold with his soldiers, something that earned him great respect. His reputation solid, General Ten Onkel was considered tough as nails. Among his peers, he was known as the "The Flying Dutchman." After the Korean War, he worked as a plan adviser at the Pentagon, but then, with his career on an accelerated tack, something happened. He developed a sudden loss of concentration. He began to take an interest in the innocuous, such as the love of nursery rhymes. At the Pentagon, his fetish for Valentine cards raised eyebrows. But what really stunted General ten Onkel's blooming career was his interest in yodeling at awkward moments, like in the middle of command briefings, or at parade, wearing one of his collection of Bavarian 'Trackten" hats with their tiny medals and feathers. Bavarian hats were not considered Army issue.

The year 1964 was to be the year of General ten Onkel's retirement. As a last duty station, and with eight months to go in the service capping his hero's career, he was given command of the Berlin Brigade. However, the Pentagon wanted to be sure there would be no problems so they assigned Bird Colonel Big Red One, Colonel James Blowhardus, as second in command. He was there to cover any screwups, should there be any.

When assigned to the Berlin Brigade, all officers were briefed and informed about the General's eccentricities. They were advised not to be cynical, or to laugh, should the impulse be there. Thus, when BrGen ten Onkel—also know as Uncle T—came into the Situation Room out of uniform it was, more or less, understood and vocally "A-hemed!" hand to mouth with a cough.

Gen ten Onkel smiled. "Hi, boys! Say, what's this alert all about, James? It interrupted my morning racketball match."

Colonel Blowhardus pursed his lips, disturbed that the General should use the familiar "James" in front of fellow officers instead of the impersonal rank and last name, as was proper.

"The Communists have blocked a convoy at Babelsberg just beyond Checkpoint Bravo, Commander. It has been several hours now," informed Colonel Blowhardus respectfully.

"Good, than let 'em sweat it out."

Startled, Colonel Blowhardus stepped back, as did some of the other officers. He was not sure if he had heard right. "Let who sweat it out, General?"

"The Russians, of course," General ten Onkel answered mildly.

"But Commander, we don't have the Russians trapped in the East. They have our soldiersa traansportation convoy trapped and blockaded!"

"Then we'll just have to wait until General Patten gets here."

His jaws tight, Blowhardus bit his cheeks from the inside. There was some muffled laughter in the room. General ten Onkel turned to Captain Michaels. "What's your name, Son?"

"Captain Michaels from G-4, Sir."

"Logistics, huh? Give me a situation report, Captain."

Captain Michaels glanced at Colonel Blowhardus, who was making every effort to hold his temper. That the general deferred to a subordinate for answers was a sign of disrespect for the Chain-of-Command. To do it in front of fellow officers was an outrage. Michaels hesitated. "Come on, out with it, my boy," General ten Onkel insisted.

Frowning, Colonel Blowhardus gave the captain a go-ahead nod.

"Well, Sir, it appears, Sir, that the Russians are up to their old shenanigans..."

"Shenanigans?" the General broke in. "I didn't know the Soviet Union allied themselves with the Irish?" Again the officers in the room struggled to control their giggling. Colonel Blowhardus cut them short with a hard glance around.

"They haven't, Sir," replied Captain Michaels.

"Then what is all this about shenanigans?"

"Nothing to do with the Irish, Sir. Figure of speech, Sir."

"Whose figure?"

"The speech's, Sir," answered Captain Michaels with an anxious sidewards glance at Colonel Blowhardus.

"I see. You must be Irish. That explains the shenanigans talk, huh? Please continue with your report, Captain."

Near by, Colonel Blowhardus wanted to weep, but he held his eye ducts. Abruptly, three desk phones in the Situation Room rang at once. No one moved to grab them. "For God's sake, get on those phones!" the Colonel snapped at his soldiers. "And you, Captain, hurry up and make your Situation Report to the General."

Nodding, Captain Michaels continued. "At 0700 this morning the

Communists blocked off one of our convoys. Apparently, the officer in charge, a Major Dimwitty, had an altercation with the Russian command."

"What do you mean by *altercation*?"

"The major punched one of the Soviet guards in the nose. The Soviet response was to blockade our convoy. The Autobahn could be next," replied Captain Michaels.

Colonel Blowhardus slapped his forehead. "What? Major Dimwitty! That dimwit! What's he trying to do? Start a war?"

"Now, now, James, let's be calm about this," said General ten Onkel, pulling weakly at the Colonel's sleeve.

Captain Michaels stepped up to the large wall map of Berlin and its environs. He asked a second lieutenant who was in charge of the five-foot pointer—his only job other than making coffee—to point out the Allied defensive positions around the city. The Brigade officers in the Situation Room listened earnestly while General ten Onkel bounced his racketball on the floor. When the Lieutenant finished his report, Colonel Blowhardus took the pointer and pointed to the map.

"From what I see, we'll have to move fast. Our convoy is situated in enemy territory. Got to see how far the commies will take this thing. We'll pull a company from 3rd Battalion, 6th Infantry and send it to our side of Checkpoint Bravo. Make a big show of it. Let the commies know we mean business. Back them up with a couple of APCs from 40 Armored. We'll have them take up positions just in case we have to go in. Do I have your okay on that, General?" Blowhardus asked, tapping the wall map, assuming a positive reply.

"Nope!" answered General ten Onkel.

Colonel Blowhardus wheeled around in disbelief. "No!"

"That's what I said, James. No! Not good tactics," said General ten Onkel with a leisurely shrug.

"But General, the Communists are threatening our lifeline into West Berlin! We may have to respond! We should be in place to jump off just in case!" Colonel Blowhardus scolded, his voice desperate.

Fingering his racketball, General ten Onkel sat down in a chair and crossed his legs. His legs were thin and hairless, the knees shiney. An aid had pushed the chair under him. "We mustn't react. It's what the Russians want. In a situation like this it is sometimes better to follow the dictates of wisdom rather than just jump."

"But there is a provocation here, Commander!" the Bird Colonel protested.

"James, do you remember what General Matthew Ridgeway once said? He said, `I always fight against hair-brained schemes that cost lives.´ Well, your scheme is hair-brained." Colonel Blowhardus took on the look of an epileptic. Behind his back there were some nods of approval. "Just let this incident play itself out. Let's see what happens, okay? Now, I'm going back to my racketball date. Keep me informed, James, will you?"

"But this is a red alert, Commander!" Colonel Blowhardus pleaded.

"Let us try to downgrade it to a yellow alert, shall we?" asked General ten Onkel, patting the Colonel's hand. "We just might avoid igniting a world war. I've been through two of them and so have you, James. Let's avoid this one Do let me know how things go." Humming, General ten Onkel left the Situation Room.

"TENSION!" ordered his aid. Everyone snapped to attention as the General left the room.

Just then SFC Pellon entered the Situation Room, a message in hand. He handed it to Colonel Blowhardus. "Ss-sir, the S-Soviets want to negotiate." The Colonel looked around. General ten Onkel had been right.

II

Slouched in the driver's seat, his knee up on the steering wheel, Yorit watched the civilian traffic thirty yards to the left. A line of heavy semi-trucks—"Lasters" the Germans call them—stood with rear doors open, cargoes on the ground for East German officials in uniform to tediously pick over. In the other bays, cars were being processed, but more quickly. Those that got cleared raced back onto the East German Autobahn, glad to get out of there.

Yorit bit into a C-ration cracker. He looked at the date on the box. It read 1949. "Yuck!" he said and tossed the cracker out the window. He opened a C-ration Hershey Bar, a part of the chocolate was covered in gray fuzz. He bit into it. "José, it looks like we're trapped."

"It's worse than that. We're fucked!" Gonzales replied, fingering a comic book he was reading.

A machine gun had been set up in the middle of the road, the barrel pointing directly at their Army jeep. Gonzales counted the number of Russian guards that surrounded them. "One light machine gun and twelve guards. Do we look that dangerous?"

"I think they want your comic book, José. Please give it to them so we can get out of here."

"Over my dead body."

"Okay, but not my dead body. I think these guys mean to play hard ball."

"They've no sense of humor," said the MP.

"That's why they want your comic book—humor."

The MP kicked at the jeep's floor heater. "Doesn't this thing pump anything other than lukewarm air?"

"If we can get up and moving again, the engine would heat up real fast," said Yorit, also uncomfortable in the morning cold.

Gonzales began to squirm. "You gun the motor and heat up the jeep, will you? I gotta go crap. When I get back I expect a warm cabin."

"Where can you take a crap around here?"

"Over there in the bushes."

The overcast sky had brightened as Gonzales stepped out of the Signal-MP jeep. It was not as cold as he thought. His intention was to walk to a group of trees near the barbed wire fence when one of the Soviet guards confronted him. The guard snarled something in Russian, indicating with the weapon's barrel that Gonzales get back inside the jeep and stay there. Gonzales, who had nothing to defend himself with except the flash of his black and white MP *brassard*, did as he was told. The sidearm he carried was only for show. It was unloaded.

"Back already? Where did you crap, in your pants?" joked Yorit from his slouch.

The MP squirmed as he sat. "Would you believe, the commie bastard would not let me relieve myself? He even poked me with his weapon."

Just than the jeep door popped open. It was the ROTC Lt. He stuck his head inside the cabin. "Out on the tarmac. There's a command call."

From out of their trucks, the twelve Tac-drivers and auxiliary drivers with them formed up. Though it was early morning and the sun on the horizon, the area floodlights were still on. The drivers all looked tired. It was their eyes that gave them away as long haul drivers; they were bloodshot, ringed, and drugged from thermos coffee, lots of it. Yorit and Gonzales joined them on the mall's checkpoint parking lot.

Maj Dimwitty, who had been talking to a Russian officer outside of the Processing Shed, walked over. "Fall in! At ease!" he ordered. "Men, our situation is serious."

"Like, no kidding," grumbled one of the drivers.

"We are in the middle of a Soviet-American confrontation. And by the looks of things, it may evolve into a confrontation between NATO and the Warsaw Pact," the major noted.

Standing at rest, Gonzales grunted with discomfort between snorts. Yorit "Shh-ed" him.

"But I gotta shit," he hissed back.

"We could be here for some time," the Major continued. "If that's the case, as guests of the Soviet Union there are some procedures we have to follow. Until further orders, you are all confined to your vehicles." A groan went up from the thin line of Tac-drivers.

With pressure building on his bowels, Gonzales raised his hand. "Sir, what if a guy's got to crap, like right now? From whom do I get permission?" (In the army at formation one must always ask permission, whatever the situation.)

Maj Dimwitty looked over at the MP. He took out a notebook and jotted down the comment. "A logistical problem. I'll bring it up with the Russians," he said as he slipped the notebook back into his pocket. He continued to drone on about the dangers of East/West confrontation, duty to one's country in rough times, and soldier discipline in a hostile environment. Though tired, the drivers listened respectfully while the convoy MP, Sgt Gonzales bit at his lips. Yorit nudged him to get him to stop hopping. Gonzales opened and closed his fists with controlled anxiety. The bowel pressure was about to reach its threshold.

"...and that's the situation here, as I see it," said Maj Dimwitty with finality. "Any questions?"

"YESSER!" bellowed Sergeant Gonzales again. "My position is tenuous, sir! I am a walking landmine. If I don't shit now I'll explode and level the parking lot! You want that, Sir?"

The Tac-drivers looked over. Yorit backed away. Maj Dimwitty stared. Grasping the seriousness of the situation, he quickly stepped over to one of the Russian officers who was standing nearby, watching them. With some hesitation from the Russian side, a quick deal was cut. Maj Dimwitty returned to the thin formation of Tac-drivers, Yorit and Gonzales.

"Men, because there are no latrine facilities available, and since we are all confined to vehicles (Gonzales was huffing and puffing his breath a cloud in the morning frost) the Soviets have given us permission to use the area directly behind our vehicles as latrines, but only three feet distance from the back bumper." He held up his hands indicating the distance. "To go further afield, other than the allowable 36 inches, is taking a chance on being shot! Drivers, dismissed!"

"That's space enough for me!" Trumpeted Gonzales, and took off running, undoing his belt as he did. He ran, hopping the final five yards into the space permitted. There, he thundered a sigh...and his bowels moved.

Near the East German town of Potsdam stood a Jugendstil villa, gray and somber. It was morning when Berlin Brigade's Col Blowhardus and his new aid, Capt Michaels, entered. Taking their seats at the large conference table they drank coffee which was served, and they waited. They did not have to wait long. Ten minutes later the Soviet chief negotiator, Colonel Bluvov, entered the room. He crossed the marble floor of the conference room with his aide, a big man, in tow. As he walked he dared a grin, revealing two aluminum-capped eye molars, the image Draculian. It was meant to frighten. It had to do with the year 1953, the year Stalin died.

Because of Stalin's death, all Soviet five-year plan productions were interrupted, including gold mining. Production dropped. With that, there was not enough gold for simple things like finger rings, watches, and gold teeth. In the Soviet Union, couples had to get married using Cuban cigar bands for wedding rings, a not altogether undesirable idea since, in case of divorce, they were easily disposed of, torn up and thrown away along, with the marriage. All Russian citizens who needed dental work, other than members of the Politburo, had their teeth capped with aluminum alloy. There was no gold. The Soviet military establishment was no exception, thus Col Bluvov's alloy fangs. It gave him the image of a tough negotiator, waiting to bite his opponent to death.

Col Bluvov extended his hand; his uniform's chest medals rattled as he did. Col Blowhardus stood up, taking it. The two colonels sat down across from each other at the large oak conference table where in 1945 President Truman, Joseph Stalin and Winston Churchill had once sat, facing each other. At the moment, neither officer smiled. Col Blowhardus fixed his counterpart with an angry stare. Not to be intimidated, Col Bluvov took out a gray Georgian cigarette. He worked it into an ivory holder. His aide, the muscular Army Captain, lit it for him.

"Just what is the meaning of this?" demanded Col Blowhardus in Russian.

"A man may smoke if he wishes," replied Col Bluvov with an air of condensation. Both men, very bright, could speak the others language. Discussions could easily pass from English to Russian, and back.

"Don't patronize me, colonel. I'm not referring to your stinking cigarette!"

"You don't like good Georgian tobacco, Colonel?"

"Smells like a page out of *Das Kapital*," said Blowhardus flatly.

"Your western humor degenerates early in our discussion," replied Col Bluvov with a rush of nostril smoke.

"Much like Communism as an economic theory," replied Blowhardus.

"You're not amusing, Colonel."

"Look, Colonel Bluvov, you have one of my convoys tied up at Babelsberg Checkpoint. My government insists—no, *demands*—that it be released immediately!"

"Tsk, tsk, tsk. My dear Colonel Blowhardus. Is this how we discuss disagreements that may exist between our two countries?" His voice had the tone of a card player who knew the hand was stacked in his favor.

Blowhardus arched an eyebrow. "You have absolutely no authority to hold my convoy vehicles. According to the Tripartite Agreements of 1945 and the Quadripartite Agreements of 1958, the United States, Britain, and France have been given free and unhindered access by air, land, and water to the Western Sectors of Berlin. For that, in 1945 we turned over to your government the German provinces of Thüringea, Salasia, and Saxony. That's the agreement, or have you forgotten?"

"I have not forgotten," Col Bluvov answered dryly.

Col Blowhardus sucked in his breath. "Than please order the goddamn barriers removed, sir!" he demanded, punching holes in the Russian's cigarette smoke with his forefinger to make his point.

Col Bluvov placed his cigarette in a large crystal ashtray that was sitting on the mahogany table where Stalin, Truman and Churchill had once sat. He glared back at his American rival. "Please do not point your finger at me, Colonel Blowhardus. I am in the position to…to BREAK IT OFF!"

"The finger that launched a thousand missiles," said Capt Michaels in a low voice behind his Commander.

Now it was Bluvov's turn to be angry. "We have reasons to hold your vehicles. One of your officers was disrespectful to the forces of the Soviet Union! He abused my soldier. An outrage!"

"Which your people deserved," retorted Col Blowhardus testily. "Your soldier climbed onto one of our trucks, the property of the United States Government. As you are aware, that is strictly forbidden and a violation of the Allied Control Agreements! I'd have punched him myself!"

"An offense to our honor!"

"Shall we duel with pistols, Sir?" suggested Blowhardus, half-standing, leaning forward, knuckles on the table.

"Shall we?" responded Bluvov, also half-standing, knuckles on the table, flashing his aluminum fangs.

"Now look, Colonel Bluvov, let's cut the Patty Cake stuff. Our forces—yours and mine—are on high alert. A very dangerous situation! We—you and I—are here to defuse it. I suggest we do it, like now!"

The two senior officers sat back down. Col Bluvov considered the opponent across from him. Would the American negotiate in good faith? No tricks? He decided to test him. "Colonel Blowhardus, tell me, what exactly do you mean by, ah, what was it, patty cake?" he asked as he lit another cigarette.

"Patty cake." Colonel Blowhardus looked back at Captain Michaels behind him, unsure if he heard right.

"It is a code, is it not?" noted Bluvov. "I observed you impart something to your man," referring to Capt Michaels. "I am not so stupid that I cannot see through your little trick. It suggests to me that you are not serious about our negotiations."

"Serious? Of course I am serious," argued Blowhardus, not sure what the Russian was getting at.

"Than why the code?" Bluvov asked, exhaling, a body language that could only mean censure.

Straightening in his chair, Col Blowhardus frowned. "What code?"

"The patty cake code, of course," answered the Russian.

"Baker's man," said Capt Michaels in a low voice behind his commander.

"Quiet, captain!" snapped Blowhardus over his shoulder.

Col Bluvov raised an eyebrow. "Ah, ha! Told your man to shut up, did you? Playing tricks again, Colonel? You are not in a position for tricks. Think of your vehicles," Bluvov warned.

"Tricks? What tricks?" questioned Blowhardus, unsure if he had understood correctly.

"The patty cake tricks. I wish the issue to be placed on the table, here, between us, for an open and frank discussion. Clean the air, as you Americans say," said the Russian colonel dryly, flashing a fang.

Col Blowhardus sat back. He looked at his counterpart, trying to pick up the thread of his argument. He turned again to his aide behind him, Capt Michaels. "Just what the hell is the bastard driving at?" he asked in an aside.

"Sir, I think he wants you to explain the Mother Goose rhyme, 'Patty Cake'. You did mention it a moment ago."

"I did? Are you sure? If I did it was a Freudian slip. Hell, I'm not even sure what a patty cake is."

The door opened and a servant, the Soviet Army equivalent of an army PFC, entered the conference room with two glasses of apple juice on a tray. He put the tray on the table and left as Col Bluvov drummed the table with his fingers. He was growing impatient.

"Sir, if it will get our convoy released, we should respond," encouraged Capt Michaels in a low voice.

"So what do I do, dance through the tulips?" Blowhardus asked, feebly. "What the hell is a patty cake anyway?"

"You got kids, sir? As babies, didn't you ever play patty cake with them?"

Col Blowhardus looked at his aide strangely, then he brightened. "Oh, you mean *that* Patty Cake!" As he talked, his eyes rolled; the frustration was getting to him. "Good God, this is insane."

"Commander, I'll recite it to the Russian Colonel if you like. Anything for country and flag, Sir," said Capt Michaels.

"No, that's my job. As second in command of the Berlin Brigade, it is my responsibility. Now, Captain, quickly brief me. How does the nursery rhyme go again?"

Whispering into his Commander's ear, Capt Michaels went through the couplets until he had Blowhardus, Bird Col of the United States Army, snapping his fingers in rhyme. He had picked up quickly on the rhythm, which was not unlike marching to a cadence call at parade back at West Point. Capt Michaels himself had learned patty cake on his mother's knee and never forgot it.

Col Blowhardus turned back to his adversary, Col Bluvov. "All right, Colonel. Quite frankly, I feel I must question your intelligence, if not your sanity on the subject, but since you insist on knowing what Patty Cake is all about, well, for the sake of peaceful co-existence between our two countries, here it is. And I repeat, this is not a code."

Bluvov nodded, a half smile on his face. Sitting back in his chair he tapped his finger tips together lightly, confident he had won a concession in the eternal game of Cold War politics. Moscow would praise him for it. "Bishop to pawn four," he chuckled to himself.

Col Blowhardus stood up. *What would Roosevelt say to this?* he thought as he placed a hand over his chest as if about to project an aria. At first he stumbled, than he picked up on the meter. "Patty cake, ah, patty cake, hmm, baker's man. Ah, hm! Bake a cake as fast as you can..." Behind him Capt Michaels snapped his fingers to the rhythm. "... you roll it, and pat it, and hm...?" Here, Blowhardus was unsure about the next couplet and glanced back at Capt Michaels who mouthed the words. "Ah yes. Gotcha. And mark it with 'B.' I'm getting the knack of it now."

Col Bluvov frowned. He noticed his own aide, the big man with the bull neck of a wrestler, bobbing his head in playful syncopation. Suddenly Bluvov jumped up. "Stop this nonsense, Colonel! What are you trying to do, make a fool out of me? Do you take me for an idiot? I see you tried to...to slip it past me, but ah-ha! I caught it!"

Perplexed, the American Colonel glared at him. "Caught what?"

"That mark it with 'B' trick!"

"Huh?"

"What do you mean by mark it with 'B'? Mark what?"

"The Patty Cake. What else?" asked Blowhardus, now really confused. "You wanted to know what patty cake was all about, didn't you? Well, that's it! You got it!"

"Nyet! You got it! Trying to pass a code signal to your man, do you? Have you forgotten, dear Colonel, your convoy is in the Deutsche Democratic Republic? Until you explain yourself, Sir, there it shall stay!" Bluvov threatened, pounding the table top with his fist, eye teeth flashing. "Mark it with 'B'? Most devious of you, Colonel Blowhardus." With that, the Russian stood up and stalked out of the room, chest medals rattling as he went, his bull neck of an aide in tow.

Later, back at Brigade Command Headquarters, Col Blowhardus gave a status report to Gen ten Onkel. The general shook his head. "James, you say he walked out, but why? Patty Cake is a lovely nursery rhyme."

Eyes swollen with concern, Bird Col Blowhardus could only stare at his Commanding General. He wanted to cry.

"Patty Cake is certainly one of my favorite nursery rhymes," said Gen ten Onkel. "When I'm back in the States I sing it to my grandchildren all the time. Perhaps I should go over to the Soviet Mission myself and sing it to this Colonel Bluvov."

In despair, the second in command of the Berlin Brigade nodded. "Commander," Blowhardus sighed, "you can try, but knowing the Soviets they have no appreciation for Mother Goose."

Back at Babelsberg Checkpoint, the Russians had reinforced their positions around the American convoy. They did not hide themselves, but walked back and forth with their Kalashnikov assault rifles at their chests. The convoy drivers remained in their trucks as ordered. Only on occasion did they go outside their vehicles to bowel-move, their attitude semi-somnolent as they watched the guards watch them. The Cold War had returned with a fury. All trading between the two forces had ceased. The mood grim, there was a sense of foreboding. The only activity permitted now was for the two of the convoy officers to move among the trucks. Every twenty minutes Maj Dimwitty would walk over to the MP-communication jeep to call Berlin Brigade Operations and ask for a situation report. Each response was not positive.

As evening approached on the third day, Yorit and Gonzales slumped in their seats. Both were uncomfortable and cold. On the floor behind them, static from the VCR-10 radio crackled.

"Say, José, is there a promotion freeze on over at the 287 MPs as well?" Yorit asked.

"You better believe it. We got guys who have held the rank of E4 for five years. We're so short of NCOs we got Corporals running the squads."

"Just like at 592 Signal," nodded Yorit, field cap low on his forehead.

"From what I hear it's the same in all the companies," nodded Gonzales, his voice tired. "The freeze is army wide. Why it is I don't know, or care. But if you want a promotion bad enough there is a back door, you know."

"And what is that?" asked Yorit, perking up.

"Re-enlist for VietNam."

"VietNam?"

"Yeah, that's what I hear. If you're a career guy and like excitement, what the hell, why not? You a career guy, right, Robert?"

Yorit opened the C-ration box. "I'm not sure. I like the Army in spite of the phobias. But a career?"

"Good thing you brought this case of C-rats with you; otherwise, we'd be nibbling on each other."

"It may come down to that yet."

Outside, the area flood lights buzzed and popped. In their oversized uniforms, the Russian guards appeared bored. Gonzales folded his hands behind his head. "West Berlin is getting to me."

Yorit licked the his fingertips. "How's that?"

"Did you ever find yourself walking down a Berlin street and hear footsteps behind you, close like, then you turn around and there's no one there?"

Yorit scratched the stubble of his beard. He looked shabby after three days of no shave, as did the rest of the soldiers. "I never really pay much attention unless they are women in high heel shoes, but yeah, maybe, now that you mention it."

"It happened to me twice on patrol. As we sit here now, stuck as we are, it reminds me," said Gonzales, meditatively.

"Reminds you of what?"

"That Berlin is a city of ghosts."

"Ghosts and clean streets," commented Yorit. "You never find a piece of paper or rubbish anywhere around here. Germans come out of their homes or apartments to not only sweep the sidewalks, but to sweep the curbs. '*Alles in Ordnung!*' they say. Everything in order. It's the German way. Remarkable."

Gonzales chuckled. He lit a C-ration cigarette from a pack marked 1952 and inhaled. "Yeah, the clean streets. Maybe it is the ghosts out there who clean them. Here in Berlin those clean streets tell stories. My Company Commander tells us it has to do with the cobblestones. They tell stories. When you do as much street patrol as we MPs do, you can't help but hear things. Especially at night. There are voices, but no people. There are footsteps, but no one is walking. Really spooky."

"Reminds me of St. Paul's Cathedral in London," said Yorit from his deep slouch. "If you ever get inside the church, up in the copula and whisper, you can be heard clear across to the other side of the dome, a fifty-yard divide."

The MP put out his cigarette. He did not like the taste. "In Berlin it's the ghosts. They murmur. It has to do with the city's past. Too many people murdered here."

"Can't be worst than the streets of Chicago," said Yorit, arms behind his head.

"There is a difference. In Chicago the Mafia murdered and gunned down folks. Here in Berlin, the murderers were the politicians. The folks here were gunned down in the concentration camps and are trying to find their humanity back by walking the Berlin streets. They say it all began with the political murder of Rosa Luxemburg and Karl Liebnick."

"Who were they?"

"Old Communists," answered Gonzales, looking out the window, watching another evening mist begin to settle. In college he had read about the city and its history. "After World War I Berlin was a dangerous place to live. At the time the city was full of political thugs, mostly Communists and Nazis Nationalists. The Communists and the Nazis went after each other with knives, pistols and clubs. They would bump each other off like the gangsters back home in the Capone days. Left a lot of dead bodies on the streets, it did."

"Where does Hitler fit into all this?" asked Yorit, interested in what his shotgun partner had to say.

"Everything. Ever hear of the Nuremburg Laws? The Nazis forbade the Jews citizenship. Ever hear of *Kristalnacht*, the Night of the Long Knives? That was when Jewish shops were shuttered and the synagogues burned. Lots of people arrested; some killed: Jews, politicians, Union bosses, journalists, professionals, anyone who defied the system. Many were sent to concentration camps, some never to come back, and their spirits never have been laid to rest. It's those dead that we MPs on night duty patrol hear and make us look over our shoulders."

Yorit pulled up the collar of his field jacket. "Are you telling me Berlin is populated with ghosts?"

"Yes, and there is another reason. Many Berliners were killed during the War from Allied bombing and Russian street fighting. The blood of those murdered and killed has seeped into the cobblestones, so I've been told."

Yorit thought for a moment. "Maybe that's why Germans have to get drunk to laugh."

Outside, in the glare of the mall's lights, one of the Russian guards signaled to the jeep. Fingers to his lips, he indicated a smoke. Yorit motioned for him to come over. Quickly, he stepped to the jeep's door. Yorit opened it and handed him a pack of C-ration Pall Malls, also vintage 1952. The Russian slipped him a bottle of vodka he had in his coat. The two American soldiers glared and praised their good luck.

"Dare we crack it now?" asked Gonzales. "We're still on duty."

"Most definitely," said Yorit, twisting off the cap, taking a good swig. He handed the bottle to his sidekick. "Only one swallow, otherwise we could get into deep trouble for DUI-ing on the job."

With a sigh, Gonzales wiped his mouth and closed his eyes. He took another swig. The two soldiers were beginning to enjoy their evening under the evening's bright lights in Communist territory. The drink warmed them. Now relaxed, they slipped into a somnolent mode when Yorit spoke up.

"Did you know the 592nd Signal Company has its own ghost?" The MP shook his head. "It hangs out here on post at the deserted SS Barracks across the street. You know, on Avenue C. It haunts the place, especially on stormy nights when the wind screams. It can be very unsettling," said Yorit, as he watched the Russian guard hunched against the cold, walking under the check point area's hard Kleeg lights. The temperature was dropping.

In their jeep, the two soldiers drowsed. Gonzales spoke up. "I got a story for you." Yorit stirred. "One of our NCOs, a Staff Sergeant Herman, told me he was once in the District of Lankwitz to visit a girlfriend. He told me how he was waiting outside her apartment block when a car pulled up to the curb—a vintage-looking vehicle. It was a Citroen, he said. You know the kind, all black with the big round fenders. Two guys in leather raincoats jumped out. They rushed the doorway. A moment later, they came out, pushing some guy in front of them. He was half-dressed and looked frightened. The guys shoved him into the Citroen. Sarge Herman had never seen anything like it, not even on TV's Dragnet. The Sarge glanced back at the apartment building from where they had come and then back at the street, but the Citroen, it had vanished! And get this. He said it didn't drive away. Sergeant Herman hasn't been back to the Lankwitz District since."

"And the girlfriend? What happened to her?"

"She's available. Want her?"

"Only if she moves out of Lankwitz."

Suddenly the jeep door jerked open. Both soldiers jumped. There was nothing to see except the outside mist curling. There was a rush of cold air, then that familiar voice. It was Major Dimwitty. They relaxed. He wanted to call Brigade Operations for a situation update.

***

Back at USAEUR Headquarters, Brigadier General Benjamin Ulysses III cursed. He had just missed a ten-foot putt on the floor of his spacious office. Before going to lunch, he had been trying for a half hour to get a hole in one, but each time the ball died at the lip of the dixie cup placed on the carpet. At that moment, 1stLt Tupple rushed in. He was carrying a file marked "Secret." He did not see the ball and booted it, then stepped on the dixie cup, crushing it. "Sir, a telex from Berlin Brigade... What the..."

General Ulysses III watched the ball scoot under the sofa near his desk. He glared at the Lt. "Are you not supposed to knock and salute your Commander before you enter senior officer quarters, Lieutenant?" The General was visibly disturbed at the interruption.

"Yes sir, but... Sorry, Sir!" he snapped, coming to attention and saluting "Here's a secret telex report that just came in, Sir."

"I don't give a damn about the telex. I'm flying to Washington for a one-week leave, and I got to get my golf game up to scratch. Now, don't come in here again like that without first knocking. Hear, Lieutenant?" The General took a chipper iron out of his golf bag. Getting on his hands and knees, he began to dig under the sofa for the golf ball. "So what's so urgent that you couldn't take time to knock?"

It took a moment for Lt Tupple to respond. He had never seen a two-star general on his hands and knees before. "Commander, the Soviets have cut off negotiations with Berlin command. The East German Autobahn is still in a state of blockade."

The general jumped up. "What? What happened to our negotiations? They were on course!"

"Collapsed at ten-hundred hours, Sir."

"Oh, damn! Okay, give me the telex report." The Lt handed it to him. General Ulysses moved to his desk. He put on his glasses and read the report. Lt Tupple stood at rest as he did so. After several minutes, he put down the report. "Is that all there is? No explanation? No reason for the shut off?" he asked, very concerned. Lt Tupple shook his head. "How can I report this to the Pentagon? It reads like a college freshman research paper. Now you listen to me, Lieutenant. You get back on your telex and get me the facts! Why did negotiations collapse? What is it the Soviets want? Who was on our negotiating team?"

"Oh, that I know, Sir. It was a certain Colonel Blowhardus. He's second in command of the Berlin Brigade."

General Ulysses gasped. "Colonel Blowhardus? You mean Colonel

James Blowhardus, the Greek? Oh, God, we're in trouble now. Between him and the Dutchman—referring to General ten Onkel—we got the Kookla, Fran, and Olli TV Show running the Berlin Brigade. I knew something like this would happen. I advised against teaming those two up for such a sensitive post—West Berlin command, but as always I was overruled. The Pentagon wanted General ten Onkel in there as a farewell posting so he could retire out of the Army in a blaze of rewards and honors, which he, I might add, does deserve."

"Why's that, Sir?" asked the Lt.

"In memory of the great officer he once was. His regiment did not collapse at the Pyongyang retreat. He saved a lot of lives. But that was Korea back then. Now we are stuck between the mule and the barn door, and the mule's a-kickin'! Lieutenant Tupple, get back on the telex and get me the facts, quick!" Saluting, the junior officer about-faced to leave. "Oh, and one more thing, Lieutenant. Before you go, run across the street to the PX facility and get me another dixie cup, will you? I got to get my golf game up to scratch."

***

At the Department of Defense, in a conference room deep inside the Pentagon, an emergency meeting of the National Security Council had been called. In the room were the Joint Chiefs of Staff of the Army, Navy, Air Force and Marines, with entourage and aides. They sat together at an oversized octagonal table. The Director of the CIA was present, as well as J. Edgar Hoover of the FBI. He scribbled notes. The military chiefs eyed him suspiciously. Chairing the meeting was the Secretary of Defense Robert McNamara. He called the meeting to order by ringing a little silver dinner bell, the same one he used when he was CEO of Ford Motor Company. Its light tinkle had the affect of cutting through the lumbering male voices and brought the room to attention. With his crew cut and clear rimless glasses, Defense Secretary McNamara gave the impression of a high school principal at assembly. The Joint Chiefs turned to him.

"Gentleman, the president has asked me to stand in for him. He has an important engagement in Hollywood, a fund-raising dinner for the Democratic Party." There were some snickers and winks around the table. Secretary McNamara frowned disapproval. He coughed into his hand. "As you all know, we have a problem in West Berlin. The situation is getting out of hand. We have a red alert crisis there where none should be. The president understandably wants it solved immediately. Thus, your cooperation, and that of your departments, is imperative." The generals nodded and murmured approval. "Mr. Pierre," noted Secretary McNamara, referring to Press Secretary Pierre standing nearby, "will you please give the Joint Chiefs an up-to-date briefing on the information we've received from, 7th Army Headquarters."

The Press Secretary moved to the podium at the end of the table. Behind him was a blackboard and an oversized wall map of East and West Germany. He adjusted his glasses. The briefing began, and typical of bureaucratic briefings, quickly degenerated into a soporific ennui, common in department monologues. Years of official Pentagon conferences taught the General of the Air Force, LeMums, to lock his eyelids in place. It gave him the appearance of rapt attention when actually he slept. Only the light rattle at the back of his throat gave away the ruse. When it came time to vote on policy, an aide who stood directly behind him would tap the General on the shoulder or take the General's hand and hold it up for him.

"At 05:30 on the morning of Oct 3," began the Press Secretary, "one US convoy, No.211, made up of twelve five-ton vehicles departed West Berlin's Checkpoint Bravo. At 05:45, the convoy entered the Soviet Control Checkpoint at Babelsberg for documentation processing. One of our officers, a certain Major Dimwitty of Berlin Brigade, was in charge, assisted by his transportation officer." Mr. Pierre looked around to be sure he had the Joint Chiefs attention. He did. Satisfied, he continued, though disturbed by an odd throat rattle from somewhere to his right. He could not place it. "Soviet military personnel immediately initiated delaying tactics by checking tires, noting seal numbers, counting and recounting vehicles."

"How many vehicles are we talking about, Mr. Pierre?" asked the Chief of the Marines.

"Twelve five-ton diesel-driven trucks of the 37th Tactical Transport Company, and one Army jeep."

"Why all that checking and rechecking? What the hell, can't the Russians count to twelve? How did they ever manage the Atomic Bomb, I wonder?" asked the Chief of the Navy, looking around.

"Please continue, Mr. Press Secretary," advised Secretary of Defense McNamara.

"A Soviet military person attempted to climb onto one of our vehicles, whereupon, after repeated warnings, Brigade's Major Dimwitty pulled him off, utilizing limited corporal coercion."

A light snore from the back of a throat became noticeable. It was the Air Force Chief's.

His aide nudged him. Blinking, the Air Force Chief refolded his arms and slipped back into the somnolent mode, eyes open.

"Sir, would you please forget the Foggy Bottom nomenclature? And be specific," said the Chief of the Army to the Press Secretary. "Corporal coercion? Was it a judo chop or a kick in the pants that got the Russian off our vehicle?"

"That Major probably pinched and scratched him if the Army training manual is anything to go by," snorted the Marine Chief. The other Chiefs laughed, appreciating the sense of humor. J. Edgar Hoover of the FBI wrote down the Marine Chief's comment, giving him a deficiency note known in civilian life as a "Mr. Meaner." It was considered an unauthorized wisecrack. Undiplomatic!

Taking offense at the Marine Chief, the Chief of the Army stood up. "That was uncalled for, Sir, considering the lousy job the Marines did at the Bay of Pigs invasion."

"We were never in the Bay of Pigs invasion!"

"That's what I'm referring to!"

"Gentleman, please," snapped Secretary of Defense McNamara. He eyeballed the two military chiefs back into their seats. "Please continue, Mr. Press Secretary."

"To get back to the question... Major Dimwitty punched the Russian in the mouth. As a reaction, the Soviets immediately drew weapons."

"Typical Army," snickered the Chief of the Marines. "Use a sledge hammer where diplomacy is called for."

Offended, the Chief of the Army was on his feet again. "We are talking about the honor of the United States of America here, General!"

"And I am talking about a potential catalyst to war!" retorted the Marine Chief.

Defense Secretary McNamara immediately rang the tiny bell in front of him to bring the table to order. "Commanders, please! Would you both sit down? I am now formally ordering your aides to keep you in your seats, with coercion if necessary!" The two generals resumed their seats followed by dirty looks, meant to frighten them. Ever vigilant, J. Edgar Hoover noted their conduct deficiency and scribbled it on his clipboard. It would go into their 201 (personnel records) files.

"Were any of our men armed?" asked the Chief of the Navy.

Press Secretary Pierre flipped through his report. "Only the Convoy Commander, Major Dimwitty. He is authorized to carry a side arm. According to the report, it was not loaded when he punched the guard."

"Now, there's a soldier for you. Taking responsibility! That looks good," said the Chief of the Army proudly, one hand forming a fist.

The Marine Chief slapped himself on his forehead. "Of all the dumb moves! Punching a Russian in East German territory when our convoy is surrounded by Soviet armor! Outrageous!"

The Chief of the Army glared at the Chief of the Marines. "Where else can an officer punch a Russian but on Soviet territory? It's where the Russians are! Take the war to the enemy, I say."

"Yes, and your man almost did. Now look what we have, General. A blockade!"

"My man stood his ground, unlike your Marines at the Chosen Reservoir!" retorted the Chief of the Army.

"What do you mean? It was your Army that threw away their weapons in retreat!" argued the Marine Chief.

"Impossible! The army was covering your Marines' asses!"

"And you left your dead behind! The Marines never leave their dead behind. We bring them home!"

The Chief of the Army jumped up. "I resent that accusation! All this would not have happened if the Air Force had blown up the Yalu River bridges like they were supposed to do! Put us all in the Chinese meat grinder, they did!"

The accusation instantly brought Air Force General LaMums wide awake and to his feet. His aide did not have to poke him. When taking 40 winks, he always had one ear open for mischief, like now. His eyes popped. He blinked. "We had our orders. Blame General McArthur," he snarled.

"I think all the military blundered on that one," responded the Director of the CIA.

The Chief of the Army tried to jump up again, but was held down by his aide, as instructed by Secretary McMac. "You have no room for criticism, sir, considering how your CIA swat team goofed the President Diem assassination!" he barked out.

"We had our instructions, Sir."

"Yes, and now we have a VietNam insurgency getting out of hand!"

Frowning, Secretary of Defense McNamara clapped his

hands lightly three times to bring the Joint Chiefs of Staff to order. "Commanders! Commanders! We are the National Security Council here, not the Colgate Comedy Hour. At issue is our convoy in Europe, not one in Korea." Feeling frustrated, he took a handkerchief from his pocket and dabbed at his forehead. He was sweating. There were days he wished he was back at Ford Motor Company where to ring his servant's bell made executives tremble, unlike here at the Pentagon where the response was the perpetual clash of brass and egos. "Secretary Pierre, would you please carry on?" asked the Secretary of Defense, suddenly tired.

"Yes Sir," replied the Press Secretary. "Now then, the Soviets have since dropped road barriers around our convoy, confining it to the Babelsberg processing area. By 1600 hours European time they had closed the Autobahn to all civilian traffic. Road repairs were given as the reason."

"Shut down in both directions?" asked the Chief of the Navy, raising his eyebrows.

"Yes Sir."

"To all military and civilian traffic?" asked the Chief of the Air Force, General LeMums. He was indeed wide awake now.

"Yes Sir."

"What about barge traffic on the Elba River, the air corridors?"

"Both are still open but with delays on the canals. Furthermore, our sources in East Germany indicate that the 7th Byelorussian and 9th Soviet Ukrainian Armored Divisions had begun active maneuvers," droned Mr. Pierre further. As he talked, the eyes of the Air Force Chief again solidified. He had drifted off.

At that moment, an aide rushed into the conference room. He handed Secretary of Defense McNamara a single sheet of paper stamped "Top Secret"! The Secretary frowned. He held up his hand, interrupting the Press Secretary. "This has just come in. The Warsaw Pact has gone on alert. The president must be notified at once."

"But he can't be disturbed," said the CIA Director, putting down his pen. "He is still in Hollywood on confidential business."

There was some murmuring. "This situation looks serious, gentleman," argued the Secretary of Defense.

"You're right. Jackie might find out about Marilyn," said the Secretary of the Navy.

Secretary McNamara glared at him. The FBI director made a note in his clipboard. Another "Mr. Meaner." "Commanders, I'm referring to West Berlin under siege, not the president's solicitations. Look, Soviet divisions on maneuvers, the Warsaw Pact on alert. Any suggestions, Commanders?"

"Yes," said the FBI director. "I suggest we take a coffee break."

"Good idea," said the Chief of the Air Force, again fully awake. The words "coffee break" had awakened him.

"I disagree," said the Chief of the Army. "This is an East-West, superpower confrontation. We must deal with it immediately. I suggest only a fifteen minute coffee break."

"Thirty minutes!" rejoined the Chief of the Marines, pushing his chair back to get up. "We Commanders need a Twinkie with our coffee. Send an aide to go out and get a package."

"I vote the thirty minutes," concurred the CIA Director. "What about you, Mr. Hoover?" he asked, looking toward the FBI Director.

Secretary of Defense McNamara stood up and rang the servant's bell and stamped his foot. When frustrated, he had a habit of copying Green Bay Coach Vince Lombardi on the sidelines during a game. "Generals, please! We are the American National Security Council! We are here to debate issues, not take coffee breaks! As the chairman of this meeting, there will be no coffee break until we have formulated a plan of action to put on the president's desk! Is that clear, gentlemen?"

The jowls of the Joint Chiefs quivered with indignation. They didn't appreciate being scolded like elementary school boys. The Chief of the Air Force, LaMums, followed with a question. "All right, let me ask this. Has the army initiated any further negotiations?"

The Chief of the Army nodded. "That is an affirmative, Sir."

"Now the Army's thinking like the Marines," said the Marine Chief confidently. "We can go for coffee."

"But the Army negotiations with the Soviets have been canceled," said Press Secretary Pierre, still standing at the blackboard.

The Chief of the Marines slumped in his seat. He needed that coffee. "Damn it! The Army flubbed it again. Never send a boy to do a man's job, I say."

The Chief of the Army leaned across the table as if to challenge the Chief of the Marines to arm wrestle. "Sir, if I'm not mistaken, were not the Marines also part of the `Big Bug Out´ in Korea?"

Immediately, the Secretary of Defense jumped up from his seat. He did not want another altercation. "Commanders, please stop arguing the Korean War! It is the past! This confrontation is in the present and in West Germany *today!* Okay! Now, Mr. Press Secretary, please tell us why the negotiations were canceled."

Press Secretary Pierre turned to the podium and flipped through his notes. "I don't really understand myself, but according to 7th Army report, the Soviets did not know how to play, ah, Patty Cake?"

The Joint Chiefs stared at Mr. Pierre. "Patty who?"

"What the hell is Patty Cake? A weapon?" asked Air Force Chief LaMums.

"No, it's the Marine Corps fight song," sneered the Army Chief of Staff.

The Chief of the Marines wanted to jump up, but was held down by his aide. He managed a growl. "I resent that, Sir!"

"Patty Cake sounds like a CIA code name to me," said the Chief of the Navy.

"Or the SAC signal to launch," said the Army Chief.

"It is neither," said the FBI Director, glad that he still remembered fairy tales from the days on his mother's knee. "Actually, it's a Mother Goose rhyme."

The Air Force Chief scratched his nose and shook his head. "Until we get to the bottom of this Patty Cake thing, I say let's mark it 'Top Secret'."

"No," said the FBI Director. "We have to mark it with 'B.' Now, let's take that coffee break."

III

It was the following morning when Col Blowhardus, followed by Capt Michaels, again entered the conference room. Waiting for them, Col Bluvov stood up. The two officers did not shake hands but immediately took their seats at the long table across from each other. Blowhardus, his tone serious, spoke first. "Colonel Bluvov, I have some positive news from my government. My government feels that there is room to meet your demands."

"My demands? Did I make demands?" asked the Russian Colonel coyly.

Blowhardus brushed aside the cynicism. "Yes, you did. You wanted to know if Patty Cake was a coded message. Well, it isn't. I can assure you of that. Here, these are documents you requested that clearly define the meaning of all things Patty Cake," he said, sliding a large manila envelope over to the Russian officer. "Also, I wish to point out that the word is not compatible to our Defense Department lexicon. In other words, Colonel Bluvov…it ain't code!" The Russian Colonel nodded approvingly as Blowhardus continued. "We usually do not give out this kind of information to an adversary, but in the interest of mutual understanding between our two countries, please keep the information." On the envelope, in the space usually reserved for the stamp 'Top Secret,' it was marked with the letter 'B.'

Col Bluvov opened it and took out the documents. "It is not written in the Russian language."

"Sir, Patty Cake does not translate well in Cyrillic," noted Captain Michaels.

"We shall study it," said the Russian Colonel, passing it to his subordinate, the tough looking body guard who stood behind him. Folding his hands on the mahogany table top, Bluvov considered his American counterpart. "And I have a surprise for you too, Colonel. I am to inform you on behalf of the Warsaw Pact nations that my government wishes to avoid problems with your government and NATO. Therefore..." he paused to dramatize the moment, "we are prepared to lift the barriers and permit your convoy vehicles to proceed. I have been told the Autobahn repairs are now complete."

Col Blowhardus who had come into the room in a temper, brightened. The only thing he could think of to say was, "Gosh!"

"At 1300 today your convoy may proceed unhindered." Col Bluvov smiled, revealing his capped molars made of aluminum. Both American officers cringed. "It is free to go as soon as you sweep away, how do you say it, `defecations´ deposited by your soldiers."

Colonel Blowhardus sighed with relief. "That is good news, Colonel Bluvov. My government will certainly be grateful. As you know, it is our wish not to be confrontational with the Soviet Union, and..." Here, he hesitated. He placed a finger to his lips, unsure of what he just heard. "Ah, Colonel Bluvov, may I ask what do you mean by 'defecations'?"

The Russian officer grunted amusement. "Yes. Your soldiers have deposited considerable defecations in the territory of our ally, the *Deutsche Demokratik Republik*. They have brought it to our attention. They feel the defecations are not only offensive, but demeaning to their sovereignty. They request it be cleaned up before your vehicles depart."

Col Blowhardus turned to his aide, Capt Michaels. "What exactly is the bastard talking about?" he whispered.

Capt Michaels leaned forward. "He is talking about defecation, sir. Shit! Soldier shit, that is."

"Soldier what?"

"He is referring to our convoy personnel. They have been relieving themselves on East German territory. Apparently the East German government has taken offense to it. They feel our American defecation—shit, that is—infringes on their sovereign rights. They want us to remove it," said Capt Michaels in a low voice, just audible enough for his Commander to hear.

Blowhardus frowned. "Shiiiit? You're kidding, are you not, Captain?"

The offficer aide shook his head. Col Blowhardus turned back to the Russian seated across from him. It was now his turn to rest folded hands on the mahogany table. He leaned forward. Being a history buff, he repeated what Br Gen McAuliffe said when the German Army Commander ordered him to surrender at Bastogne. "Nuts!"

Puzzled, Col Bluvov checked with his aide about the definition of nuts. He stood up. "Are you saying *Nyet*, Colonel Blowhardus?"

"No, I am saying nuts!" stated Blowhardus.

"You speak of peanuts, then?" asked the Russian.

"Yes, peanuts! Cashew nuts! Walnuts! Nutmeg! You name it. NUTS! The United States Government does not, nor will it recognize the sovereignty of the German Democratic Republic. Therefore, Sir, we will not clean up the—what did you call it? Defecations?"

Col Bluvov shot a vilifying look across the table, his molars exposed. "Listen, Colonel Blowhardus, we have 16 of your people in our zone. They have been there for four days. They have deposited considerable defecations on the sovereign soil of the DDR. It is offensive! It is an insult! You shall remove it—immediately!"

Suddenly calm, Blowhardus sat back. "Now, now, Herr Colonel. Tsh, tsh! Are you really going to let a couple of turds stand in the way of peace and harmony between our two nations?"

Bluvov glowered. He looked back to his subordinate and whispered something to him. The subordinate quickly took a Russian-English dictionary from his briefcase and flipped through the pages. He could not find what he was looking for and shook his head. Col Bluvov turned back to the table and Col Blowhardus, across from him. "What exactly is a turd?"

"It is shit, Sir! In your face! Crap! Defecation, if you will!" snapped Col Blowhardus, losing patience. "Look, Bluvov, if you don't let that convoy go right now I'll order my Brigade to smash their way through and take your checkpoint! Then you'll really know what it means for Shit To Fly!" he yelled.

"You talk of war?"

"I talk of my guys sitting in the cold for four days! It's hardly an issue of war, but an issue of...of nature calling!"

"My point precisely," stated Col Bluvov, wanting to save the negotiations as he was instructed to do by his superiors. "I suggest a compromise. My people will supply brooms and shovels if your people will clean it up."

"I would prefer if you supply a portable latrine. Then we would not have the problem, thank you!"

"The Soviet Union does not give comfort to the enemy!"

"How can it when the Soviet Union does not know the meaning of the word, 'comfort'!"

"The fact remains, the American defecations are American!"

"No longer! It is now an integrate part of the Soviet Occupation Zone, the DDR, earned by right-of-conquest, according to the Tripartite Agreements of 1945 between President Roosevelt, Prime Minister Churchill and Stalin. The defecations are yours!" argued Blowhardus.

"I don't believe there is a paragraph on defecations written into protocols of 1945. The defecations are yours, Colonel!" Bluvov argued back.

"Oh, I see, we are back now to Patty Cake, huh?" said Col Blowhardus, his eyes burning from exasperation. (He had slept little since the blockade had begun). "Even if my country wished to clean up the mess, our hands are still tied."

"Oh? How?"

"According to International Law, no nation or state is permitted to occupy or carry off one square inch of another state's sovereign territory, and that includes any foreign matter that may have been deposited in a zone of occupation. Brooms and shovels won't help! The defecations are yours!"

The Russian arched an eyebrow. "Might I remind you that the *Deutsche Democratik Republik* is not an occupation zone, but a sovereign state and an ally of the Soviet Union. The defecations are yours, Colonel!"

Growing desperate, Col Blowhardus held up a finger. "Sir, look at it from the point of view of Socratic reasoning. The stuff may have once belonged to American soldiers, but since its release from bodily apertures in the persons so defined and dropped into the DDR, the defecations, as you so delicately call it, are yours!"

"You call that reasoning?" vocalized the Russian.

"Most definitely!" stated the American. "The defecation has become an internal part of the Soviet Zone of Occupation. And since you are sovereign by right-of-conquest on all matters on the ground pertaining to your zone—and that includes the defecation, whether American, British or French—all are yours! Absolutely! Besides, your state can use a little fertilizer. *You* clean it up!"

Col Bluvov folded his arms and flashed one aluminum molar. "*Nyet*!"

Blowhardus shook his head. He was not getting through. He made one last attempt. "Colonel Blovuv, Sir, let's take it from the point of view of science. Human excrement is not unlike a meteorite falling from the sky. It is a thing unto itself. It wings through space belong to no one until, low and behold, it hits the earth. It hits in Russia, let us say. What are you going to do? Dig it up and throw it back in space? No, you keep it! You now have sovereign right over it. It is the same with human excrement. What my drivers dumped on your Autobahn—not that they wanted to, but they had no choice since you blockaded them in—has become an intricate part of ther Soviet Zone, under the control of the Hammer and Sickle. It can't be shoved back into the body. It's messy stuff. You have no choice. You have got to keep it. The defecations are yours! That simple."

"Hm!" mumbled the Russian thoughtfully. He glanced at his subordinate whose blank stare told him his mind was not much above the level of Patty Cake, and therefore worthless.

Feeling he was at last getting through, Blowhardus pushed what he thought was the advantage. "Look at it from a political point. That is something you Russians are masters at. Let's say you go to Iran and shit in the desert. Five years later you go back. Do you dig up the shit and take it back to the Soviet Union? No! The shit belongs to Iran. It is Iranian. Who else should it belong to? Whether it's five years or five days, a physical and political metamorphosis has taken place once the defecation strikes the ground. The poop can no longer be yours; it has become a fundamental part of the state of Iran. Now, doesn't that make sense?" he stated in Russian with an accent, hoping Col Bluvov would finally understand.

Pausing, a glare of light coming into the room through the windows, the Russian Colonel lit up yet another of his stinky Georgian cigarettes. He blew a smoke ring across the table at the American counterpart. "Your logic smells."

Blowhardus stiffened. "Not as much as shit does!"

The Russian fixed on him. The tension was building. "A compromise," suggested Bluvov. "We sweep it up and give the shit back to you in a paper bag."

"Cannot be done! The metamorphosis has already taken place!"

"We do not speak of bread and wine, here."

"Only if it is made of excrement!"

"You are a fool, Colonel Blowhardus!"

"And you are a jerk, Colonel Bluvov!"

The Russian's face took on color. His jowls bulged above the stiff collar of his uniform. He gagged, trying to to speak, his patience at a threshold. "Now listen to my logic, Sir! Are not these your vehicles? Are not these your drivers? And did these drivers not defecate in the sovereign territory of our ally, the DDR? Then it follows, the defecations are yours! You sweep it away, and I mean immediately, or face the wrath of the Soviet Union!" On their feet and leaning on the mahogany conference table, the two colonels—one Russian, the other American—glared at each other across the impasse.

***

The weather had changed abruptly. A warm wind blew up from the Atlantic Gulf Stream, sending temperatures on the North German Plain into the middle 50s. Suddenly, for the drivers of convoy 211 it was not so bad to be stuck on a barren checkpoint somewhere between Holland and Poland. It was like Boy Scout camp. The sky had cleared. The sun came out. The soldiers opened the doors of their vehicles. Major Dimwitty secured permission from the Soviets to allow the men to step out, stretch, and walk around. They could do some PT—the side-straddle-hop. Pushups. By the afternoon they were congregating in small groups and becoming chummy with the Russian guards.

But the nights were still hard. It had to do with the temperature drop. The Russian guards, now very friendly with the American drivers, supplied them with the occasional bottles of Vodka. It had the Americans singing well after midnight and made that morning physical training even more essential. On the evening of the fifth day, snacking chocolate bars in their jeep, Yorit and Gonzales watched the Russian changing-of-the-guard ritual.

"I'll tell you, Yo, I sure am glad you brought these candy bars with you," said Gonzales, taking a chocolate bar out of the brown paper bag on his lap. It was one of several bags Yorit had brought along. The bag was filled with candy, gum etc. They had already eaten the bananas. "Another can of C-rat spam and I might throw up. But why so many paper bags?"

"I'm making a statement for democracy," said Yorit, still slouched in his seat, one knee against the steering wheel.

The MP bit into the Mars Bar. "How can candy be a statement for democracy? Hey, what's this in the bag? A yo-yo?" He held it up.

Yorit reached over and took it. Fingering the yo-yo, he looked around to be sure no one was near. The two officers were over by the trucks. "If I tell you something, José, promise not to tell anybody?" The MP nodded. "Okay. Driving convoy as long as I have, a couple of years now, I got to feeling sorry for the East Germans farmers out there. Every time we drive past them on the Autobahn we see the poor bastards hoeing their fields—men, women, and kids. I mean in every kind of weather. You never see a tractor. It seems they plant and harvest all by hand like they used to do in Kansas. Can you imagine? I'm sure them folks are miserable. From my perspective, East German farmers don't have much except maybe a shared pot to piss in. That's Socialism. So I fill up a couple of brown paper bags with western decadent goodies like gum, chocolate chip cookies, C-ration cigarettes, Hershey Bars, stuff that will rot your teeth. And as our M151 Ford jeep passes by on the Autobahn, I toss the bags out to the farmers working in the fields I must have spent a fortune on commissary Twinkies."

"Better be careful or you'll turn the East Germans into sugar junkies," Gonzales warned.

Yorit laughed. "They already are. When I toss, they drop their hoes and dash for the bags and fight over 'em. That's why I toss out several bags at a time, to keep the farmers from killing each other. It's against Army regulations, I know, but hey, we're Americans. We're here to help Germany. If I ever got caught tossing, I'm sure I'd be busted. So, José, shh! Don't tell anyone, please."

"Great idea, Robert," said the MP. "On my next convoy run I'm going to do the same thing."

***

Back at Heidelberg, West Germany, dressed in a windbreaker, sweat pants, and tennis shoes, General Benjamin Ulysses III was just walking out the door of his office at 7th Army Command when 1st Lt Tupple, rushed up. He had another message in hand marked "Urgent to Secret." He saluted. "Oh, you're leaving headquarters already, Sir? It's only 1400 hours."

"I'm assistant basketball coach over at Patrick Henry High School. We are having a practice game. If the message can wait, give it to me first thing in the morning."

"It can't wait, Sir. See? It's marked 'Priority'," said the Lt.

The General rolled his eyes. "So much for basketball practice. The kids will have to wait. Okay, let's have it."

Taking the envelope, the General tore it open. It read: "Negotiations concerning Berlin-Helmstedt convoy No. 112 have been suspended."

"Oh, shit!"

"How did you know, Sir?" asked Lt Tupple.

"How did I know what?"

"That that negotiation had been suspended because of soldier shit."

Startled, General Benjamin looked at his junior officer. "Tupple, you watch your language! There are civilian secretaries walking around here."

It was morning in Washington as the National Security Council officials filed into the Pentagon conference room, followed by their entourage of aides and advisors. The Chief of Staff of the Air Force, General La Mums, came in last. One of his aides, an airman, carried his awards and medals on a velvet pillow. The other Chief of Staff members looked on, envious. They did not have as many awards on their velvet pillows. One medal General LeMums was particularly proud of was given to him by President Kennedy himself. It was for endurance during the Cuban Missile Crisis. He never once fell asleep during the many non-stop National Security Council meetings.

Secretary of Defense McNamara had already taken his place at the head of the octagon conference table and waited for the chiefs and their entourage to take their seats.

"Commanders," he began, "the president has asked me again to chair this meeting. The crisis in West Berlin has been reclassified to Level Red II." The Generals sucked in their breaths. Red Level II meant the world was that much closer to a nuclear exchange.

"Where is the president? Another Hollywood conference?" asked the Chief of the Navy. There were some snickers.

"It seems you know his agenda better then I do, General," said Secretary McNamara, brushing the crack aside. J. Edgar Hoover of the FBI jotted down the conduct deficiency note next to the chief's name. Leaning forward, his fists on the octagon table, Secretary McNamara talked slowly, giving the situation the gravity it deserved. "We have a crisis on our hands that is getting out of control. Now, all traffic coming into West Berlin has been temporarily stopped. Extended road repairs are the reason given by the Soviets. Sirs, we have to get this situation under control, like now. It's getting worse instead of better. The president needs your advice. Mr. Press Secretary, the situation report, if you please!"

Press Secretary Pierre got to his feet. He adjusted his glasses to deflect the glare of the brass arrayed in front of him and began the briefing. "The East German Autobahn from West Berlin to Helmstedt, West Germany is currently in a permanent state of blockade."

The Chief of the Marines looked up. "Wait a minute! I thought we resolved the conflict with the Patty Cake issue."

"That is correct, Sir. The Russians responded favorably to the negotiations. Another problem, however, has arisen. A more serious one," noted the Press Secretary. "It is so serious that it prompted an extension of the blockade." The Chiefs looked at one another. "Apparently after five days of enforced incarceration, the drivers of the 37th Transportation Company out of Kaiserslautern had fouled the parking area with human feces. The Russians want it cleaned up before they release our convoy. It has to do with respect for East German territory, or so they say."

"Now what the hell is that supposed to mean?" interrupted the Chief of the Army, his voice filled with exasperation..

"It means Army shit in someone else's backyard. They don't like it and neither would I," humphed the Chief of Air force, eyeballing the Army Chief as he spoke.

"That is correct, Commander," said Mr. Pierre. "The Russians consider it not only unhygienic, but an insult to the dignity of their ally, the German Democratic Republic. Their party secretary, Walter Ulbricht, complained about it."

"Well, if that's the only issue holding up the convoy have the boys police the shit. Can't see why a couple of turds should cause a super power confrontation," suggested the CIA Director, observing his finger nails.

The Chief of Staff of the Marines looked at the Chief of Staff of the Army. "Another East-West standoff and it's all your fault, General! Your service has absolutely no discipline! Now we're into it up to our ears!"

"No, only up to the ankles," noted the CIA Director.

The Chief of the Navy looked up. "You mean we are on a Red Level II alert, the Warsaw Pact facing NATO forces, weapons drawn and threatening, all because someone shit in a parking lot? I mean, really! I've heard of the face that launched 1000 ships, but the turd that launched a thousand missiles? I'm just glad I'm in the Navy. There we throw our crap overboard."

The CIA Chief scratched his head. "I could understand it if the Army crapped a red, white, and blue residue, but this?"

"Why are the East Germans complaining?" asked the Chief of the Army. "The South Koreans love the stuff. Chuck full of nutrients, our doodoo. You know the South Koreans even pay us for the privilege of picking up our On Post excrement and hauling it away. They sprinkle it on their rice paddies, then eat the rice. It makes them feel American."

"We are not in South Korea, Sir; we are in East Germany. It's all your fault we're in this mess, General!" snarled the Air Force Chief.

Fearful of another confrontation between the services, Secretary of Defense McNamara immediately stood up. "Generals! Generals! Please! The question here is a plan of action, not who is to blame. What should we do? We've got to defuse this refuse thing otherwise West Berlin will starve."

"Rectal corks could help," said the Navy Chief, ever thoughtful.

There followed the distinct sound of reflection, a gnashing of teeth and a snarl or two when the General of the Army spoke up. "I suggest we launch a rescue mission. Why not? Our new UH-1H, Hueys are here on depot in West Germany. We're using them in VietNam with some success. Why not here?"

A captain, the Chief of the Army's aide, whispered something to him. The Army Chief grumbled and glared at him. "Capt'n, are you trying to embarrass me?" and turned back to the table. "My assistant tells me we do not have any UH-1H Hueys on depot in West Germany. Such a strike is out of the question."

"How about if we send in some armor, say three tanks?" suggested the Marine Chief. "That should be enough to bring our convoy out. After all, what are we talking about here? A mere 3000 yards inside Communist territory?"

"I'd go for that," said the Director of the CIA, "except the Soviets could counter with three divisions and three hundred tanks. They are right there on the spot."

"Generals, why not just clean up the feces, if that's the issue?" suggested the Navy Chief.

"A negative to that," said Secretary McNamara. "According to the Potsdam Agreements, US military is not permitted to interfere, that is, to do road maintenance in the Soviet Zone. To police the Autobahn of any matter, organic or otherwise, would be a flagrant disregard of the Four power Agreements of 1945. The Soviets could claim we interfered in the internal affairs of their Ally, the so-called GDR. It would give them a propaganda victory and use it as an excuse to scrap all agreements between our two countries. With no international agreements to stall them, the Soviets could sign a unilateral peace treaty with Walter Ulbricht and accordingly march into West Berlin. Legally and tactically, we would not be able to stop them, given that the city lies 110 miles behind our lines. Also, if we tried, it would give Khrushchev an excuse to pull out all the stops and launch strikes from their Communist satellite countries such as Cuba, North Korea, North VietNam, Syria, as well as attacks across the whole of the Iron Curtain. It could mean a nuclear exchange! Do we want to take that risk, gentlemen?"

The Chief of the Navy's face went pale. "And all because of an army turd," he grumbled.

"Not just a turd. More like a pile of turds," noted the Director of the CIA. "My department research shows that when confined to a small space, 14 to 16 soldiers on a diet of C-ration spam and chocolate can double body waste, analytically speaking, of course."

"Maybe the Russians do have something to gripe about after all," said Air Force Chief, General LaMums.

"I agree. Maybe they do have a gripe," whined the Marine Corps Chief. "But a blockade?"

Growing concerned, the Generals looked around at one another.

They scratched their chins and conferred with their aides, nodded, asking questions, looking for a way out of the dilemma.

"Well, Commanders?" asked Secretary of Defense McNamara.

The Chief of the Navy jammed a cigar in his mouth. "If we could find some neutral authority to clean up the excrement we could solve the problem. But who?"

For a moment the room fell silent for thought. The Chief of the Army took out a handkerchief and whipped his forehead. The Chief of the Marines contemplated the back of his hand. The Chief of the Air Force snoozed, albeit with his eyes open. The Director of the CIA asked his aide for a layout copy of Washington's underground bunkers; he wanted to review which one was his since he might need it. The unflappable Director of the FBI, J. Edgar Hoover, doodled. There were no conduct deficiencies to be noted.

"Commanders, as the advisory council to the President of the United States, have you, the Chiefs of Staff of the United States, reached any conclusions?"

The Chief of the Navy stood up. "Yes! I move we take a coffee break."

***

The convoy drivers were tired. They were uncomfortable. They were irritable. After five days, going on six days of sleeping behind steering wheels, sitting in the cold, eating C-rations and inhaling the rising stench that emanated from behind their vehicles, especially as the day warmed, they felt they had a right to complain, out loud and vocally. They did, sometimes with a scream. "Awe, shit!" shouted a Gonzales, frustrated.

The jeep door jerked open. Both he and Yorit jumped. They were on edge. It was the ROTC Lt. "Don't do that again!"

"Don't do what, Sir?"

"I'm not sure what."

"Yes Sir."

"Get Brigade Command on the radio. The Major wants to talk with Operations," he ordered with a tired bravado.

Two minutes later, Major Dimwitty stepped over to the MP-Signal communication jeep.

Yorit handed him the handset. "Sir, the batteries on the VCR radio are running low. We're working off our reserves. May I suggest we cut back on communication? Otherwise the radio might shut down. Black out," he warned.

Major Dimwitty, who was beginning to resemble an apostle after five days of no shave, looked at Yorit who was also beginning to resemble an apostle. "It wouldn't dare," he said. "Piss on it if you have to, Soldier, but keep that radio operational."

Though the reception was weak, Yorit was able to raise Brigade Headquarters. Major Dimwitty held the handset to his lips. Since the batteries were weak, he had permission to drop the code formalities and talk straight away. "Hello, Operations? We're running low on rations and battery power. Situation critical. Any news? Over!" he asked, his tone languid.

Ten minutes later the return communication was, "Delegate supplies with care. Situation not yet resolved. Out!"

Major Dimwitty threw down the hand set. "You!" he pointed to Yorit. "You tell the Lieutenant to call a formation."

Under an unusually clear sky, the drivers of the 37th Transportation Company assembled on the parking mall in front of Major Dimwitty. Beyond, bored, and cradling their weapons, the Russian guards watched them. Yorit and Gonzales took their place at the end of the sloven looking line of soldiers. A "Snap to!" order was out of the question. The usually sharp looking outfit now looked more like grease monkeys after a hard day in the mechanic's pit: facial beards, eyes glazed over, uniforms rumpled. Tired.

Rubbing the back of his neck, Major Dimwitty observed his crew. "Men, I have bad news. We're stuck! Negotiations are going nowhere. The Russians will not let us depart unless somebody polices up the shit behind our vehicles. They won't do it and we're not authorized to do it. What all the fuss is about, I don't know. It's a stand-off of which we, unfortunately, are in the middle. I know it sounds dumb. It's one of those hard nose east-west confrontations that don't make sense. They never do. Nevertheless, we have to stand firm. The survival of a free West Berlin depends on our resolve not to shovel the shit."

The solvent line grumbled. "Sir, if it'll defuse an East-West conflict, I'll gladly sweep it up," offered one of the trans-drivers.

"Your heroic gesture is noted for the record, Soldier."

"Sir, I say let's all shovel the shit," another driver warily suggested. He had picked up a dose of cabin fever.

"Not permitted," interrupted the ROTC Lt.

Yorit raised his hand. "Sir, why not let the East Germans do it?"

Major Dimwitty looked at him. "Do what, Signalman?"

"Let the East German border guards, the Vopos, let them clean up the doodoo. After all, it's in their territory. It'll get both Moscow and Washington off a diplomatic hook and us the hell out of here. We keep our honor clean, not to mention our hands, and the Russians will keep theirs. Everyone will be happy. No one will lose face. Let the East Germans shovel the shit, Sir."

"I'm sure those high level negotiations at Potsdam already discussed that option," said Major Dimwitty, sounding aloof.

"But, Sir, the question is—have they?" asked one of the trans-drivers, skeptical .

Looking tired, Major Dimwitty scratched at his beard. "You know what, soldier? I'll ask." He turned to Yorit. "You, Signalman, the man with the bright ideas, get me Brigade Operations on the radio again."

Three hours after the call, the East German Autobahn was open for traffic. The barrier pole at the Soviet controlled Babelsberg checkpoint was lifted and the spiked slats under the rear tires of the rear trucks pulled away. With that, diesel engines coughed, motors sputtered, and again, like Corsairs off a flattop, convoy No. 122 of the 37th Transport Company out of Kaiserslautern began to roll. Destination: Helmstedt, West Germany.

As the American Army convoy pulled away, a detail of East German security men in green uniforms and combat helmets with machine pistols strapped to their backs stepped out. They began brooming at what might be defined as "deposits of contention." The American Army defecation! Shoveling it into wheelbarrels as they did, the East German security police (Vopos) did not look happy.

"What do you suppose they're going to do with our shit deposits?" asked Gonzales, looking back; he and Yorit were both glad the convoy was on the move again, their M151 jeep in the lead.

At the wheel, Yorit thought for a moment. "Probably ship it off to Communist North Korea. They could use the stuff for their rice paddies."

***

The six-day West Berlin blockade was now over. Both sides, Soviet and American had stood down. It did not make the headlines. There were no parades. In the Army's *Stars and Stripes* newspaper only one small column referred to the incident. Then it was just history.

Because of Yorit's suggestion, the six-day Soviet blockade was lifted, and if one wished to stretch the imagination, a super power conflict avoided. To Yorit's surprise, back at 592nd Signal Company, he was recognized at the company's 1700 formation. Recognition was something that rarely happened to simple soldiers. Standing in front of the company, he was given an Army Certificate of Achievement Award and a handshake from Company Commander Capt Mellon. A weekend pass followed, of which one day was rescinded. Dust balls had accumulated under his bunk while he was on convoy duty.

Because it was said he kept his cool in a dangerous situation, Major Dimwitty received the Army Commendation Medal. At government expense, the Army flew him and his wife to Washington and a reception dinner was given by Secretary of Defense McNamara for a job well done.

As for the sloe-eyed drivers of the 37th Transportation Company out of Kaiserslautern, the sons of the Red Ball Express, the outfit that kept the army supplied in war and in peace, what happened to them? Nothing! There was no award. There was no ceremony. There was no time off. They were back on the West German roads and Autobahns in their heavy tonners, gas pedals to the floorboards, rubber to the pavement, somewhere between Bremenhaven and the Fulda Gap, doing what they do best—their job.

Pay Call

Several students from the Berlin Conservatory of Music had set up a jazz band. It was a hobby and an alternative to their strenuous studies. The idea was to play the latest and greatest of American jazz and blues: Zoot Sims, Count Basie, Dizzi Gillespi and other music notables. They advertised themselves as a "combo" and worked gigs at the local Schöneberg and Charlottenberg district clubs. They had already developed a name for themselves when the saxophone player, a Dixieland fan, quit. He had wanted more Dixie in the group's repertoire of music which, more or less, did not fit the style of the clubs where they gigged. There were conflicts, and he quit the combo. After a month, unable to find a replacement, the combo (now a trio) went to the only jazz source where they might find a sax man willing to work for little pay—the American Berlin Brigade.

PFC Kevin Kantwell was leaving the post snack bar. He had just drunk a milkshake and was on his way back to Signal Company for afternoon formation when a note on the entrance bulletin board caught his eye. He stepped back, pushed his glasses to the edge of his nose and looked closely. He jotted down the name and the phone number on the card. It was an offer to play saxophone with a German jazz group. The possibility appealed to him.

Private First Class Kantwell was not the typical Army enlistee. He did not drink, he did not smoke, and he did not hang out at bars with the boys. And women? They did not interest him much. Such behavior made him, more or less, the company oddball in a macho environment of mighty drinkers and tactless studs. He was the square plug that did not fit the round hole of the Army mold. This meant he was often alone. His bad case of athlete's foot did not invite friendship either, for his quarters stunk, and no one would bunk with him.

The foot infection was a Basic Training strain, easy to pick up and difficult to shake. He blamed the daily 10-mile hikes that opened blisters on both feet and the common showers where soldiers played the game of "Slip the Soap." Posted overseas, the infection had gotten worse despite the numerous powders and disinfectants given him. One clinic physician in Landstuhl, West Germany, a major on TDY (temporary duty), diagnosed his athlete's foot as gangrene and wanted to amputate. A second opinion by a junior officer physician, with the rank of 1ˢᵗLt who had just completed his medical internship when he was drafted, advised against it. The Major promised Kantwell a medical discharge and a sure 30% disability pay from Uncle Sam for the rest of his life should the operation fail, as the Major was that eager to operate. Kantwell wisely followed the 1ˢᵗLt's advice. He refused.

Thus, at the end of a workday and alone, PFC Kantwell would hang his boots out the barracks window to air out. With no roommates, he would sit in his quarters and read, write, compose, or play one of the two instruments he had mastered—the cello and the violin—all in solitude.

In civilian life, music had been his first love, and it still was. Tchaikovsky was his hero. As a student of composition at Julliard School of Music in New York City, he had trained in string instruments. For a hobby, though, he played the saxophone. On occasion, he would get together with fellow students from Julliard to "jam" at the local bars. It was a way to relax. He was happy living the life of a Fine Arts academic until a personal relationship interfered, causing him to drop out of school and enlist in the Army--just to show HIM! It was a decision that devastated his parents. At the MEP station (Army In-Processing Center) he had the first of several "Bend-over-and-part 'em!" physicals. The physical shocked him. What shocked him even more—he liked it.

A year later, in the Berlin Brigade, PFC. Kantwell was more or less isolated with his creative impulses that a professor once called "bordering on reverence." With little to do but hum, he saw the German jazz band as an opportunity to get away from Army life for a few hours. It meant rubbing shoulders again with real musicians instead of the local finger-pickin', hoot-n-anny, Beatle and Rolling Stone crazed yokels in the barracks. Noting the address and phone number of the jazz band leader, he decided to call.

***

A week later, it was 0700. Morning chow was over. The soldiers of the 592nd Signal Company fell out for the extra formation. With his arms folded, 1stSgt Persilla watched them. One after another the PltSgts ordered, "FALL IN! COVERRR!" Shifting and shuttling, the platoons lined up.

"Companyyy, 'TENSION!" the 1stSgt ordered, followed by the call of "STRAKE TROOP!" (Sharp soldier)

"STRACK TROOP!" the three platoons thundered back from attention.

"AT EASE!"

1stSgt Persilla read out the Orders of the Day from his clipboard. "As you all know, this is the first day of the month and 'Pay Call'." There were rumblings of anticipation from the ranks. "Following Pay Call there will be a stand-by inspection by the Company Commander," he announced. "No exceptions! All doors to quarters will be open! All wall and foot lockers will be open! Any questions?" There were none. "Platoon sergeants, see me now. Companyyy, 'TENSION! Fallout!"

The formation collapsed. The soldiers, now a mob, rushed for the barracks entrance to be the first in line for Pay Call. However, one soldier, Spc-4 Yorit, decided he wanted to make a statement for individualism, something frowned upon in the army. Defiant, he sauntered toward the barracks entrance instead of hustling, as was the rule. "I refuse to be coerced into such mindless behavior!" he stated out loud.

3rd Plt Sgt Sweechek walked up behind him. "You, Yorit! You better hustle. I hear the Commander is going to shut down the Pay Call line early because of the inspection. If you want your money, hustle!"

With a "You got to be kidding, Sarge," he took off running with the pack. So much for individualism.

In front of the Orderly Room, the Pay Ccall line had already formed, and just like the chow line, it meandered. First, it meandered the length of the hallway, then it meandered around the corner, then down the stairwell stairs, leaving the soldiers at the end of the line grumbling.

Pay Call was a once-a-month ritual and the only time soldiers did not complain about having to stand in line. They were to get their bucks, their "Base Pay," money-in-hand, as they say. It was cash on the barrel head! $65 for E-3 pay, $90 for E-4 pay, $120 for E-5s and up. Twenty-four hours later, most of the soldiers would be broke, their money blown, drunk up, with barely a memory of what happened to it. With free room and board and medical, the army Pay Call was a freebee. Play money. Fun stuff to be blown at leisure, especially if you were 19 years old and the first time away. from home.

In the orderly room, Captain Mellon, the Company Commander, sat at 1st Sgt Persilla's desk. On the desk were stacks of $50s, $20s, $10, and $1 bills, the cash used to pay the soldiers. The regimen was thus: a man would enter the orderly room (stiffly, of course), stop two paces from the edge of the desk, salute, and report his name, rank, and serial number as loud as he could. "Specialist Fourth Class, Thomas Hatnoy, 358-46-9864, reporting for pay, SIR!" And get paid. That was the company Pay Call.

If there were rainmakers in the company, they were the barracks loan sharks. Every company had one or two. They were mostly Dago soldiers form Philadelphia, Chicago, New York, or Detroit's Little Italy who pimp-rolled as they walked the line. They collected 50% usurious interest on money loaned out the month before. To ask more than 50% was considered unethical. With their Neanderthal enforcers walking behind them—big strapping guys like 2nd platoon's Corporal Angelo who weighed 210 lbs, all of it muscle and no gut—the loan sharks would demand debt payment on the spot, and get it. And woe betide the man who couldn't pay up. Like, BOP!

Standing at the back of the line, Yorit folded his arms and gave one of those "Oh, shit, here we go again" sighs, that is, out loud, breathy, indicating boredom. It was immediately infectious. Bravo and Pereski yawned. Jonas yawned. O'Malley dropped his shoulders and let his knuckles drag on the floor, the way the Irish do. Robuck, also bored, watched him. "Say, Pattie, are all Irish guys built like you—long arms, big knuckles?"

"Only if your grandfather picked potatoes in Killarnie," interrupted Bravo, who stood in front of O'Malley.

"Or if your father was a New York City cop," said Pereski, who stood in front of Bravo. "It comes from the long arm of the law chasing Waps in Jersey. Say, Frank, you're a Dago-Wap, right? Ever been chased?" Bravo glared at Pereski and made a fist. Pereski glared back.

O'Malley shrugged. "The long arms come from shooting too much pool, not being Irish. All that stretching, you know."

"Stretching will do that to you?" asked Yorit, who stood in front of Jonas. "I'll stick to playing marbles, thank you."

Like the Army chow line, there were the grumblings, but unlike the Army chow line, the Pay Call line moved steadily. The soldiers were glad of that.

Slouching, Yorit looked around. "Do you guys have any idea how much time we waste standing in lines?"

"Don't have to tell us. We live it," said Robuck.

"I know, but just think about it. This morning at formation we stood in line, then we stood in line for chow, then we stood in line for mail call, now here we are again standing in line for Pay Call. Four times waiting in line and its not even 0900! Is somebody nuts?" The men around Yorit nodded in agreement. "And tell me," he added, "what do we get for all that standing in line?"

"Varicose veins?" answered Kantwell, also in line.

"No, a wasted of life," Yorit replied. "25% of Army life is spent standing in front, behind, or next to someone with beer breath, every day, 24 hours a day, and that's twelve months a year! For years! What a waste of manpower."

Fingers to lips and thoughtful, the other men grumbled. "Na, so-what?" "Big deal." "Fug it." "Shit!" Then someone farted. It cut the grumbling short.

"So what's your point, Yoyo?" asked Lavoss from his place in the Pay Call line.

"That's just it. There ain't any." And Yorit began to cry.

"But there is a point, there, soldier," came the rough but familiar voice. The men looked around. It was the 2nd Platoon's Sergeant Oats; he had come up behind them. "A soldier actually spends 33% of his Army career standing in line, and you want to know why? So we Sergeants can be sure you men don't screw up, that's why. By the way, Yorit, you seem to be bitching a lot lately. Gonna have to talk with your Section sergeant. You may need an extra work detail or two to get your mind off of thinking." Turning, Plt Sgt Oats walked away, leaving Yorit expressionless.

Pereski pressed his thumb to his chin. "Guys, we must stop being negative here. There are advantages of being in the Army. Take the Army base pay, for instance. You earn $90 a month. Now, divide that $90 by 30 days, then divide that by 12 hours a day. You are thus earning... ah, who's got some college around here?"

"Twenty-five cents an hour," said Robuck.

"Exactly! Tell me one job in the world where you can stand in a line, do nothing, and get paid 25 cents an hour for it? Come on tell me."

"The Cuban Air Force, maybe?" said Bravo

"It's like Ol' Sarge Sweetcheeks says," Pereski went on. "Pull your finger out of your ass and bite the bullet. We're in Uncle Sam's Army!"

"Or bite the finger and pull the bullet out of your ass."

"I'd rather bite the finger."

"It depends whose finger you're biting."

"Or whose ass it was stuck up."

"Or whose finger."

"Not my finger."

"So shall we bite the bullet?"

"Not if it had been up the ass."

"Then what do we bite?"

"Let us bite neither."

"Ye-ah," said Jonas in southern, singing. "We 's in the Army now..."

Bravo then pitching in "...we're not behind the plow... ." With that, the other signalmen in the Pay Line picked up on the old World War II soldier's melody. "...we're digging a ditch, you son-of-a-bitch, we're in the Army now!" They all laughed. And the pay line moved up.

In short order the men were in and out of the company Orderly Room. Having gotten paid, everyone was all smiles until they hit the Chinese Wall. The debt tables! They were just outside the Orderly Room. Call it the gauntlet. Call it what you will. There was the hair cut table, the Red Cross table, the tailor's table, the government EE-US Bond table, and the loan shark table, which wasn't a table at all but an extended hand, palm up and pay up—the debt table. Following the debt table payouts, some soldiers came away with a shell-shocked look and two dollars in change left in the pocket. "Where'd my dough go?" And the line moved up.

"Next!" ComCom Captain Mellon called out from inside the Orderly Room.

Waiting at the door, it was Jonas' turn to get paid. Smartly, he stepped into the Orderly Room. At the demarcation line in front of the pay desk he saluted. "Specialist Cecil Jonas, 573-34-080, SIR!"

"At ease!" snapped back Capt Mellon. 1st Sgt Persilla stood behind him. He had a sidearm strapped to his hip should anyone be foolish enough to grab for the pile of dollar bills on the desk and run.

From the door, O'Malley looked over Yorit's shoulder. Yorit was next to him in the pay line. "1st Sarge looks tall for a midget," O'Malley mused. "Is he standing on a box behind the Commander or wearing high heel boots?"

"It's the weapon he carries," whispered Yorit. "It makes everyone look tall."

Jonas took his pay in hand, saluted, about-faced, retreated, and stepped smartly out of the Orderly Room.

"Next!" snapped Com Mellon.

Now it was Yorit's turn. He brushed his sidewall haircut, checked the buttons on his fly, and his fatigue shirt. All were lined up. Stiffening, he stepped into the Orderly Room and up to the so-called demarcation line, two paces in front of the pay desk. He saluted. "Specialist E-4 Robert Yorit, 873-226-165, reporting for pay, SIR!"

Leaning back in his chair, Capt Mellon, a West Point graduate, looked critically at him, noting his appearance: haircut, shave, brass, the boot shine, the buttons on Yorit's fly. Satisfied, he read over Yorit's pay statement, then, taking dollar bills from the stacks on the desk, he counted out $90, an E-4's pay for a month. He set the currency teasingly at the edge of his desk, a little out of reach. It required a precipitous bow from the waist (call it homage to the officer corps) for the enlisted man to reach out and take his money.

Just as Yorit began the demeaning descent from the waist, Capt Mellon stopped him at mid-bow. "Hold on, there, soldier," he said, shuffling some papers in front of him. "I see you have an unpaid bill here that needs adjusting. You bought a photo camera on time from a German camera shop and didn't pay." He held up the invoice. "I've received a complaint— two payments overdue. Now, why haven't you paid your bill, Soldier?"

"Sorry, Sir. Drank up the money. You know how it is, Sir. But I swear..."

"I agree," interrupted Capt Mellon. "I will just take $50 off the top toward that camera. And here's a $15 PX bill you still have open. We'll clear that, too. Now, tell me, how much are you supposed to send home to your mother?"

"$20 a month, Sir!" Yorit answered smartly.

"And are you doing that, Son?" Capt Mellon asked, looking up at his soldier who was a year older than the Captain himself. Both had college, but Mellon had graduated.

Yorit looked embarrassed. "Not for a couple of months, Sir, but I have an explanation..."

"Hold the explanation. I'll just take $20 off the base pay. There!"

Yorit watched his CO as he stuffed the money into separate envelopes. Reaching back, he handed the envelopes to 1st Sgt Persilla, standing at attention behind him. "Take care of this, will you, Top?" he said, and looked back at Yorit in front of him still at attention. "Here, Specialist," he said, sliding a lone five-dollar bill to the edge of the desk, "Here's your base pay for the month. Spend it wisely." The cynicism in his voice was noticeable.

A light scream (more a gag) emitted from the back of Yorit's throat. With a bow from the waist, he stretched and took the fiver from the desk, for he dared not cross the white demarcation line painted on the floor in front of it. "Aren't you forgetting protocol, Soldier?" Capt Mellon scolded.

Immediately, Yorit snapped a smart salute. "NOSIR! Thankyousir!"

"Yes, and one more thing," warned Capt Mellon, not yet returning the salute, "I will not tolerate any deadbeats in my company. From now on you WILL pay your debts! You WILL pay your bills! You don't, and I'll pull your gate pass and confine you to barracks till all debts are cleared. Do I make myself understood, Specialist?"

"YESSIR!" Yorit shouted, his throat constricting, the salute still in place at his forehead as if taped there. Capt Mellon returned the salute. With that, Yorit dropped his hand and about-faced, stepping from the Orderly Room and away from the Commander's fixated glare. He felt it singe the back of his neck.

"NEXT!" came the command order.

Outside the Orderly Room and standing in the hallway, Yorit held up the five dollar bill, all that was left of his month's base pay. "What can a man do with five bucks?"

"Play the slots!" said Robuck, who was still in the pay line.

Just then Pvt Milano, one of the company loan sharks from the 1st Platoon's Mafia, walked up. He snapped the five-dollar bill out of Yorit's hand. "Thank you, Robert. I'll take that."

"Huh?"

"You've just cleared your debt with the firm. Congratulations," said Pvt Milano, turning to the man standing next to him, a six-foot, 210 lb enforcer. It was Cp; Angelo from 2nd Platoon. "Scratch Yorit off the shit list, will you, Angie? One guy less you have to punch out tonight." Cpl Angelo looked disappointed.

With Pay call over, the soldiers returned to their quarters to get ready for the company inspection. They had already waxed the floors and dusted every square inch of flat surface, for at 592nd Signal Company, quarterly inspection was serious stuff. The rooms had to look immaculate. Boots and shoes were spit-shined, the soldier bunks made, the army issue, brown wool blankets with the capitol letters "U.S." printed on them, pulled tight, the blankets stretched and taut over the bunk's four corners. All foot and wall lockers were open and on display. With that, the soldiers stood at stand by, hands folded behind their backs and in position. They waited, knowing that Capt Mellon, 1st Sgt Persilla and the Plt Sgts would soon arrive, cynicism and clipboards in hand. In their quarters, Lavoss, Yorit, Robuck, and Pereski waited. They bunked together.

"This ain't a white glove inspection, I hope," said Lavoss, looking around.

Robuck cocked his head. Standing next to the door, his job was to shout, "Attention!" when the Commander's team entered. "White glove inspection? That's as absurd as the finger-in-the-oil pan inspection at the Motor Pool."

"Not quite, but close," said Lavoss. "The CO wears a white glove to check out the nooks and crannies of each room. If he finds dust, it spells trouble." The soldiers looked worried.

Back on the first floor of the barracks, the inspection team had already checked most of the soldier quarters when Capt Mellon noticed the door to the Day Room. "Say, 1st Sergeant, why is that door not open. It is part of the barracks inspection, isn't it?"

Before Persilla could respond, Capt Mellon pushed open the door. Inside, the Day Room was stuffy with tobacco smoke. The windows were shut. At a table, four men sat playing five-card stud, a hefty pot in front of them. They were dressed in shabby fatigues and unshaven. Off to one side, an ashtray was filled with dead butts; half drunk cups of coffee were on the table. The men were Charlie, Marly, Curly, and Mo. Standing behind Capt Mellon, MSgt Sweechek gave the ordere. "Attention!"

Nothing happened. The four men continued their game. It was as if the senior staff had not entered the Day Room at all. An order of "Attention!" should have whip-sawed the four men to their feet, according to the laws of nature and the Department of the Army. It had no effect. One of the players, Charlie, dared to flagellate as if in defiance at the intrusion. The disrespect was blatant.

"What is this outrage, 1ˢᵗ Sergeant?" demanded Capt Mellon.

"What outrage, Sir?" the 1ˢᵗ Sgt answered calmly.

"These four men, here, of course!"

"What four men?" 1ˢᵗ Sergeant Persilla said again, looking at the card players.

Startled by his reply, Capt Mellon looked directly down at his 1ˢᵗ Sgt, standing next to him. He was indeed short, in spite of the high heel boots. "These four soldiers in front of us, or rather, Raggedy Ann dolls, by the looks of them. They are out of uniform! And they are playing cards! And smoking cigarettes in my presence!"

"Oh, these men," answered Persilla, his voice surprisingly calm. "They're not here, Sir."

"Wha'? What do you mean, they're not here? What am I looking at, chimpanzees?"

"No, Sir. Human beings."

"Ah ha! Then you do see them after all!"

"Yes, Sir. Of course," answered the 1ˢᵗ Sgt.

"Then what's the meaning of this?"

"Of what, Sir?"

The answer snapped the Commander's head around as if he had been punched. "First Sergeant???" he hyped. He was beginning to wonder if his right hand man had lost it all.

Though Capt Mellon had been Company Commander for over a year, he had never before seen Charlie, Marly, Curly, and Mo before. What he didn't know was that during inspections, they and their floating poker game always floated to the broom closet on the second floor, there to hide. The Company Commander turned to his inspection NCOs. "Master Sergeant Sweechek, do you see these four men?"

"That's affirmative, Sir," he answered.

"And you, Sergeant Cabul?" The NCO answered the same, as did Plt Sgt Oats. "Then you all agree that there are four unshaven, unkempt, crummy-looking sad sacks here in my day room and sitting at this table, gambling. Is that not correct?"

"Yessir!" the Plt Sgts answered in unison.

"Then why are they not on their feet recognizing my presence as their Commander?"

"Because they are not really here, Sir," answered MSgt Sweechek with a straight face.

"What, Sergeant? You too?" Capt Mellon stepped up to the card game and slammed his fist on the table, bouncing the pot of money, startling the players. He grabbed one of them, Charlie, by the collar and pulled him out of the chair as if to give him a smack. "Is this shit-head a mirage?"

Struggling, Charlie tried to break the grip. "What your Sergeants are trying to tell you, Mister Cap'n, is we're not in the Army anymore. You ain't got no authority over us. We's civilians. And if you don't put me down, I'll make my first civilian arrest!" he threatened.

Startled by the arrogance, if not the man's nerve, Capt Mellon dropped Charlie back into his chair. "What is this piece of garbage talking about, Top?" he asked Persilla.

The 1st Sgt hesitated, and then threw up his hands. "It's like he says, Sir. They're not officially in the Army anymore. They've been processed out over a year ago. Their tour of enlistment has expired. The company has no jurisdiction over them. Only problem is, Sir, their orders never came down to ship them back to the States and home. The orders got lost. Records fucked up."

"Fucked up?"

"Yes, sir. Unless we get command orders to return these four men back to the States—regulations, you know—we're stuck with these grease balls, Sir."

"In other words, they are here, but they ain't," added PltSgt Cabul.

Putting his fingers to his temples, Capt Mellon pressed them lightly. "This is the damnedest thing I ever heard!"

"Yee-ah! And I'm mad as hell at the Army too, Mister!" complained Mo, not pleased with the game's interruption. He was holding a full house and a winning hand.

1st Sgt Percilla's voice dropped to a growl. "Until Department of the Army cuts orders, we got to house and feed these four bums, Sir." The three PltSgts nodded in helpless agreement.

"You mean these bums can eat company chow, sleep in company quarters, but not draw work details because their term of enlistment is up?" asked Capt Mellon in disbelief.

1st Sgt Persilla could only shrug. "Sir, they're officially not classified as 'present-and-accounted-for', although physically they are here. They are not required to follow orders, nor are we permitted to give them orders. The regulations, Sir."

Finally comprehending, and looking like a kid caught trying to put slugs in a bubble gum machine, the Company Commander's voice dropped to a waffling "Oh." Capt Mellon looked back at the card game. The pot was hefty with dollar bills.

"Care to join us, Commander?" invited the player known as Marly.

The CO raised an eyebrow. He glanced at the pot in the middle of the table. "Well, if you men are not recognized as present, then that means there ain't no card game in progress, and if there ain't no card game in progress, then I ain't playing poker if I sit in. Since that's the case, deal me in boys. Oh, and carry on with the barracks inspection without me, will you 1st Sergeant?," said Capt Mellon, pulling up chair.

Fifteen minutes later, the inspection team, minus the company commander, was on the second floor of the barracks. The first soldier quarters they walked into belonged to PFC Kantwell.

The room appeared to be in tip-top condition: floor waxed, bunk tight, laundry bag in its place at the end of the bunk. Both his foot locker and wall locker were open. 1st Sgt Persilla glanced at Kantwell's footlocker display. Satisfied, he looked into the wall locker with its contents of dress greens, khaki, and civilian clothes. Again satisfied, he was about to turn away when he noticed something at the back of the locker. He reached in and took it out. It was a violin case. Under the bunk he found a cello in its case. He frowned. "Soldier, I thought I told you at last inspection I do not want to see non-military objects lying around your quarters, that you either ship it home or store the instruments in the Arms Room."

Still standing at rest, hands behind him, Kantwell glanced at the wall locker. "I thought it would be all right if I kept the instruments out of sight, 1st Sarge."

Percilla fixed on him. "Soldier, your first mistake was you thought. We got a Brigade IG (Inspector General) inspection coming up and this stuff has got to go. That's it!"

"But where to?"asked Kantwell, weakly.

1st Sgt Persilla put his hands on his hips, the way D.I.s (drill instructors) do, and leaned into his soldier's face. "Didn't I say either ship it home or place it in the Arms Room? Now I want those instruments out of here, along with any other whistles and kazoos you may have stashed away Like RIGHT NOW! This is a military barracks, not an orchestra pit! Got it, Soldier?"

Kantwell, himself short in stature, was still head-and-shoulders above the 1st Sgt. He looked down at him. "But 1st Sarge, you can't just mail away wood instruments. Instruments have to be crated properly," he whined.

"Then into the Arms Room they go!"

"The Arms Room? Impossible. String instruments are not weapons, 1st Sarge!"

"They may not be to you, PFC, but that violin bow could poke out someone's eye!"

Outraged at the suggestion, Kantwell cleared his throat. "1st Sarge, I can't do that. The Arms Room is damp and cold. In there, even the weapons rust. It'll be worse for my cello. It can alter the dynamics of the wood. Warp the construction!"

A hint of a smile, albeit a crooked one, appeared on1st Sgt Persilla's face. He saw his authority being challenged. The other Plt Sgts, Sgt. Sweechek, Sgt. Oats, and Sgt. Cabul, watched and wondered how he would assert his authority. Sensing this, Persilla looked up sternly at the taller soldier. The fire in his eyes flared for a moment, then cooled. "Are you saying 'no' to a direct order, PFC?"

1st Sgt Persilla loved trouble makers; they made command a challenge. It meant he had to come down hard on his soldier to get him to conform. Draftees especially had to be disciplined, coerced if necessary, winnowed down (the army called it the "Enlightenment") in order to change a can't-do attitude into a can-do, Gung-ho, Banzi! one. The Army taught there was no place in the ranks for negatives; it was something to be stamped out at the roots, otherwise the ability to wage war would be compromised. The Code of Conduct, General Orders, and Chain-of-Command would be meaningless. Without enforced discipline, a man might not attack the enemy with a bayonet between his teeth or blow an enemy track with a charge strapped to his chest or attack a machine gun nest with a police whistle, if so ordered. In Korea, the 1stSgt saw how a Can't-do, no-I-won't attitude lost skirmishes. Back at garrison, loose discipline was not an issue. On the battlefield, it was. It could cost lives! Persilla took a step back, like a sheriff about to draw a six shooter in a B-western movie.

Upon hearing the commotion, some of the men from the other room quarters gathered at Kantwell's doorway. Word had spread that there was going to be a shoot-out. The Maestro, Kevin Kantwell, the soldier with stinky feet, had challenged the system!

With cheeks twitching, 1st Sgt Persilla took on the look of a hangman holding the cantilever to the trapdoor. "Tell me, Master Sergeant Sweechek, did one of your soldiers just say 'I can't'?" he snapped over his shoulder to his PltSgt.

"That's affirmative, 1st Sergeant!" he snap-answered back, annoyed that the man about to be disciplined was one of his own, a third-platoon soldier.

The 1st Sgt trip-wired. He fired off a broadside salvo that echoed the length of the hallway. "Snap to, PFC! Shape up, Puccini! You're in the Army now, not the Boston Pops! Pull your head out of your ass and take them whistles and kazoos down to the Arms Room like I told you, or else I'm going to have to chew you up and spit you out like a BB!" Persilla had been a drill instructor at Fort Hood, Texas and knew how to hammer green 'cruits.

Kantwell withered. "But 1st Sarge..."

Persilla turned back to Sgt Sweechek. "Platoon Sergeant, your man's deaf. Pull his post pass. If he still refuses to follow orders, we'll cut paperwork for a company Article 15. The kid is begging for a transfer over to 6th Infantry and the trenches."

The men standing at the doorway sucked in their breaths. The 6th Infantry! That would mean rifle company responsibility. It would mean 24/7 field training ten months a year with time off only for Thanksgiving and Christmas and the Easter Bunny, if that. In a rifle company there was little room to practice scales.

From the hallway door, Bravo watched. He turned to Pereski, standing next to him: "Which reminds me, Paul, I better hide my Jew's harp before the 1st Sarge finds it," and ran back to his quarters.

Having made his point, 1st Sgt Persilla turned and left Kantwell's room to continue the inspection of the barracks, the three Plt Sgts— Sweechek, Oats, and Cabul—following in his jet stream. The men in the doorway had already dispersed to their quarters.

Hurt, rebuffed and hyperventilating, Kantwell stood in the middle of his room, his body's reflection undulating above the polished wax floor. His face had turned beet red, as if the skin had been peeled back by dragon breath. Actually, it had. He took his beloved string instruments out of their cases and cradled them as if they were living things, family pets about to be gassed. Then, head bowed, he returned them to their cases and carried them down to the Arms Room for a lock-up. Back in his quarters, he threw himself on his bunk and cried out. "Fuck the Army! Goddamn it! Fuck-the-Army!" It was language he never used.

Just then Pereski, Robuck, and Bravo walked sprightly into Kantwell's room. Their own quarters had passed inspection, and they were now free to move around the barracks. Bravo told them what had happened to the Maestro. The three men decided to see how he was taking it. Kantwell was, after all, a man of the 3rd Platoon, and, quirky or not, one of the guys. The FTA—"Fuck the Army"—scream greeted them as they entered. It was a common cry among soldiers suffering depression.

"Hey man, watch your tongue. You're spitting them FTA slugs all over the floor," said Robuck, as if the metaphor was a bug to be squashed and swept up.

Pereski pretended to slip. "Oops! I just stepped on one of them bug critters."

"Got one!" said Bravo clapping his hands pretending to whack a fly.

"Got what?" asked Robuck.

"That FTA bug. The fuck-the-Army one."

Kantwell looked up from his bunk, eyes swollen. "Will you guys please leave me alone?"

Pereski closed the lid of Kantwell's foot locker and sat down on it, crossing his legs. "Come on, Maestro. Don't take it so hard. 1st Sarge is a good guy. He barks, then forgives. You'll have your off-post pass back in no time."

Face flushed, Kantwell sat up. "The hell with the pass! It's my string instruments I'm concerned about! He had me put them down in the Arms Room!"

"Most contrite," affected Robuck, checking his nails.

Bravo took a stick of gum out of his pocket. "Maestro, I know how you feel. The 1st Sarge found my Jew's harp and took it away from me. I'm crushed."

Kantwell gave him a venomous stare. "Bravo, you are crude. You're all crude! You and the Army! You are unable to grasp anything beyond a fifth-grade education. You just don't abuse fine-tooled musical instruments like that! Wood expands! It contracts! It splinters!"

"If that's true, my rifle stock should be match sticks by now," reasoned Robuck.

"You can't compare the wood of a stock rifle to a cello's fine surface," said Pereski, coming to Kantwell's defense. "It's…it's like comparing apples to woodpeckers. A rifle is scientifically designed to withstand Arms Room temperature extremes and battlefield conditions. Cellos and woodpeckers are not."

Bravo snapped his fingers. "Wait a minute, guys. Got the problem solved. Rubber bands! I got three of them on my webbing. Maestro, here, they're yours."

"Rubber bands? For what?" he asked, staring at Bravo.

"To keep the violin's wood from splintering."

"Are you serious?"

"Of course I am. It's my last three rubber bands."

Flailing his arms, Kevin Kantwell, the Maestro, fine arts musician-turned-soldier-turned-signalmen, jumped up from his bunk. "Get out of here, all of you! You're a bunch of animals! Assholes! Out of here!" he cried out, distraught.

"Now, really," said Robuck, feigning affront. "I come by to offer you solace and what do I get for it? I'm called an asshole."

"In your case, I'd call that insight," said Bravo, heading for the door.

Back in the company hallway, the three friends walked quickly toward the stairwell. They had to hurry to get to the motor pool, for the day's training was about to begin.

"Would you say the Maestro is good re-enlistment material?" asked Robuck, skipping down the hallway stairs.

"Not after this inspection, he ain't," said Pereski.

"How about you, Frank? You're-enlistment material, right?" Robuck repeated.

"Me, re-enlist? No way. Yourself?"

"Nah! I don't want to end up in Southeast Asia."

"If none of us are re-enlistment material, who is?" asked Bravo, talking, not really caring. "Somebody among us has got to be re-enlistment material, otherwise who is going to do the fighting? Hey, Cecil! How about you?" Jonas had just joined them on the stairwell.

"How about me, whaaat?" asked Jonas in southern.

"Would you re-enlist for a tour in Vietnam?"

"I don't have to. Rosenblum did that for me. By the way, Lavoss is thinking about it."

"But you can too, you know, Cecil."

"Who's you?"

"You!"

"Me? I'm a non-entity."

"How do you know?"

"Platoon Sarge Sweetcheeks calls me that all the time."

"Calls you what?"

"Who knows?"

"Sure!"

The front doors of the barracks burst open and out stepped Pereski, Robuck, Bravo, and Jonas into the cold gray Berlin morning,. They chatted and joked. Like tenth-graders on the way to class, they jostled each other, oblivious of the pained distant wail coming from the barrack's second story where stinky boots hung out the half-open window. It was Kantwell's quarters. "Ahhh! Ah! Ahhh!"

That evening, after chow, Yorit lay on his bunk, his nose buried in J.D. Salinger's novel, *Catcher in the Rye*. He found he could relate to the main character, Holden Caulfield, and his sense of lost identity. As a civilian, he had an identity, or so he thought. Here in West Berlin, in a military environment, he was beginning to question it. "Who am I? What am I? Why am I here?" he asked himself. In the Army, original thought was frowned upon. Personal opinion was discouraged. Questions tossed. A man had to play the game of Follow-the-Leader, even though the leader might be a blooming idiot. Most NCOs were not. They were doing a tough job, running young male men who did not want to be soldiers, nor want to be in West Berlin. Although Yorit felt himself devoid of an identity, he was thankful he still had the one thing which made him a person that identified him as relevant—a social security number.

He put down the *Catcher in the Rye* and glanced at his watch. It was 18:30. He considered going to the Orderly Room to pick up his off-post-pass from the staff duty desk before some busybody Sgt volunteered him for whatever there was superfluous to be done, like starching shoelaces, or mopping sidewalks. He sighed an "Oh, the hell with it!" kind of a sigh, and turned over. Comfortable in his GI bunk, he continued to read.

There are some things in the Army that do make life almost lovable: reading a good book in one's own bunk (also known as the "fart sack") is one of them. Lying there, curled up, flipping pages can transcend all the animal noises which barracks life (and college dormitories) dump on you. Yorit felt content. He was steeped in that moment's sentient tranquility and was grateful. Stretching, he took a deep breath and sighed. "Ahhhh!" It was then the door to his quarters banged open. The door hit the wall, startling him. Holden Caufield went sailing into the air. An uninvited guest stormed into the room. It was Kevin Kantwell, the Maestro. "Bullshit!" he raged, kicking the door.

He walked up to Yorit's wall locker and punched it. Then he kicked one of the footlockers, tilting it on its stand.

Yorit watched him. "Hey, bimbo! If you must trash a room, trash your own, not mine!"

"Done that already!" Kantwell stormed.

"Oh, and that makes me next, huh?"

Still in his rage, Kantwell grabbed a footlocker by the handles and lifted it as if to throw it, contents and all, across the room. Having second thoughts, he set it back down on the metal stand. It was heavy. His anger spent, he dropped onto one of the four bunks in the room and put his face in his hands. Yorit watched, saying nothing.

That afternoon at chow, Robuck had told Yorit what had happened, how during the barracks inspection Kantwell had been ordered to put his beloved instruments in the Arms Room. He protested, and it brought the 1st Sgt down on him. If it happens often enough, a soldier can develop something known as "barracks fatigue." In war time they call it "battle fatigue." It comes from living in a disciplined environment at close quarters with only men, not unlike a penitentiary sentence. Without the occasional off-post pass to let off steam, a soldier could go wacky. Pounding metal lockers and panic screams were the first outward signs of barracks fatigue, or burnout. Punching your SecSgts (the assumed tormentor) would soon follow. After that, it was a matter of time before there were psychiatric tests and a "profile," and finally a medical discharge—or worse, a transfer to the Pentagon's Center for Behavioral Research and Rehabilitation, also know as..."the Infantry." Every post had such a center. In the Infantry, the fatigued soldier could scream to his heart's content with impunity into a 3x3x5 foot element, known as the foxhole! The one he had just dug. Kantwell's behavior suggested he was on that track. Yorit had seen it all before and he felt sorry for the man.

Yorit sat up and looked at his company buddy. "Listen, Maestro, acting like this will only get you confined to barracks and extra duty. You want that? Or how about a transfer to the 42nd Engineers? That's Infantry, man! You think Signal Company is tough, wait till you soldier with them. You'll be humpin' heavy mortar and sleeping with your rifle between your legs. And in case you don't know it, cellos don't hold up well in the trenches. Just keep talking back to 1st Sgt and smacking wall lockers."

His eyes swollen with emotion, Kantwell held his head in his hands. "My instruments are my only friends."

Yorit wanted to empathize with him, but didn't know how. He had been trained for combat situations, not hand-holding psychotherapy. "Now calm down, Kevin, and tell me what exactly happened that so freaked you out?"

Kantwell, who was 20 and looked like 14, gnashed his teeth as if he just had taken a bite out of someone's ankle and come up with a mouth full of sock. "1st Sarge took away my instruments."

"Yes, I heard about it."

"He had me store them in the Arms Room."

Yorit thought about the guys who bunked in the next room—Jonas and Lightpony. They would be overjoyed at the news. The Maestro's composing and instrument tuning penetrated the barracks walls and drove them, if not most of the company, up a wall. "So they're stored in the Arms Room? So what?"

"So what? It's outrageous, that's so what!"

Yorit got up. He crossed the room to where the musician-student-turned-soldier sat on Robuck's bunk; he placed an understanding hand on his shoulder. "Okay, it's done and you can't do anything about it. I suggest you forget it and move on."

"I hate the 1st Sarge! I hate all Sergeants! They make my life miserable!"

"Don't blame the Top. He and the other senior NCOs have a tough job to do," said Yorit, trying to be sympathetic. "To be the 1st Sergeant of a company of soldiers isn't easy. Its kinda like a conductor directing a 120-piece symphony orchestra, only the musicians can't read the music. They don't teach music appreciation at non-commission-officer leadership school. To the 1st Sarge, a violin looks like a weapon. Look, if it's not in the Soldier's Manual, he don't get it. Comes from being a career man. He doesn't understand things civilian anymore. The 1st Sarge even took away Bravo's Jew's harp."

"I thought Bravo was kidding when he told me that," said Kantwell, slowly becoming resigned to his situation.

Yorit moved to sit down on the room's only desk chair. "Look, Kevin. You enlisted for this—good, bad or indifferent. My advice is to take it on the chin, tough though it is. You do that and a change of attitude will get you past the Army rough stuff. Stay cool. That would be the smart thing to do. Next time the Top asks about the instruments, tell him they are tools which can help you understand, oh, map co-ordinance, let's say. He won't know what you're talking about and maybe he will let you keep the instruments on the floor in the broom closet."

Kantwell dabbed his knuckles with a handkerchief; he bruised them, punching the wall locker. "He didn't have to make me lock them up."

"If an object has a point, it goes into the Arms Room. You know that. It's in the regulations. They even keep Jimmy Lightpony's tomahawk down there."

"You are missing the point, Robert. The Arms Room environment is damp!"

Yorit shrugged.

"And do you know what happens to wood in such an environment?" Kantwell asked, sternly.

"The strings rust?"

"No, the wood splits. And there's mold!"

"Gee whiz, that is serious," said Yorit, glancing at the ceiling, not knowing what the man was talking about.

"On top of that, the Orderly Room pulled my off post pass."

Yorit's eyes widened. "They pulled your pass? Now that is serious stuff. Hell, I can relate to that. Come on, let's go trash the wall lockers together."

The Maestro got up and began to walk back and forth. "And tonight of all nights when I am suppose to pick up my new saxophone."

"Your new saxophone? What are you talking about?"

"Some German university students have a jazz band. They play at the local dives around here in Berlin and need a sax player to make up their combo. You see, I play the saxophone as well as string instruments, but just for fun. When I lived in New York I used to do gigs to support my school tuition at Julliard."

"You mean you play horn instruments as well as string instuments? Kevin, you're a genius." Yorit was impressed.

"Yes, alto sax. If I can get in with the band, it would keep me from going nuts in this barracks life. I was supposed to pick up the instrument tomorrow from a house in the Wannsee district. The German musician there has one and will let me borrow it. It would give us a chance to get to know each other. But now I can't go. My pass is pulled. I'll tell you, Yo, the army is driving me nuts!" Kantwell wailed, getting up from the bunk and walking to the door. "I apologize, Robert. I didn't mean to bother you with my problems."

Yorit thought for a moment. "Look, Maestro. Tomorrow is Saturday. I could pick the saxophone up for you if you want."

Kantwell stopped. He swung around. "What? You'd do that for me?"

"Well, what I mean is..." Yorit bit his tongue and flinched under his breath. "Now what did I say that for?"

"You're a real buddy. How can I ever repay the favor?"

Yorit thought for a moment. "You could start by giving me carfare."

Doing an errand for someone who had athlete's foot was the last thing Yorit wanted to do. He would rather use his company pass—a privilege really—to go across the street to the Golden Sun bar and booze up. Yet he could not say no. It had to do with those "right neighborly" mid-western values programmed into him growing up as a kid in northern Ohio. He blamed his family, the neighbors, and the Sisters of St. Joseph for those values. In grade school each morning, the Sisters had him and the class say the Pledge Allegiance to the Flag. Then they had to memorize the Sermon on the Mount and the Parable of the Good Samaritan—and live it! When Yorit wanted to say "No, I won't," he could never do it. Instead it always came out, "Yes, I will." It became his nature to help the other guy. The Monsignor at St. Vincent de Paul, Father Flannigan, once told him it was the best way to get to heaven. In those harsh Cleveland winters such training had him shoveling a neighbor's sidewalk and pushing stranger's cars out of snow drifts. In summer, those Christian Midwestern values had him cutting old Mr. Mallard's grass and doing errands for neighbors like the widow, Mrs. Rote, who lived on West 135th Street. Then, as a grade-schooler, he was hoping he would get to heaven that way. Yorit guessed helping Kantwell would too. And he kicked himself in the butt.

Yorit sighed with resignation. "Okay, Kevin. Get up off your knees and stop worshiping me. I'm not Jesus on the cross. Just give me the address. Where do I have to pick up the saxophone?"

The Old Man

The train trembled. The benches trembled. The bodies trembled. The trembling passed up through the floorboards, through the seat of the pants and up the back of the passengers to the neck. There it wedged, lightly shaking the heads affirmative. None of the passengers seemed to notice. They were too moored in their own galaxy of thought, barely conscious of the Berlin subway trembling as its high sped toward the Wannsee district.

Outside, beyond the streaked windows, was a No-man's Land of old roadbed and disused track. Shiny rails shimmied and slid in and out of each other like strokes in a Paul Klee composition. Sections of torn-up rail lay on the ground next to barren roadbed. Stunted trees and wild shrubs dotted the landscape. Here and there, bomb craters from the war could be seen, even after 18 years; they had yet to be filled in. There were abandoned switch houses and the occasional water tower, *Jugendstil* in design, that stood majestic against the sky. The train passed an unused station resembling a U-Boat's coning tower, its walls chipped and bullet-riddled from a long ago battle. The late afternoon's sunlight glowed golden against it. Beyond, in the distance and looking like toy blocks cut from cardboard, were the tenement houses from the Wilmersdorf district.

This was the *S-Bahn*, a yellow subway train with a huge network of track, a lot of it unused, that ran above-ground and over the city's street traffic. West Berlin's other subway was the *U-Bahn*. It was the underground rail. Then there was the dead *Bahn*. It was made up of old track that went nowhere. It couldn't. It dead-ended at the Berlin Wall and the broken bridges along the Spree River.

The intricate web of the *Bahn* track was dominant; it reached out and touched the whole of the city, east and west. It was a network that daily force-fed a million and a half people, 20% of them war widows, into the confined space of the anthill known as West Berlin, turning the city's 513 square miles of territory into a frothing kettle of activity, a storm in the proverbial teacup, only it was a teacup made of barbed wire, 110 miles behind the lines.

The train slowed as it entered the District of Zählendorf, where the vistas altered. The apartment houses of the inner city thinned, then vanished, to be replaced by purple-hued forests and noble *Tannen* trees that half hid the villas and restored homes of Berlin's political elite.

"Nikolasee!" garbled the chipped loudspeaker above the door. The *S-Bahn* train stopped to let off passengers.

Turning away from the window's meditative contemplation, Yorit got up and stepped off the train. It was early evening and the mist had begun to creep out of the forest. This was the Wannsee district, very rural and very deserted. The scent of the evergreens was everywhere. Inhaling, Yorit pulled out the city map Kantwell had given him. The street he was looking for was only a couple of blocks.

It was an elegant neighborhood. Partially hidden homes poked out from behind pine trees and hedgerows. Cast iron fences ran parallel to the curb. It did not look like a war had once been fought here. Checking the address, he soon found the street, a cobblestone one and empty of traffic. There were two parked cars, one with a flat tire. At house number 25 Yorit stopped. It was the address. He pushed open the gate, an ornate one designed for a cemetery, and walked up the flagstone pathway to the house. It was a *Gründerzeit* turn-of-the-century villa, noble with its large windows, stucco facade, and a portico with two Dorian pillars. That was the right half of the villa. In the twilight of the evening, the left half looked like Berlin 1945. It had been hit by some high explosive that blew out two walls, causing the thick roof timbers to collapse into a gigantic lean-to. It had never been repaired, no doubt for lack of money.

In West Berlin, it was not uncommon to walk past a row of manicured neighborhood homes only to be startled by a surreal hole in the ground, an exposed cellar that had once been a house, or a front yard with steps that led up to nowhere. It had once happened to Yorit. He and Bravo had parked their jeep on a side street in front of such a hole-in-the-ground where a home had once stood. The only part of the house, or villa, still in tact was the five stone steps that led up to the non-existent front door. As they sat in the jeep at the curb, working the Army net, transmitting and receiving messages from Brigade HQ, a lone woman walked up the street towards them. She was attractive and wore a fur coat to the ankles and one of those pheasant feather hats weathly Berlin widows were fond of. She passed the parked jeep and stopped in front of a small iorn gate. The two soldiers watched her. She pushed through the gate and slowly walked up a path that led to the stone steps. She climbed them. At the top of the steps she could go no further. Where was once a house stood there was now a hole in the ground, surrounded by broken stones. She looked around. Was she reminiscing? Was this hole once her home? Was she about to do what many lonely West Berlin women did after the war and suffering depression? Jump into the hole in the ground, gas themselves with the kitchen stove, or jump off a bridge into the River Spree? Was she about to leap from the steps into the basement below? It was a long drop.

Statuesque, she stood, looking like Wagner's Brunhilde, outlined against the fulminating sky. In Berlin the skies never stop fulminating. After several minutes of reflection she threw up her hands, mouth open, her scream voiceless, then let her hands drop as if resigned to some hated fate.

Yorit considered this as he studied the half ruined part of the villa. It resembled an abstract sculpture—its one exposed wall, a Jackson Pollock painting. Thirty feet up from the ground and etched in to the tatty wallpaper of the wall was the outline of what had once been a staircase. It looked surreal. Of course, in cold war Berlin everything looked surreal.

Reflection aside, Yorit pushed the door buzzer; it was not a knocker like most Berlin homes, but a bell buzzer. A moment later the door opened, but only a crack. A shadowy eyeball glared out at him suspiciously. He wanted to say, "No, I'm not the Gestapo," but thought that impolite. Kindly, he said, " *guten Abend!* (Good evening) I'm the American calling about the saxophone." The door opened further.

The eyeball belonged to the head of an older woman, 65 or 70. She looked Yorit over, as he did her. She was dressed as if from another century—shawl tight at the shoulders, her hair streaked white and pulled into a bun. *"Wollen Sie Zigaretten verkaufen?"* (Do you want to sell cigarettes?) she asked, her voice all cracks and scratches, the jaw working as if feeling for a bad tooth.

Yorit was not sure what to say. "Ah, I'm here to pick up a saxophone, an instrument from a Mr. Dietsch. Does he live here?"

The woman responded with a doubtful, "*Wie, bitte?*" (What?) Her steely gaze made him uncomfortable.

He wondered if she had ever been interrogated by the *Polizei* back than. "Perhaps I have the wrong…*die falsche Adresse. Tut mir leid,*" he said in a weak German, and turned to go.

"Hello, wait!" a male voice called out from just inside the door. The door opened further. "I am Horst Dietsch. I have been expecting you." The old woman gave Yorit a disapproving scowl and withdrew. "Do forgive my aunt; she does not address strangers well," he said, extending his hand. The young German man looked fresh, with a blush to his cheeks. He had a fine nose and sandy hair, the advertised image of what Germans were known to look like. "You must be Robert Yorit. Mr. Kantwell telephoned me that you were coming."

"That's right," Yorit replied. "Kantwell asked me to pick up a saxophone for him that you have, I hope."

"Yes, I do. Please do come in," Dietsch invited in good British English that Yorit did not expect, not in post war Berlin.

Inside the large foyer, the walls were starkly barren as if the room had been robbed of furniture. Dark spots near the ceiling told of a dampness seeping through. Here and there some wall molding had broken away and was in need of repair. A lone chandelier gave off a weary light; one bulb was burned out. As they talked, their voices echoed hollow off the wood floor.

"Are you a jazz musician too?"

"No, I'm a Rock and Roll fan," answered Yorit, looking around. "My friend, Kevin Kantwell, he's the jazz man in the company. He told me something about wanting to join a band—your band, I guess. That's why I'm here. He could not come tonight."

Dietsch nodded. "Yes, we need someone like him for our group: We have been unable to find the right kind of jazz musician. Oh! Forgive me. May I invite you in for a drink?"

"No thank you," said Yorit appreciatively. "Just bring me the saxophone and I'll be on my way."

"Please, I insist," said the young German. He was glad to meet an American. He knew none and did not want to let him go so quickly.

Yorit figured he did not have anything to lose and answered, "Yes, why not? I have some time, Mr. Dietsch."

"My name is Horst. Call me Horst."

"Okay. I'm Robert Yorit. Call me Yoyo. My friends call me Yo." They shook hands.

Yorit followed Dietsch up a flight of stairs to the second floor and a dimly lit room. It was the family room, with heavy worn furniture and a very large cylinder coal stove. The heat of the stove made the room stuffy. The windows were covered by Persian carpets to keep out the harsh winter drafts. There were two bookcases and a baby grand piano that, together, suggested wealth and culture gone poor. In the middle of the room was a dining table; it had a small pile of newspapers and some books on it. Yorit noticed that one of the books was a thick Lutheran Bible with leather ribbons sticking out from the gilded pages. Though the room was well furnished, one wall was flat-empty. Nothing was placed there—no photographs or paintings, no furniture. It looked out of place in the room's over stuffed environment. Oddly, the empty wall's only decoration was a door that looked like it came from a church sacristy. It was a heavy oak door, painted in a faded green color (not Army OD). It reminded Yorit of Rosemary Clooney's chirpy little jingle popular in the 1950s, "What's behind the Green Door?"

"That one wall doesn't seem to fit the room's decor," Yorit noted.

Dietsch nodded. "When it rains here, and it rains a lot in Berlin, the damp comes through. It is why the wall is empty of things."

"And the door?"

"It once led to rooms which are no longer there. That part of our villa was destroyed in the war. You noticed it from the street, I'm sure," he said, moving toward the table. "Please sit down and tell me about your friend, Mr. Kantwell," Dietsch invited. "Is he a true musician? We only talked briefly on the telephone."

"Absolutely," said Yorit, taking a seat in a tired overstuffed chair; it was next to a floor lamp whose heavy shade blocked the light, giving the room a gloomy cast. "Kantwell is next to brilliant. He studied music at the Julliard School of Music in New York. The best!"

"He studied the saxophone?"

Here, Yorit smiled. "No, string instruments—violin and the cello. Saxophone is his hobby. He composes too."

"Composes? Most unusual," noted the German with a touch of respect for this unknown saxophone player who was about to join his band. "I'm really looking forward to meeting him."

"He likes to think of himself as a protegé of the Russian composer, Peter Tchaikovsky," Yorit added.

Dietech took some papers that were on the table and moved them aside. "We do not need a Tchaikovsky here. We need a Zoot Sims."

Yorit grinned. "So let us call Kantwell 'Zoot Tchaikovsky.'"

Dietsch stood up and rubbed his hands. "Forgive me. You are my guest. I will prepare a tea for us." He left the room before Yorit could say no. If there was one thing he was not, it was a tea sipper. No one in the company drank tea, but even Mess Sergeant Nast's tinted adrenalin-popping Mess Hall coffee would have been welcome right now.

Yorit looked around the living room. Never having been in a German's home before, he did not know what to expect. The Hollywood image of Germany was of the Black Forest, castles, battle axes, suits of armor, and creepy type characters like the actor Peter Lorie. There were some photographs hanging near the coal stove. He got up to look at them. They were studio photographs, perhaps 15 in all. A few were patina-edged, of women, children, obviously the family. They were arranged in such a way that they circled three portraits of young men in military uniform as if to draw attention to them. One of the photographs showed an officer supporting a mustache and a chest full of medals. He stood, looking proud, next to a seated woman in a flowing Victorian gown with puffy shoulders. Neither subject smiled, but glared into the camera as if angry about something. Another photograph was of a young man dressed in what appeared to be a West Point Cadet uniform. The figure gazed off into the horizon, seeming confident of the future. On a table next to him was a peak helmet, the type servicemen wore in World War I. The third photograph was more recent. It was of a youth in the field dress of a Wehrmacht officer; the picture had a signature and a date: *Mai 1940.* What made the three photographs intriguing was that all three of the men wore little metal crosses around their necks like bow ties. It was Germany's Iron Cross for valor. The Iron Cross was the equivalent of the American Army's Bronze or Silver Star. One real Iron Cross hung on the frame of the Wehrmacht soldier photo. The metal was tarnished and the ribbon frayed. This was obviously a family that was proud of its sons. Yorit poked the medal with his finger.

Dietsch returned with a pot of tea on a tray. Setting it down on the table, he went to a floor cabinet and brought out a bottle of clear liquor, a German *Korn*, and two shot glasses.

"You come from a military family, I see," said Yorit, indicating the photographs on the wall.

"Yes, my family has a long military tradition. It goes back to the time of Napoleon." He filled the two shot glasses.

"Who is the gentleman with the beard?"

"My great-grandfather. He was a soldier in the Prussian War against France in 1871. It was called 'Bismarck's War' because it united Germany, making it a nation state. This is Great-grandfather's house," he said looking around the room, rich in family heirlooms and tradition.

"Nice house."

"Yes, it was once, before the war. We are now trying to restore it, but money is a problem."

"Money always is. And that second photograph?"

"My great uncle. He was in World War I," replied Dietsch.

"And this one?" asked Yorit referring to the third photograph, the one of the Wehrmacht soldier with the Iron Cross ribbon around the frame. He was still curious.

Dietsch paused. "My father. He never returned from Russia."

"Oh, I'm sorry to hear that."

Dietsch raised his shot glass. "*Prost!*" Yorit raised his. "Bottoms up!" (*Zum Wohl*) And they drank.

"Yes, my aunt—you met her at the door—will not let the family forget that they all died for *Das Vaterland*. They were German heroes, although today in German society to be a hero is something to be ashamed of. That is why she arranged the *Fotos* this way, with the family around them. The meaning is for us, our family, to remember and never to forget that they were heroes. It is our *Alter Junker* tradition." He sipped his tea.

"And what are those traditions?" Yorit asked, curious.

" *Für Gott, König und Vaterland.*, Junker traditions steeped in Christian values like discipline, courage and honor. These values were once part of our state, or so my uncle tells me. *Vaterland* means the family."

"Is that the German thinking today? God, Chancellor Adenauer, and *Vaterland*?"

Deitsch laughed. "No, today the perspective is different. In our *Bundesrepublik*, the family and German democracy stand together. Adenauer will be out of office in a couple of years."

Impressed by Dietsch's knowledge of English, Yorit said, "Let's drink to the family and the *Bundesrepublik*. "

"Yes! *Prost!*" "Cheers!" And the two young men drank. Dietsch set down his glass. "Are you a musician?"

"No, I just listen to musicians," said Yorit, this time pouring himself tea, which was customary after drinking the *Korn* drink.

"I have managed to get a saxophone for your friend, Kantwell. You will bring it to him, yes?"

"Of course. That's why I'm here. Do you have some scores—I mean sheet music—he could look over? He told me to pick up whatever you have."

"Yes." Dietsch put down his cup of tea and got up; he walked over to piano and turned on a small lamp. "May I give you an idea of what we play?" Sitting down, he began with Earl Garner's "I Only Have Eyes for You," but without the groaning.

Yorit poured himself another *Korn Schnapps.* He liked what he heard, though it lacked Garner's soul and silk touch.

"Can you sense the passion in this composition? *Schön, nicht wahr?*" (Beautiful, isn't it?) he said, his eyes closed, feeling the mood. "Now, if only we had a Charley Parker on the saxophone."

"You have one," said Yorit. "Kantwell used to play at Soho neighborhood gigs."

Dietsch did not seem to hear, but leaned over the piano and groaned. "Is this real Earl Garner stuff?"

Yorit coughed into his hand. "Yeah, sure," and sipped his *Korn Schnapps.* "By the way, Horst, did you know that Earl Garner could not read sheet music? His piano was pure, from the soul."

Dietsch bobbed his head. "Cool, man, yeah!" he uttered, trying to perform like an American night club entertainer, but falling short. The accent was not quite right.

Yorit took the bottle of *Korn* and helped himself to another shot. He was beginning to enjoy the evening. "For a German, your English is good. Very correct. Better than mine. You must have lived in England."

"Yes, a year," Dietsch answered, running his fingers over the piano keys. "Here in Germany we are taught the fundamentals. We begin to learn language at age ten, then, we go abroad to study."

Yorit took a cookie from the tray. "The only language we learn in high school is Spic."

"Spic?"

"That's slang for Spanish."

Dietsch covered the keyboard and got up. "I also speak French, but English is my second language. It is something my uncle insisted I learn. He told me the English language is the language of the future."

"Too bad the Russian *Politburo* doesn't see it that way," said Yorit, with a touch of wit.

From behind a chair, Dietsch brought out a black case. He set it on top of the piano and opened it. Inside, tarnished and somewhat scratched, was an alto saxophone. "I have two reeds. They are not very good. I will get some new ones for your friend, Mr. Kantwell."

"I have an idea," said Yorit. "Why don't you come over to Lichtefelde with the group? We'll sign you on post. You could do a practice session there at the BSB Theater. It's available, and there is a piano. It will give you a chance to meet the Maestro himself; that's what we call Kantwell. You can jam together. Get to know each other. A dry run, so to speak."

The two young men continued to talk about the possibilities when something inserted itself into the conversation—a squeak. At first it was subdued, then more persistent, repeating itself as if a child nearby was bouncing playfully on a bed spring.

They both looked around. Moving in the shadows from across the room was the outline of a figure. As it drew toward them, Yorit saw it was a wheelchair. It glided, ghost-like, over the worn carpet. The squeak came from one of the wheels.

"*Onkel! Ich dachte dass Du schläfst.*" (Uncle! I thought you were asleep.) said Dietsch, a little surprised.

The wheelchair wobbled as it approached. Yorit could see it was made of a reed material with a high back and ancient wooden wheels, a relic from another era. Pushing at the wheels was the shrunken figure of a man, or someone who had once been a man.

For a moment the wheelchair hung at the edge of the floorlamp's light, as if waiting for a shove. Only the legs were visible, and the largest pair of hands Yorit had ever seen. The hands were out of proportion with the bony wrists; they had knuckles the size of walnuts, either from hard work or from too many youthful punch-outs. With another creak of the wheels, the rest of the uncle slid into the light and with him the distinct smell of rubbing alcohol.

Yorit drew back. He could only gasp. He was not sure if the uncle was dead or alive. His skin was a pale yellow, lips razor thin, the blond-gray hair slicked back, "Joseph Goebbels" style. He was a slip of a figure, with boney shoulders poking up through a white shirt that was closed at the collar. A wool vest covered his pencil-thin chest, while over his lap a wool blanket lay flaccid; it covered the profile of the two cucumbers hidden there, the thighs. But it was the eyes that caught him; they were the palest of gray and spoke of either cold intelligence, or spent iniquity.

The uncle touched the base of his throat at what looked like a bicycle tire patch stuck there. "*Ich horte unbekannte Stimmen,*" he croaked. (I heard unknown voices.)

Yorit looked around. Did someone turn on a transistor radio? Only when the uncle touched the patch at the base of his throat a second time did he realize the voice was wired to a small speaker inside the wheelchair's left wheel.

Sucking in his breath, Yorit wanted to get up and run, but he didn't. What shocked him was not the throat patch nor the sunken eyes or the unfortunate condition of a man who obviously knew great pain; it was the lower jaw, the way it opened and closed. It flapped! It was as if the uncle was being jerked by a ventriloquist's unseen string.

The jaw bone itself appeared to be made of a synthetic, Bakelite material, cold and bloodless like the texture of a window mannequin's smooth cheek. The jaw's movement was completely out of sync with the voice. The upper lip of human flesh was chapped. It quivered with each flap of the Bakelite jaw. Looking closely, he noticed a barely discernible hairline crack just below the ears, and the two stainless steel nuts set there. The reference, "Frankenstein's cousin," was not without merit.

Yorit look away, then back. He could not help himself. He looked again. He was both drawn to the grotesqueness of the emaciated creature in front of him and appalled by it at the same time. The uncle had all the fascination of the dead before the casket closed. The uncle's upper lip, the fleshy one, quivered and puckered as if about to engage a soda straw. Opening, it revealed a cruel orifice that was the mouth. Sucking in his breath, Yorit got up and headed for the door. He had reached his shock limit.

Touching his jaw, the uncle croaked, "Young maan! Return *selbst* to position...*sofort!*" he ordered, followed by a gentler croak of, "I begs of youfs."

Yorit stopped. Embarrassed by his own behavior, he swallowed hard and returned to his chair. In his Army career he had been ordered around by lots of loud-mouthed Sergeants, not to mention officers, but never by a wheelchair's left wheel.

"Horst," the uncle croaked diabolically, "*bringst Du mir ein Glas Rotwein, bitte.*" The nephew got up and crossed the room to the cabinet; he took out a bottle of red wine and a glass. The uncle then turned to Yorit. The jaw jerked. "Youfs are ein Amerikaner?" he asked in a circuit buzz.

Yorit nodded weakly.

"Youfs come to sells *Zigaretten*? I buys all you hafs," the wheelchair's circuitry buzzed again. The English, though croaking, was presentable.

Caught up in the drama of the jaw's movement, Yorit did not answer at first. The orifice had to repeat itself.

Yorit shook himself. "My ration card allows me only four cartons a month. I smoke most of that myself. I'm sorry, Sir."

The jaw worked silently as if trying to throw some internal switch to synchronize sentence pronunciation between croaks. "I am most disappoints," it managed.

Yorit pulled an open pack of Lucky Strikes from his pocket and passed one to the uncle. He immediately took it and stuck it into an enamel cigarette holder he produced seemingly from nowhere. Curling a large knuckled finger around the holder, the uncle pushed it into the orifice that was his mouth. It wedged there between the chapped upper lip and the rigid Bakelite plate of the lower one. He clicked the orifice shut, gripping the cigarette, then lit it.

" *Onkel, Herr Yorit ist hier...* I mean, Mr. Yorit is here to collect the saxophone. It has to do with my jazz band," said Dietsch respectfully.

"*Na, ja! Der Saxophonefs, huh? Das Nikker instrumenfs,*" he replied, a lock of hair falling across one of the shallow eyes; it give the uncle a Carl Sandberg look, only without the sagacity. He brushed it back. A long drag on the Lucky Strike seemed to stimulate one eyelid. It fluttered. The other eyelid stayed shut, as if in meditation. Clucking, he opened his orifice. "Real *Tobaccofs, der Ami*. No dirty French *Gauloise*," rattled the jaw's orifice.

"The French cigarettes do not have a good tobacco?" asked Dietsch, curious about the uncle's comment.

"Greek ist their tobaccofs," said the transistor-sounding left wheel, the jaw opening and closing. "French tobaccofs comes von *Griechenland* (Greece). Der soil, it ist not good for tobaccofs, no, not efens for der Vinefs! Tastes like *Hunde Scheize!* (Dog shit). How cans a land kissed by the suns and hot womens make such *Hunde* tobaccofs," the uncle uttered, his scratchy voice raising and dropping among the wheel spokes.

Yorit watched the uncle tremble as he lip-sucked the cigarette holder and talked. He wondered if his broken accent had to do with the vibrating spokes of the wheelchairs. Feeling sorry for him, he pushed the whole pack across the table. "Keep them, Sir. I have a supply."

The uncle glanced airily down his nose at the youthful American. Taking the pack, a gargle emitted from his orifice. He pressed his throat's black tab to speak, "Most good gracious of youfs, young mans."

Dietsch stood up. "*Lieber Onkel, darf ich Dir zur deinem Zimmer zurückbringen?*" He had become embarrassed by his uncle's presence and wished to bring him back to his room.

"*Nein,' no! Darfst Du nicht,*" he gargled, irritated that his nephew should ask, the left wheel's vocal negation shifting to the right wheel. "*Nein*, no. I vishes to knows our *Amerikaner* guest, here. It ist an opportunitys mes to talks der English. Ve haf not often such der privileges of such guests to our estate." Dietsch sat down. The uncle turned again to Yorit. "Mein conditions, as you sees, it frightens der peoples. It makes dem most discomfortablefs. Are youfs not most discomfortablefs, Herr Yorit?"

"Nn-no! Not at all." The squeal in Yorit's voice suggested otherwise. He was not sure where to reply—the right wheel, the left wheel, to the uncle's chomping orifice? He was not sure where the transistor radio voice was coming from. But good manners made up his mind for him: he would talk to the uncle's smooth forehead. "Please go on, Sir. I'm just fine."

"*Onkel, ich bitte Dich,*" (Uncle, please.) Dietsch pleaded.

The uncle clicked his fingernails on the arm of the wheelchair. Glowering down, he pressed the throat patch again. " *Neffe*, (nephew) dis ist an opportunityses for mes to speaks der English. Youfs knows it how most fond I am of things English. Efen *der Amerikaner* of things. I vas so once a student der English, trained so in the grammars. One must use der few opportunitiesfs one hafs to speaks der language," the jaw pronounced, hissing the way Germans sometimes do when they talk.

"*Was Du willst, Onkel,*" (What you will, uncle) replied Dietsch respectfully.

Again the uncle turned to Yorit, the upper lip protruding. "Youfs sees, young man, many years ago I lifs in London, a most pleasurables der experience. *Ah, die Frauleins* (girls). So innocents, so slights, so fine," his tinsel voice uttered, one eyelid fluttering with nostalgia. "But, dat vas before der wars!" the right wheel stated vociferously, startling the two young men.

"Dear uncle, you must not shout," insisted Dietsch, glancing at his guest, embarrassed. "We are here next to you."

The *Onkel* slapped at his throat patch and growled, "*Das weiß ich.* (Right you are.) But vhats I's to dos? It is *der verdammte Schalter!* (damn circuits) Hic-up! Da ist it agains." Reaching down, the uncle began to fiddle with something under the seat of his wheelchair. That done, he stiffly sat up. Trembling, he took his glass of wine and raised it to his orifice.

He drank, slurping, the glass clicking on his teeth. Now content, he turned again in his seat and eyed Yorit, a quivering question on his orifice. "And now, Mr. Amerikaner, may I asks, what do youfs tinks of our Berlin here, hm?" his snap quirky.

Yorit looked away. It was not easy to meet the uncle's tremulous stare head on. "Yes, Berlin is okay, I suppose, if you mean all the new construction going on here. There are still lots of ruins to be cleared away from what I see."

Nodding, the uncle pressed the throat tab again. This time it was the left wheel that spoke. "Youfs supposes? Do youfs not knows Berlin vas vonce der jewels of monumental architectures? *Der Baroque, der Romanesque, der Jugendstyle, die Grunderzeit.* But nows,　　*Leider* (unfortunately), it ist ein monuments to ruins.　Vat vas onces too grandeur ist no more. Most sad, do youfs not tinks?"

"You have a point, Sir," said Yorit, looking at Dietsch as if to say, "So what's your uncle driving at?"

"So much von der vars destroys and explodes avays. Boom! Boom! Like so-s."

"Yes, it looks that way, especially the closer one gets to the Berlin Wall," noted Dietsch, still uncomfortable about his uncle's presence.

The old man coughed, or rather the right wheel coughed. The circuits chuckled a 'Zzzz', then stopped. "Do youfs knows, young mans, dats here in West Berlin ve hafs a mountains?" Yorit shook his head. "Der mountains, they ist called *der Teufelsberg*—the Devil's mountains. You sees Poland von our mountains. You finds it in *der Grünewald*, our forest. It is composed of a million cubics the meters of stone, all broken: art deco stones, *Jugendstiel* stones, neoclassic stones, rococo stones, *Gotik* stones, a dousand years of *Deutsche Zivilization* stones. It ist alles stones vich are broken so likes my body here. Do youfs understands mes?" Yorit hesitated. The orifice continued, "*Der Teufelberg ist ein* monuments to our once glorious *Deutsches Reich!*" he said out loud, his drink in his hand as if to toast. Legs trembling, the uncle tried to stand. The drink was getting to him.

Yorit and Dietsch looked at each other.

"Does youfs know our *der Reichstag*, Herr Yorits?" the uncle continued. "It vas suppose to be der foundationfs ofs our *der Demokratie*. It nefer vas to be. No, today, it sits dere on *der Spree*, our rivers, awaiting for the returns," the lower lip quivered, the right wheel trembling.

"Return of what, Uncle?"

"*Unser neues Deutschland.* Ha!"

Yorit looked up, puzzled. Did the voice just shift to the left wheel again? It was as if the word syllables threaded the chair's spokes.

"Can that happen, after all these years, Uncle?" Dietsch was himself a student of history at the Berlin Free University and knew of the tragedy that was the City of Berlin.

"Ah, Neffe, (nephew), let us prays it vill happens. It must happens." said the right wheel with a mild croak, the jaw chomping, the upper lip quivering. Yorit was not sure which wheel he should pay attention to. The discussion, prompted by drink, was animating the uncle. "*Yawol!* Yes!" he burst out. "*Ein Deutschland von Aachen bis Danzig, Flensberg bis Konstanz, und Niedersachsen, Sachsen, und Ost Preussen. Alles zusammen!*" (together)

Dietsch looked hard at his uncle. "*Danzig? Sachsen*? Why, you are talking about parts of Poland and the DDR. Today, East Prussia is a part of the Soviet Union. *Onkel*, German unity is not only impossible, it is dangerous."

With the upper lip rigid, the lower lip again quivered. "Ah, but *Deutschland* vill be again togeder only it vill be *ein democratische Deutschland*. I predict its! It vill be in der evolutions of tings und 'dann, und dann', (then) ve Deutschen vill govern us from *der Reichstag*. It ist der vishes of all der peoplefs."

"And the Wall?" asked Yorit.

The uncle glared at him. "*Der Mauer*, it vill be historyses!" pronounced the orifice again, opening and closing, sputtering, sounding out of sync with the wheelchair's transistor. "Youfs notice my vords, young mans, make youfs notice my vords! It vill happens!"

Dietsch jumped up. "*Onkel, bitte!* (please) You must not shout. *Denk an deine zustand.* (Think of your condition.)"

Holding up his hand, the uncle sat back. "I tinks on my conditions most times, Horst. I hafs no choices, but please, do forgifs me, yes?" enunciated the right wheel. "It ist my vounds; dey makes me so. My body hurts." Here the uncle paused, as did the two youths. In the room's faded solitude, Yorit sipped his *Korn Schnapps* and wondered about the uncle's broken body, and Dietsch sipped his tea. The uncle, bound to his wheelchair, shifted and sighed uncomfortably, his teeth clicking between sucks of his Mosel drink. "Tell me, Herr Yorits, pleases. Do youfs haf other opinions of our city?"

Looking around the room, Yorit considered the question. "Yes, well, Berlin, hm. It is an interesting city, but a bit gray. Still too many ruins in spite of all the new construction going on. If there is one thing West Berlin does have though, it is character."

"Quite so, young mans!" the upper lip quivered out loud. "For an *Amerikaner* vits small knowledge of *Europa*, yous are most obserfants." Yorit was not sure if he had just been insulted. "Indeed, Berlin once had much characterfes! *Die alte Stadtmitte* (middle of the city), it vas vonce famous for it is cultures and theatres, 49 of dems like *Schauspielhaus, der Staatsoper Staatstheatre, and Unter den Linden.* It vas drama vitout pauses! But todays?" the voice dropped. "All ist vanquished. It ist tributes to der inexact sciences and der madnesses of *Krieg* (war)."

The uncle's occasional shouts between syllables did not shock Yorit anymore. He could only wonder how the uncle was able to coordinate the speech process: upper lip, Bakelite jaw, the chair's right wheel to left wheel and still be coherent—scratchy but coherent.

Suddenly the right wheel gave a buzz, a whrr. Yorit thought a circuit may have shorted out again until he realized it was the old man himself; he was chuckling. "Zzzt. Zzzt." This was getting to be too much. He looked toward the door and a possible run for it. As if reading his mind, the uncle pressed hard on his throat patch: "Stay youfs in der chair!" he ordered, followed by a conciliatory "Pleases."

Yorit did not move. Again, the room fell silent. The uncle took another drag on his cigarette, triggering one eyelid to flutter. He slurped his drink, clicking the glass against the bridge. Physically, his body was in a total state of discord: skeletal, snapping jaw, a head that jerked from side to side; yet his mind was clear, or so it seemed. Dietsch asked him again if he would like to be removed to his bedroom.

" *Neffe,* your Herr Yorit makes statements most toutful. My vishes ist only to aggrandizes upon thems." Dietsch shrugged and sat back.

The orifice tried to smile. "Yous sees, Herr Yorit, our villa, it ist an examples of our old Berlin. One parts is masterpieces of 19th century architectures, the other parts a masterpieces of madnesses." Here the uncle paused to draw a handkerchief from his pocket and wipe the saliva from his plastic jaw. "Yous haf sees our villa, *der fascades*, yes? It ist part ruins, and forgifs youfs me, it is part broken and vhy?" Here the uncle hesitated. "Becauses of youfs."

Yorit sat up. "Me!" Dietsch glanced at his uncle. The accusation was unexpected. "Me?"

"It ist youfs, young man. Youfs make the faults," the orifice repeated vociferously as if Yorit had flown the plane which had dropped the 500 lb. bomb that blew away half of the family estate, and the rest of Berlin with it. "Youfs and yours the B1-7s did its to us. Youfs! Youfs destroy Berlin, Hamburg, und our *Köln*! (Cologne) Shames to youfs!" accused the left wheel's spokes vibrating from the sudden unsynchronized rage.

Wide-eyed, Yorit stared at the lower jaw opening and closing and chopping. "If you'll excuse me, Sir; in 1944 I was five-year old and not a bombardier on a B17 Flying Fortress."

The uncle continued. "*Und am schlimmsten* (the worst) war *die Stadt Dresden*! Vhens youfs bombs die *Stadt* Dresden, youfs bombed Paris!"

Now it was Yorit's turn to fix on the uncle. "And what about you, Sir? You're German *Luftwaffe* bombed Warsaw and London and Rotterdam! And let us not forget little Coventry in England. Your Luftwaffe leveled the city. Equally outrageous, don't you think, ah, Sir? All bombed to the foundations, as you say."

The uncle frowned. The wheelchair's tone, a moment before aggressive, hesitated. Thoughtful, the right wheel croaked, "Yes-s, most tragics vas its."

"Indeed, war is an inexact science," said Dietsch, speaking up.

"Well, not always," said Yorit, remembering something he had read in the art section of *Playboy Magazine*. "When Cologne—your *Koln*—was bombed, our 8th Air Force leveled the whole city except for your Cathedral, the 'Dome' I believe you call it. It is a great medieval treasure. It was spared by what we call "precision bombing." War can still be an exact science if need be."

The uncle moved as if to reply, but didn't. Dietsch rubbed the saxophone case lightly with a finger; it was against the chair. Yorit slouched. He was putting on a buzz. It had to do with the mix of black tea and the *Korn Schnapps* drink. He helped himself to a refill.

The room with its heavy furniture, book shelves, photographs and paintings seemed to drift in the shadowy environment. It had grown strangely comfortable, inviting reflection in spite of the uncle's outbursts. Only the one wall, the empty one with the singular green wood door, spoke of a dissonance. *What is behind the green door, really?* Yorit wondered.

The uncle pinched out the end of his cigarette with his fingertips, burning the skin. The two youths could smell it. Taking a change purse out of his flaccid trouser pocket, he snapped it opened and began to field-strip the used cigarette butt.

Yorit watched him. A German civilian field-stripping a cigarette? Most unusual! he thought. Only in the Army did soldiers do that. What Yorit did not know, what he could not know, was that back in 1945, with the war over and the German population hungry, all of Germany was field-stripping cigarettes and repacking the left over tobacco to make new cigarettes. And sell them to buy food! American cigarettes were once the German currency of trade. As a currency, the state's *Reichsmark* was worthless. With the nation's economy in ruins, Chesterfield Cigarettes, Old Gold, Pall Mall and Lucky Strikes became the new currency: 7 Reich Marks for ein Cigarettin. It was the time of the black market where a half-a-pack of butts could buy a woman; where heirlooms were traded for bread; where everything was traded, and re-traded to feed desperate families. Every half smoked butt, known as a *Kipper*, held intrinsic value to a starving population. When recycled and sold, a *Kipper* put food on the table. It compelled whole families—husbands, wives and the kids—to follow occupation soldiers around, especially American soldiers, waiting for them to toss away their half-smoked butts. People would snatch them up from the gutter, sometimes fighting over them. In kitchen laboratories the Berliners would field-strip off the paper and repack the tobacco. Ten half-smoked *Kippers* made up one full-bodied cigarette of mixed tobacco, not excluding a little sawdust, and sold on the Potsdamer Platz black market. A whole cottage industry grew up on R.J. Reynolds residue. It made a few Germans rich. Such habits, field-stripping cigarette butts, die hard among the post-war generation of which the uncle was one. He snapped the purse shut.

Yorit felt a twinge of sympathy. "Look, Sir, next pay day I'll see if I can swing a carton of Lucky Strikes for you."

The uncle eyed him suspiciously, the way Germans do, with that arched eyebrow. "Most kind of youfs, young man, but I prefers der Chesterfields if you pleases!" shrieked the wheelchair abruptly. Yorit and Dietsch jumped. It was as if as if someone had just poked the wheel with a sharp stick. Again, the circuitry.

The uncle could only shrug. *"Es tut mir leid,"* (I'm sorry) and drained the rest of his *Wein* drink, the Bakelite jaw clicking the edge of the glass. Yorit and Dietsch relaxed. "Tell me, Herr Yorits, where is youfs, *die Kaserne*? Is its *Tempelhof*?"

"No, Sir, that's Air Force. I'm posted at Andrews Barracks Berlin Brigade. That's on *Finkenstein Allee* in the *Lichtefelde District*."

"Aah ja, Lichtefelde. Most interestings. In my days, ve calls it, *Die Kaiserlishe Hauptkadetteanstadt*," the right wheel answered placidly, for once, as the uncle dabbed at his throat patch.

"Why is that interesting, *Onkel*?" asked Dietsch, not familiar with things military.

"Do yous wishes to know, *meiner Neffe*?" Dietsch nodded. The uncle viewed him and Yorit, his expression a riddle.

Yorit spoke up. "Well, Sir, since I'm posted in the Army at Andrews Barracks Berlin Brigade, I'd like to know too."

The uncle's jaw opened and closed, static followed. The voice crackled. "Youfs Andrews Barracks Berlin Brigade, or shoulds I calls it *die Konzerne*, it vas once a military academyfs. It vas parts of our *Deutsches Reich*, an officer trainings institutionfs. It vas similar to yous, der Vest Points." the left wheel buzzed. "Many pupils vhich learns there became most high officers in our Kaiser Wilhelm Army. Over 3000 officers. The best families of Prussia and Germany sends der childrens dere to studies at *der Kaiserliche Hauptkadetteanstadt.* "

"Andrews Barracks at West Point?" Yorit was not prepared to accept the revelation. "Hard to believe. I thought it was some sort of Nazi compound, or so I was told."

The uncle's jaw chomped. " *Ah ya, das auch.* (that too) It was *die SS Leibstandarte Adolf Hitler, der Fuhrer's military regimentfs*. As youfs sees, Herr Yorits, youfs Andrews Barracks Berlin Brigade, or so youfs calls it, ist in possessions of a most dark history."

Drink in hand, Yorit wondered, could that be the reason for the giant Druid stones at the Yankee Stadium football field? Or the relief sculptures of Superman and Wonder Woman on the wall facade of the post Olympic swimming pool? "Hm," he mumbled

Shifting in his chair, Dietsch coughed out loud, hinting it was time for his guest to go.

The uncle glanced at his nephew. "No Horst, not yets, not befores ve completes der questions. Vhats vas its? Ah, ja, der Andrews *Barracks Berlin Brigade*. Tell me, mein Herr, do yous knows ofs der Ernst Rohm *Putsch, oder (or) der Putsch* against Adolf Hitler hisselfs?"

"I'm not sure," Yorit answered; "National Socialist history was not taught in high school civics class."

The old man's upper lip quivered "Den I shall inform youfs. You sees, in 1934 dere vas *ein Putsch* against an organization called *der SA, Sonderabteilung* (the Special Department). Ernst Rohme vas der leader ofs der SA. He vas der number two peoples in *die Nazi Partei*. He vas also a homosexual, an outrages to die *Eliten*. Dis person, Rohm, he controls all der SA regiments. Hitler had hims and many of der SA leaders to executes. It vas for political reasons. Peoples all over *Deutschland* vas arrested. In Berlin some of dems, the peoples, vas brought to your Andrews Post *Konzerne*. Interesting, no?"

Dietsch shook his head. "*Onkel, das klingt schrecklich.*" (that sounds horrible)

"*It ist die Realitat, Neffe,*" quivered the right wheel's spokes, almost giggling. The uncle's eyes appeared to swell. "Dey vas executed on the spots, I believe dey says in English."

Yorit stared at the old man. "Executed at the Andrews Barracks Berlin Brigade? I better check back at the company for blood stains. Not happy campers, them SA guys."

"Happy c-camps...." the uncle repeated, unfamiliar with the metaphor.

"It is an American expression. It means 'not nice,'" said Dietsch, looking over at Yorit to be sure. "But *Önkel*, why do you tell us this?"

"History, *meiner Neffe*," flapped the jaw as if trying to applaud. "In da times of July 1944 dere vas a second *Putch*, this times against Adolf Hitler hisselfs. It vas done by senior officers *von der Wehrmacht* Army. Most courageous, dems. But *der Putsch*, it fails. *Die Leibstandarte*, the bodyguards as you say, dey comes from your *Konzerne*," chatted the chair's right wheel. "*Da Leibstandarte*, dey stops the coup against Hitler. *Die Leibstandarte*, it vas loyal to *der Fuhrer* unto the ends.

"And the *Putchs* officers who tried to kill Hitler, what happened to them?" asked Yorit, fascinated by the story.

"They vas condemed, all."

"And shot," said Dietsch.

"Yes, many vas shots. In *Deutschland* there vas 4000 executes over all. Here in Berlin der leaders of der coup vas executes. They vas hanged to hooks at *Plötzensee*."

Yorit looked up at the uncle. "Well, so much for the class reunion."

There followed an odd buzzing as if someone was shaving with an electric razor. Zzz! Zz-zz! It was the wheelchair's right wheel. It was chuckling.

Dietsch stood up, shocked that his uncle should find such an outrage amusing. "*Lieber Onkel*, how can you laugh at such a thing? Execution? An outrage!"

Hand trembling, the uncle pressed at his throat tab and croaked, "Horst, amused I am nots. It ist an outrages, *yawol*! I tell youfs, if dere ist efil todays, dey dwells at the *Kaiserliche Hauptkadetteanstaldt*. In youfs, Herr Yorit, youfs army *Koncerne am Finkensteinallee!*"

Yorit shrugged. "Now I understand why our NCOs are so grumpy."

There was a crackle. It was as if a needle on a record player had skipped its track. Abruptly, the wheelchair burst into shout. "And dere ist spirits too!" Yorit and Dietsch looked at each other again. The uncle sounded crazy. Hearing himself crackle, the uncle immediately reached under his seat. It was the circuitry again. He fiddled with something.

Observing him, Yorit thought about what he just said about spirits. On post, over at the band company, the 298th Army Band, one of the musicians once told him that the barracks doors sometimes opened and slammed shut during the night, and no one knew why. Spooky stuff. Than there was that ghost phantom in a black tunic sometimes seen standing in the window of the abandoned SS barracks across from Signal Company. Could the uncle be right, that the post was haunted? Yorit weighed all this as he watched the old man correct the wheel chair's circuitry.

The left wheel coughed another squawk. The chair's circuits were still overloaded. The uncle's seemingly emotional excesses apparently had shorted out some fuse. The circuitry board was not wired for extended conversation. Again, the uncle reached under the wheelchair's seat to the miniature switchboard. Again, he adjusted it, tapping at his throat tab as he did, opening and closing his mouth. Finally he sat back, exhausted from the effort. Dietsch filled his wine glass. Nodding, the uncle drank thirstily.

Both fascinated and revolted, Yorit now understood what nurses in a hospital ward must feel like when inured in a patient's dementia. He ceased to be repulsed by the grotesque presence of the thing in front of him, or the smell of rubbing alcohol, or the crunch of the Bakelite jaw's slurping a drink, or the exclamatory squawks and shouts emitting from the wheelchair's transistor circuitry.

"Why did those officers try to kill Hitler?" Yorit asked pointedly, not caring now if he offended the old man.

The uncle raised a nicotine-stained finger. *"Um das Vaterland zu retten!"* the uncle croaked. "To safe Germany! To stop da Nazis! To stop da insanityfs! *Deutchlands'* heroes— Colonel Graf von Stauffenberg, General von Witzleben, General Gudenauer, und Colonel von Tresko— dey all tries to do so, but fails, and vas executed for its. Most sad. Most sad."

"I am impressed from what you tell me, my dear *Onkel*, but why did these officers not try to save the Jews too?"

The question seemed to catch the uncle by surprise He shifted in his chair, then raised his eyebrows as he focused on his nephew. *"Um diese Zeit, die Juden, lieber Neffe, waren nicht Menschen."* (At this time the Jews, dear nephew, were not people.)

Dietsch opened his mouth as if to comment. *"Onkel*, when you say that you make me ashamed to be *Deutsch."*

"Yous must nots, *Neffe.* Its ist not vats you tinks. Ve vas not evil peoples, die *Deutschen.* Remember, ve toos vas prisoners to *der National Socialismus. "*

Listening to the discussion, Yorit had to ask, "How's that? I read the German people voted for Hitler to govern the country."

"Not soos!" the left wheel and chomping chin insisted loudly as if Yorit had said something offensive. "Vit evil tricks der Nazi *Parti* got controls of governments, and da court places, and der radiofs, and der *Polizei* toos. In dose days, to defy National Socialismus infites fisits."

"Visits?"

"Oh yes, fisits from der *Gestapo! Yawol*, inside our homes ve doubts Hitler; ve curses him. But outsides on the streets, it vas most different. There, ve must to shouts *Zieg Heil*! and applaud or ve gets da visits."

"And the Jews?" asked Yorit.

"Der Nurnburg Laws makes dem unpeoples. It vas der realities!"

"But the Jews were Germans, " insisted Dietsch.

"Yes," the uncle whispered, the shame in his voice visible. "It vas terrible things. *Schrecklich!* You sees, ven die Nazis placed *die Juden* into der camps, dey places German genius into der camps toos. They destroys our *Humanismus.* Today, youfs only have to looks around at der new German architecturefs, or hear our most modern musicfs to see what *Deutschland* most lost. Instead of giants like Wagner and Mendelssohn, ve must tolerates der pops and vhistles *von* der so-called composers like Stockhausen and Hindemith. Their music abstracts. In medicine, it vas der sames. "*Damal, Moabit Krankenhaus* (hospital), once *Deutschland's* most famouses facilitys der medicines and *Vorschung*, (research) is today, vhat? Most *mässig* (mediocre). Our universities, toos *mässig*. Before 1933, did you knows most of da world Nobel Prizes for Medicines and da Sciences goes to wes *Deutschen*, many of dems Jewfs. Today, no more! Our great vriters, musicians, directors of film, again vas Jewfs. Dey must flee *Deutschland*." It was then that the uncle began to name names. "Kurt Weill, Max Reinhart, Fritz Lang, Ernst Lubitsch, (Again, the transistor's speaker under the wheelchair began to break up.) Albert Einstein, Sigmond Freuds. Grrrr! *Eine Schande! Eine Schande*! (Shame! Shame!) Here in Berlin you haf been to ours, der department stores, KaDeWe and Herte, yes? Dey belongs onces to *Juden* families Wertheim and Tietz. Bot family vas deported. An absolute *Schande*!"

Behind them the drapes moved. It gave Yorit a start. Was there a draft? He was getting spooked. So much tragedy, he wondered... So much history lost. Was this the reason Germans rarely laughed?

A long silence followed, Dietsch, Yorit and the uncle all lost in reflection. Moved to change the subject to something lighter, Yorit nodded toward the wall and the family photographs. "Sir, I see you come from a military family. Which photograph up there is yours?"

The uncle stiffened. He was about to sip his wine, but didn't. He put it down. "I am not present in our family panteons."

Dietsch looked up from his folded hands. "Yes, that's right. I never thought to ask, *Onkel*, but tell me, why is your photograph not up on the wall? The whole family is there. You were military too."

Here the chair's right wheel hummed. The left wheel squawked, "Scr-scr". It was as if the two chair wheels could not decide which one should spin first. Had the drink loosened too many spokes? With the uncle's orifice opening and closing, his emaciated hand reached up and pushed at his throat tab. Other-worldly, the right wheel began to rattle. "Youfs *Tant*i (aunt). She burns up my fotos."

"*Aber warum?*" (But why?) asked Dietsch. Yorit's ears perked up.

"Becauses I was *ein Polizist*. Youfs must understands, after der var der times, it vas dangerouses for me, so she burns my fotos."

Disturbed by his uncle's revelation, Dietsch pursued his point.

"*Aber was für ein Polizist?*" (What kind of policeman?)

The Uncle's Bakelite jaw flapped; the upper lip twisted into a curl. To answer was to struggle. "My positions vas most administratives" Again the curtains moved. The room, a moment before so comfortable, now chilled.

"What position, *Onkel?*" Dietsch insisted, wanting to know. Yorit looked at his drink. He sensed this was getting serious, a private family question.

"Perhaps, *Neffe*, you pushes me backs to my roomfs."

"But I wish to know, *Onkel*, please."

Again, the jaw opened and closed in rapid succession. The old man pinched out the end of his just-lit cigarette with is big fingers. There was a smell of burned skin in the air. He sat up and fixed his gaze on his nephew. "If you must knows, in dose days I possesses a most high of positions in *das Reichsicherheitshauptamt*."

Yorit looked up from his *Schnapps*, the glass of *Korn*. He thought he had heard the name before, but he was not sure. He repeated it to himself: *das Reichsicherheitshauptamt*. Then he remembered. It was that patch of ruined ground on the Prinz Albrecht Allee in the Kreutzberg district, near Checkpoint Charlie and the Wall. He had been there often on Army radio patrol. It was where he had once met the witch, the woman who called the ground there a cemetery.

From 1933 until 1945 *Prinz Albrecht Strasse* was known as the location of the *Geheimsicherheitspolizeihauptquartier*. Gestapo Headquaters! It was a name that chilled the blood. When one went into the *Geheimsicherheitshauptquartier*, one often never came out, but was processed and sent to one of the many concentration camps, like Dachau and Sachenhausen. Besides Jews, the German socialists, Union leaders, officers, politicians, priests, ministers, educators, even the rich and the powerful, anybody and everybody who dared question National Socialist authority passed through the ornate doors of Berlin's *Geheimsicherheitshauptquartier*, the Gestapo Headquarters. Of those Germans who survived and managed to return home, the experience left them traumatized.

Appearing stunned at the revelation, Dietsch, the nephew, sat back. Had his uncle been an administer for the *Gestapo*? An interrogator or an executioner? Was this the reason for his big knuckles? Did he give people beatings? Dietsch sucked in his breath. *"Onkel, das ist nicht wahr? Du warst nicht eine von Ihnen?"* (That is not true. You were not one of them?)

Both the nephew and the uncle stared at each other. The uncle did not answer but rubbed his polished chin thoughtfully, his thin body squirming. There was hesitation—a silence, a moment of solemn tension.

" *Onkel*, you were not a Nazi, *oder*?"

"I vas responsible for our familyfs, *Neffe*."

"So you were one of them."

"To be a National Socialist did not mean one vas a Nazi in der hearts."

"You mean when the *Gestapo* executed people, they did not mean it in the heart, is that what you are saying, *Onkel*?" Dietsch blubbered, very concerned.

The old man raised his hand to challenge the question. "The *Gestapo* did not executes. We vas securitys!"

Dietsch looked at him, his beloved *Onkel,* the man who had raised him from childhood, someone he admired, who he respected. Now this. "I cannot help it. I am disturbed."

"As youfs must to be," the uncle replied. "Horst, understand der times. *Deutschland* vas a state occupies. Efil had fallens upon our *Vaterland*. Our peoples lived with fears. To protest meant punishments; to do ones dutys vas to survive."

Dietsch got up. "Then, as a policeman, you must have known about the Jews, the deportations, the mass executions?"

"Of courses I knows of *der Juden*." uttered the right wheel's tinsel voice. "Eferyone knows of *der Juden*, or suspects."

"And you did not try to stop it?"

Stressed by the accusation, the wheel chair began to tremble. Suddenly he burst out, "Who mes? I vas a little mans. I only follow der orderfs!"

Yorit stiffened in his chair.. There it was again. That excuse. He had heard it before, several times. He had read about it too. It was the national confession which Germans used to refute, deny, and negate any participation or association with the National Socialists party, or to refute, deny, and negate any participation in the hunting down of the Jews. It was the excuse the Allied interrogators heard over and over from people of all walks of life, whether a politician, postal clerk, military officer, housewife, manager, railroad engineer, bureaucrat, or a simple soldier, soldiers who claimed they had all served in Norway during the war. "Who, me? I-was-a-little-man. I-only-followed-orders." It was the way, the only way for the guilty to absolve themselves of the national shame. "Blame the system," they would say. The collective was at fault and not the guy a step or two down in the hierarchy. During his defense at the Nuremberg Trials even Hermann Göring had said it: "Who me? I-was-a-little-man. I-only-followed-orders."

It was the same with the deep-pocket corporate managers of large German cartels like Krupp, Siemans, Volkswagen. When the directors and managers were asked why they used enforced concentration camp labor on production, the answer often was, "Who me? I-was-a-little-man. I-only-followed-orders." The denial was so prevalent among the population, US Army psychiatrists had to classify the excuse as a syndrome. However, what the excuse mentality could not excuse away was that thing known as "whistle blowing."

Under the National Socialism, many in the German population had become voluntary whistle blowers. They stoolied on one another. Every apartment house had a warden *(ein Gauleiter)*, every apartment block a *Policist*. A wisecrack overheard or a slip of the tongue could bring a visit by the *Polizei* and an invitation to *Gestapo* Headquarters. To live in Germany in the 1930s and 40s was like going to a football game where fans played the referee. If one did not cheer the home team, a whistle blew and the game stopped and the fan was arrested.

Shifting in his chair, the uncle spoke up. "You must understand, Horst, *unsere Abteilung* (our government department) it vas in a carrousel of papers, der stamps, and schedules and lists—endless lists! These names goes to Dachau; thoses names to Theresian Stadt. Der calculations vas-s most complicates. *Juden*, Communists, priests, Union leaders, politicians, Socialists and liberals, and journalists, especially journalists; dey all had to process. Anyones who vas-s suspect had to be interrogates!" the wheelchair wheels rasped loudly as the uncle tapped at his throat patch as if sending a Morse code message. "For me, peoples vas only pieces of der papers. Ja, peoples was papers, like dis."

From the ashtray he picked out a cigarette butt, one Yorit had smoked; it was not field stripped. With practiced precision he stripped it and rolled it into a paper ball, then flicked it across the table to make his point. "Peoples was *nichts*! (nothing) Dey vas documents to processes," he said, followed by a series of squawks and garbles. The uncle grabbed again at the throat patch.

"But there were human beings behind those documents!" insisted Dietsch.

Again the uncle rubbed his Bakelite jaw as he spoke, his voice scratchy. "In dose, der days, *das Deutsche Volk* forgets the meaningfs of da word 'humanities.' Me toos, I am sorry to speak. As I says den and I says now: I-vas-a-little-man. I-only-follows-der-orderfs."

Yorit felt he was becoming part of a family feud, only in the English language. Why they discussed the subject of National Socialism in his presences intrigued him. "May I ask a question, Sir?" he interrupted.

"If you vishes," answered the uncle gruffly, drawing another cigarette from the open pack still on the table. He slid it into the cigarette holder.

"What ever happened to the Nazi functionaries, the men who ran the German government at the time? Today, one never hears anything about them. Are they still around somewhere, in prison or dead? Where are they?"

The uncle turned his clear gray eyes upon his guest and glared. The look made Yorit quiver. *How many prisoners has the old man terrified with that look*? he wondered. The uncle's upper lip trembled. Pressing the patch at the base of his throat, the left wheel squeaked. "I tell youfs, young mans, todays dey sits in most high positions, *höhe Beampton in unsere Regierung.*" (high government officials)

Startled, Dietsch shifted in his chair. "*Önkle*, you mean Ex-Nazis work as bureaucrats in our government?"

"*Yawohl*! (yes) In der governments dey are," the right wheel echoed this time.

"That can't be, *Onkel*!" stated Dietsch, his voice pitched as if he had been threatened with a thumb screw. "Do you say that our Chancellor Adenauer, or SPD's Herbert Werner, or old Ludwig Erhart were Nazies?"

"Oh, no-nos. Chancellor Adenauer had to hide from dems because of his criticisms. Herbert Werner vas a hero. He fights die Nazis. But you looks fife steps downs in our systems and you finds dems, the old Nazis. They works *als hohe Beampten* (as high officials), only dey changes der hats. Dey gets the old jobs back and now sits *auf ihre dicke Po* (like asses) and, as before, dey stamps der documents, a faforite past times."

Now Yorit spoke up. "I'm not sure I understand, Sir."

The uncle glared at him. "As Beampton officials, the National Socialists, dey returnes to deir old posts!" the right chair wheel shouted out. "Take youfs our Dr. Adolf Kittell of der CDU and odder peoples like hims. He ist examples. He vas in the Goebbels Propaganda Ministry. A Nazi, him! Amazing, is it nots? Der var done, dese peoples turns and bows and kisses der shoes of *der Amerikanern*, and der British, toos. For kissing der shoeses dey gets *die Persilscheinen* (a document that exonerated officials and politicians of past misdeeds). Todays dey plays der good citizens. Dey collects high incomes and goes to official balls, and talk *der Diplomatie*. In Brussel dey vears der sash! Most convenients, no?" Breathing deeply, the uncle fell back in his chair, the left wheel huffing, "Yes, most convenients. Peoples do not to know vhat dey once vas—Nazies!"

" *Und unsere Richtern?*" (And our judges?) Dietsch asked, slipping into German.

"Ah, *Die Richtern!*" Here, the Bakelite jaw flapped rapidly. The question had opened an old grievance, a pent up one that ran deep in the old man. "*Die Richtern! Die Richtern!*" he repeated with a screech of the wheels. "I burns to tinks! *Die sind die grossten Schweinen überhaupt!* (The judges are the biggest pigs of all!) Scratches youfs one the skin and youfs scratches a Nazi! *Die Richtern,* dey never holds the whips; dey pointfs der fingers! It vas dem vat condemnfs our peoplefs! It vas dem vat sent tousands to the campfs and executions!"

Suddenly there was a snap. It was the Bakelite jaw. It dropped to the uncle's chest and hung there, held by two cat-gut wires. The orifice exposed a cadmium red hole with a flailing tongue darting in and out, snapping like a cobra wanting to strike. Yorit and Dietsch watched, horrified. "If Freisler lived," the cadmium red hole trumpeted, "I assure youfs he vould sits todays on our *Verfassungsgericht!*" (the Supreme Court)

Dietsch jumped up, hands out in an effort to interrupt the right wheel's diatribe.

"I can name the names! Go youfs! Go open der Dahlemer Archeifes! Dere, youfs finds der proofs! All secrets dark! *Die Schweine!* Dey dwells in elegances vile ve of the *Polizei* dids their *Schmutzarbeit!* (dirty work) Ve knows der truth of dems! Ve knows der trut!"

"*Onkel! Onkel! Dein Kin, bitte!*" (Uncle, your chin, please!) Dietsch managed to interrupt.

The uncle looked down the bridge of his nose. Startled, he grabbed at the wayward jawbone hanging there. Turning away, he fiddled with it, managing to click-click it back into place. He opened and closed the jaw several times. With a chuckle of embarrassment, he turned back to the two young men in front of him. "Zzz! Zzz!" the left wheel chuckled as he gave the Bakelite jaw a light cuff. "*Na, ja*! Shits happens," he said, adjusting the stainless-steel bolts under each ear.

Yorit watched and wondered what he would do if the uncle should have a seizure. Dare he give an old Nazi mouth-to-mouth resuscitation as the Army had trained him to do? He felt he had enough of the ghoulish sideshow, and got to his feet. "That's it!" he said to himself with finality.

The uncle glared at him the way Germans sometimes do. "*Setzen Sie sich*! " (Sit down!) he ordered. "Horst, dis embarrassments infites us to one last *Schnapps. Die Flasche*, (the bottle) if youfs pleases."

Yorit sat back in his chair. "Okay, Sir, but only one drink."

Dietsch went to the cabinet. This time he took out a bottle of *Weinbrand* (brandy). He poured three shots. With the shock of the moment passed, the three men relaxed.

Gripping his shot glass the way Germans do, from behind with two fingers, the uncle scolded a "*Prost!*" he toasted and tossed the drink into the open hole that was the orifice, the Bakelite jaw clicking on the glass edge as he swallowed.

Yorit coughed. The drink was strong stuff. In the tired light they quietly licked their lips and contemplated the brandy taste. Then Yorit spoke up. "Sir, may I ask one question? Why did those *Schwein* judges, as you call them, get their jobs back if it was known they were Nazis?"

The uncle did not answer right away, but continued to tighten one neck bolt. "You must first knows a little history, young mans. In 1949 vhen der *Bundesrepublik* becomes a land vith vhat you calls states, *Deutschland* had few judges. At das times, most official, *Beampton* vas still to be seen as 'National Socialisten' and not to be trusted. Dere vas no untainted officials to fills the high positionfs of Government. Der *Lander*, like Bayern, and Baden-Wüttenberg, Hessen, all needs judges. Your Allied commanders haf no choices but to stamp the *Jurist Puselscheinen* (permits) as clean. Vith dis, der old jurists, dey receive deir robes and dey returns to the benches, as you *Amis* say. Nazi officials vas again *Richtern*, but now judges for a new system, der *Deutsche Democratic Republik*. Most disturbing, no?"

"Was it the same in the Russian zone?" asked Dietsch.

"No, der *Beampton* officials dere, dey vas sent to Siberian."

"Did the Russians send the *Gestapo* officials to prisons too?" Yorit asked further.

The uncle did not respond, but sipped his drink.

Dietsch looked at him; "*Onkel*, today we have the 1960s. After all these years, surely the truth must come out about our justice system, that many jurists and judges here were once members of the Nazi party."

"*Ya, Na und*? (So what.) Youfs know vhat shall happenfs? *Nichts*! (Nothing) Dat ist der reasons for *Namen und Taten* (names and deeds) documentfs, dey sits in der Dahlem archivefs. Dere, the secrets are locked up. Should scholars dares to research and exposes dems, many officials, some in the *Bundestag*, must den resign for shames. *Die Beamten* bureaucrats too. Dey shall all be exposes, guilty to sympaty, collaborators to murder."

"Do you say the misdeeds of our German past are something to be forgotten?" Dietsch questioned, a whine in his voice.

The old man shook his head. "Yes. It ist because our beloved *Bundesrepublik* vould loses high officialfs, important peoples, some *Bundestag* peoples. I knows dem. Should high officials or our generals be found in disgraces or shamed as Nazis, dey vould go into rooms vith a pistol and shoots. Dat ist der vay. It is our traditions."

"Shoot? Shoot who?"

"Theirselfs! It ist that, or to lives in disgrace. *Wir Deutschen können nicht ohne Ehre leben.*" (We Germans cannot live without honor.)

"That so?" said Yorit. "I think our local politicians back home could learn something from your German traditions."

"I do not approve," interrupted Dietsch. "Such tradition of honor belongs to the 17th century, another age."

"It's better than the French alternative," said Yorit with a nod, hinting of humor.

"French alternative. Vhat you means?"

"The guillotine."

Dietsch tapped his fingertips together, his brows knitted in thought. "If there are people in high places who committed crimes against the state, then *Onkel*, if you know them why do you not speak out? The newspapers, *der Morgenpost, die Bild Zeitung, Die Welt*, all would be happy to print your story for sure?"

The old man twisted in his seat at the question. The right wheel spoke up. "Horst, dat I cannot dos. Is it not my duties to name da names and make da vorld avares vho deses officials and politicians might be. Dey should be brought to justices by justices. Not me!" The slip of a body appeared to tremble. The right wheel wheezed. "You sees, should

I speaks dere are dangers. I must tink of our familys. My responsibilitifs ist heavy. Familsy first. I must remain der silents. To speak outs ist foolish."

"You fear something, *Onkel*?"

The uncle snapped his *Weinbrand* back. Again, he worked the bolts at the neck, opening and closing his jaw as he did. "Peoples in high places can be most dangerouses. Dey can be cruel and..." Suddenly, the left wheel burst out in a sudden, rejuvenated shout, startling the two youths. "...in my supine positions it ist vise to keep, to keep der SILENTS!"

The chair's wheels seemed to be losing control. Again, for the forth or fifth time, the uncle reached down and adjusted the circuit network under the seat. He continued.

"Does der name General von Gatten means sometings to youfs? No, of course nots. I shall tell youfs. Von Gatten, he vas responsibles for der Fuhrer's, the spy networks. *Der Abwehrdienst*. (Secret police). Todays, he ist again responsibles to do the sames police networks, only nows for *der Bundesrepublik Deutschland*. Vas he a Nazi? *Ja und egal! Der Amerikaner* positions him to the posts. So you sees, as long as he and peoples like hims sits in power positions, peoples like me must remain der silents."

"But why?"

The old man looked at the two youths in front of him, his fierce gray eyes suddenly gone soft. The light in them seemed to fade to the room's deep shadows, drop by drop, the body fading from life. Having exhausted so much energy talking, the transistor voice turned static like a radio signal between programs. The uncle pushed hard at the throat patch to vocalize. The static retreated. "Horst, my boy, looks you at me. Vhat sees youfs? I am a broken man. I hafs pieces of metal here and here," the static said, the uncle pointing to his hip and neck. "I am in no a positions to be der heros. Most of my generation peoples are like me, brokens. Der pride in our *Vaterland* ist—vhat you calls it—vanquished. Ve must valk in der shames for vhat we to have dones to *die Welt* (world). Derere are no more der symbols to make *die Deutsche Volk stolz* (proud), deeds dat makes der chest to swells. Today, *Deutschland über Alles* ist vitouts meanings. In many countries ve Germans are spitted upons and maligned. I, too, am most bitter. So, to speaks out? No! It changes notings. It ist der reasons to remain here in der silents. No more *Sieg Heil*! You understand?"

The uncle winced. A sudden muscle spasm pinched his back. One leg began to shake, forcing him to reposition himself. He moved it with some effort. *"Wir Deutschen leben in Ungnade!*(dishonor) Our *Militar* it ist in *Ungnade*! Our industry ist in *Ungnade*! The churches, institutions, cowards them all, ist in *Ungnade*! Our traditions, culture ist ignobles; our history ashes! *Die Deutsch Aufklärung* (enlightenment), music, literature and science all made to ruines in just twelf disgrace yearfs of *National Socialistismus! Scheize!"* (Shit!) The bony fist hit the table, rattling the glasses. The liquor glass bounced. Both Dietsch and Yorit listened, saying nothing. Fascinated. *"Der Fuhrer*, he says *der Deutsche Reich* shall last one tousands of years. He vas correct! It vill last one tousand years in der mind of mans as…as abominations!"

Yorit watched, fearful that the jaw would again slip its hinges. It didn't. The uncle reached out. "Vhat vill save us is our youthfs. Yous, Horst. My generations, *der Schwein* generations must first to vanishes. Our hearts are too hard!" the left wheel shouted. Pausing, the wheel's utterance dropped to a whisper. " *Ja wohl*! Yes! Only in youfs, der new German mans, ist dere hopes. But you must be morals, be tolerants, and haf der compassions for odder peoples and deir cultures. Only den vill *Deutschland* have a place-es in old Europe."

Having said that, the uncle's head dropped to his chest. He seemed close to tears. Dietsch reached out and rested his youthful hand on the aged one.

Taking it all in, Yorit sat up. "Yes, sir, I'm sure Germany will again have its place, but until then, the Allies in Germany are here on patrol, just to be sure."

The uncle looked up. He gave Yorit an aprising look when the circuits lit up, ringing. "Quite sooo, young mans! As long as der Allies are on der patrols! And do yous know vhys yous *Amerika, Englander, und Französen* must patrols us?" Yorit was not sure what the uncle was driving at. "Becauses yous and der rest of der vorlds still fears our *Deutschland*!" quivered the upper lip as if, attempting to curse.

"That is nonsense, Sir."

"You *und die Welt* fears us and our machines!"

"More nonsense!"

"Our disciplines! Our organizations! *Das was ist Deutsch*!" (That which is German)

"I doubt that," said Yorit.

"Der Allies dey vishes to squeeze *der Deutsche Volk* to keeps us *schwach* (weak), from a-rising up to kick yous all out!" croaked the left wheel with a burst of national pride, a pride that still smoldered in the emaciated body.

Yorit stood up. It was time to go. "Quite frankly, Sir, if I might talk as an American citizen and soldier, we don't give a shit about your machines, or for that matter, what you Germans think. The US Army is here to stay…and patrol! We're here to defend you—Berlin, and West Germany—against Communism, whether you like it or not. If we were not here, this hole-in-the-ground of a city would be 'Red' and Walter Ulbrich your chancellor. Your nephew, Horst, would be standing in bread lines instead of going to college. Who knows, Sir, where you would be? Probably strung up in Siberia, from what you told us. Now, if you will excuse me…" Yorit grabbed the saxophone case. "…I'm leaving! Thank you for the hospitality. Horst, I'll tell Kevin to call you."

"Robert, just a moment!" Dietsch called after him.

"*Lass ihm*," (Let him go) said the uncle, indignant.

"You don't have to show me out," said Yorit, unsteady from too much drink. Taking his jacket, he crossed the room to the green door and looked back as he pulled it open.

Both the uncle and Dietsch cried out, "Halt!" "Stop!"

"Good-by!" said Yorit—and plunged. With a gasp and a scream, he found himself hanging on to a pair of door handles and kicking at the night. He was two stories above the ground and swinging out over the bombed-out half of the villa. "Fuck-n-aaa!" The saxophone case hit the ground somewhere below. Now he knew what lay behind "The room's Green Door" and Rosmary Clooney's popular song. Nothing! "Fuck-n-aaa!" Yorit cried out. Only later would he find out that the uncle's green door was never locked. The old man used it to pee from, and to empty his cigarette ashtray.

"Give me your hand!" Dietsch called, holding on to the door frame and leaning out the door to grab Yorit, if he could.

Yorit kicked for leverage to get the door to swing back toward the house. Suddenly there was a loud crack. The weathered wood around the handles began to splinter. In desperation he lurched, missing Dietsch's outstretched hand and dropped into the darkness below, his last words an unforgettable, "Shiiit, last again!" There followed a thud.

***

The night sky was clear. The stars were out. The forest scent was sweet to breathe. He opened his eyes and looked up. The flashlight's weak light glared in his face. He blinked. It was Dietsch; he had come out of the house. His voice was tremulous with concern. "Robert, the saxophone! Is it damaged?"

***

Later, back at 592nd Signal Company, Yorit limped into the Orderly Room. His face was bruised and his jacket torn. He dropped his off-post pass on the Staff Duty desk and picked up a pen to sign in. Sitting behind the desk, Sgt Cabul eyed him curiously. He had been reading a Daffy Duck comic book when Yorit interrupted him.

"Good God, Soldier! What the happened to you? You look like you had your ass kicked."

"Not quite, Sarge. I fell down a flight of stairs."

"A flight of stairs does that to you?"

"No, only the first step."

Old Eden Saloon

Outside, the evening was damp and cold, the air chilly, the trees swept of leaves, the streetlights barely illuminating. Up and down the street the apartment buildings were dark, all the window shades (*Rolos*) were down. It was as if the occupants were trying to hide something. The past? In Berlin it was the past that prompted one to look over their shoulder and with a shiver ask, "Who's there?" It was the *Damaschkus Strasse,* a cobblestone street, where Jews had once dwelled. It was in the Halensee District

It had to do with their good soldiering. Both Yorit and Lavoss got a "Good-Till-Midnight" company pass. It had been a rough week of training, 16-hour days, some extra duty, and a short field exercise and twice, KP duty. Tonight, free of Army drill and regimen, they had but one goal—to party! They were desperate to get away from the company, if only for a couple of hours. At the main gate the MP guard checked their passes and inquired where they were going for the evening. In a fit of passion Lavoss shouted, "Out on the town! Out on the town! Away from the Army, damn it, and out on the town!"

Startled by the outburst, the gate guard apologized for the delay and returned both men's passes without examining them. He understood their emotions.

Yorit and Lavoss crossed the street to the Golden Sun bar for that quick "wet your whistle" ritual. Inside, they found their company mascot, the woman, Death, sitting alone. She had already drunk some, and she seemed contrite. Her boyfriend, SFC Oats, had stood her up for the evening. Both men felt a pinch of guilt. They didn't have the nerve to tell her what every man at 592nd Signal Company knew: that SFC Oats was in hiding.

SGT Oats had gotten into Death's pants with a promise of marriage. He deflowered the old flower, then broke off the engagement without bothering to tell her, though he did boast at the NCO club, "Guys, got me one more notch on me rifle stock." He stopped returning her phone calls and did not answer her letters. Death soon became suspicious, the way older single woman do when they are desperate for marriage and a family. Still, she remained hopeful. She shrugged off the disappointment with the excuse, "Well, you know how Americans are." She never expected she was part of the game of "Draw the Straw," all of them short. Yorit and Lavoss knew it and felt sorry for her.

Putting an arm around her shoulder, Lavoss suggested she join them for a trip downtown and some night life. "After all, Death dear, you are the company mascot," he complimented her. Unsure of the meaning of the word "mascot," she agreed to go with them. Had she known the meaning of mascot she would have still gone with them; being with fun guys is better than an un-fun evening alone in her flat. A few cheer-me-up shots later and walking arm-in-arm, the three of them boarded the streetcar *Strassenbaahn* for downtown West Berlin.

A short time later they reach the *Kurfürsten Damm, Uland Strasse* intersection. Call it the   West Berlin's Fifth Avenue. Though it was bitter cold, the *Damm* was crowded with shoppers. Christmas was not far off. Stepping along briskly, they mingled with the crowds, taking in the festive atmosphere.

In front of the cafe known as *Kranzler's*, a war veteran on one crutch languidly worked his street organ. Some shoppers stopped to watch. He appeared not to have the Christmas spirit. He tried to look cheerful with his rakish top hat, but he could not pull it off. His parrot had just died. It had caught pneumonia. The veteran blamed overwork and the cold evenings. It happened during the German equivalent of a "Polly-want-a-cracker" routine. "My bird dropped dead, just like that," he told Death in German, snapping his fingers. "Fell off his stand, he did. Now what was I to do? The show must go on. It's that, or back to the flophouse." He had kicked the bird into the gutter. With his hat still rakish and his collar up, the veteran continued to pump the street organ with one hand while doing the old soft shoe with his crutch. He had lost a foot during the war.

Observing him, Yorit asked, Dancing on crutches? Hm… Think that would fly on television back home?

"Maybe it would on the Arthur Godfrey Show or Dick Clark's

American Bandstand. It's entertainment," said Lavoss, referring to the popular talk and television show hosts back in the States. Death dropped a German Mark into the veteran's tin cup, and they moved on.

Half a block up the *Kufürsten Damm*, in front of a boutique's plate glass window, a mime performed on the street. He had a chalk face and wore a clown's hat. Nearby, a magician did tricks. It was not the kind of night to do slight-of-hand, too cold, but he did it anyway. He did card tricks and pulled coins from people's ears. He surprised his audience when he handed them money. No one realized the money was theirs. He had pick-pocketed the audience while performing. He was that good. Death told Yorit and Lavoss she knew the magician; he was a reformed pickpocket. He was sometimes hired by the local Social Democratic Party to raise money for the party coffers.

Further up the *Damm*, a ventriloquist performed with string puppets. Each puppet had its own child-like voice. It amused the pedestrians. He drew light applause, especially for two of his puppets; they went at it on the sidewalk in a miniature bed. Yorit looked at Death. "I don't know about you, honey, but I'm getting turned on. Wha-do-ya-say, you and me hit the sack?" he invited her, wiggling his eyebrows.

Death looked at Yorit with a half-smile. "Why not? But can we fit on that tiny bed?"

"And what about me?" asked Lavoss.

"You get your own puppet," said Yorit.

Taking a break from the cold, they went into one of the many cafes that lined *Kudamm Boulevard.* Inside, they took a table and ordered drinks near three women who were sitting together. They were dressed elegantly, in widow black: fur coats draped at the shoulders and large felt hats with arched pheasant feathers sticking out of them. As they chatted, they sipped yellow egg liquor, *Eierlikür,* from thimble-sized cups.

Curious about the long hat feathers, Yorit asked Death about it. "Feathers that long are a bit bazaar, don't you think?"

"A Bavarian tradition," Death noted. "The feathers are for tickling "males of interest," should they pass by. It gets their attention."

"Couldn't they just ask the `male of interest´ to join them at the table?" asked Lavoss, admiring one woman with an especially long feather.

"Oh, no, not here in Berlin. That is not how the game of romance is played."

Yorit thought for a moment. "Oh, you tickle first then go on a date? I thought it was the other way around, to date then tickle."

Lavoss and Yorit learned that the Berlin women who wore such long feather hats were widows. Dressed in black as they were, it told of their past: widows of traditional wealth, some of it National Socialist.. During the war their diplomat husbands had vanished on some foreign front. Today, with little to do and much wealth sitting in Switzerland, they strutted the glass and mirror cafes of *Kufürsten Damm* like Toulouse Lautrec figures, hoping for a pick-up and maybe an affair. Very elegant and very dignified, the "Great Dames" of West Berlin, as they were called, sipped their liquor while at the same time studying the mature males who passed by, voyeuring them as if they were applicants for a fashion photo-op. The widows rarely smiled. They would not or could not, for their makeup, like their age, was rigid. Now poised and sitting in a cafe sipping egg liquor, the Great Dames waited for something to happen—some event, hopefully cataclysmic, like a David Niven character rich in sophistication to approach them and shock them out of the hated void left by their dead diplomat husbands. Sometimes tipsy, they would primp themselves while stealing a peak into the gilded wall mirrors to check their lipstick or powder their nose. If a lip developed a smudge (blame the excessive chatting) it was immediately touched up—for the ninth time. That done, the Great Dames would turn back to the coquettish business of male-scouting and liquor-sipping and of course, chatting.

Death knew of them and considered their game a bore. It was because the widows were too much like her. A hunter! The only difference? Death was without wealth. She could not afford the fashion or the cafe lounge lifestyle. She had to work ten hours a day to pay the rent. She stood up. "Boys, I do not like this cafe. We go somewhere else. I suggest the Old Eden Saloon."

"A saloon, here in West Berlin? Sounds like back home," said Yorit.

"Yes, there is live jazz and the drinks are cheap," she added. "It is a favorite place for the Berlin inside crowd."

"Sounds cool," said Lavoss, eyeing one of the Great Dames. She had arched an eyebrow, giving him an invitational shake of her pheasant feather.

Death watched him watch the dame. "The Old Eden has an interesting mix of people," she added, "Rosa Luxemburg types: leftists, journalists, lawyers, homosexuals, street prostitutes." She "poofs" on a pause from the cold."

Yorit got up. "So what are we sitting here for? Let's go check out the homos."

Eyebrow raised, Lavoss looked up at him. "Hey, Robert, you're still in the Army. This is not the place to change lifestyles. Later maybe, but not now."

They paid and walked toward the door. Passing one of the Great Dames, her over-extended pheasant feather nipped Yorit at the cheek. He had just been targeted. Turning in the direction of the feather, the Great Dame gave him a nod. She was in her fifties, elegant, wore a pearl necklace, and was fashionably dressed. She offered him a condescending, yet licentious smile. It meant "You may hustle me if you wish, Sonny Boy, but be quick before I change my mind."

"Forget her," said Lavoss, picking up on the eye contact. "We're on a date with Death, remember?"

Yorit blinked. "A date with… I'm not sure I want that."

Glancing back at the Great Dame, he shrugged an apology, but she had already castrated him with a snap of her pearled necklace. She returned to admiring her aging self in one of the gilded mirrors. Yorit had taken five seconds too long to respond to her feathery invitation.

Outside, on the street, they hopped the city's double decked *Omnibus*. Several stops later, they got off. It was the *Demaschkus Strasse* stop. The street lights were dull and the apartment buildings dark. A light winter mist hung in the night air as they walked the cobblestone street. They spoke little, but sensed there was something more in the air here than just the winter chill. Lavoss stopped. "What was that?"

Yorit looked at him. "What was what?"

"I don't know? That!" he said, looking over his shoulder.

Yorit followed his gaze. "Al, there's no one there."

"But I thought I heard a voice."

"You did," said Death, walking between them. "You heard the past."

Drawing closer together, they gripped each other's arm and moved quickly, hoping to pass the oppressive feeling of that something which haunted those who dared walk the *Demaschkus Strasse*, day or night. One dark building stood out on the street. A dull neon sign hung out. It read, "Old Eden Saloon." They were there.

A short line of people waited out in front of the entrance. A bouncer stood at the doorway. He was not letting anyone in, not yet. Tonight, Friday night, the Old Eden Saloon was crowded. Only when a patron came out of the bar would the bouncer step aside and let the next patron pass and enter.

"Looks bad," said Lavoss, the night's condensation spilling from his mouth. "I fear we'll freeze and be AWOL before we get inside the club."

"I thought this was supposed to be an exclusive joint," said Yorit, a little disappointed. "By the looks of it, the Old Eden is just another G.I. bar only with a cover charge."

Death shivered in the cold. "I said prostitutes come here, and where the prostitutes are the crowd is. They make the Old Eden exclusive."

"Really! Then I'd like to meet one," said Lavoss.

"Me too," said Yorit.

They watched as two couples came out of the Old Eden arm-in-arm. Four people went in. The line moved up. Lavoss thrust his hands into his pockets. He looked at Death. "Maybe this is not the time to ask you about it, dear, but do you really care all that much about Signal Company's old Platoon Sergeant, Sergeant Oats? He's a bit strange, you know."

Death thought the question odd. "To you maybe, but not for me. Together, we have an understanding. Maybe it is enough for us to fall in love."

"After the first or the second baby?" quipped Yorit.

"Shouldn't you try to fall in love with a German guy instead? After all, you are German," said Lavoss, thinking over her relationship with a platoon NCO.

Again the thoughtful look. "German men? Terrible lovers with small *Portemonnaien*." (change purses)

"Soldiers have the same problem," said Yorit.

"Not me," said Lavoss. "My *Portemonnaien* has the right proportion. I'm an irresistible lover."

"She's talking about your other *Portemonnaie*," said Yorit. " It's too small,"

"How do you know? Have you seen it?"

"Yes, I've stood next to you in the latrine."

From the waiting line, two more people entered the Eden Saloon. Nearby, a man in a suit complained to his girlfriend about the wait.

Yorit rubbed his hands together. "Brr. You know, if this is what civilian life in this city, I mean the lines and all that, we may as well hang out on our Army post. At least there the lines move."

Lavoss nodded. "Yes they move, but all backwards."

Death began to shiver. She wore only a leather waist jacket, too thin for the night. Lavoss opened his jacket. "You're going to catch a death of cold, Death. Here, snuggle up to me." She slid under his arm.

Yorit looked at her. "Hm, how can Death catch a death of cold when she is death? Ha, ha!"

"Not funny, Robert. I suggest we go somewhere else. I really don't want to wait in the cold. Besides, our company passes are only good till midnight."

"I know what we do," said Death, reaching into her handbag. She took out a pair of sunglasses.

"What's that?"

She held out the sunglasses. "I wear these when I go to the Negro soldier bars."

Taken back, Lavoss stared at her. "I didn't know you went out with niggers."

Death looked at him, puzzled. "Yes, why not? They are Americans too, *oder*…" (or)

"I know, but…oh, forget it."

She pushed the sunglasses into his face. "Albert, you have nothing to say about who I go out with. Here, play blind and dumb."

"Ya, Al, be yourself," coaxed Yorit, laughing.

Death pulled up Lavoss' coat collar then spun him around several times to get him to stagger, which he did. Taking him by the arm, she pretended he was a blind invalid and walked him, staggering, to the front of the line. She apologized to the other patrons as they went. The Germans, ever respectful, stepped back for what they assumed was a real blind man. Together, when they reached the Old Eden's entrance, the bouncer, the image of a veteran wrestler, muscle-faced and all, stopped them.

Looking above the bouncer's head, Lavoss began his performance. He felt for the bouncer's shoulder muscles, then his face; he grabbed his nose and squeezed it. The bouncer slapped his hand away as Death explained to him in German that her friend was blind.

Although a hard guy on the outside, inside the bouncer was a soft touch. Just then, two people stepped out of the saloon and passed them. Grunting, the club bouncer pushed open the entrance door. "You three may go inside." Greatful, Death slipped him a two mark tip, and the three entered the Old Edan Saloon. Once inside, they dropped the charade.

"Death, dear, that was an original," Yorit declared jubilantly, giving her a hug. "Who knows how long we'd have been outside at the front door if it wasn't for you?"

Looking around, they noticed Lavoss was still playing the game of blind-man's-bluff. He had stepped into the bar crowd. "Hey, where are you doing? Come back!" Yorit called out.

"What for?" Lavoss answered back, still wearing the sunglasses. "It's a great way to fill my tin cup!"

Darkly lit, the Old Eden Saloon was thick with cigarette smoke. Bodies were jammed from the entrance to the deep interior. To order a drink, a customer had to cry out, "*Bier hier!*" and wave an arm as if to salute dictators. Beer, half-liters, quarter-liters, and shot glasses of *Schnapps* flowed in a procession, passing from hand to hand over the heads of the crowd. The money, *Deutsch Marks*, flowed back the same way, from hand to hand over the heads. A bartender in a white apron played traffic cop. He directed the orders to the recipients while the cashier, a fat lady in a yellow floral dress who resembled a female Humpty Dumpty, made change. She was the owner of the Old Eden Saloon, lovingly known as "Mama Lisa."

Mama Lisa sat behind the bar, high on a four-legged stool, her oversized bottom consuming the seat. She was the perfect image of a smiling Buddha, only a feline one. From her vantage point she had a view of the carnival below her. She smiled continually, never losing that quiescent Buddha or Humpty Dumpty look. With her massive *Übergewicht* (weight), heavily rouged cheeks, pig eyes and rakish red hair just out of pin curlers, she was a one-woman sideshow, with the Old Eden Saloon her stage.

Lavoss held up a hand, indicating three beers. Nothing happened. He tried again to get recognized. "What you got to do to get served around here?"

"Try shouting *Sieg Heil*," suggested Yorit above the noise of the throng.

"*Sieg Heil!*" Lavoss shouted. It got the attention. The Germans around glared at him. In the crowd a man compressed next to them also flashed a disapproving look. Lavoss looked back at him. "And what am I suppose to say, tea for two?"

The closer they got to the bar, the denser the crowd. Body heat became a problem. It made everyone thirsty, which meant more hands went up, which meant more drinks were passed, which meant more money paid, which made Mama Lisa grin all the more. Because of the room's density, once an arm was raised it was stuck there in a Fascist-like salute. How to get it down was a problem; the human crush was that great. The only place to rest the salute was akimbo, the elbow on the head or shoulder of the person squashed directly in front. Should your nose itch, to scratch it was out of the question, but one could scratch his neighbor's nose if requested.

Three full *Krugen*, mugs of beer, were finally passed up to them. Lavoss stuck a ten Mark note in the hand of the man in front of him, not sure if he would ever see the change, but he did. The change, seven *Marks,* was passed back. The routine was for the man in front of Lavoss to pass the ten *Mark* note to the man in front of him, who passed it to the person in front of him, who passed it up the line until it reached Mama Liese at the cash drawer. She ordered the *Bier*, made the change and handed it back. Germans, being an honest *Volk*, passed it back. Back down the line the change went, following the hand trail it had traveled until it reached Lavoss. It impressed him. "Wow! Germans you can certainly trust. Back home in Chicago we'd never see the change, or the beer for that matter."

"It proves one thing," said Yorit. "The Germans might gun you down in battle, but you can trust them not to steal your watch."

Suddenly the slate of humanity shifted, sucking Death away from her companions and into the crowd. She let out a scream. Lavoss reached out to grab her, but missed. Instead, the crush pushed him up against the backside of a man in a leather coat who was in a state of perspiration. Lacross could feel the man's heat and became anxious about such close proximity. He called over to Yorit, several bodies away. "If I was a fairy I'd say this is as close to Paradise as you can get, but since I'm not—HELP!"

Yorit, himself in a squash, answered back over to him, "Ten more minutes in this crowd and you will be!"

Not far away from her companions, Death stood, stuck in the crush. It was then she felt a hand grab her rump with a full-born squeeze. She jerked her head around and saw her molester. He grinned. "Try and do something about it," he provoked her in German.

"Just pretend I slapped your face!" she snapped back at him over her shoulder.

"Since you cannot stop me, enjoy my velvet touch," he added, still grinning, giving her another full-born squeeze of the butt.

"Pervert!" she cried out in German.

"Of course," he spoke into her ear, breathless with excitement. They were that close.

With only one hand free—the one holding the *Bier*—she tossed it over her shoulder and into the face of the pervert. He ceased his velvet touch. "Bitch!" he cried. Death could only smile. "You're welcome."

Again, the human tide shifted, this time drawing Lavoss up against her. "Death, dear, we got to stop meeting like this," he huffed, but before she could reply, a short, balding man, an attorney by the shape of his head (pointed) slipped between them. He apologized for the interruption and promised to slip away at the first opportunity, crowd permitting.

The Old Eden Saloon went from a rip tide to a gridlock, and back. No one moved in the human ice pack except by consent of the masses, and only than in groups of four or five.

There was a sudden push. A crevice opened up. In a swirl of heat and bodies, Death was jerked away yet again. In her space plopped a male replacement who smelled of dead fish, one eye open and unfocused, the other shut. He had the expression of someone dead drunk. His arms flopped onto Lavoss' shoulders. Lavoss tried to push him away, but the pressure of the crowd kept them together like a pair of unwashed towels in a laundry basket. The unlit cigarette in Lavoss' mouth broke on the drunk's forehead. Riveted as they were, he had no choice but to accept the creepy situation, sip his *Bier* with his one free hand and dance an odious waltz with the drunk.

Not far away, Yorit called out, "Al, buddy! Who's the boy friend?"

"I don't know," he shot back, "but as soon as he wakes up I'll pass him over to you!" Lavoss was worried that someone from the Army Central Intelligence Division (CID) might be in the crowd and recognize him and turn him in. The proximity to the drunk would certainly be misinterpreted and could cost him his Secret Clearance, if not his Army career. In the crowd, they resembled two gays grinding on each other.

Yorit pushed closer. Now he could talk to him without yelling. "Where's Death? Have you seen her?"

"Never mind Death! Help me get this maggot off of my body!" Lavoss begged.

"Okay, but how?"

"Cut his throat!"

Lavoss raised his free arm in the Fascist salute for two more beers. "This is worse then standing in line with a bunch of Polacks with garlic breath!"

"And just how do the Polacks stand in line?" Yorit demanded, not amused since he was Polish.

"That's just it; they don't! They can't read the signs."

Yorit chuckled. Lavoss was right.

Miraculously, and much to Lavoss' relief, the crowd shifted again. The drunk shunted off, dragged away by the ebb tide, his head bouncing onto another shoulder—a woman's. Horrified, she looked around for help, but no one could come to her assistance. The crowd had fused the pair in a repulsive embrace.

A stranger in a trench coat, the collar up, was now shoved up against Yorit. They faced each other, both helpless, both suspicious, both unable to move, each supporting a beer glass in the one free hand. "*Sind Sie Schwule?*" the stranger asked him. (Are you queer?)

The question was not unusual. West Berlin was a city with a large homosexual community, many of them closet types. They came to Berlin because the city was open, liberal, and tolerant. West Berlin was for them a playground where one could live out one's eccentricities. It was where perversion and excess was accepted; it was the reason for Berlin's creativity: the brilliant theater plays, "Avante Garde" art, and lively street life, a contrast to East Berlin, where the sidewalks rolled up at nine o'clock. In West Berlin the bars were open all night. Decadence was above-board with gambling clubs and the slots, plenty of them. The prostitutes themselves had a functioning Trade Union, as did their pimps. The city was also a magnet for the business community running away from West Germany's oppressive tax code. Here, *der Bundeswehrs*, the Army draft dodgers could also be found, as well as gangsters, transvestites and Soviet spies. One knew the spies by their trench coats and lumpy pockets where hidden cameras bulged. With that kind of a socio-economic broth, when the stranger asked Yorit, "*Sind Sie Schwule?*" The question was not out of place.

"No, are you?" he answered back.

"*Naturlich nicht. Nein,*" the German replied, relieved he was not rubbing up against someone with an alternative life style. "Look, if you pull this way I'll pull that way, and we can forget we ever met like this," he suggested in broken English.

"Only if Allah wills," Yorit agreed.

"Also, *ziehen!"* (So pull!) the German ordered just as a crevice in the crowd opened up. And the two men separated.

Looking around, Yorit could see neither Death nor Lavoss. They had vanished in the smoke and haze of the saloon. He was alone and beginning to feeling claustrophobic. "Albert Lavoss, where the devil are ya?" he cried out loud, anxious.

"I'm a heartbeat away," came a breathy voice behind him.

Yorit glanced around. The crowd had shifted and pulled Lavoss around behind him. He rested his chin on Yorit's shoulder. "Where are those beers you ordered? I'm thirsty."

"Haven't arrived yet. Here, take this." Lavoss reached up and pulled down one of the foamy *Bier* mugs passing overhead and gave it to his buddy. Yorit drank. It slackened his thrust. Satisfied, he handed the half-empty mug to the procession of drinks bouncing down the line to the patron who ordered it.

In the crowd, another aperture opened up and shut, but not before a middle-aged woman was thrust up against Yorit. She startled him. Her breasts dug into his chest, rattling his teeth. The pressure elicited a voltage charge in the vicinity of the groin. Given their range (in millimeters) and her deep stare, Yorit succumbed. He was instantly in love. "Introduce me," said Lavoss, his chin still resting on Yorit's shoulder.

"Al, will you please depart? Go away! Can't you see I got a thing going with this lady here?"

"The crowd won't let me," he answered, the crowd's vice pressure against his back.

"Well then, close your eyes. It's not every day I have something this wonderful happen at such close quarters." Yorit tittered , talking out of the corner of his mouth while eyeball-to-eyeball with the woman. He saw thatshe had a high forehead, full erotic lips and penetrating pale gray eyes. "What's your name, lady?" he asked, his lips to her ear.

"What's your name, baby?" Lavoss repeated, his chin still on Yorit's shoulder.

"Al, please!" Yorit snapped around.

Lavoss chuckled. "Where did you learn to be a smooth-talker like that, reading a Wheaties boxtop?"

Yorit tried an over-the-shoulder Three Stooges fork-finger poke-in-the-eye maneuver, but only succeeded in jamming his knuckles into his friend's forehead. "Ouch! If I could turn around I'd let you have it!"

"If you could turn around I would dance with your girlfriend!"

Pressed up and a nose distance away, the woman watched the two talking G.I. sidewall-haircut-heads argue in English. She found them entertaining.

Whether it was the heat of their bodies or the drink or both, Yorit and the woman realized they were indeed attracted to each other. Without a word, they kissed. From his position millimeters away, Lavoss could only observe. He puckered, but no kiss.

With her eyes wide open, her lips hung lightly on Yorit's. She stared at him, absorbing the unexpected pleasure of an American romance. To him her breath was sweet, the flavor of malt, her touch a sheer tingle. In the tight atmosphere and barely moving, the three of them—the woman, Yorit and Lavoss—tangoed

Growing frustrated, Lavoss nudged his friend. "All right, pal, my turn." There was no response; Yorit was too absorbed in the execution of another kiss. Pressed againt him as he was, Lavoss waited, his eyes rolling, waiting for the crowd to shift him away. "Damn it!"

Gradually, Yorit's own position grew to the point of discomfort. Buried in his pants, and fighting to escape, was that distended member known as "the hard-on." It was protuberant. At the moment, it threatened to bust the confines of his trousers. The woman ground her hips against his, coaxing a response that made him lush with animal in spite of being hog-tied by the crowd. To him this was rapture. A joy. There was an effervescent ecstasy in spite of his buddy's chin digging into his shoulder. "Al, will you please flake off?"

Then, just like that with a snap of the finger, she was gone. She vanished as suddenly as she had come, abruptly jerked away by the human ice pack. Once again, the mob had shifted. Yorit tried to hold on to his mystery woman, but she was already out of his arms, locked in another people constellation. He called after her. She reached out for him. But it was too late. She disappeared in a landscape of talking heads and Fascist-like salutes calling out for drinks: "*Bier hier!*" "*Bier hier!*" Yorit could only bury this face on the neck of the man in front of him and weep.

"Welcome back to the real world," said Lavoss, pulling down the two drinks he had ordered from overhead. They had finally arrived. He handed up the payment to the waving hands to be passed along and up to Mama Lisa at the bar.

"Oh, you still there, Al?"

"Do I have a choice? I'm stuck. Gotta pay for our drinks," Lavoss groaned. "Besides, while you were kissing your girlfriend I was nibbling on her ear. It was why she was moaning." He handed Yorit his drink.

"She was the woman of my dreams."

"Mine too." slurred Lavoss. "From now on we double team all the chicks here. What do ya say?"

The two friends continued to be jerked to and fro by the crowd, separated, then coming together. Lavoss looked around. "We got to get out of this hammerlock environment. Say, see that alcove over there to the right at the far corner?" Yorit looked over. "It's a hallway of sorts and there ain't much of a crowd from what I can see. Let's make for it, Yo," said Lavoss.

At that moment again the crowd shifted; it moved to the left, only this time without Yorit. He felt himself shrink. "Hey, wha'…"

Lavoss felt him slip down against him. "Now Yo, what are you doin'? This ain't the place to genuflect."

"Who's genuflecting? I'm not genuflecting!"

Lavoss stared at his buddy against him. "Then why are you getting short on me?"

"Something's got my foot," Yorit cried out, beginning to panic. The crowd shunted this way and that with him getting shorter by the moment. Yorit's head now rested at Lavoss' chest. Seeing what was happening, one of the German boozers tried to assist him, but could only grab Yorit by the ear with his free hand; the other hand held a *Bier*. It was not enough support. Yorit slipped further. Growing desperate, he cried out like a swimmer caught in an undertow. "Al, I'm going down! Do something!"

"Gimme your drink. I'll hold it."

"That's not enough!" .

"Give me your wallet then."

Yorit made another effort to free himself from the lock at his foot, only to slip further. Now he was below chest level.

Holding the two beers in his hand, both his and Yorit's, Lavoss could do nothing but watch his buddy slip further. "Help!" Another of the Germans tried to save him, but it was not enough; there was no leverage. Yorit gave one last desperate cry, then vanished under the Old Edan crowd.

With a plop, the space once occupied by Robert Yorit, a soldier in the U.S. Army, slammed shut. The human pack resealed itself.

Horrified, Lavoss could only stare down at the slot into which he had disappeared. Yet he was thankful. He had saved both *Biers*.

***

There was an indistinct rumbling, a shuffling, a sentient feeling of tranquility. Taking a deep breath, Yorit opened his eyes and looked around. He found himself lying on his back and paddling like a fish in an aquarium. Then he sat up. He bumped his head against something soft. He looked. It was a rump. A rump? Confused, he was unsure where he was. Around him was a sense of twilight, the environment medieval. It was as if he was in a deep forest of oddly-shaped objects that resembled stunted tree trunks—undulating stunted tree trunks. They moved and shifted from one leg to another. "Huh?" One leg to another they shifted. It was then that Yorit noticed the crotches; they surrounded him. They were of every shape—some lumpy, some smooth, some pointed. Leaning forward, he touched what looked like an ankle. It startled him. Attached to it was a calf and a knee; it was a leg in a skirt. Yorit gasped again. It was an ankle indeed! Now he understood where he was. He was not in a medieval forest of stunted tree trunks, but an anatomical manage of shifting torsos and pelvises, all in motion to a soundless rumba. The indistinct murmurs he heard above were not a volcano's rumbling, but muffled voices. He was still in the Old Eden Saloon, only now under the crowd; he had been pulled down from above, but by what? In the twilight of this nether world, he looked around and saw what it was that brought him down: a footstool of sorts. It had caught his leg in the crush. "Damn it," he grunted. On the edge of panic and gasping, Yorit screamed, but the cry had no penetration in the undulating anatomical environment.

Threads of broken light emitted from the fault lines that ran zigzag along the vaulted roof of torsos. From above, muffled voices sometimes turned to laughter, but here below, where he was, all was quiet, the world semi-dark. Yorit wanted to cry. A cigarette butt dropped into his hair. He brushed it away. Along one fault line nearby there was a sudden rush of liquid. Someone had spilled his drink.

Breathing deeply, Yorit now realized he could not...no, he dare not panic. He fought to concentrate on where he was. Considering his situation, he realized he might be trapped, maybe for hours, until the crowd thinned, or until the Old Eden closed. The more he thought about it, the more anxious he grew. Should the crowd stampede, he would certainly be crushed to death. The mere idea of it caused more anxiety. In desperation, Yorit tried to stand up and force the fault line between the torsos. No luck. He pounded shoes with his fists. The shoes kicked back. He hit a knee; it jerked and caught him on the chin, dazing him. Another knee dropped on his shoulder as if to rest. He pushed it off. The knee did it again. Again, he knocked it away, only this time he tied the tormentor's shoe laces together. "Problem solved!" he yelled up. The situation looked hopeless. He wanted to panic but knew to panic was foolish. "What do I do?" he groaned to himself, helpless.

He broke out into a sweat; it was getting hot down under. Reaching into a nearby pants pocket, he felt for a hankerchief and took it out. Too much humidity, he reasoned. He knew he would need water if he was to survive. It was then he noticed the puddles on the floor. Spilled drink? "Well, at least I won't go thirsty," he said out loud.

He meditated. The more he reflected on his situation, the more Yorit realized it was the torsos above him that had the problem, and not him. The Old Edan crowd was locked in a massive body crush. Here below, in this nether world, though on his hands and knees, he could roam at will, if he wasn't trampled to death first. Then an idea occurred to him: *Hey, I'm free of the Army!* He did not have to take orders any more. There were no senior NCOs around to bawl him out. No routine. No discipline. In this situation he had the power to poke crotches at will if he wished to, or to unbelt trousers and feel up skirts, and all with impunity. Down here in the nether world he was—what else? The king! The thought made him giddy. To prove the point, Yorit unzipped a nearby trouser fly. There was no resistance. He considered unzipping a few more, but decided not to. As a king of the nether world of undulating torsos and leg limbs, one had to have principles.

Looking around, Yorit noticed a pleated skirt and two very shapely calves. He smiled to himself deviously. Dare he? Yes! Forgetting the king's principles, he ran his hand up under the skirt. There was a garbled scream from above. He giggled and pushed his hand further up the skirt to the warning track, the panties. That was when the knee kicked. He took the blow on the chin, knocking him backwards. "Foolish!" he grunted, critical of himself. This was not correct behavior and he decided to leave the calves alone. He crawled away

Continuing his four-legged crawl, Yorit placed his hand on a still-lit cigarette butt that had slipped to the floor from above. He yelped, cursing its owner. Immediately, a blister formed on his palm. Still, he continued his crawl and took another kick, this one in the ribs, then one in the neck. Someone stepped on his leg. He cried out in pain. He felt as if he was taking a beating. Now a foot stepped on his hand. He bit the foot's shin to get it off. It did, but an undulating knee caught him unexpectedly on the bridge of his nose. The blow stunned him. Yorit sat back, his nose slightly bleeding. He felt in his pocket for the handkerchief he had pinched earlier, but it was gone. Reaching around himself, he grabbed the edge of a nearby skirt and dabbed his nose with it. He was thankful. The skirt's cloth had stopped the nosebleed.

Trying to orient himself, Yorit continued to crawl forward. After some minutes on his hands and knees he found he had crawled back to where he had begun the crawl, at the unzipped fly. He had crawled in a circle! Perspiring from the effort, he sat back to re-evaluate his position. It looked hopeless.

It was then he saw it, there in the twilight shadows, a body; it was on the floor and unconscious. It was to his left. Looking again, he saw that the forest of undulating torsos and legs were stepping all over it. Shocked, Yorit immediately crawled over to the prostrate body. Turning the bruised head to him, he saw it was the one-eyed drunk who had waltzed up against Lavoss earlier in the evening. In his unconscious state, the drunk had apparently slipped to the floor and was now a doormat slowly being stomped to death. He took the drunk's pulse. He was alive, but barely. Army training had taught him about sucking chest wounds and combat first aid, but this?

In desperation Yorit hammered on the pair of legs that stepped on the prostrate body; one leg stepped off only to step back on him. He drove his shoulder up between the torsos, hoping to force them apart. No luck! He beat on shoes and screamed, but he got kicked for his effort. Above, the world was unaware a human being was being stomped to death below them. Yorit began to tremble. "This could be me," he groaned fearfully.

He knew that he had to get out from under the dense environment, and fast, or he might not survive the night. Chin in his hand and contemplating, he became aware of the shoes; they all pointed, mostly in one direction, no doubt toward the bar. He figured if he moved at a right angle to the shoes, it just might bring him up near the hallway-alcove Lavoss had mentioned earlier. If he was right, with any luck he could resurface over there. Pushing away a leg that stood on the drunk, he whispered into the drunk's ear, "Hang in there, fella. I'm going for help," and scrambled away on all fours.

Yorit moved as quickly as the undulating shanks and limbs around him would allow. Because he crawled fast, he took more blows and hits to the body. Again, he put his palm on a lit cigarette lying on the floor. "Ouch!" he cursed. Taking a moment's rest, he sucked at the burn wound. It was then he noticed a pair of interesting legs. It was to his left; they had a refined well-formed shape. Slim and muscular, they were packed into dark gray leotards. In the twilight of the nether world of undulating torsos, the form radiated an honest sensuality. He knew this was not the place to get turned on, but nevertheless, he was. He crawled up to the leotard and stroked one ankle where skin was exposed. It responded to his touch. Pleased, Yorit stroked the other ankle with the back of his hand. Instead of a swift kick he expected, the leotarded leg raised its knee and nudged his shoulder. It liked him. He glanced around to be sure no one was watching, but who could be watching him down here in the nether world? A pair of kneecaps? No. In the world above, what he was doing would be defined as kinky, freaky, weirdo. But here in the nether land, who cared? Yorit kissed the ankle. It responded by rubbing his cheek. Bewitched, he moved his hand up the muscular thighs. He turned his head into the leotard's crotch and whispered. "Who are you, my dear?" The leotard communicated with him the only way it could—with a subtle bump-n-grind. Excited, Yorit begged to know the person who belonged to the upper half of the leotard. If she was anything like the leotard's lower half, he would propose.

Though tempted to draw down the leotard to expose the navel, he denied himself. He had to move on. He had to get out from under the crowd or the deadbeat drunk lying there might be crushed to death. Bidding the lower torso's leotard a poignant farewell, he crawled away.

This time it came from his right—another human groan. Yorit stopped to listen. Squinting, he looked into the forest of shifting leg limbs. "*Helf mir, bitte*," (Help me, please!) came the sobbing moan of a woman's voice. Yorit thought he recognized it. But, no, it couldn't be… or could it? "Death? Impossible," he said to himself. Crawling in the direction of the groan he found it was indeed Death. She, too, had been sucked down into the nether world of limbs and torsos.

Falling into his arms, she did not know it was him. She was in shock. Her stocking pants were torn and her eye shadow was all over her face. One eye was bruised and swelling from a kneecap blow. She was close to hysteria when Yorit found her. "Gosh, this place is getting crowded. Death, it's you. But how…" She was unable to reply. He touched her hurt face. "You poor dear. They've pummeled you too. Tell me, which leg kicked you and I'll de-cap it at the knee."

"*Niemals in mein Leben…*" (Never in my life) she sobbed, almost incoherent.

Yorit gripped her by the shoulders and shook her. "Death, it's me. Robert. Snap out of it!"

"Rob…ert?" she looked at him wide-eyed and bewildered. "How?" and began to cry.

"A long story, *Schatz* (Sweetie). Here, wipe your face with this," he said, taking the hem of a skirt that had brushed them. "Can you crawl?" She nodded weakly. "Then hang onto my ankles and follow me. I'm going to try to pull us out of here, but you have to crawl!" he ordered, drying her mascara-smeared eyes. She nodded.

With some effort, they squirmed together and twisted around the catacomb of shifting limbs. Though it seemed like an hour, it was only minutes. As Yorit had hoped, the crowd appeared to thin out and the twilight brightened. He now saw what he was looking for, a break in the flow of compressed torso humanity. He crawled toward it. Getting to his feet, he pulled Death after him. They were up...and out.

***

Free from the nether world and the human catacomb, Yorit saw they had indeed crawled to the far side of the bar room and close to the vaulted hallway. Bruised and gripping each other, they headed for it. Nothing had changed. The Old Eden Saloon was still a squash of humanity, dense and loud, money and drinks floating overhead. They had survived the ordeal.

Lavoss waved. He stood at the alcove waiting for them. They pressed forward, Death reached Lavoss and fell into his arms. He embraced her. "Good God, dear! What happened to you? You look like death warmed over. I mean…"

"Frank, she is Death and she is warmed over," said Yorit, joining them, brushing himself off.

Leaning on Lavoss' shoulder, she sobbed, almost incoherent. "*Es war schrecklish*! Horrible!" she gasped. "*Ich muss zum Klo.*" (The toilet) Nearby was the WC, the ladies room. Unsteady, she made for it.

"Man, what the hell happened to you two? Why is your nose swollen?" Lavoss asked, glad to find his Army buddy alive.

"We were under the crowd," said Yorit, still breathing heard from the escape effort.

"You mean you were actually down under this crowd?" Lavoss could not believe it.

"How many crowds are there here tonight?"

"When I saw you go down over there in the middle of the room, I thought you were a goner."

"I was, thanks to your no support. A real buddy you are! You let me sink!" said Yorit wearily, not a little angry in the smoke-filled room.

"So that's the thanks I get for saving your drink. Here!" Lavoss handed Yorit his half empty glass of *Bier.*

"It's warm!"

"It's beer."

He drank. "Another please."

Lavoss stepped into the crowd and pulled down a mug that was passing overhead and handed it back to his buddy.

"Why did you let me slide down like that?"

"In this crush, I had no choice. My arms were pinned above my shoulders and I was holding our mugs. It was either grab you or spill the drinks," Lavoss replied, not liking to be grilled. "Tell me what made you drop."

"I tripped."

"That's what they all say. Find anything down there under the crowd, treasure maybe?" asked Lavoss, handing Yorit a handkerchief.

He wiped his face and dabbed at his nose. "Actually, I did. The leotard of my dreams."

Lavoss frowned, then laughed. "The leotard of your dreams? Like, was there anything in them leotards? A body maybe to fill your dream?"

"Sure was. A whole lot of body."

Lavoss found the statement odd. "Did the body have a head?"

Yorit drank deep from the mug. The cold beer was refreshing. It relaxed him. "I don't know if it had a head. I only got to know the torso from the waist down."

"No head, huh? The best kind. But don't ever bring the leotard home to meet the family; it could cause a panic."

"It was fabulous," Yorit began to croon. "The thighs were strong, the ankles thin, round hips. A terrific rump. It was my dream torso. But down there under the crowd I had a problem: how do you ask a leotard covered torso out for a date?"

"Find the upper half!" Lavoss advised, still chuckling.

Yorit snapped his fingers. "Oh, my God! I almost forgot! The drunk!"

"The who?"

"There's a drunken bum down under the crowd. The guy who slopped all over us earlier in the evening, remember? I found him unconscious on the bar room floor with people standing on him."

"It serves him right."

"Al, if we don't get him out of there he could be crushed to death. We got to tell someone—the barkeeper." Yorit then told him about his adventure in the nether world of twilight and body vaults, of torsos, legs, and crotches and about how he found Death near death. Lavoss listened.

"Robert, you're right. We gotta to do something. Look, you go to the men's room and get yourself clean up. You're a mess. Take care of that bruised eye. The men's WC is over there. Me, I'll get to the bar and tell them folks about the drunk on the floor. See if we can save him." Yorit agreed.

With some trepidation, and following one last swallow of his drink, Lavoss charged into the crowd of compressed humanity. Yorit called after him with a warning. "Whatever you do, don't trip!"

The struggle to get to the bar was not easy. He was thrown back twice. Eventually, after much pushing and shoving, he reached the bar and pounded on the oak wood top to get some attention.

Sitting at her cash drawer was Mama Liesa. From up close she was not just fat; she was huge, like the slug curled on top of the mushroom in the film, "Alice in Wonderland." To call her Humpty Dumpty was no exaggeration. Her body had the shape of a large ostrich egg precariously balanced on top of a four-legged bar stool. Like many overweight people with an obvious glandular problem, her features were compressed between pink, bulbous cheeks and tiny lips that made her appear as if she was about to blow a soap bubble. She didn't. Instead, she offered a benign smile. Sometimes she chuckled, though there was no apparent reason other than, perhaps, the kick she got from counting *Deutsch Mark* notes, or making change from the overstuffed money drawer. She continually tapped the piles of notes into slots, playing with them and fingering them like a master *croupier* at the casino. Occasionally a five or ten *Mark* bill would slip to the floor. Her size prevented her from bending over to pick it up. The bills stayed there accumulating until enough of a pile warranted a call to one of the bartenders. He would come along with a broom and dust pan and sweep up the *Marks*.

"Dear *Frau*, a man...*Kaput!*" Lavoss tried to explain in German. "He can be dead. *Tot! Da!* Over there!" he pointed into mass of humanity behind him. You must call the *Polizei!*"

Puzzled by his gestures, Mama Liesa looked at the stranger in front of her who spoke horrible German. Unable to understand him, she continued to smile benignly, her piggy eyes full of secret humor. Lavoss tried again. Listening, Mama Liesa leaned back on her stool, which looked as if it would collapse from her weight, and called over her shoulder to one of the bartenders. Wiping his hands on a dish towel, the bartender came over to her. She said something to him. He looked doubtful at Lavoss. "*Kann Ich...be ofs da disposables?*" he asked in mangled syntax.

Lavoss was glad someone spoke the *Dinglish*, a mix of the German and English languages. "There's a guy under the crowd there, passed out," he said in desperation. "He's lying on the floor. People are standing all over him. He'll be crushed to death if we don't get him out. He might even be dead by now. You got to call the police!"

The bartender glanced at Mama Lisa, then back at the American. "*Na und?*" (So what?) was his unhurried reply.

His indifference surprised Lavoss. "*Na und?* He'll die if you don't do something! People are jumping up and down on the poor bastard!"

"No one dies tonights," replied the bartender passively as if to stand on prostrate bodies was the most natural thing in the world at the Old Edan Saloon.

"How can you be sure?" Lavoss remonstrated, raising his voice, desperate.

"Because *Morgans* (in the morning) we alvays *finden der* peoples," said the bartender.

Lavoss could not believe what he just heard. "You mean this happens in here all the time?"

"*Jawohl!* We slappen dem, the peoples, in the faces; give dems a *Koffee*, and theys goes homes. No one to *tot* (dead). Sure!" the bartender said with a shrug, his English a disaster.

Mama Liese leaned toward Lavoss. Close up, her three rolls of chin looked like powdered pancake batter. When she talked, her small lips puckered as if threatening to blow the soap bubble she chewed. *"Schau mal, Ami,"* she chided. *"*you goes *dahin und you finden ihm the man, dann calls you me-s die Polizei, ja!"* With a grin she sat back, proud of her destroyed English. The expected soap bubble never materializing.

Lavoss was about to protest further but gave up. He looked back at the surging crowd. "I see. You take the poor bastard's drink money than let him perish." Mama Liesa nodded, smiling as though she understood him, the contours of her moon face unaltered.

Slapping the bar top in a show of disapproval, he turned into the crowd and worked his way back toward the archway where Yorit and Death both waited, refreshed from their clean- up, though somewhat bruised. "Well, what about the drunk under the crowd?" asked Yorit when he reached them.

"The guy's okay. After the crowd's gone, he'll be swept up, put in a body bag and sent home in time for breakfast. At least, that's what Mama Liese says."

Yorit frowned. "That is reassuring. I mean, that they sweep him up, but can he eat breakfast inside a body bag?"

The mob continued to sway back and forth as more people came into the Old Eden Saloon. After his experience in the down under nether land, Yorit considered it a miracle to be still alive. Death too. She drank three quick shots of *Schnapps* to calm her nerves. Now, feeling better, she took a cigarette from her handbag. "I must be crazy. When ever I go out with you *Amis*, strange things happen to me, like tonight. Just once I wish to go out and have a normal rendezvous with a man, have dinner, and go dancing. I should date officers; at least they are gentleman, or so I have been told."

"Well," said Yorit, not a little offended, "we of the lower ranks may be animals, but we are heroic animals."

"Eloquently spoken," praised Lavoss. "Indeed, we are heroic."

"Heroic, how?" Death asked, exhaling smoke with a toss of her head.

"I rescued you, deary, didn't I?" Yorit replied. "If I didn't come and get you, you'd still be down there under the crowd. Isn't that heroic enough?"

"Yes, and thank you. Still, strange things do happen. It must be your *Ami Kultur* (American culture). There are no rules about how to escort women. No control. *Wie sagt man das: Euch seid Hemungslos."* (Americans behave without shame.)

"No, I'd call it unrestrained," said Yorit with a note of pride, thinking of the Keystone Grunt antics their squad often pulled, on and off duty.

"Blame the media," added Lavoss. "If you grew up watching the Three Stooges, Jerry Lewis, and Jackie Gleason on TV you would be *Hemmungslos* too, as you say."

Yorit shook his head. "Don't blame Larry, Curly, and Mo. Blame the Army."

"Why the Army?" she asked.

Yorit sipped his drink. He looked at Death, tolerant of her ignorance. "Well, dear, first of all, when you attend Basic Training the Army unscrews your head and emptys it of any behavior defined as civilian, then they reprogram you on how to be a basket case, a disciplined basket case, that is. Guys are not permitted to think for themselves anymore. They have to think as a company, a platoon, as a squad. It's called being brain dead to the count of four, right, Albert?"

Lips pointing, Lavoss nodded agreement. "The Army molds you that way. It's why soldiers go AWOL, fight, gamble, get drunk, and eat shit-on-a-shingle in the chow hall. Just look at Yoyo here. He loves the stuff. It shows he's brain dead."

Death frowned. "What is shit-on-a-shingle?"

Lavoss pretended to gag. "SOS? You don't want to know it."

Pursing her lips, her face a shadow in the room's alcove's gloom, Death thought for a moment. "Do you think maybe that is why your Sergeant Oats, he behaves so strange to me? He is a brain dead person?"

"For sure!"

Yorit put an arm around Death's shoulder and gave her a squeeze. "Congratulations, dear. You have just come to understand what it is that motivates the American fighting man: the demise of the brain."

"It's how we win wars," Lavoss added. "You got to be brain dead to sit in a fox hole and wait to be shot at."

Ever thoughtful, Death nodded. "Yes, I think now I understand."

"Understand what?" asked Yorit.

"Your Sergeant Oats. His behavior. He was in Korea, yes?"

Yorit and Lavoss looked at each other. Lavoss spoke first. "I'd think twice about him, sweetie. I mean, you heard about the pipe he smokes. It's made of human bone. Creepy stuff!"

"Robert told me the story," she said, a sadness in her voice.

"Anyone who smokes a bone pipe is demented, for sure."

"That's right," said Yorit with a wink. ""No one is sure which national hip bone the pipe is carved from. Could be North Korean or a Chinese hip bone."

"Or his first wife's," added Lavoss.

Death gasped, shocked at the revelation. "His wife's hip bone?"

"With Platoon Sergeants, you never know," said Yorit.

Frowning, a cigarette between two fingers, Death flicked the ash away. For her age she was indeed an attractive woman. "I will tell you boys something. The last time I saw your Sergeant Oats, that was three weeks ago, we visited his Army NCO club. Oats met an old friend there, someone from his Korea days. He introduced me to his friend, also a Sergeant. And do you know what this friend does?" Yorit and Lavoss shook their heads. "He fell on the floor and tried to look up my skirt."

Shocked, Yorit could only respond with, "Outrageous!"

Lavoss said the same. "Unbelievable! Did Oats punch him in the nose to defend your honor?" Lavoss asked, shocked by the statement.

"No, he joined his friend on the floor."

"Senior NCOs are known for that," said Yorit with conviction. "They can get away with it, unlike us enlisted man. We could never..."

Lavoss put his finger to his chin. "Death, dear, whether you believe me or not, you have been honored. Two Americans looked up your skirt at the same time."

With a toss of her head and half a laugh, Death reached out. She grabbed the two soldier friends in front of her and pushed them both up the dark hallway. "*Euch seid beide Blurdies!* (You're both knuckleheads!) Come now. Let's go. I want to show you the other rooms here in the Old Eden Saloon."

II

Refreshed from the drinks, the three chums moved down the short hall and entered a room that resembled the interior of a Chinese pagoda. It had red-shaded wall lamps, the lights low. The guests sat at small lacquered coffee tables. In the middle of the floor, a musician bent over a saxophone. He and his base player were playing a Lionel Hampton jazz repertoire. In the room, the guests sipped drinks and bobbed their heads to the rhythm like New Yorkers at a Village bar. There was light applause when the musicians finished. Yorit bought drinks.

"I love this kind of environment," said Lavoss, standing in the doorway and looking around. "Say, will you check out that woman sitting by herself? Boy, would I like to meet her."

"Why don't you?" encouraged Death.

"But how? I don't know her."

Yorit lit a cigarette; the match dropped to the floor. "It's easy, Al.. You know Jefferson, the black guy from 298 Band Company? Plays trumpet. He once told me how on a bus he saw a woman who turned him on. The bus was crowded. So, pretending the gentleman, he got up and gave her his seat, then sat down on her lap. The people around on the bus were shocked. You know how Germans are. If you don't behave by the rules, they give you the evil eye. Well, being an American and black, the whole bus evil-eyed him. They glared him down, so he told me."

"So what happened to the woman?"

"Apparently she liked his sit-on-me come-on. They hit it off and made a date. Several dates. The rest is history."

Lavoss nodded, a trace of admiration for Jefferson. "What a great way to meet chicks. I'd call that pure Keystone Grunt. Ballsy! Okay, I'm going to give it a try. Jefferson, ol' buddy, move over!"

Taking a table, Death and Yorit sat down and watched as Lavoss stepped over to the table where the woman sat by herself. With a half-bow, he introduced himself. She looked up at him, unsure. Then he sat down on her lap, the Keystone way. Flop! Startled, she protested. Two men from a nearby table got up and came over to her. Feeling foolish, if not embarrassed, Lavoss got up. There was an exchange of words. One of the man clinched his fist.

"Uh-oh!" said Yorit, half rising. It looked like a fight was about to take place. With a nod of apology, Lavoss turned and beat it back to their table.

"What happened to your girlfriend?" asked Death.

Lavoss shook his shoulders. "She was in denial," he said, disappointed.

Death glowered at her two American escorts. "This is what I mean about you *Amis*. Everything you do is a *Witz* (a joke)."

"But isn't that what life's all about?" said Yorit.

"No, definitely not, not if you are a woman alone here in West Berlin and struggling to survive."

"What do you mean?"

Death sat back in her chair and took a sip of her drink. She looked at her two soldier friends. "This city is not an easy place for single women." There was a strain in her voice. "Jobs do not pay much and the flats are expensive. As for German men, they are by their nature cold, their marriages even colder. Maybe it has to do with the weather, or the war, or both. There is little in West Berlin to make women laugh except maybe you *Amies*, black or white. You are an escape for many of us, those of us who know you. You are a breath of fresh air in a hard city."

"Hopefully not bad breath," said Yorit, sensing her mood change.

"And the Spics?" asked Lavoss.

Death shook her head. "What is a Spic?"

Lavoss chuckled and reached out and took her hand. He was moved by her emotion. "Listen, dear, there is another side to consider—the soldier side. Without you and the other Berlin *Mädels* to dance and schmooze with, we soldiers would suffer. Thank God you're open to us, black, white or Spic Ain't that right, Yo?" Yorit could only nod a positive silent reply.

Death grinned. "Come on, let us check the other rooms."

Getting up from the table, they moved together to another semi-dark room of the Old Edan, The atmosphere there was more relaxed. A female cabaretist, the German equivalent of a stand-up comic, was performing before a small audience. Half-singing, half-talking, she strummed her guitar as she sat on a bar stool. She was doing a satire about the West Berlin's mayor, Willi Brandt.

"When the Wall went up," she sang in German, "he got up. The result? the Wall stayed up! Thank you, Willi Brandt, the defiant." There were rumbles of appreciation from the audience. She sang about the mayor's excessive drinking. "*Weinbrandt Willi*! Oh, you silly..." There was more applause from the audience.

"Mayor Brandt sounds like our kind of guy," said Lavoss. "Let's invite him over to the Golden Sun some night for a booze-out."

The cabaretist sang about Walter Ulbricht and the East German Communist Party, jokes that could have earned her being kidnapped by the STASI Security Police who operated with impunity in West Berlin. "How does a worker earn money in the Communist Paradise?" she sang to the appreciative audience. "The worker pretends to work, and the government pretends to pay." The small crowd applauded.

With that, Yorit and Lavoss got up and left to explore the next room. It was at the end of the hallway. Death did not go with them and remained in the room. It was a rare chance for her to enjoy German cabaret humor.

***

Entering the last room of the Old Edan they saw it was designed like the inside of a barrel, with a large curved ceiling. The room was crowded, semi-dark, the atmosphere smoke-filled. A bandstand had been set up at the back with spotlights. Taking their drinks from the bar, they looked around for a table.

"The band must be a trio by the looks of the instruments," said Yorit, pointing at the piano, base and guitar instruments.

"Or a combo," added Lavoss, noting one chair where a beat-up alto saxophone on it.

Yorit nodded. "Yeah, and if the combo can play some decent rock-n-roll maybe we can get out there on the dance floor and make the ol´ Joe smoke. You dance, Al?"

"In high school, ya, but not much lately; been too busy marching in cadence."

Near the bandstand they found an open table and sat down. They drank.

"You know, back home on Cleveland's West Side to dance was to breathe," said Yorit, as he watched two women walk, dressed in tight sweaters and with strong legs, their hair all fluffy. Lavoss growled after them. Yorit sniffed out loud. "Yes, every Friday and Saturday night we'd—I mean me and the guys—would suit up. We would Brill Cream the hair—got to get that pompadour just right, ya know—and go shake, rattle, and roll. We'd go anywhere to dance, even across the mighty Cuyahoga River to the East Side of Cleveland and East 55th Street.

"Scovol Avenue was the place. It was the coon neighborhood. There were a couple of cool dance bars there. I'll tell you, when it came to the dance, the black guys were the best. They used to laugh at us Whities trying to keep up. We'd give them a run for their money, though, I can tell you."

"That was taking a chance, wasn't it, I mean going into a black ´hood?"

"Not really. Folks in Cleveland got along. Race didn't matter much. Back at my high school, West Tech High, we'd practice dance in the hallways; we'd practice dance in gym class, dance in the school parking lot; we'd even dance on the street by ourselves. Cars would drive by and honk their horns. I'll tell you, a man couldn't keep the feet still at West Tech High School. It was the same with all the schools in Cleveland."

Another attractive Berlin girl passed their table. The two soldiers stared after her, mesmerized by her every step. "One more like that and I'll break into a sweat," hissed Lavoss.

"I already have," blubbered Yorit, hissing out loud.

Lavoss turned to Yorit, drink in hand. "So tell me. What happened on those Friday and Saturday nights back in Cleveland?"

Yorit grinned at the memory. "Well, Friday night was a dance at St. Vincent de Paul Gym; Saturday night it was at St. Ignatius Hall, or St. Edward High School in Lakewood. I mean, at Catholic schools a guy had to genuflect first in order to ask a girl to dance. The priests were watching. Then we had the Knights of Columbus Hall on West 130th. No genuflect there. We danced. The Irish-American Club on Madison Avenue held Friday festivities too. That's where I learned the jig."

Lavoss sat up. "You, a Polack, can do the Irish jig? You're kidding."

"Had to, or Patty would have thrown me out, head first."

"Don't ask me to make a holiday in Dublin."

"But the roughest place to dance," Yorit went on, "was St. Rocco's Parish Hall on the lower West Side of Cleve. There, you had to be careful. The Dago Bombers, another name for Italian punks, would walk around like they thought they were Marcianos, Grazianos, and Jake Lamottas, ready to fight."

Lavoss rubbed his chin. "So you were a Tony Zale. He beat Rocky Graziano for the middle weight championship of the world, you know."

"The Dago guys all wore zoot suits with combed pompadours. Sal Mineo types. But when it came to the jitterbug, they couldn't match the Polaks, the Patties and the Hungies. And wo-ah to you if they lost a dance competition. You'd have to fight them outside." Yorit, pointed to his chipped front tooth.

"You failed to duck?"

"No, an Italian head-butted me. Been tasting garlic ever since." And they both laughed.

Just then the band came in to the club room—three musicians by the way they were dressed. They wore suits and ties. They hopped up to the small bandstand and took up their instruments.

Yorit looked toward the door. "I should get Death in here. We dance cool together."

Then a fourth musician stepped to the bandstand. He was dressed casual, only his hair was short, too short for a civilian; it had the cut of Army sidewalls. "Kantwell!" they both gasped.

Immediately, they got up from the table and crossed the open floor. "Kevin, what are you doing here?" asked Lavoss, surprised at the unexpected surprised.

Glad to see his Signal Company buddies, Kantwell gave a broad smile. "1ˢᵗ Sarge gave me the okay. I got my off-post pass back. These here are the guys I play jazz with."

"I thought you were playing with Horst Dietsch and his band," said Yorit.

"Sometimes I do, but tonight I gig with this German group. They're good, and into the rock-n-roll scene. Hey, how'd you find out I was here?"

"Just kind of sensed it," said Lavoss, with a subtle nod.

Kantwell picked up his saxophone. "You going to join the dance contest? It's up next."

Yorit's eyes widened. "A dance contest?"

"Yeah, we'll be starting shortly. Our break is over."

The band leader sat at the piano; he tapped out a few bars on the keyboard. It was the signal to begin. Kantwell gave the leader the thumbs up and stepped to his place on the bandstand. Yorit and Lavoss returned to their table. The music began. Two German girls moved to the dance floor. Yorit glanced around the room. The boys sat at tables or leaned against the wall.

Lavoss folded his arms. "I'm with them. I don't want to be the first guy on the floor and have everyone stare at me. I'd feel foolish."

"After four years in the Army, white socks and sidewall haircuts, you should be used to everyone staring at you."

The beat of the music thumped cool. The women, growing hot, grooved and rocked where they stood, waiting for the boys to move in on them. The German males watched and talked.   Most of them were Free University students who sat at small checkerboard tables the way students do, discussing everything political and philosophical under the sun. They talked, gesticulating between slurps of *das Bier*, their interest still focused on current issues.

And what were the current issues of the day? It was the state of the

German Federal Republic. Will Germany one day unite? Will the Allies abandon the city? Is it better to be Red than dead? She's cute! You can't trust Politburo Chairman Khrushchev. NATO could get along without the West Berlin appendage. If only Hitler had listened to his generals. Where is Vietnam? Will Great Britain join the EEC? De Gaulle is the greatest living Frenchman since Napoleon, that is, except for Briget Bardot? Can Willi Brandt, a boozer, govern a divided city? Is there going to be a second Cuban blockade? If President Johnson puts the squeeze on Cuba, will Khrushchev put the squeeze on West Berlin? Will Bavaria ever secede from the Federal Republic? What is this issue in America called Civil Rights? All discussed to the band's warm-up beat of the Beatle toon "It's Been a Hard Day's Night".

Observing the girls, Lavoss turned to Yorit. "You got to admit one thing: the Berlin ladies are attractive. They could all be on a catwalk."

"Yes, and if the Kraut guys here don't move on them soon, you and I can lock and load!" glowed Yorit, fixing on one girl in particular.

"Yeah, lock and load!" Lavoss was warming up.

The band leader went to the microphone and made an announcement: "*Meine Damen und Herren! Jetzt gehts los!*" (Ladies and gentlemen! Let's go!)

With that, the base player snapped out a throaty beat. At the tables around the room some of the boys broke off their descussions and moved to the women. Lavoss got up and crossed over to the bandstand. "Hey, Kevin, what's up?"

"Dance contest. Winner gets two tickets to the opera or a Japanese transistor radio," he said, putting the saxophone to his lips.

Back at the table Yorit asked, "So what's going on, Al?"

"It's the dance contest."

"Is there a booby prize?"

"Yes, the winner gets to date the base player."

"But he's a male."

"That's why he's the booby prize."

There was a scraping of chairs as the contestants got up and moved to the dance floor. The floor began to fill. The atmosphere grew tense. The band flipped to a Rolling Stones repertoire. All talk subsided. The dancers were taking partners.

Yorit could not sit still. Grabing his chair he got up began to hop with it.

Lavoss watched him. "I didn't know chairs turned you on," he chuckled.

"Only if they have four legs and a cushion. Ooh, I can't keep my feet still. The beat is too cool."

"So, go Cleveland go!"

"Yeah!"

Boogying, Yorit stepped around the room, looking for what he hoped was the right partner to jitterbug with. He spotted one girl who rolled her shoulders and wiggled to the Rolling Stones beat. He approached her. "*Wie heissen Du*, baby?" What's your name? he asked in terrible German, a glint in his eye.

"*Güdruin*," she answered, not sure about the flake boogying with a chair in front of her. Yorit had dragged it along.

After a fumble through the language barrier, the girl named Güdruin managed to understand that he wanted to dance with her. She accepted. It was either her or the chair.

Güdruin was nineteen and wore a fluff skirt and a blouse. With her blonde pony tail, green eyes and flushed cheeks, she had the look of virgin innocence. Yorit liked his choice. Leaving the chair behind, he took her hand the way boys do and led her to the dance floor, popping his fingers as he went, his pimp roll fully exaggerated. He was back in his high school element.

The two of them began to dance to the music. Almost immediately, Yorit realized she was not of his caliber. She danced as if carrying a goldfish bowl. American jitterbug was not quite *Bayrische Hofbrauhaus*. With his own personal "whippy-do" dancing style, he tried to make them both look good. He sprang and pirouetted while she moved to the harmony of a silent waltz. He countered with a pizzicato tempo. She made an effort to follow him. He smiled and winked. She could only groan, "*Depp!*" the German equivalent for the word "Creep." To her, Yorit was too alien for her taste. He didn't fit her idea of a goldfish bowl. Frustrated, she gave up and walked off the dance floor.

In an adroit maneuver Yorit thought slick, he turned and found her gone. He was dancing by himself, the audience staring. A Fred Astaire he was not. Embarrassed, he slithered, reptile like, from the dance floor. From the bandstand, Kantwell watched him go and blew him a D flat of capitulation on his saxophone.

"Show off!" snipped Lavoss when Yorit returned to the table.

"The bitch shot me down," he muffled.

"You'd have been better off dancing with the chair."

"But a chair doesn't have tits and hips. Say, Al, who was the girl I saw you dancing with?"

"I didn't get her name. I should have. She let me bite her on the neck."

Yorit looked at him. "On the neck? On the first dance? Where's her dance card, I want to put my name on it."

"Too late. I got the next ten dances," Lavoss boasted. "Then I'm going to take her back to the barracks and bite the rest of her body."

Abruptly, the music ceased. Taking the microphone, the band leader announced for everyone to get ready. Counting, "*Ein, und zwei, und drei!*" he nodded to Kantwell who began to hiss into his saxophone with a feel of deep reverence. Slowly, he opened the throttle to that enigma known as soul music. Everyone recognized it. It was music from the track called "Night Train." The dance contest was on.

At that moment, Death walked into the barrel room. Yorit saw her and jumped up. He ran over and took her arm. "Come on, baby. We're rockin´ tonight!"

From her years of hanging out with G.I.s, Death knew all the American dances from the jitterbug to the Rolly-Polly to Chubby Checker's Twist. Yorit knew if he was going to win the dance competition tonight, he would have to do it with her as his partner. She had the technique and hip-hop which most German girls did not—could not have. She could even do the West Side shag, what the infantry boys from the South called "Yankee mule kickin'!"

One of the bartenders was named the contest judge. He moved along the edge of the dance floor, noting the dancers performance as "Night Train" chugged along. He placed a hand on the shoulders of one couple. They were eliminated. Then another couple. After several minutes another couple washed out. As the "Night Train" picked up speed, others, though good, were asked to leave the dance floor. One pair especially had to go; they were doing the Tango. Another pair danced what looked like a Scottish jig. They were eliminated too. It did not fit the parameters of soul music. Lavoss also had to leave the dance floor. His partner had quit on him. He had tried to feel her up. Offended, she walked off, leaving him alone among the shagging dancers. "Oh, shit!"

When the "Night Train" pulled into the station and stopped, there were still three couples left on the dance floor, Yorit and Death among them. The band took a quick pause before the final push to choose the winners. It gave the dancers a moment to size up the competition. "You win for the both of us, Yoyo!" Lavoss called out from the sidelines.

Taking his handkerchief, Yorit dabbed Death's forehead. "We got the game in the bag, dearie. I can taste first prize already, although I'm not sure the opera is my thing."

"What is the second prize?" she asked, waving at someone she knew across the room. That someone gave her the "thumb-in-the-fist" flash, the German expression for "good luck."

In the middle of the dance floor, Yorit enjoyed the moment's adulation. It energized him. The girls on the sidelines were talking and pointing. They chatted, saying things in German like, "Ain't he cute?" and "Oh, can he dance!" Feeling confident, eyes half-lidded, Yorit gazed casually around. Then he stopped. Something caught his eye.

Through the haze and gossamer of the cigarette smoke, a tall figure emerged like a phantom from the back of the barreled room. The figure had been watching the competition with keen interest. Stepping around the tables, Yorit watched him. He wore a dark, shark-skin suit and needle point shoes that clicked on the wood floor as he walked; his whole movement suggesting the smooth grace of a high school track star loosened up for the race. The shoulders were broad and his fingers basketball thin, but it was his hair that gave warning of things to come. It was a black guy's Nat King Cole process It gleamed and shined Vaseline in the room's overhead lights.

Yorit watched him approach the floor, for the "Cat"—a name the neighborhoods gave slick guys who could dance and fight—looked like a tall Sugar Ray Robinson, the World Middle Weight champion.

"What's the matter with you?" Death asked him, aware of Yorit's sudden hard silence.

"Baby, we got competition," he said through tight teeth.

Holding up one hand and flashing gold cufflinks, the Cat turned around and snapped his fingers toward the tables. It was the signal. It brought her out—his German moll, a blonde bombshell. She was dressed to kill: thigh hugging leather skirt and a super tight sweater, cashmere and white. Her appearance was a contrast to the rough, though good styled, Golden Sun women. Stepping on the dance floor, she turned all male heads.

Then their eyes met—Yorit's and the Cat's. They locked on each other. Yorit nodded, for he understood. He had seen it all before. It was Cleveland, East 55th Street all over again, and Saturday night at the dance. He knew now he was in the ring with Sugar Ray.

"Where does a coon get a chick like that?" asked Lavoss. He had come out onto the floor. Kantwell, too. Carrying his saxophone, he walked over to Yorit. "Looks like you got competition, Robert."

"Don't I know it."

"We win anyway," said Death, for she was determined.

"The blonde bombshell spoke to the judge briefly. He directed the new team to the floor with the other waiting dancers. Yorit turned to his partner, Death, "Well, what do you think?"

"Wir kicken der Arsch!"

"What does that mean?"

"It means, we kick ass," she answered, having learned her American colloquial well.

The music began. It was a Cosy Cole's number, the "Drum Boggy." The adrenaline jumped. Like thoroughbreds out of the starting gate, the four couples—two German and two American—were off and running. The German dancers, though good, immediately fell behind.

Death swung easily, moving in and out, back and forth, controlled by Yorit's steady hand. The other dancers jumped, hopped, and skipped, attempting to defy space, while on the sidelines the crowd "be-bopped!" But one after another, the other dancers were eliminated. Their jitterbug was no match against the two Americans from the hoods and their molls. In the end, only they were left: Yorit and Death, and the Cat and his blonde bombshell. For them the dance floor was now wide open. The question was, who would dominate it?

At that point the band's drummer slipped into a solo made famous by Cosy Cole. Rat-tat-tat! Rat-tat-tat! Perspiring profusely, the dancers jitterbugged more above the floor than on it. People came in from the other rooms to watch. They were surprised to see a first class floor show in a dead beat joint like the Old Eden Saloon. Most of the audience had never seen anything like it before. It was "American Bandstand" come to West Berlin.

As his shoe taps clicked the floor to the beat, the Cat's shark suit flashed in the spotlights. It was a gimmick, and a good one. It was gimmicks that won the battle-of-the-band competitions. When the Cat moved into peripheral view, Yorit noted his grace. His timing was super smooth. He and his blonde bombshell were a perfect match. She read him and knew by the subtle twitch of his wrist how to move, where to go, how to...sliiiide. They were tops. Indefatigable. And totally unbeatable.

Yorit felt heavy in the thick-soled Army issue black brogans. He had put them on for the evening, not expecting he would be in a dance contest. He pulled Death into a shag move. He revved her like a souped up '49 Ford waiting for the street light to change and drag race. He accelerated her, then slowed her, then sexily sped her up, hoping to impress the judge and the crowd.

Pushing Death away, he caught her wrist. He spun her, drew her in, and shag-shagged. Then Yorit brought up his heavy guns, that part of a competition that won him numerous contests at West Tech, St. Ignatius, St. Ed's and St. Rocco's dance. The white handkerchief! He stopped and dropped it on the dance floor.

Now he and Death picked up the rhythm again. They moved quickly, dancing inside the handkerchief's parameters. It brought a howl from the crowd, made them stomp, made them clap. But Death, for who knows why, began to flag. Her timing fell off like a souped up car engine in need of a tune-up. Yorit pushed her hard, but the drummer's beat pushed harder. Thumpity thump, thump! Thumpity thump, thump! They were good, but the Cat and his blonde bombshell were better. They kept the tempo and the skip. The judge's hand dropped on Yorit's shoulder. Eliminated!

The Cosy Cole's drum solo continued for a time to the howl and applause of the crowd. Then it was over. It was some of the best dancing the club's Berliners had seen since the 2nd Armored Division rolled into the bombed-out city in the summer of 1945.

With the competition over, the bartender-judge announced the winners: Alex Brown and Suzanne Hofschmied. They went up to the bandstand to collect first prize: two tickets to the opera. That done, the bartender-judge called out for the winners of the second prize, the Japanese transistor radio. Death, smiling, walked up to the bandstand proudly, happy to receive it. It was the prize she wanted anyway.

Too humiliated to present himself, Yorit crawled under a table and pouted. All the dance contestants got a round of "on the house" drinks, while Alex Brown, the Cat, and his blonde bombshell stood to one side where they autographed beer cards.

Lavoss knocked on the table's top. "For God's sake, Robert, will you come out from under the table? Get out there and shake the winner's hand like a man!"

"I can't."

Lavoss knocked again on the table top. "I mean, really! Be a good loser, will ya? Where's your sportsmanship?"

Still grumbling, Yorit climbed out from under the table. He brushed himself off. "You're right, Al," he said and crossed the dance floor to the autograph line.

It was a short line, mostly girls. When Yorit's turn came, Brown looked at him. "Oh, it's you. If you want my autograph, you've got to give me something to write on," he said in a condescending tone of an East 55th Street `hood..

Yorit brushed the slight aside. "You're good, fella, but you're a motherfucker." He knew he was taking a chance on getting slugged, but he was angry. "You didn't play fair, Brown. You walked in here prepared and practiced and dressed slick, you and your doll. She was not a pick up. She was professional! You made the rest of us look like foot-stompin' locals at a barn raising." Brown nodded, understanding Yorit's disappointment. "Yeah, man! Against the Germans, your tap-step was a one horse race,. But, bro, not against me."

Yorit glared at Brown. "I gave you a run for your money, dude. I'll tell you what, if I'd have been suited up and had the right chick at my side, I'd a whipped yo' mo' fuckin' ass," he said, talking jive.

Brown's grin was pure arrogance, his smile pearly. "I see you can't take getting `womped', m' man. I had to step in and clean yo' house, else you'd-a walked out-a here thinking you was too-o goood. I had to knock you down a peg or two. Besides, I have to think of my reputation."

Yorit shrugged, shook his shoulders and extended his hand in concession. Brown took it. They shook. "Well, Brown, if I was going to lose, I'd rather lose to a one of my own people, an American. Where'd you learn to dance like that? New York, Chicago, L.A.?"

"West Virginia. Wheeling, West Virginia, m'man," Brown answered with obvious pride.

Yorit's mouth fell open. "Wheeling, Wha´? I thought folks down there only danced the Virginia reel and coal mined."

"In Wheeling, we's cool, m'man," said Brown in jive, laughing. "You wanna learn how to dance, you come to our clubs in Wheeling and we'll show you a trick or two. Who knows, you might even win the next contest." Still chuckling arrogantly, Brown snapped his thin fingers next to his ear as if rattling dice in a crap game.

Too fucking cool, thought Yorit, though he didn't like the gesture. It grossed him out. "Hey, we're neighbors. I'm from Ohio," he was about to say so when a female fan who had been talking to Brown's blonde bombshell partner turned to him. "*Sie waren einfach super!*" she effused. (You were simply terrific!) Brown, the Cat, nodded with the indifference of someone use to female adulation. He scribbled on the girl's beer card. "By the way, what unit are you with, m' man?" Brown asked Yorit.

"The 592nd Signal Company over at Andrews Barracks Berlin Brigade. And you?"

"Bravo Company, 2nd Battalion, McNair Barracks. We's cool at McNair, you know."

"You're an infantryman and can dance like that? You're going to have to teach me the Foxhole Twist," laughed Yorit. He just had to hit back. "Why ain't you in the field with the rest of your battalion?"

Brown gave a cynical smile. "Can't be! Got to be here to womp yo Special Troops' butt!" He scribbled another card autograph handed to him by an admiror. "Like I said, m' man, get in a little practice, than when you are in my league, you know, anytime, anywhere. Now, if you don't mind, m' man, I gotta think of my public."

Starting to fume, Yorit replied, "M' man, you wait till next time," and walked away, leaving "The Cat" Brown chucking behind him.

Back at the table, Yorit joined Death and Lavoss. Kantwell came over, carrying his saxophone. "You were damn good tonight, Robert, but unfortunately not good enough."

"Next time I will be," he grumbled.

"What is the problem with you?" asked Death testily, not understanding his behavior. "So we did not win. `*Na und*!´ " (So what!)

Yorit looked at her. "Dear, I can take losing a competition to a kid from New York, or a kid from Chicago or LA, but to lose to Wheeling, West Virginia? I'm humiliated!"

"Wheeling, Where?" asked Lavoss, not sure if he had heard right.

"Exactly my sentiments," said Yorit. "Down there they don't even know how to spell the word `jitterbug,´ let alone dance to it."

"Tonight they did. Apparently Rednecks can spell and dance," said Kantwell. "Wait, what am I talking about? That fella ain't no Red neck. He's a nig… ."

"We did get second prize, the Japanese transistor radio," Death interrupted.

Lacross slapped Yorit on the shoulder in an effort to console him. "Come on, buddy, don't take it so heard. It was only a dance."

"I can't help it, Al. I'm frustrated. I want to cry."

"Be glad you lost, otherwise you'd be stuck with two tickets to the opera. You want that? Hey Yo, where are you going?" Lavoss called out as Yorit walked away. He headed for the hallway.

"I'm going up front of the Old Edan club," he answered back over his shoulder.

"It's not time to go back to the barracks yet."

"I know. I'm going to throw myself under the crowd."

"What for?"

"There's a half-a-torso dressed in leotards that appreciates me."

"Wait, I'll come with you. I'd like to meet the leotard's other half."

Death watched her two soldier friends go. She turned to Kantwell, fingering his saxophone. "What is a half-a-torso?"

"I'm afraid to ask."

The Soldier

It was another day, like any other day, and the day before that day, as each day always is in the US Army. that is, the same: repetitious, redundant, excessive, forever and eternal, or so it seemed. It was 0530 in the morning when the whistle blew for reveille. It was followed by a formation, thEn roll call, thEn sick call, than PT (Physical Training) and thEn another roll call to make sure no one had bugged out. There was morning chow, then mail call, and still another formation followed by the command of "FORDWAAARD 'ARCH!" by PlTsGT Oats. And the 592nd Signal Company moved out for the Army's Wednesday morning training. Marching down the *Altdorfer Strasse*, they turned and continued to march down Avenue C. There, and fifty yards later, the company came to a halt in front of the post theater to the order of "COMPANEEY HALT!" Step, step. "RIGH' FACE!" Step. There followed a pause, a hesitation, a period…or was it a comma? "Ah, whatarewewaitingforsarge?" were some utterances from the three platoons. One minute passed, two minutes, but the affirmation order to "AT EASE!" failed to materialize. It was than that 1st Sgt Persilla stepped into view in front of the three Signal Company platoons. "Thank you, Sergeant Oats!" he bellowed. The two NCOs saluted each other.

Without acknowledging the presence of the three platoons, stiff and still at attention, 1st Sgt Persilla looked up at the old four-story *Kaiser Kadet* building in front of the company. It was a renovated structure that looked like any high school structure back home: Baroque, big windows, large doors, all red brick and granite, suggesting academia. It was used to billet NATO's Pentomic Army Infantry Battalions on rotation from the States. The Army battalions would fly into West

394

Berlin every three months to support the Brigade and remind the Soviet Union that there was a million man back-up force somewhere ready to fight them should war be declared. For this year's quarter period it was the 3rd Infantry Division, 2nd Battalion out of Fort Steward, Georgia, which was on rotation here in West Berlin. But for the soldiers of the 592nd Signal Company at attention in front of the *Kaiser Kadet* building the attitude was, "Na, who cares?"

In front of the Signal Company formation, two PFCs and a Pvt from the battalion were working on beautification detail. The three soldiers were doing lawn maintenance, pushing rakes and a broom, all in slow motion. It is what you do on detail: slow motion. Still at attention, necks stiff, backs straight, the three Signal Platoons had no choice but to face and watch them until further orders.

1st Sgt Persilla turned back to his company. He rubbed his hands together, for the morning air was chilly, then he stiffened. "COMPANYYY!" he ordered, "STAND AT--EASE!" Step, step. The formation could finally relax...and flatulent.

"The word is out!" the 1st Sgt began, his voice grating against the morning sunshine; it was the first real sunlight Berlin had in a month. "Gonorrhea has broken out in Brigade Special Troops!" There were some chuckles in the ranks. "Therefore..." he paused to let his words sink in, "...there's been a change in training schedule." The chuckles turned into doubtful mumbles. "Brigade has ordered all companies to have an emergency briefing on personal hygiene!"

Someone from 2nd Platoon raised his hand. The 1st Sgt recognized him. "Top, does that mean Brigade is gonna teach us how to skin it back?" The question generated some "Har-hars!" from the ranks.

"Only if you're not Jewish," said Pereski from his place in the 3rd Platoon. The men around him chuckled.

"At ease back there!" PltSgt Sweechek warned over his shoulder. He had overheard the wisecrack and thought it had merit.

"No, soldier!" answered Persilla to the 2nd Platoon man's question. "And you won't have to bend over and part'm either like they do back at Basic Training." The three platoons looked relieved. "But there is to be a five-hour block of hygiene training for the next couple of weeks, beginning immediately, as ordered!"

From the ranks, eyes rolled. The grumbling was noticeable. The signalmen knew what that meant: five hours of monotone lectures by a Toastmaster reject, usually a 23-year old ROTC (Reserve Officer

Training Corp) Lt who had never been laid but happened to have a degree in accounting. Or the briefing could mean a lecture by a deep South NCO who enunciated in Louisiana Cajun while playing the Jews harp around a campfire. There was more eye-rolling.

As he lectured, 1st Sgt Persilla began rocking on the high heeled soles of his boots. He tried everything to look tall and authoritative in front of his soldiers. He waited for the groans to subside, then he barked, "Now you men pay attention! Gonorrhea's serious stuff! Before this thing gets out of control, we got to lick it!"

"I'd rather not, 1st Sarge," came the response from someone in the 1stP platoon. The company laughed, including the PltSgts.

Persilla looked over, a scold in his eyes. "Who said that? You weren't recognized, whoever! This ain't funny! Sergeant Kabul! Your platoon!"

PltSgt Kabul immediately about-faced. "Whoever made the wisecrack, drop and give me twenty!" he ordered.

Knowing if he didn't step out, the whole platoon would have to drop and do pushups, so out stepped Sp E-4 Robert Zunt. He dropped to the ground and began counting, as was the rule, out loud. "A-one, sergean'! A-two, sergean'! At push-up number twenty he jumped up and returned to his position in the ranks and thanked PltSgt Kabul for the discipline, as was the rule.

The 1st Sgt noted SPC Zunt's name on his shit list, the clipboard he carried. "Now, I don't want to see any of you men falling asleep during this briefing! It's that important! Senior NCOs will be walking the aisles, checking for cat-nappers! Any questions?"

Following the three platoons' loud and unified reply of "NO FIRST SERGEANT!" Persilla turned the platoons back to PltSgt Oats, who called the company to order, then to "FALL OUT!" The three platoons broke rank and hustled toward the Post Theater entrance for their morning class briefing.

"It don't make sense," complained O'Malley, hurrying. "Why does the Army need five hours to explain to me the subtleties of male rectal hygiene? I'm already an expert."

Yorit hustled with him. "Yes, but do you use soap?"

In the foyer of the theater, Robuck hustled next to Bravo. "You know, Frank, 1st Sarge must have had your pecker in mind when he called the briefing."

"No, way. I'm Catholic, circumcised, and don't have to skin it back."

As they moved into the theater hall with the other signalmen, Pereski spoke up."Where does Gonorrhea come from anyway?"

"It comes from not washing your hands after Kitchen Police duty and masturbation," said Jonas in front of the hustle.

"If that's true, then we all got the disease."

"Gosh, and I had Kitchen Police duty yesterday," said Robuck, pushing with the crowd.

With a cry of "Ugh!" Jonas and Robuck stepped away from him.

Inside the theater, the soldiers were loud and lively. They moved down the aisles to the sloping rows of seats. They jostled one another while talking dirty, the way soldiers do. "Ma' fuck!" "Shiit'!" "Move yo ass!"

The theater had a stage with a proscenium arch, unusual for an Army Post. The rows of seats were twenty across, with two aisles that ran along the walls. The seats quickly filled. In the middle of one row Lavoss sat down, the rest of the commo squad around him: Robuck, Pereski, Yorit, Hatnoy, Kantewell, Bravo, O'Malley, Jonas, and Jimmy Lightpony the Shoshone. The men from the other sections did the same, everyone talking at once, out loud.

"You know, this is the third personal hygiene briefing in a year," said Hatnoy to the group. "If only guys would learn to put a rubber on straight we wouldn't need hygiene classes."

"Pereski looked at him quizzically. "Oh? And how do you put a rubber on straight?"

"By the numbers, what else. It's in the Army regulations."

Kantwell looked puzzled by the statement. "By the numbers? You mean like 1-2-3-4, humpf?"

"That's right," said Lavoss, "otherwise you might put the condom on backwards."

"And how do you know if a rubber is on backwards?" asked Robuck, inquisitive.

"You look for the label."

"The label?"

"Yes, it's the part that tickles."

On the stage, standing at the speaker's podium, a moody looking captain watched as the company filed in. He looked around. He had a tough but tired-guy look, legs apart, arms akimbo. He gripped a blackboard pointer as if it was a javelin to be hurled should anyone dare fall asleep during his briefing. He was an officer and a medic from the 279 Hospital Company, the instructor of the day.

One man from the 2nd Platoon who sat near the stage eyed him cynically. "By looks of his complexion he might have the disease himself." There were chuckles around. (The captain suffered from a bad case of youthful acne.)

"All right, pipe down there!" ordered SSgt Oats, standing near the stage. "The briefing is about to begin!"

The Captain leaned the board pointer against the podium and looked at the indifferent audience in front of him. "Good morning, Signal Company! "he called out, followed by the infantrymen shout of, "HU-AH!"

With that, the three signal platoons jumped to their feet and responded with a unified return shout of, "HU-AH, SIR!" as they had been trained to do.

"Soldiers! Take yourrr, seats!"

And the class briefing began.

Call it an anomaly, and no one has yet to figure out why, but US Army briefings are always conducted in overheated rooms, usually after a heavy morning or afternoon chow. It goes without saying that it can invite slumber, and no one slumbers better than the American soldier. After the captain yelled, "Good morning Signal Company, Hu-ah!" half the signalmen dropped back into their seats and dozed.

1st Sgt Persilla had anticipated this; he caught it right away. Like any good company 1st Sgt, he had the innate ability to sense the controversial, anticipate the unexpected, and solve the unintentional before they happened. From his long experience, he knew his soldiers and had a solution at the ready. A bamboo pole.

He kept several bamboo poles stored in the company Arms Room. He brought them with him and passed them out to the PltSgts who walked the aisles. What made the poles unique were the 12-ounce boxing gloves attached to one end; it was tied on with duct tape. During a briefing, those men who dozed nearest the aisle merely got an elbow nudge to wake them up. But for those soldiers who dared to dose off in the middle of the row, they got a whack by the bamboo pole with the 12-ounce boxing glove attached. There was no escape. They tried to dodge the boxing glove. They tried to block it. They slumped in their seat to avoid it. It was all to no avail. The 12-ouncers always found their mark. Thud! Whack! Smack! It was worse than a nun's four-knuckle jab that seventh graders got for not kneeling straight in the pew at church Mass. In the company's post theater briefing it made Catholic boys especially anxious.

A blow by the bamboo pole's boxing glove could turn a cheekbone raw. Not a few soldiers got knocked out by it. Bravo was one of them. He had a glass jaw from too much CYO boxing in grade school and was unable to take a punch. He requested a "profile" not to attend training briefings because it was dangerous to his health. The request was denied. He was stuck. He had to attend military briefings, though he knew that should he doze off he would get a whack. At the end of his four-year tour of duty, when asked what it was he got most from his service in the United States Army, he would answer, "Cauliflower ears." Then he would wiggle them.

No one ever really got upset or objected to the bamboo pole's punch. It was the way things were in the Berlin Brigade in the 1960s. In fact, the signalmen found it to be a badge of courage to get punched in the head by a bamboo pole with a 12-ounce boxing glove attached.

They had all gone through worse, like Army Basic Training. Nothing in the Army was as bad as that. If soldiers did not behave themselves, discipline was to be expected. In 592nd Signal Comapny one man did question the punch discipline. He was PFC Stanton Preston of the 1st Platoon.

***

PFC Preston was different in character. Academically, he was a cut above the rest of the soldiers. He had a Ph.D. in engineering from University of Michigan. Upon graduation from college he took a job with General Motors, drawing a super salary. Life could not have been better. He was planning to get married when he got drafted. His deferment had jumped from 4A to 1A—a shock! He had never expected it. His father, a local politician, did not have enough pull to get the "stand-by" 4A deferment reinstated. It was unusual, since the sons of politicians rarely got drafted for active duty. To the Army Reserve, yes, but to Active Duty? No! For PFC Preston it meant his wedding had to be put on hold; it was the reason for his eternal griping. What woman would marry a Ph.D. in engineering with a rank of PFC and an income of $70 a month, the Army base pay?

Upon being drafted, Dr. Ph.D. Preston reported to his MEP station for enlistment. He was in line with a group of mostly unemployed fellows—Detroit ghetto blacks, high school dropouts, and down-state, back woods hillbillies. They were to be his roommates all through Basic

Training and much of his Army career. Preston's mother had to hold up his hand when he was sworn in. At the ceremony he was weeping like a baby. Fourteen weeks later and twenty pounds lighter, Preston arrived Berlin Brigade with the noble rank of "Private First Class" to add to his doctorate title.

Dr. PFC Stanton Preston griped about everything military. He griped about the draft, how unfair it was for the well-educated to be drafted; he griped about the mundane work details; he griped about the bad-smelling roommates; he griped about the chow (who didn't); he griped about being forced to listen to country music in the barracks 24 hours a day. He even griped about the German women—too many hair follicles in the wrong places. He griped about everything and everyone. "You are all so beneath me," he would sometimes utter, and let every one know it. He once reported to 1st Sgt Persilla to complain about Sgt Barmodus, his section NCO. The 1st Sgt listened, smiled, than put him on extra work detail for having "an attitude." PFC Preston then went to the company commander, Capt Mellon, with his complaint. When the Company Commander realized Preston did not follow the Chain-of-Command to register his gripe, he threw him out of the Command Room, but not before adding a work detail for good measure.

"Is this anyway to treat a PFC with a doctorate?" Preston fumed back at his quarters. He was determined to show the Army a thing or two.

Now, following the Chain-of-Command, he went to the BrSgtMaj with his complaint. The SgtMaj made Preston stand with his nose against the blackboard. Not getting satisfaction, Preston approached the Judge Advocate Office (JAG). He was told him to turn the other cheek. Finally, in desperation, the PhD turned PFC wrote his state senator.

Two weeks later, Preston received a letter back from the august gentleman from the State of Michigan, a man noted for his sense of balance and high values to the electorate. In his letter, he told Preston what it was like to be a Marine in World War II, island-hopping in the Pacific. He had fought in the Battle of Tarawa, Pelalu, and Iwo Jima.

If a Marine was dissatisfied with the job, the senator wrote, or faked a nervous breakdown, or played shell shock, he was given an aspirin, a slap on the back, and pushed into a forward foxhole position, accompanied by his trusty M1 rifle. "It's the best cure for whatever ails ya," he wrote.

The wise old senator from Michigan then wrote his constituent further. "Absorb Uncle Sam's discipline for that's what it is. And be thankful you're not in forward foxhole facing a Japanese *Banzi!* charge. So shut up and listen to your NCOs! They know what's best for you, PFC!" Preston did not vote for the senator in the next election. The senator won anyway.

"Wack!" The punch startled him. Preston had just been hit again by the bamboo pole with the 12-ounce boxing glove attached. He had nodded off during the dull gonorrhea briefing. Jumping up, he was ready to fight back when he remembered what the wise old state senator had written him. Rubbing his cheek, he sat back down. "Pay attention!" he told himself. Army Sgts know what's best.

***

With the briefing half over, and half the company dabbing at sore cheeks and brows (the sergeants had been indeed zealous with their bamboo poles), the signalmen departed the post theater. Outside, on avenue C, they formed up again into the three platoon at-ease formation. There they waited. Looking around, they wondered. They saw there was no one in command to march them back to barracks. The company PltSgts had vanished, but to where?

What the soldiers did not realize was that their PltSgts, Oats, Sweechek, Cabul, and the other NCOs, including 1st Sgt Persilla, had all gone for a quick coffee break at the snack bar. It was around the corner from the theater. Taking breaks is one of the privileges career NCOs delighted in. Carrying a clipboard of authority was the other delight. Now, standing in formation at parade rest, the question among the signalmen was, "Gosh, guys, what do we do now?"

In the 3rd Platoon, Kantwell turned to O'Malley. "Pattie, what did you get out of today's gonorrhea lecture?"

"What lecture? Oh, you mean the briefing," O'Malley corrected.

"Yes, the briefing. The one the captain just gave us. What did you get out of it?"

"I don't know. I was wearing earplugs."

Kantwell turned to Bravo in rank on the other side of him. "Frank, what did you get out of today's briefing about gonorrhea?"

Bravo thought for a moment. "To soap it down before you have sex with a German woman."

"Will that prevent gonorrhea?"

"Who is talking about gonorrhea? I'm talking about her armpits."

Still waiting, the men in formation talked, ho-hummed and shuffled their feet. It was becoming another one of those "Hurry up and wait!" approaches the Army is famous for. Growing impatient, someone shouted, "Aw shit!" followed by a "Mudderfucker!" expletive and a "Wha' we standing 'round fo'?" danced through the three grumbling platoons.

The soldiers looked at each other, looked around and "Humpfed!" Still no senior Sarge or someone in authority to march them back to barracks. According to Army regulations, a formation is not permitted to move unless dismissed by a person of rank, E5 or above. An individual may decide to say "What the hell!" and waltz away, but not three platoons made up of 95 soldiers, three squads deep. That is a definite no-no! A person in authority has to be in command to give the order for a company to move. "Forward! March!" A two-stripe Corporal could, but the company had none. Only E-4 Specialists and below. So, with that, the three platoons waited at rest, fermenting. It was the reason for the expletives: "Aw shit!" "Mudderfuck!" "Wha' we standen her' fo'?"

Squeezing a pimple, Robuck began to whine. "So what do we do now?"

"Will someone please march us back to barracks?" begged Yorit, nearby. "I gotta pee!"

There was no response. Throughout the company the griping grew vocal. The men kept looking over their shoulders, hoping some senior somebody of rank carrying a clipboard would appear, take authority, and order "Attention! Dismissed!"

A StSgt from Headquarters Company happened to pass by. Robuck asked him if he would march Signal's three platoons back to barracks. The StSgt said it was not his responsibility and walked off.

An E-7 sergeant from the 42nd Engineer Company came within shouting range, but he pretended not to hear. A Capt pulled up in a jeep to asked directions to the motor pool. When asked to dismiss the formation, he said he wasn't the company's commanding officer, and drove away.

"Will somebody please dismiss us?" one desperate voice cried out.

Meanwhile, across the street from Signal Company, the infantry soldiers on "beautification detail" stopped to watch them. As enlistees and draftees, they understood the frustration.

The signalmen whistled to themselves. Others bit their nails.

O'Malley turned his face to a moment's sunshine, hoping for some cheek color. Pereski looked up too. There was a small dark cloud overhead. "Just our luck we get rained on," he said. And they did. It was a quick shower. It came with a gust of wind. The dark cloud overhead emptied itself on the all three platoons like an animals bladder. Then the rain stopped.

"This is ridiculous!" complained Yorit with a scuff. "Hey, Al, you got time and grade. What the hell! Call us to attention, right face the company and march us the fuck back to barracks! It's that or my bladder is going to pop. What do ya say?"

"Time and grade? I'm only an E-4 like you," Lavoss called over from his place in the ranks.

"But you'll be an E-5 Sergeant one day. May as well get in some practice...like now," Yorit encouraged him.

"Ya!" Lavoss called back, "And get busted to rank E3 for impersonating an E5 Sarge. No way!"

"Aw shit!" raged Bravo, growing frustrated with company's isolated status.

Lavoss stomped his foot. "No, man! You know how the Army is. They misinterpret such behavior. Fart in the ranks and they think you volunteered for a work detail. No man, you do it!" Yorit dropped the idea.

From the other side of the street, one of the 3rd Infantry Division soldiers, the PVT-2nd Pvt was getting bawled out by his StSgt in charge of the work detail. He was loud. It caught the attention from the signalmen in formation. They watched. The Sgt had come by to check on his three soldiers. He did not like what he saw: slow motion sweeping. In the Army, bawl outs are second nature. They happen all the time. It comes with the rank. You hear it in the Orderly Room, at formation, in the field, on duty, off duty; No one in the Signal Company formation paid much attention until the soldier, the Pvt, humiliated beyond tolerance, swung and punched his StSgt. It was a sucker punch. It caught him in the jaw. Stunned him and dropped like a brick to the ground. The Pvt took off running.

"Hit'm again!" Jonas cried out. He was watching, along with everyone else in the Signal formation. Some of the men laughed. "An NCO finally got his due!"

The infantry StSgt got up and rubbed his jaw. He gathered the two PFCs on the work detail and together they ran after the Pvt-2 who had disappeared into the company Kaiser Kadet barracks.

"I sometimes wish I had the guts to do that," said Pereski. "I recall a time when..."

"What's going on over there at 3rd ID?" asked 1st Sgt Persilla. The company Sergeants had all just returned from their break. Satiated from their coffee and donuts, Sgts Oats, Cabul, and Sweechek now stepped to the front of their platoons, with 1st Sgt Persilla at the head of the company. Looking around, he saw his soldiers frown resentment. They had waited too long. Still, the Sgts took no notice. Stretching, 3rd PltSgt Sweechek burped with contentment. 1st Sgt Persilla asked again, "Say, men, what is going on over there?"

"Little punch up, Top," Yorit called out. "An infantry soldier just kicked his detail Sergeant's ass. Took one order too many, I expect." There was some laughter from the ranks.

Persilla shrugged. "Oh, I guess I better behave myself around here, huh?"

He was about to call the company to attention when, from an upper story window, there came the crash of glass. Someone had shattered the window pane. The three platoons looked up. It was the 3rd ID, Pvt-2 soldier, the one who had punched his StSgt. He had a shovel, his trenchant tool in hand, and was trashing his quarters. "I can't take it any more!" he yelled out above from the broken window. A foot locker appeared on the window sill's edge. With a shove it came crashing down to the ground. It was followed by a set of dress greens, shoes, and polished display boots, one boot after the other. A bunk and mattress followed. Then the laundry bag, half full. Still looking up and standing in formation, the men of the 592nd Signal Company watched, taking it all in.

1st Sgt Persilla shrugged and turned back to the formation. "Now, men, there is an example of a soldier with a bad attitude! Don't yo' all pay him no mind!" Stiffening, Persilla gave the command of, "Companyyyy! 'TENTION!"

The three platoons snapped to, chest out, heels together, hands and fingers along the seam of the field trousers. Weeping, the 3rd ID private climbed to the edge of the window sill and stood there, hands on the frame, looking down. Inside the building there was the loud sound of a door bang and desperate cries of, "No, soldier! No!"

"Right face!" 1st Sgt Persilla ordered from below.

"I can't take it any more!" the Pvt cried out again from the third story window.

"Forwaaard!"

He jumped.

"Maaarch!"

Plop! The PVT-2 hit the ground.

"Yo' lef'..."

"Did he bounce?" Bravo asked Yorit next to him as they marched.

"Yo' lef'..."

"Sounded like he did."

"Yo' lef', righ', lef'..."

"That soldier had potential."

"How's that?"

"Haw, hay, yo' lef, righ´, lef˝..."

"He committed suicide by the numbers."

"Yo' lef'..."

"It don't get no better than that."

"He should-a been in Signal Company."

"Yeah, definitely communication material."

"Yo' lef'..."

"I'd give him a promotion—posthumously, of course."

"Righ' lef'..."

"Where do you suppose he come from?"

"Yo' lef'..."

"New England, by the twang of his scream:"

"Shut up in the ranks back there!" bellowed MSG Sweechek.

"Yo' lef', righ', lef˝...hey, yaw, three, fo´! Yo´ lef˝..."

Cookie Nast

"I'm buying."

"No! I'm buying."

"Okay, then I'll mooch." said Yorit,

It was how the evening began. Yorit and Jonas, the Alabama golden boy, went into the Golden Sun *Lokal*, the soldiers dive, for a quick `*Bier'*. Inside, Sweettalkinmarge, one of the women nicknamed, tattooed, and branded by generations of Berlin Brigade soldiers, was sitting with two men at a table. Jonas dropped a coin in the jukebox and walked over to her. He smiled his Fido-like grin, that is, the tongue hanging out, eyebrows wiggling, and asked her to dance. She thought him ridiculous and gave him the cold shoulder and a gentle, "Fuck off, boy!" The two men sitting with her laughed. Jonas, his male ego dented, walked back to the bar where Yorit stood downing his suds. Despondent from the put-down, Jonas ordered a *Bie'*. He drank it in silence.

Yorit looked at him. "What did she say?"

"She told me to fuck off," he replied mournfully.

"That's why they call her 'Sweettalkinmarge,'" said Yorit. "It's her way of saying you're cool."

"And after all I did for her."

"What did you do for her?"

"Taught her how to swear with a twang. Fick yo´all, honey!"

"You and every other GI in the army," said Yorit, finishing his drink.

Jonas straightened. "Come on, Yankee. Let's go."

"Where to, Reb?"

"Who cares? Downtown? Got to find us some women!" Jonas drawled out.

Outside, the two men hopped the tram heading for the Friedenau District and the bars there. Paying their fares, they took a seat.

"Say, Cecil, what happened with Sweettalkinmarge, really? Why'd she put you down? I saw you dancing with her the other day."

"It was those two guys next to her. They blocked me from my hustle. If it wasn't for them, she would be running her fingers through my brush hair right now."

"And maybe passing on to you a good dose of her clap. She may have done you a favor by putting you down," said Yorit, noting the venereal diseases briefings the company just had.

As the tram clanged along, the two buddies talked energetically, the way soldiers do, cynical about everything military: the discipline, the duty, the training, the command.

Jonas slouched in his seat. "Remember that 3rd I.D. guy who jumped out the window?"

"Yeah, what about him?"

"I've been wondering. Why do you suppose he jumped?" (The event was still the hot topic back at the company.)

"I don´t really know," said Yorit, thoughtful. "The army is a rough place. It can knock a guy down, as we both know, especially if you can't get an off-post pass once in a while."

"Yes, but not so rough that you throw yourself out a window."

"It is not just a question of why he jumped, but why head first?"

Jonas sat silently for a moment. "You can see he didn't go to Army Jump School, otherwise he'd have hit the ground and rolled. Probably be alive today too."

"Lack of training." speculated Yorit, looking out the tram window.

"Think so?"

"What else?"

"Too late now."

"Poor fucker."

"Nah! He's one of the lucky ones. He's out of the Army now ."

On the *Rhein Strasse*, car traffic was light for this time of evening; the apartment houses were dark, a contrast to the Netherlands where the people never draw the living room curtains. It had to do with the Dutch culture. Friendly by nature, it was the Dutch tradition to have parties, celebrate birthdays, embrace, quarrel and make love in front of the living room window for all to see. It kept the neighbors entertained, those who happened to pass by. By contrast, the Germans were more reserved. They not only drew the curtains, they would drop the *Rolos* (the shutters) and bolt the doors. It was why German towns were so dark at night. A shopkeeper once told Yorit that it had to do with life under National Socialism. At the time, people snitched on one another to the authorities. It created a sense of distrust among residence. Though National Socialism was long gone, such snoopy habits still tended to linger among the population, even 18 years after the war. It was the reason apartment house buildings in West Berlin were so dark and had that formidable fortress look. Distrust!

"*Saar Strasse!*" the tram driver called out.

Jonas nudged Yorit. "We're here," he said and they got off the tram. It was the wrong stop.

Yorit looked around, then slapped Jonas on the shoulder. "Dummy! Our stop is still some blocks up the street! Now we have to walk."

"So we gotta walk," snapped Jonas with a shrug, not appreciating the slap. "We're trained for it, ain't we?"

"I hope so. I'm still wobbly from that Berlin *Kindel* beer we drank at the Golden Sun."

With hands in their pockets and collars up against the night's cold, the two soldiers quickly hustled down the street, passing several shops. Approaching one of the local bars, they picked up on the weak neon-colored sign. It blinked and had the configuration of a cat. They stopped and stared. It was the *Schwarze Katze Lokal*, the Black Cat bar, one of the few all Negro bars in the city and off limits to white soldiers unless invited as a guest. In West Berlin, Negro soldiers had their hangouts where they drank and danced, and the white soldiers had theirs. The Golden Sun was one of the white man bars; the *Schwartze Katze*, a black soldier one. Though the Army had been integrated years ago by a Truman presidential decree, there was an unspoken rule among servicemen: "Each race unto itself." On duty the races mixed; off duty, they didn't. The *Schwarze Katze Lokal* was one such example.

"Hey, will you check out them chicks going in there? Do they look good!" drooled Jonas, a little surprised at the quality of the German women standing at the Black Cat entrance. "What them Negras got that we ain't got?" his southern accent rumbled at a low ebb.

"Money," said Yorit. "Those guys spend their whole base pay on a woman to get a little."

"Oh really?"

"Sure, if you want to get laid it's what you do," said Yorit as they passed by the outline of the neon-lit Cat.

Jonas stopped. "Let's go in."

"Huh?"

"Yeah, let's go in, Yoyo."

Yorit grabbed his buddy by the arm. "Cecil, wait! We can't. It's a black G.I. joint. If we go in, there's bound to be trouble. We're white guys. I'm not ready for a punch-up tonight because of my race."

Jonas thumped his chest. "I'm from Alabama, boy, and a proud southerner. If anybody knows how to handle Negras, I do," Jonas toughgrunted in his tar-paper accent.

"Well I'm from the North and Ohio, and from where I come from black guys will punch you out if you cross their line. We're not far from our white man's bar. It's up the street at the corner. Come on!"

Jonas stood his ground. "I'm buying and you is-a moochin', that was the agreement, right? I say we drink some at the Black Cat, then we'll head up the street to our beer joint."

Yorit hesitated, unsure. He was reluctant, but... "Hm, okay Cecil, but only under one condition."

"Was's dat?"

You keep your mouth shut. As soon as those guys in there hear your Billy Graham twang, they'll know you're a Redneck and we're in trouble. It'll be Birmingham in reverse, and I'm no Martin Luther King.

"Agree-ed!" Jonas laughed, giving Yorit the high five slap.

At the door of the *Schwartze Katze,* two NBA types who looked more at home on the full court press than in a Cold War city, stepped in front of them. They were the club's bouncers. "Yo, `Chalky!'" His voice had that Ghetto flavor. "Yo is goin' the wrong way. Yo fishin' hole is up the *Strass-e* there, man," he said, pointing.

"But we heard the music is better down here at your club," said Yorit politely.

"Yo still goin' the wrong di-rection, ma-man" repeated the NBA player. "Beat it!"

"Why don't you invite us in?" Yorit suggested, giving the big bouncer-player a grin.

Standing nearby, the other NBA type laughed. "Why should we, m´man?"

"Because we love good soul music: Ray Charles, Ella Fitzgerald, Louie Armstrong," answered Yorit, undeterred.

"That may be, but when yo chalkies come in,' yo' goes for our chicks too, and m´man, we don' like dat."

"We're not after the women here, only the music. The bars uptown don't have such great soul and jive. Come on, dude, give us a break and let us in your digs," said Yorit trying to relate to the Negro toughs.

Still suspicious, the two NBA types looked them over. "Well, what d' ya think, Davy? Should we let the chalkies in?" the one bouncer asked the other.

The other NBA type, Davy, at six-foot five, also towered above the two signalmen. He had hands the size of Goose Tatem's of the Harlem Globe Trotters and shoulders just as broad. "Ah, what the hell. Let 'm a-go in. If they's gets-a-sassy, we c'n kick butt. C'n give us entertainment. Tell Eugene inside the door the two chalkies is okay." Davy than turned to Yorit. "Say, man, what company you with?"

"592nd Signal over at Andrews Barracks. How about you doods?"

"We is 3rd Battalion, the 6th out of McNair. Most of the guys in here are from 6th I.D., and I'll tell ya, we is mean modderfuckers. So behave yo'self, hear? This is our dive," he cautioned.

Yorit and Jonas passed Eugene, who looked like a Baltimore Colt middle linebacker, five-foot five and squat. He gave them a warning look and let them pass. Sucking in their breath, the two signalmen entered the black soldiers bar.

The *Schwartze Katze* was a *Lokal*, as the Germans called their neighborhood bars. It was a large place where the bar top ran along one whole wall. It had a dance floor with spotlights that drilled the dancers, a contrast to the rest of the room, which was dark and shadowy and ideal for lovers wanting to slip into the corners to kiss. Most of the women looked Scandinavian—pale skin, blonde, boyish, their skirts teasingly tight. Jonas and Yorit gawked. Neither had ever seen black men hustle white women before. It just was not done north OR south of the Mason Dixon Line.

"Jus' look at them chicks, will ya?" whispered Jonas, catching his breath. "Phew-ee!"

Yorit glanced around the room, still uncertain. "This is not my kind of playpen, Cecil. It's dangerous."

"But them chee-icks. Man-ooh-man,n!" Impressed by the clubs environment, women, the more Jonas talked the more he slipped into Alabama.

"Shh, Dixie! Don't you dare talk southern in here. Remember what the bouncer at the door said," Yorit warned him furtively.

They did not recognize anyone they knew since most of the patrons in the *Katze* were from the McNair barracks and the Infantry. Though they stood out as the only white guys in a black man's bar, the hostility Yorit expected did not materialize. There was no reproach concerning their presence. Everyone was too busy having a good time drinking, laughing, and trying to make out with the Scandinavian-looking German women. Yorit and Jonas relaxed. They ordered *Biers.*

Out on the dance floor no one jitterbugged or did Chubby Checker's "The Twist" like they did uptown at the white guy bars. Instead, the couples danced a kind of a hip-boogie, pelvis on pelvis, rump to rump, followed by an erotic grinding that was a turn-on just to watch. Bug-eyed, Jonas and Yorit watched, "Gosh-ing!" each other.

"Down home, Negras would get strung up for messin' with white chicki-dos like this," said Jonas, his voice a little loud.

"So will we, Cecil, if you don't hold you tongue. Can't you talk like you're from the North?"

Jonas only chuckled. At the bar, the more they drank the more he exaggerated his heritage, inviting suspicious looks. "Somethin' wrong with the ways I talks, Robert?"

Yorit looked at his friend, sternly. "In here there is, Rebel, so shut up. Please!"

Confident he had everything under control, Jonas held up his beer glass. After twenty minutes of observing the floor show, he leaned toward Yorit. "Boy, have I got a problem!"

"What, got to urinate?"

"No, got me a hard-on and it hurts. Who-ee!"

"Well, don't play with it in here. Wait till we get outside and find a tree to bump."

"Nah, I'd like to let one of them women play with it."

"I think its time for us to go, Reb," said Yorit nervously, finishing his drink. Just then Jonas moved down the bar to a niche. It was closer to the dance floor and the lights, Yorit behind him. "Cecil!" he hissed after him.

"Would I like to get to know that bab´ girl over there. My type."

"Yeah, me too. And that one, and that one, and that one... ."

One girl on the dance floor caught Jones' fancy. Her shape was perfect and her smile inviting.

"Whew-ee! If that ain't Sophia Lo-rain, no one is. I certainly don't understand it. In our white guy bars we get mostly them over-the-hill mamas like Death and her sister Sin, or Sweettalkinmarge. The Negras, here, they get the cheer leaders from Tulane."

"Kind of makes you want to go back to college," said Yorit. "Oh, well, come on Reb, time for us to go. I don't feel comfortable here any more. We're getting too many looks."

Then it happened. Little Richard music came up on the juke box. Couples moved toward the dance floor. Hopping up and down, Jonas set his drink on the bar "Yo, buddy, I can't stand this anymore. Gotta dance!"

Before Yorit could stop him, the golden boy from Alabama, Cecil Jonas, was moving among the tables toward the one Scandinavian type he liked. Some heads turned. There was critical mumbling among the black patrons. Around him, Yorit sensed disapproval mounting. Out on the dance floor, Jonas and the girl danced the "Monkey" together, the eyes of everyone at the bar watching. When the music stopped they stayed on the dance floor under the spotlights and talked.

From the bar, two men stepped away and moved toward them. They were not smiling. One of them confronted Jonas. There was an exchange of words. Jonas opened his mouth. That was it. He blew his cover. That mellifluous accent, that farm boy sloth…it was a red flag. He was pushed. Someone grabbed him from behind. Jones turned and was punched. The girl fled.

Cursing, Yorit quickly moved to the dance floor. He knew he had to give some back up, and be quick about it. It happened. He did not see it coming, a sucker punch from out of the blue. It caught him and staggered him. A second punch missed. Nearby, Jonas too was defending himself. A table went over. Women screamed. But just as quickly as the fight started, it broke up. The two NBA types and Eugene stepped in. The bouncers had been watching from the door, waiting for just such an altercation to happen. Davy grabbed Jonas from behind and jerked him out of the melee. Off balance, he got slugged again. Pushed to the door, he was thrown out and landed on the sidewalk. It was "Jack and Jill went down the Hill" and Yorit came tumbling after. One of the bouncers tossed him with a boot in the butt.

"I done tol' yo'll honkies behave yo'selves'!" warned the NBA, standing at the entrance.

"Damn niggers!" Jonas balked back at him, his lip bleeding.

"Ain't you had enough, trash?" shouted Davy, the other bouncer.

"You better thank your lucky stars we ain't back home in Alabama, black ass!" Jonas snapped, blood on his face.

Yorit thought it odd how similar the two men sounded shouting at each other in southern, one the skin color black, the other white. It was as if they were both country cousins.

Having had enough of the back talk, the two NBA type stepped away from the entrance toward Jonas and Yorit, ready to fight. The two signalmen took a stance. A small crowd watched from the door. Eugene shouted a warning. Everyone stopped, for there at the curb, parked on the *Haupt Strasse*, was an M.P. jeep on patrol. Inside, the two MPs from the 287th Military Police Company watched the action develop.

"You just better skee-daddle, white trash!" Davy yelled. Both NBAs turned and went back inside the *Schwartze Katze Lokal* and closed the door. The small crowd that had gathered dispersed.

"Asshole Infantry!" Jonas called after them.

Neither man said anything until they were well out of range of the bar. Yorit felt his cheek as they walked up the *Haupt Strasse*. Only now did he feel the results of the sucker-punch; his cheek had swollen. "Cecil, you asshole, you just had to dance with that girl, didn't you?"

Jonas grinned. His eye was turning black where he had been hit; his nose had stopped bleeding. "Yes, but what a girl! Say, thanks for the back up, Yo. I won' forget it."

"Neither will my cheek. Say, did we get our butts kicked, or didn't we?"

"But it was fun, wasn't it?" grinned Jonas, walking fast, faking a punch.

Yorit thought for a moment. "You know, you're right. It was." Both men laughed. They had lost a fight, were kicked out of the bar, yet they felt undefeated. Call it the Cro-Magnon high. In life, a couple of awkward punches measured young men and their manhood. Street fight or a prize fight, win or lose, afterwords there is always a feel of exhilaration. Thus, arms around each other, pulling each other, faking and fainting, they pimp-rolled up the West Berlin *Haupt Strasse* talking bravado, ready to take on anyone who dared look cockeyed at them.

Jonas beat his chest and howled. "Heavy Motor? Fuck'm! Light Infantry? Who cares? Andrew's Special Troops just took on the McNair's 6th Infantry!"

"Yeah!" snapped Yorit, feeling pugnacious himself. "Them wimps!"

"Let's go back again and take'm on again." Jonas was feeling his oats.

Yorit grinned, still punching the air. "Sure, but next time,"

Now determined, they walked fast up the *Haupt Strasse* boulevard, heading for the white soldier's bar and some soldier riot drink. It was after hustling two blocks that they noticed the figure of a large man. He was staggering along the sidewalk, obviously drunk. He leaned against a tree for support, then fell. Whoever he was, both men knew the West Berlin *Polizei* would find him and sweep him up. The German police were sticklers when it came to public order and behavior. They called it "*Stadtliche Ordnung.*"

As they passed the drunk, Yorit stopped. He glancing back. "Hey wait a minute. That guy laying there. There's something odd about him. What? Look, he's wearing white socks. Is he one of us? Germans never wear white socks."

Crumpled and trembling, the figure lay with his face under an arm. His trousers had jerked up, revealing the white socks. He wore a thin blazer, too thin for the evening's cold. Yorit and Jonas stepped over and turned the figure over. Startled, they jumped back, for there on the ground in front of them was the scourge of the Signal Company Chow Hall, Mr. Kitchen Police himself, StSgt, "Mess Daddy" Cookie' Nast. He was passed out and lying in the fetal position.

"Well, will ya look-y-yall wha' we gots her'? A drunk coon!" said Jonas, slipping into his southern accent again.

"Gosh, is he stinko-ed," said Yorit, tapping him with his foot.

Sgt Nast popped open one eye. Moving, he struggled to get up, took a couple of steps sideways—the drunkard's gait—and collapsed again.

The two signalmen watched, concerned. "Our Cookie doesn't seem to know where he is." What to do? That was the question.

"Oh, let him lie there. He can handle it huimself," said Jonas.

"I don't know. In his condition he might stumble into the street and get run over," said Yorit, unsure of what to do.

Jonas folded his arms. "If he does get run over it serves him right, after all that shit-on-a-shingle chow he been force-feeding us. I once asked him why he don't take the grub off the menu, and you know what he said? 'What was good for Teddy Roosevelt and the Rough Riders is good for me.' Can you imagine? The army had been feeding us soldiers shit-on-a- shingle ever since Teddy Roosevelt charged up San Juan Hill!"

"Well, it got the Army up San Juan Hill, didn't it."

Jonas laughed. "It sure did. The Rough Riders had no choice; the porto-potties were all up there at the top."

Both men leaned over their drunken Mess Sgt. "Wake up, Sarge!" There was no response. Changing his tone, Jonas slipped into a tired Delta slang. "Hey, yo there Nikker boy!" he scolded. "Yo' haul yo ass up and move them cotton bales, hear me?" There was still no response except for the twitch of a wrist. Jonas stepped back. "Wow! He's really knocked out. That should've had him up and on his feet and-a `foot-stompin'`."

Yorit took Sgt Nast's pulse to see how close to death he might be. "Cecil, we can't leave the Sarge here on the sidewalk like this. He's one of our guys." Reaching down, both men grabbed him by the arms and propped him against the tree. "We got to bring him back to barracks."

Jonas protested. "What? If we do that the whole evening will be shot! Our passes are only good till midnight."

Yorit shook his head. "Nasty ol' Mess Sarge or not, we got to. We can booze at the Golden Sun later."

"You're right. Can't leave him here like this," said Jonas. Dropping his deep South accent, he stepping into the street and hailed a passing taxi.

Back at the Army post main gate, they hauled the big man out of the back seat of the taxi and paid the driver. Half carrying, half dragging Mess Sgt Nast, they walked him toward the entrance. The gate guard waved them through without checking their passes. "He's the third guy this evening they've carried in, and it isn't even 2200 hours yet," said the guard.

The BAQ, senior NCO quarters, was separate from the enlisted men's three floor barracks. It was a flat brick building that had more the look of a Florida motel off a Tallahassee highway than a home for unmarried senior NCOs. Pushing through the door, they shuffled down the narrow corridor, checking the door names until they reached Sgt Nast's quarters. His name was on the door. Jonas took the room key out of Nast's pocket and unlocked the door. Inside, they dropped him on his wood framed bed. (Sergeants don't sleep on metal bunks like the enlisted men do.)

Now asleep, he began to snore. The two soldiers turned to leave when Yorit paused. "Wait!" he said, looking around. The room was simple, spartan, and neat. There was the bed, a desk, a dresser, an arm chair. No decorations were to be seen except on the wall above the desk; there, several awards hung; they were dining facility awards that Nast had earned during his years of service. Two awards, however, were different. One was a Purple Heart, the other a Bronze Star—a Bronze Star for bravery. "Cookie was a hero?" Yorit and Jonas looked at each other. There were also photographs of units he had served with. One photo was of a whole company, all black soldiers, in field dress with their white officers; the officers sat in chairs in front of the company like hunters back from a safari, their worriers around them. The company yard arm read, "Charlie Company, 24th Infantry Regiment." The date on the picture was 1950. There were other photographs too. They were of young men grinning, horsing around in front of the camera. Nast was easy to pick out; he was the largest man horsing.

On the bed behind them he groaned. Suddenly, he began to thrash. He tried to get up. Jonas stepped over and pushed Nast down. Though unconscious, the Mess Daddy moved to get up again. This time, both Yorit and Jonas jumped on him to keep him down. There was a struggle with Nast carrying the two men like flyweights across the room until they dragged him back into his bed.

"What do we do now?" asked Jonas, catching his breath.

"Tell me and we'll both know," said Yorit, feeling as if he had just ridden a bucking bronco. "Now I know what the Lilliputians were up against with Gulliver."

For the third time, the big man with the Popeye forearms sat up in bed. He fell back. He trembled. He shook. He tried getting up again, but Yorit and Jonas were ready on him and held him fast. In his delirium, Nast called out a name. "Leroy!" Then he dropped into a mumble, barely discernable. "The bridge!" Again, "mumble, mumble."

"Damn if he ain't got the DTs," said Jonas, struggling to hold his shaking arm.

"I say we call the staff duty NCO," said Yorit

Nast called out the name several more times. "Leroy! Leroy!"

"Boy, is this nigger her' ornery," grunted Jonas, still holding down one powerful forearm arm. "Worse than tryin' to break an Appaloosa back home, he is."

"What's an Appaloosa?" asked Yorit, struggling with the other arm.

"A white colored horse with spots. Hey, black boy! Settle down!" Jonas scolded.

After some minutes the Mess Sgt seemed to find his rest and began to breathe deeply. The two soldiers let go of him and stood up, wondering what to do next. It was then his eyes popped open—wide open. "They's a comin', Leroy!" Nast cried out. "They's a-comin!' Mumble... Ammo! Ammo!"

"Here we go again!" Jonas called out.

With an impossible strength, the Mess Sgt pulled himself up, tossing his two oppressors to one side as if they had the weight of Barbie Dolls. Swaying unsteadily, he stepped to the middle of the room and up to a chest of drawers. He pulled open one drawer and took out a metal object; it was an army .45 caliber.

Yorit tackled Nast from behind. Jonas grabbed the weapon. The three men fell over the desk chair, smashing it. The floor lamp knocked over. Wrestling, the gun dropped to the floor. Yorit kicked it under the bed. After what felt like minutes, though it was only a seconds, Sgt Nast relaxed, Yorit and Jonas on top of him. They waited, then let go.

"We ought to let the son-of-a-bitch shoot himself," grunted Jonas, his face a storm from the effort.

"Good idea, Cecil, but we can't. Got to see this through. Now! After what just happened, you and I could get charged with breaking and entering NCO quarters. Attempted murder even. Without a witness, what just happened would look suspicious. We're stuck, man. We got to save his black ass to save our white ones."

"You'r right. Let's get Cookie back in the sack," said Jonas.

Again in his bed, the Mess Sgt began to snore deeply. Watching him, the two men stepped away.

"Look, you go to the orderly room and report what happened," said Yorit. "Me, I'll stay here a little bit just to be sure he's okay."

Jonas thought for a moment. "And the weapon? For sure they'll write Cookie up for ahving an unauthorized weapon in his living quarters. He could face charges, or we will."

Yorit frowned. "Let's just play it out. No one knows about it except us. Shit!"

Jonas left the room, leaving Yorit alone with the inebriated St Sgt. He had no love for the scourge of the KP roster, but he stayed on to be sure the Mess Daddy didn't do something stupid to hurt himself. The .45 caliber remained where it was—under the bed and out of reach.

Nast was breathing heavy, his mind functioning and not functioning. A swirl. Yorit sat down in an armchair in the corner of the room, and waited. Taking out a cigarette, he lit it. Five minutes passed. Just as he thought he could get up and leave, the big man sat up and looked at him. He blinked. He glanced around, his expression as demonic as King Kong's crashing through the jungle. Nast flashed his stallion teeth, and winced.

Oh, shit, here we go again and I'm alone, thought Yorit, ready to jump him.

What Yorit could not hear was what the company Mess Sgt could hear—incoming! Whiz-boom! Whiz-boom! "Leroy! You there?" Nast cried out. "Leroy, you okay?"

From his chair, Yorit hesitated, still unsure of what to do.

"Leroy!"

"Yeah, I'm okay," Yorit replied, tremulous.

"I'm scared shit, Leroy," Nast slurred, staring into space. "Here comes ag'in!" The big man shook and pressed himself up against the backboard of his wood-framed bed.

Yorit watched him. Hoping to quiet him down, he got up and stepped to the bed and put his hand on the Mess Sgt's shoulder. He shook him. It was then the NCO grabbed him and pulled him down on the bed. They struggled. Yorit was locked in the big man's bear hug. Unaware and unconscious, Nast began to whimper and rock; he rocked back and forth, Yorit in his arms with him. "Ain't no use, Leroy. Ain't no use," he wailed out loud.

Bound as he was in the Popeye-shaped forearms, Yorit felt foolish. He wanted to jump up and give him a whack along the side of the head and yell him to, "Snap out of it!" Instead, in the dim light of the room he let himself be embraced by the black Sgt. They rocked. How Yorit wished they had left him back on the street. "Ain't no use, Leroy! Ain't no use, I tell ya!" Whiz-boom!

In the embrace, Yorit had no choice; he relaxed. He hoped no one would come into the quarters. How would it look? Him in the arms of a Sgt's embrace? "Its okay, Cookie," he said in a low voice, the room bathed in the soft glow of the overturned floor lamp. Yorit stayed embraced, stayed wept on, a white man in a black man's arms. "It's all right, Cookie. You're not alone," he said gently. And the night dragged on.

"What is going on in here?" It was the staff duty NCO, Sgt Cabul. Jonas had told him what happened. He came over to check on Nast.

Struggling, Yorit freed himself from the loathsome grip and jumped up. "It isn't what it looks like, Sarge. Cookie here is as drunk as a skunk. To squeeze me was the only way to get him to calm down."

Sgt Cabul looked at the tipped over floorlamp and the broken desk chair. "Jonas told me what happened. Real decent of you two men to bring Cookie back to barracks. Where's the weapon?"

Yorit stepped over to the bed and reached under it, pulling out the .45 cal. He handed it to Sgt Cabul.

"I'll put this in the Arms Room for safe keeping," he said.

"You won't report Cookie or any of us will you, Sarge?"

"I should, but no. Not to worry yourself. You go back to your quarters and hit the sack. I can see Sarge Cookie here is finished for the night."

Yorit set the floorlamp back up, then walked out of the room, glad to be out of there.

***

Two days later, at morning roll call, both he and Jonas were ordered out of Army formation and told to report to the Mess Hall. They said looking at each other, "Uh-oh!" Behind them, the Platoon chuckled. They knew what a "report to Mess Hall" meant. KP! Kitchen Police! It meant that both Yorit and Jonas had been involuntarily volunteered for extra duty. Departing the formation, the two soldiers entered the barracks. Behind them, they could hear MSgt Sweechek counting cadence as the company marched away for PT, the morning's physical training.

Walking down the well-lit barracks hallway toward the swinging green doors of the Mess Hall, Jonas began to complain. "Why they always pick me for work details and not the other guy?"

Yorit looked at him. "What do you mean, pick on you and not the other guy? I am the other guy! Shit!"

They pushed through the swinging green doors and entered the company canteen. Inside, it was pungent with the smell of coffee, toast and burnt bacon. They passed the empty counters and entered the crew kitchen. The on-duty KPs in fatigues had their sleeves rolled up and were mopping the floors and cleaning whatever; the cooks in waist aprons ran around preparing the strap pans for the morning chow following PT. Flapjacks were piled next to the grills. One of the KPs, a Pvt Moran from 2nd Platoon, sat in front of a metal pale, breaking eggs, a hundred of them; they were to be scrambled. Another KP, Howie Small from the 1st, was in the dining hall setting miniature flower vases on the officers and Sergeant's tables. On a duty room door marked

"Company Mess Sergeant" they knocked. From inside the duty room a voice rumbled. "Enter!" They entered.

Mess Sgt Nast was checking over the list of supplies he would need for the next month's meals. He looked up at the two soldiers as they stepped up to his desk. "Reporting for KP as ordered, Sergeant!" they said together, standing at rest, arms at the small of the back.

Sergeant Nast had the usual mark of scorn on his face that senior NCOs reserve for table flies and all junior enlisted soldiers. The lower the rank, the deeper the scorn. He leaned back in his chair and considered the two signalmen in front of him. He growled, "I called you down here because..." the authority in his voice, a threat, abruptly softened "because I want to thank you men both for dragging my ass back to quarters the other night."

Yorit and Jonas looked at each other. "Huh?" The Mess Sgt's voice was surprisingly cordial. They had not expected this kind of reception, not from him—Cookie Nast, the scourge of the company Mess Hall. They thought they were about to get hammered with a KP detail and peel potatoes the rest of the week. "Sergeant Cabul told me what you both did for me, and I want you to know, I'm grateful."

Again, the "Huh?" The mess Daddy smiled. Yorit looked over his shoulder; he thought he was smiling at someone behind them. It was the first time he had ever heard a Mess Sgt—*any* Army Mess Sgt— say "Thank you!" in the four years he had been in the Army.

"Specialist Jonas, close the door behind you, will you please?" (Did an NCO just say, "please"?) Jonas did as he was told. "Sergeant Cabul told me how you found me, DUI-ed in the gutter, and how you put me in a taxi and brought me back to the company. If the MPs had picked me instead of you, I'd have been written up for sure. Thank you, signalmen."

"Forget it, Sarge," said Jonas. "You'd have done the same thing for us."

Sgt Nast swiveled in his desk chair. "Tell me, how did my room get trashed? I don't remember. What exactly happened?"

Grateful they were not there to pull some KP duty, the two soldiers relaxed and told him what he wanted to know. Sgt Nast listened, nodding. "You mean to tell me you did all that for me, old bastard that I am?"

"Old bastard or not, you weren't yourself, Sarge," said Yorit, both soldiers still in the rest position.

"We had to," said Jonas. "We're all Uncle Sam's soldiers, regardless of rank."

Yorit nodded. "Actually, we were protecting ourselves. When you pulled the weapon, we weren't sure if you were going to use it on yourself or on us. We couldn't take a chance."

"Had to knock you down and wreck the furniture," added Jonas, apologetic.

The Mess Sgt looked at the two men. "Hm, yes, that weapon. It's an old army .45 cal. from Korea. I could have been charged with unauthorized weapon in quarters, as well as drunk and disorderly conduct. It's an incident, you know. Serious stuff! A court marshal offense, if reported.

"You mean Sarge Cabul didn't report it?" Yorit asked.

"No, but you still can." he said, gravely. "As soldiers, it is your responsibility to report me."

The two men looked at each other. "What's there to report?" said Jonas.

Yorit shrugged. "There was no incident from what I could see."

"We just accompanied a buddy home. So he was a little drunk. Off-duty, who ain't drunk in the army?" said Jonas with a smirk.

Yorit wondered about Jonas. To him, black people were all niggers, but if Jonas knew you, he was your blood brother—black or white or Indian.

Observing the two soldiers in front of him, Mess Sgt Nast realized they were giving him back his career, the only career life he knew. "I want you both to know, I'm grateful."

"Say, Cookie, tell me, was the gun loaded?" asked Yorit.

"Yes, I'm afraid it was. Damn stupid of me."

"Would you have used it?"

"I don't know. That's just it; I don't know. I been depressed lately," he said, his brows knotting. "Anyway, the weapon is in the Arms Room now. Like I said, men, I'm grateful."

Yorit was beginning to feel uncomfortable: Nast, a St Sgt, talking to them civil-like, as if they were Father Confessors. They were not used to it, not from a Sgt with rank.

"If there is anything I can do for you two men, let me know."

"A couple of beers will do just fine, Sarge,"said Jonas, now grinning.

Outside in the mess hall they could hear the clatter of trays and loud talking. The three platoons had returned from PT training. "Is there anything else before we go, Sarge?" Yorit asked.

"Yes, as of today you two men are permanently relieved of Kitchen Police duty. I'm sending the request up to 1st Sgt Persilla. He'll okay it. He'll do what I ask."

Startled, both men were relieved. They did not expect a miracle. "Our turn to be grateful, Mess Daddy," said Yorit warmly.

Standing up, St Sgt Nast came around from his desk and shook their hands. "Now go out to the servicing line and help yourselves to some chow before the rest of the company gets in here. We got hot muffins this morning and they go fast."

They shook hands again. "Thanks, Cookie!" said Jonas. "By the way, we may joke about the chow, but its okay."

The Mess Sgt winked at him. "I know it is. Wisecracks go with the job. I've heard them all in my fifteen years in the service."

The two soldiers left the duty room. Returning to his desk, Mess Sgt Nast picked up the next month's supply chart, the one he had been working on before Yorit and Jonas entered the duty room. There was a knock. "Say, Sergeant Nast?"

He looked up. It was Yorit. "Forget something, Specialist?" he asked, his expression now serious.

"Not really, Sarge, but I got a question. Been thinking about it."

Suspicious, the NCO raised an eyebrow. "Oh yeah, what is it?"

"Who is Leroy?"

Nast put down the food chart. "Where'd you hear that name?"

"In your delirium the other night you called out the name 'Leroy' several times. You also called out the words 'ridge,' 'ammo,' or something like that."

The Mess Sgt looked down at his desk, frowning. Yorit realized he may have made a mistake. Had the question opened a painful experience long buried? He shifted from one foot to the other in front of the desk; he considered excusing himself when Nast stood up. "PFC Leroy Robinson was the best damn soldier in the US Army. Ever hear of the 24th Regiment?"

"No," Yorit answered, but he did remember the photographs, the ones he saw on the wall in his quarters.

"I figured you wouldn't. No one does today," said Nast. "Well, I'm going to tell you a story, Soldier. You listen carefully and you'll learn something you won't find in the history books." Yorit wondered what he was driving at. "The 24th Regiment was an all-black soldier outfit run by white officers. Our traditions go back to the Civil War. We were America's original Buffalo Soldiers. In the 1870s we fought outlaws and Indians. In the 1890s we ran down the bandit, Poncho Villa, in Mexico. Ever hear of San Juan Hill? We were there! The 24th fought in Cuba, the Philippines, and World Wars I and II. Lots of glory, the "Double Four," as we were called back then. We were a proud outfit."

"I'm impressed," said Yorit. "Ah, what do you mean by '*were* proud'?"

Mess Daddy Nast picked up a pencil and tapped it on his desk as if about to make a point. "I'm coming to that. You see, Soldier, Korea was a disaster for the 24th Regiment. In 1950 it was stationed in Japan; our mission was guard duty. When Communist North Korea attacked South Korea, President Truman announced a police action. That was in June of that year. The 8th Army threw us raw 'cruits with little or no training into battle to stop them. We had some success at Inchon, but for the most part the 24th performed badly."

"That sometimes happens in battle, doesn't it, Sarge?"

"Not quite like this. We were in a poor defensive position on the edge of the Pusan Perimeter. There was a lot of pressure on us. When the enemy hit our lines, they whipped us. Whipped us bad! We broke and ran. Ever hear of an Army outfit doing that?"

"Retreat, maybe, but not cut and run."

"And do you know why we so-called cut and ran?" Yorit shook his head. "I'll tell you why. Because our officers, the white officers that led us, broke and ran, that's why. They left the 24th Regiment out there to face the North Korean attack alone!" Nast waited a moment to let what he had just said sink in. "Our position had been hopeless from the start. The officers knew it and cut. Only they forgot to tell 'Rochester.' We's won't worth it, ya'll know. We's only Niggas!" he said, imitating a plantation field hand. "No leadership, low morale and no ammo, and cut off. The 24th took the hit—better believe we took the hit! Most of our NCOs were either wounded or dead. You had PFCs trying to lead squads, Corporals trying to call in artillery. It was either run or be overrun. The experience haunts me to this day!"

"Was it proven that the officers abandoned their units?" Yorit asked, not believing what he had just heard.

"The official report states that we, the black soldiers, deserted them, the white officers. Can you imagine that? When really, it was the other way around. They abandoned us! In the investigation that followed the officers all played the old Army game of CYA, 'Cover Your Ass.' You know the game. They kept passing on the blame game until the only ones left to blame were the simple soldiers. The 24th enlisted got blamed for the debacle. Called us cowards, they did. Shamed us! Someone wrote a song about us. Ever hear it? You wouldn't! It's called the, 'Bug Out Boogey.' Goes like this: 'When the Chinese mortars begins to thud, the old Deuce-four begins to bug.'"

"And your buddy, Leroy Robinson? Where does he fit in?"

The Mess Sgt sat silent for a moment, fingering his pencil. "Yes, Leroy," he said, his voice monotone, without emotion, a contrast to his preacher-man barks that kept the Mess Hall operational and the signalmen fed. "Yes, Leroy. That day there was a lot of confusion out there in battle. A half a dozen men out there should have been awarded the Medal of Honor for valor; Private First Class Leroy Robinson, my buddy, was one of them. When our battalion was overrun, Specialist Robinson was killed saving my life. And me? I only lost a trigger finger when I should have lost my life." he said, holding up his hand where the knuckle was shot away. "I guess it's why I booze. I'm still alive."

Beyond the glass window of the Duty Room, the company soldiers were at the serving line. The KPs had already laid out the strap pans and stood behind the counters. Nast got up. He took his skimmer, the ladle, off the wall, the one that had once been a North Korean tank fender. He slipped the leather strap over his thick wrist. "The ol' Buffalo Regiment was really a good outfit till the Army had it deactivated."

"I'm sure it was," said Yorit.

Together, they stepped to the doorway. In the Mess Hall the strong fragrance of breakfast chow filtered the air. "Oh, by the way, Yorit, I heard you were thinking of re-enlisting for Vietnam. That right E4?"

Yorit looked up at him, surprised that the Mess Sgt knew about it. "Who told you that, Sarge?"

"Signal Company is a three-platoon company, a hundred guys; word gets around."

Yorot nodded. "Yes, I was thinking of re-enlisting. The re-enlistment NCO, Sgt Chuckles, promised me the E5 rank and a bonus if I sign up for South East Asia duty."

Sullen, the big black Sgt looked down at him. He tapped Yorit on the chest with his ladle. "Now listen to me, Son. There's a big war a-coming on. You don't want to be caught in the middle of it, not if you can avoid it. You did me a favor; I'll do you one. It's this: get out! Get out of the service! You paid your dues to our country, God bless it. Take the GI Bill and go home and go to college. Don't re-enlist! War makes soldiers age—fast! Just look at Platoon Sergeant Oats; he isn't all there in his head," he said, tapping at his temple. "Stay in the Army, noble though it is, and you'll be right in the middle of something that may be too big for you. We Grunts are always in the middle of every conflict. It's our job. Vietnam is going to be another Korea all over again. Mark my words."

"How do you know, Sarge?"

"Because it is Asia. I been there, done that. The politicians will say you'll be home by Christmas like they told us in 1950. They were right. 30,000 casualties later we soldiers were home for Christmas, only it was 1953 and not 1950. Three years late!"

"I'll give it some thought," said Yorit, disturbed.

The Mess Sgt looked at him gravely. "Do you know what a soldier does when flares light up the night and 10, 000 Chinks come at you blowing their bugles, their whistles and screaming? Do you know what he does?" Yorit shook his head. "He wets his pants, that's what he does."

"You wet yours, Cookie?"

"Many times, Specialist. You age on the spot! You are never be the same again. You even fuck different and cry when you do it, and the woman next to you will ask, 'Honey, what's the matter?' No, soldier, you go home and go to college. Keep your virginity. Have a life."

The Mess Hall was loud now. Tins and trays clanged and banged. The KPs and cooks ladled in the chow to the soldiers bellyaching over the too-fried bacon, and the-too hard boiled eggs, and the cereals that tasted like a deck of cards. Yorit watched.

Big as lumber, black as spades, St Sgt Mess Daddy Cookie Nast took his place behind his KP servers, fielding the soldiers' wise cracks and complaints. As he watched him, Yorit now understood. Staff Sergeant Nast was not only growling at the men, he was laughing at them. Sharing his Army with them. He was enjoying the job.

"Hey, Cookie, do you pass out purple hearts with this grub?" asked one soldier in the chow line.

"Right, Son, and you'll get one when I put your name on my KP roster!" The signalman went pale.

"Cookie, you call this stuff chow?" asked another wiseguy, daring.

"If it's good enough for Fido, it's good for you!" responded the Mess Sgt.

"Say, Cookie, what color is the coffee today? Black or purple?" asked another.

"Purple! To brighten your day! What's your name, smart guy? You can use some KP duty." The soldier bit his tongue.

Looking around, Mess Sgt Nast saw Yorit watching him. He gave him a wink. Yorit winked back. The scourge of the company Mess Hall was an okay guy.

Vietnam I
1964

To Robert Yorit
From Saul Rosenblum
Berlin, GermanyBien Hoe, Vietnam

Dear Yoyo,

It's Rosie here. Rat,tat,tat,tat,tat! Boom! Rat-tat-tat-tat! Hey, this Vietnam is cool. Rat,tat,tat, Boom! Puff! Will ya look at that?

Well, the Army has kept its promise. At Ft. Polk, my promotion to sergeant E5 came through just as Re-up Sarge Chuckles promised. I am now an ass-chew'n, barf-bark'n, nasty ol' three stripe NCO. And would you believe it? I've humped 'cruits, too! And not only that, I was permitted to carry my own personal clipboard. With a little practice I should be able to count to four in no time. But that's all behind me now.

Went to PLDC school, then gunnery school, and now find myself— would you believe it—in Vietnam. Boom! Boom! Rat-tat-tat! I didn't think the Army would give me Nam, what with all this talk about pulling out. It's what President Lynden Johnson said he was going to do. Pull out! He didn't, and I got orders. Now, here I am.

One problem here in Nam, as far as I can see, there are too few E-3s and E-4s that I can dump on. As Sgt E-5, I'm still the bottom of the totem pole. Everyone else in my section is SSgt, SFC, MSgt. I may as well be back in the Berlin Brigade on work detail for all the good the new rank does me. There ain't no one here I can pass the buck to. I AM THE BUCK!

My re-enlistment did not go down well with the family. They

wanted me to come home and get on with the family business like my older brother did. But, crazy as it may sound, I like the Army, bullshit and all. We—you me and the guys back at the company— talked about it, remember? I figure one more tour then I could settle down. What the hell. Anyway, when orders came through for Vietnam, the family got upset, especially my father. He said I was carrying this duty thing to one's country too far, and him a Marine in World War II.

When my home furlough was over, everyone came to Grand Central Station to see me off—except Dad. Mom told me he went to the Temple to pray. It's what my grandfather did when Dad was shipped out to the Pacific in 1942, and Uncle Sid to Korea back in '51. Jewish traditions die hard.

My father fought on islands in the Pacific. He never talked about it. As a kid I used to ask him. However, two days before I was to depart to AIT, he took me into his den. We had a man-to-man talk. He revealed things to me that I would have never dreamed he was capable of, him a fat guy with Mr. Peeper glasses. I only know him standing behind the counter of our family shop on W 44th Street wearing a Yarmulke, the magnifying glass screwed into his brow, counting carats. We own a jewelery shop, you know. I can't imagine him carrying a weapon and wearing a helmet and tossing hand grenades at the Japs. Yet, he did. He explained to me how to survive in the jungle—both jungles, Pelalu and New York.

I told Dad not to worry. Vietnam is not a hot war. The army is only there to supply and train the ARVN, the South Vietnamese Army, so it can fight the Viet Cong guerrillas themselves, or so I was briefed. America is only there as logistical support. Not to worry, Papa, I told him. Still, he went to the Temple.

Rat-tat-tat! Zing! Zip! Boom!

Your Buddy,
Rosie

About the Author

Robert Marabito grew up in Cleveland Ohio and was a fan of the Cleveland Indians. His father died when he was young, so from age 12 Robert worked at various jobs to help support the family, like setting pins in a bowling alley. In high school he had a side job at a mortuary carrying bodies to be dressed for funeral services. Later, he cut down trees for the Cleveland Light and Power Company. At the time, and with no direction, he enlisted in the US Army for 3 years and served in occupied West Berlin during the Cold War. There he fell in love with Europe.

After the service he attended Kent State University and graduated in 1969. Later, he attended Thunderbird Graduate School of International Management in Phoenix, Arizona, where he was the editor of the graduate school's first newspaper, *Das Tor* (The Gate). With the 1973 economic crash and no job in site, he went off to Europe. He landed in London, where he worked as a welder at a Thames River shipyard. Again, after a year and with no future in site, he got on a boat and crossed the North Sea only to land in the harbour city of Hamburg. He was back in Germany.

His first job was to carry beef on his shoulder and help load ships. At night he attended Hamburg University where he studied the German language. After 6 months he could speak the language, slurs and all. With that, and again no future in site, he moved to Holland and the town called The Hague. There he teamed up with a Thunderbird School chum. Together they set up a retail and wholesale company, importing and marketing American fashion design. It was there he met his wife, Anita, fell in love (Americans always fall in love with German women), sold his business and moved to Bonn, Germany. Together they have two grown daughters, Frances and Charlotte.

After some intense re-education, Robert became an investment advisor for 1st Armored Division soldiers in Wiesbaden. He could finally use his education. The business was successful until the soldiers went off to Iraq. With no soldier market, he turned to teaching Yankee Doodle English at several language schools. Today, he still works as a language teacher at the ripe old age of 70 something. For him, life is still an adventure.

Lightning Source UK Ltd.
Milton Keynes UK
UKOW05f0616230813

215808UK00002B/49/P